HISTORY OF WOMEN IN THE UNITED STATES

HISTORY OF WOMEN IN THE UNITED STATES
Historical Articles on Women's Lives and Activities

Edited by Nancy F. Cott

Series ISBN 3-598-41454-4

1. Theory and Method in Women's History
   ISBN 3-598-41455-2 Part 1
   ISBN 3-598-41477-3 Part 2

2. Household Constitution and Family Relationships
   ISBN 3-598-41456-0

3. Domestic Relations and Law
   ISBN 3-598-41457-9

4. Domestic Ideology and Domestic Work
   ISBN 3-598-41458-7 Part 1
   ISBN 3-598-41475-7 Part 2

5. The Intersection of Work and Family Life
   ISBN 3-598-41459-5 Part 1
   ISBN 3-598-41476-5 Part 2

6. Working on the Land
   ISBN 3-598-41460-9

7. Industrial Wage Work
   ISBN 3-598-41461-7 Part 1
   ISBN 3-598-41693-8 Part 2

8. Professional and White-Collar Employments
   ISBN 3-598-41462-5 Part 1
   ISBN 3-598-41694-6 Part 2

9. Prostitution
   ISBN 3-598-41463-3

10. Sexuality and Sexual Behavior
    ISBN 3-598-41464-1

11. Women's Bodies: Health and Childbirth
    ISBN 3-598-41465-X

12. Education
    ISBN 3-598-41466-8

13. Religion
    ISBN 3-598-41467-6

14. Intercultural and Interracial Relations
    ISBN 3-598-41468-4

15. Women and War
    ISBN 3-598-41469-2

16. Women Together: Organizational Life
    ISBN 3-598-41470-6

17. Social and Moral Reform
    ISBN 3-598-41471-4 Part 1
    ISBN 3-598-41695-4 Part 2

18. Women and Politics
    ISBN 3-598-41472-2 Part 1
    ISBN 3-598-41697-0 Part 2

19. Woman Suffrage
    ISBN 3-598-41473-0 Part 1
    ISBN 3-598-41696-2 Part 2

20. Feminist Struggles for Sex Equality
    ISBN 3-598-41474-9

HISTORY OF WOMEN IN THE UNITED STATES

Historical Articles on Women's Lives and Activities

5. The Intersection of Work and Family Life PART 1

Edited with an Introduction by

Nancy F. Cott
Yale University

K · G · Saur
Munich · London · New York · Paris 1992

Publisher's Note
The articles and chapters which comprise this collection originally appeared in a wide variety of publications and are reproduced here in facsimile from the highest quality offprints and photocopies available. The reader will notice some occasional marginal shading and text-curl common to photocopying from tightly bound volumes. Every attempt has been made to correct or minimize this effect.

Copyright information for articles reproduced in this collection appears at the end of this volume.

Library of Congress Cataloging-in-Publication Data
History of women in the United States : historical articles on women's lives and activities / edited with an introduction by Nancy F. Cott.
p. cm.
Includes bibliographical references and indexes.
Contents: 1. Theory and method in women's history -- 2. Household constitution and family relationships -- 3. Domestic relations and law -- 4. Domestic ideology and domestic work -- 5. The intersection of work and family life -- 6. Working on the land -- 7. Industrial wage work -- 8. Professional and white-collar employments -- 9. Prostitution -- 10. Sexuality and sexual behavior -- 11. Women's bodies -- 12. Education -- 13. Religion -- 14. Intercultural and interracial relations -- 15. Women and war -- 16. Women together -- 17. Social and moral reform -- 18. Women and politics -- 19. Women suffrage -- 20. Feminist struggles for sex equality.
ISBN 3-598-41454-4 (set)
1. Women--United States--History. 2. Women--United States--Social conditions. I. Cott, Nancy F.
HQ1410.H57 1992
305.4'0973--dc20 92-16765
CIP

Die Deutsche Bibliothek - CIP - Einheitsaufnahme

History of women in the United States: historical articles on women's lives and activities / ed. with an introd. by Nancy F. Cott.
- Munich ; London ; New York ; Paris : Saur.
ISBN 3-598-41454-4
NE: Cott, Nancy F. (Hrsg.)
Vol. 5. The intersection of work and family life.
Pt. 1. - (1992)
ISBN 3-598-41459-5

Printed on acid-free paper/Gedruckt auf säurefreiem Papier

A Reed Reference Publishing Company

Printed in the United States of America
Printed/Bound by Edwards Brothers Incorporated, Ann Arbor

ISBN 3-598-41459-5 (vol. 5/part 1)
ISBN 3-598-41454-4 (series)

Contents

Part 2

Series Preface

In the space of one generation, women's history has become the fastest-growing area of scholarship in U.S. history. Since the resurgence of feminism in the late 1960s and 1970s, insistent questions about the historical meanings of "woman's place" have sowed and reaped a garden of scholarship. Where scholarly works used to be bare of mention of women, academic enterprise has now produced a vigorous growth of books and articles, bringing to light diverse women of every region, race, class and age. This research is marked by a renovating intent that refuses to accept as "human" history a history of men. Interest is lively and debate is stimulating and sought after: attendance at the Berkshire Conference on the History of Women rivals the size of the annual convention of the American Historical Association.

While books in women's history are daily increasing in numbers and strength, as in any fast-developing field the scholarly literature in the form of articles is most expansive and up-to-the-minute. All the history journals now publish articles on women's work, domestic settings, family relations, household matters, female politics and organizations and so forth, and new journals have sprung into being to concentrate on such topics. Women's historians publish in numerous regional and thematic history journals as well as in feminist outlets and in journals of other social science disciplines. This series brings together a collection of outstanding articles from the field, almost all written in the past twenty years and more than half published during the 1980s. It brings together, in volumes organized by topic, essays otherwise widely dispersed. These volumes reprint only articles that originally appeared in journals, not chapters of books; review articles are not included. Articles have been chosen for overall quality and for range. Each one was chosen for one or more of the following reasons: because it is the standard authority on its subject matter; represents an important statement on a topic by a recognized scholar; presages an important book to come; provides a first look at new evidence or new methods; or opens an untapped area or new controversy. Older articles have been reprinted if their data or interpretation have not been surpassed or if they marked an important stage in the historiography, even if since superseded.

The historical coverage of the series extends from the Revolutionary era to the 1960s. The articles themselves are dated from the 1940s through 1988. Volumes are organized by topic rather than time period. Within each volume, the articles are ordered chronologically (with respect to substance), so that the whole can be read as an historical overview. The only exception to this ordering principle is volume 1, on Theory and Method, in which the contents are arranged in order of publication. Within each volume there is an attempt to include articles on as diverse kinds of women as possible. None of the volume topics is regionally or racially defined; rather, all volumes are topically designed so as to afford views of women's work, family lives, and public activities which cut across races and regions. Any volume in the series stands on its own, supplying as full a treatment of a designated subject matter as the scholarly literature will provide. Several groupings of volumes also make sense; that is, volumes 2 through 5 all center around domestic and family matters; volumes 5 through 9 consider other varieties of women's work; volumes 9 through 11 concern uses and abuses of women's bodies; volumes 12 through 14 look at major aspects of socialization; and volumes 15 through 20 include organizational and political efforts of many sorts.

As a whole, the series displays in all its range the vitality of the field of women's history. Aside from imbuing U.S. history with new vision, scholarship in this area has informed, and should continue to inform, current public debate on issues from parental leave to the nuclear freeze. By bringing historical articles together under topical headings, these volumes both represent accurately the shape of historical controversy (or consensus) on given issues and make historians' findings most conveniently available for current reference.

Introduction

Today, with the majority of adult women in the paid labor force, the issue of women's combination of work and family life--work and motherhood, in particular--is much in the news, as though it were an unprecedented phenomenon. Historians of women have shown, however, that women's combination of productive economic activity and childrearing has been more the norm than the exception in past time; only a small stratum of prosperous women, for a relatively short period of years in the nineteenth and twentieth centuries, were ever able to devote themselves wholly to child care and housekeeping. What is unprecedented in our own time is the extent to which women perform their work outside of the household rather than in or around it, for a wage or salary rather than for barter or "in-kind" services. The articles in this volume detail how women of various ethnic and racial groups have managed the necessary combination of economic and familial tasks, in both rural and urban settings.

In rural society the intersection of women's work with their family responsibilities was taken for granted. In the agricultural setting, both women's and men's work revolved around the household and fields; childrearing did not separate itself out as a separate task. Examples from Native American women to black slaves in the Old South to homesteading families in late nineteenth century Colorado make that clear. Of course for slaves, circumstances were much harsher and not under their own control: whether a woman had family members with her was a matter of the master's ability to buy and sell her and her kindred. On plantations where slave families were intact, however, a woman's work was of two sorts: for the master, and for her own kin. Many narratives relate slave women's bringing their nursing babies to the cotton fields with them, but slave children once old enough to do useful work were put to use by the master. It was in the latter kind of work--cooking, mending, quilting, nursing in the slave quarters--that black women's interweaving of family responsibility with necessary labor was most visible, on the general model of rural women's work that black women would also manifest after emancipation.

Not only agricultural production but most crafts were, in the era before industrialization, organized around the household: there, in the large hall or perhaps in an adjoining shop the master craftsman, journeymen and apprentices worked, women and children nearby or participating in part. The sense of separation of "work" from "home" did not come about until, in fact, towns and cities were numerous enough and commercial development sufficient to create worksites separate from homes, where numerous employees worked. This reorganization of work, occurring gradually over a long period of time, and scattered in location, was transformative enough to create a very great awareness of change among those forwarding it, participants in urbanization and commercialization. One major way that individuals understood, rationalized and accepted the change was in terms of gender roles: the separation of work from home was seen as appropriate if the home was understood as woman's place, the world of work man's.

This ideological construction of the differences between "work" and "home," a construction abuilding since the 1820s, arose in part from realistic observation among prosperous middle-class men and women, in whose families one male earner in business or profession sufficed to support the rest of the family. But it was a realistic observation for only a small portion of the population when it began, and for a century or more afterward. It is ironic, and more than ironic, that in the same decade when publicists first championed the home as a haven from the world of work and loudly glorified the woman at home as mankind's moral savior, large numbers of girls and young women were drawn out of their domestic occupations by American industrialists to work in textile factories. The rhetorical separation of "work" from "home" and identification of the one with men and the other with women undermined societal respect and even the self-respect of women who worked outside of the home. It also, just as invidiously, hid the work that still went on at home, the extent to which the home was still, and would continue to be, for *women* a workplace, even when it served as a respite from work for men.

What women accomplished in the home was not only the unpaid work of domestic service, but often work that was income-producing and essential to family economic survival or advancement. If the modern conflict between mothers' wage-earning and childrearing seems to be new, that is not because mothers in the past did not contribute to family income but because they took industry into their households, or took laundry into their households, or took boarders or lodgers in, to create cash value. Beginning in the early nineteenth century, rural women not only sold their butter, cheese and eggs but also braided straw hats or baskets at home or sold surplus cloth to the local store. In cities, manufacturers of ready-made clothing found their most exploitable labor force among poor and often widowed women who "finished" piles of shirts or pants at home, with miles of stitches, so that they could watch their children and earn money--meager as it was--at the same time. By the end of the century this manufacturing system of "given-out" work operated on a mass scale, employing thousands of immigrant women in their tenement homes, making mass-produced jewelry, trimming hats, and other similar tasks, as well as sewing. Black women found one alternative to domestic service in white families' homes by taking other people's washing into their own homes. During the mass immigration of the late nineteenth and early twentieth centuries, many women increased their own domestic burdens but made cash by giving space to a lodger or feeding a boarder.

Thus in many ways wives and mothers added to family income, stretching their strength perhaps to the breaking point, but without even appearing on the census takers' rolls as "in the labor force." Not until the 1920s and 1930s--by which time most Americans lived in urban places, and state regulation had foreclosed much "given-out" industry, and compulsory school laws kept children at school rather than earning wages for the family, and federal restriction of immigration greatly reduced the flow of transient lodgers--did wives and mothers in any large proportions enter the recorded labor force. At that point the problem of child care for working mothers, and the conflict between work and home, was perceived to be pressing, as these have ever since. The coverage in this volume, from Native American and slave women in the early nineteenth century, through pioneers and immigrants, to modern college graduates in the mid-twentieth century, gives a compelling overview of the persistent weightiness and consequence of wives' and mothers' economic roles.

The Intersection of Work and Family Life

ECONOMIC ORGANIZATION AND THE POSITION OF WOMEN AMONG THE IROQUOIS[1]

by

Judith K. Brown
Oakland University

ABSTRACT

The relationship between the position of women and their economic role is examined by comparing ethnohistoric and ethnographic data relating to the Iroquois of North America and the Bemba of Northern Rhodesia. It is concluded that the high status of Iroquois women reflected their control of their tribe's economic organization.

INTRODUCTION

My purpose is to investigate the relationship between the position of women and their economic role. Three possibilities are suggested in the literature. Lowie (1961: 201) felt that in determining women's status economic considerations could be "offset and even negatived" by historical factors. Malinowski (1913) maintained that the considerable economic contribution of Australian aborigine women was extorted from them through male "brutalization" and confirmed female subservience. The opposite point of view is expressed by Jenness (1932: 137):

> If women among the Iroquois enjoyed more privileges and possessed greater freedom than the women of other tribes, this was due . . . to the important place that agriculture held in their economic life, and the distribution of labour . . . [which left] the entire cultivation of the fields and the acquisition of the greater part of the food supply to the women.

His explanation for the high status of women among the Iroquois is essentially economic, stressing the extent of their economic contribution, but failing to deal with their place in the economic organization. Other authors have suggested that matrilineality, matrilocality or a combination of the two explain the high status of women among the Iroquois.

That matrilineality and matrilocality are hardly unrelated to economic considerations had been suggested by Stites (1905), and has been again more recently by Gough (1961), Aberle (1961), and D'Andrade (1966).

In the present study, an attempt has been made to hold matrilineality and matrilocality constant by comparing the Iroquois with the Bemba. If the two tribes are far removed from each other in time, location and tradition, the Bemba were also essentially matrilineal and matrilocal (Richards 1939: 17), and Bemba women enjoyed high status. In both tribes women made a considerable contribution to subsistence activities. However, the economic organization underlying these activities differed markedly, and there were important differences in the status of their women.

The relationship between women's status and women's work is more complex than the three points of view above would suggest. An analysis must begin with careful definitions for both "status" and "work." More than the extent of women's economic activities must be known. The economic organization of the subsistence activities must be considered. It is for this reason that no simple relationship exists between the extent of women's economic contribution and women's status. The latter is related to women's place in the economic organization of subsistence activities, not simply to the proportion of the food women produce.

THE POSITION OF WOMEN AMONG THE IROQUOIS

The Iroquois have been treated as if they had been a homogeneous group by most authors, and in the *Ethnographic Atlas* (Murdock 1967), and will be considered as such here. The six member nations of the Iroquois Confederacy do not appear to have differed on the variables under consideration.

The accounts giving fullest information on the relevant variables describe the Iroquois during the 18th and 19th centuries. This was hardly a time of stability for the tribe, and economic organization and the status of women did not remain constant over the period. Cara Richards (1957) has pointed out the increase in the decision-making powers of Iroquois women, and Noon (1949) has noted the increase in their economic responsibilities in the early part of the period under consideration.

In dealing with the status of women, two factors must be clearly differentiated. High status may be inferred from deferential treatment, or may consist of an actual position of power over basic resources and important decisions. The two need not coincide and should be considered separately (D'Andrade 1966).

Among the Iroquois, women were not accorded deferential treatment. Morgan (1962: 324) noted with Victorian bias that such amenities signal the advance of civilization. He observed, "The Indian regarded woman as inferior, the dependent, and the servant of man, and from nurture and habit, she actually considered herself to be so."

However, the position of power that Iroquois women held has been pointed out by numerous authors such as Beauchamp (1900), Carr (1887)[2], Goldenweiser (1912), Hewitt (1933) and Randle (1951). Murdock's (1934: 302) statement can be taken as a summary: "Indeed of all the people of the earth, the Iroquois approach most closely to that hypothetical form of society known as the matriarchate."

An early, detailed and much-cited appraisal was made by Father Joseph Lafitau of the Society of Jesus. Lafitau's (1724) charmingly illustrated four-volume work carries the inscription *avec approbation et privilege du Roy*, but no doubt helped to promote the revolutionary idea of the noble savage.

Lafitau differs from other early sources in that his account is not anecdotal but descriptive. The tone of the book is scholarly, and the information it contains is based on Lafitau's five-year stay in Canada, material supplied by another missionary who worked in Canada for sixty years, and on material in the *Jesuit Relations*.

According to Lafitau (1724: I: 66-67):

> Nothing, however, is more real than this superiority of the women. It is of them that the nation really consists; and it is through them that the nobility of the blood, the genealogical tree and the families are perpetuated. All real authority is vested in them. The land, the fields and their harvest all belong to them. They are the souls of the Councils, the arbiters of peace and of war. They have charge of the public treasury. To them are given the slaves. They arrange marriages. The children are their domain, and it is through their blood that the order of succession is transmitted. The men, on the other hand, are entirely isolated. . . . Their children are strangers to them [my translation].

This passage must be interpreted with caution. Lafitau does not specify in these often-quoted lines exactly which *Ameriquains* he is describing. It may be the Iroquois, the Huron or both. The particular section from which this quotation is taken attempts to establish similarities between tribal customs and those of antiquity, thus foreshadowing much of late 19th century anthropology. Moreover, a number of the unusual powers enumerated were not vested in all Iroquois women, but only in the matrons, the elderly heads of households and works groups. However, such a position was achieved and could be aspired to by all women, as Randle (1951) had noted. Unfortunately, there is no detailed description of how matrons were chosen. Fenton's (1957: 31) statement, which suggests that women made the selection on the basis of personality traits, "the mild person who speaks easily and kindly succeeds to public roles which the women withhold from the over-anxious person," does not specify the sex of the would-be officeholder.

The evidence for statements such as those of Murdock and Lafitau must be evaluated by examining the role of Iroquois women in the political, the religious and the domestic life of the tribe. In the political sphere, Iroquois matrons had the power to raise and depose the ruling elders, the ability to influence the decisions of the Council, and occasional power over the conduct of war and the establishment of treaties. Although women could not serve on the Council of Elders, the highest ruling body of the League, the hereditary eligibility for office passed through them, and the elective eligibility for office was also largely controlled by them. Goldenweiser (1912: 468) gives a retrospective account of the power of the matrons to raise and depose the ruling elders (whom he called chiefs):

> When a chief died, the women of his tribe and clan held a meeting at which a candidate for the vacant place was decided upon. A woman delegate carried the news to the chiefs of the clans which belonged to the "side" of the deceased chief's clan. They had the power to veto the selection, in which case another women's meeting was called and another candidate selected. . . .

The actions of the new chief were closely watched, and if his behavior deviated from the accepted norms, he was warned by the woman delegate. If after several warnings he still did not conform, she would initiate impeachment proceedings.

It is surprising that Lewis Morgan, whose *League of the Ho-De'-No-Sau-Nee, Iroquois* stands as a classic to this day, should have taken no particular note of the political power of Iroquois matrons. His account of the raising of the elders in *Ancient society* (Morgan 1963) differs in some details from the account given by Goldenweiser. Speaking of the election he states, "Each person of adult age was called upon to express his *or her* preference. . ." (Morgan 1963: 72; italics mine). The right to depose "was reserved by members of the gens. . ." (Morgan 1963: 73). Thus Morgan's observations do not contradict the fact that the matrons had a voice in these important matters. But for some reason, he did not find this remarkable, or did not choose to comment upon it. However, in a later work, Morgan (1965: 66) quotes from a letter written by the Rev. Ashur Wright (who had been a missionary among the Iroquois for forty years) as follows:

> The women were the great power among the clans, as everywhere else. They did not hesitate, when occasion required, to "knock off the horns," as it was technically called, from the head of a chief and send him back to the ranks of the warriors. The original nomination of the chiefs also always rested with them.[3]

Morgan's (1965: 66) next paragraph begins, "The mother-right and gyneocracy among the Iroquois here plainly indicated is not overdrawn." He ends his paragraph with a footnote to Bachofen. It is therefore surprising when twenty-odd pages later he states:

> But this influence of the woman did not reach outward to the affairs of the gens, phratry, or tribe, but seems to have commenced and ended with the household. This view is quite consistent with the life of patient drudgery and of general subordination to the husband which the Iroquois wife cheerfully accepted as the portion of her sex (Morgan 1965: 128).

In his earlier work, however, Morgan (1962) noted that women had the power of life or death over prisoners of war, which must certainly be regarded as an influence reaching beyond the household. Furthermore, the women could participate in the deliberations of the Council through their male speakers, such as the Council of 1791 (Snyderman 1951), the Council of 1804 (Beauchamp 1900), and the Council of 1839 (Parker 1916), and had a voice concerning warfare and treaties. Schoolcraft (1860: III: 195-196) sums up these powers as follows:

> They are the only tribes in America, north and south, so far as we have any accounts, who gave to woman a conservative power in their political

> deliberations. The Iroquois matrons had their representative in the public councils; and they exercised a negative, or what we call a veto power, in the important question of the declaration of war. They had the right also to interpose in bringing about a peace.

It appears from the evidence (some of it Morgan's), that the political influence of the Iroquois matron was considerable. The nation was not a matriarchy, as claimed by some, but the matrons were an *eminence grise*. In this respect the Iroquois were probably not unique. What is unusual is the fact that this power was socially recognized and institutionalized.

In addition, Iroquois matrons helped to select the religious practitioners of the tribe. Half of these "keepers of the faith" were women, and according to Morgan (1962: 186), "They had an equal voice in the general management of the festivals and of all their religious concernments." Furthermore, as Randle (1951) has pointed out, women's activities were celebrated in the ceremonial cycle, and female virtues of food-providing and natural fertility were respected and revered.

Kin group membership was transmitted through the mother, and since there were rules of exogamy, the father belonged to a kinship group other than that of his wife and children. Morgan (1962: 84; 326-327) describes the rules of inheritance and succession as follows:

> Not least remarkable among their institutions, was that which confined transmission of all titles, rights and property in the female line to the exclusion of the male...
>
> If the wife, either before or after marriage, inherited orchards, or planting lots, or reduced land to cultivation, she could dispose of them at her pleasure, and in case of her death, they were inherited, together with her other effects, by her children.

Marriages were arranged by the mothers of the prospective couple, and they also took responsibility for the success of the union thus created. Both marriage and divorce involved little ceremony. The latter could be instigated by either the wife or the husband. In the case of a separation, the children usually remained with the mother (Morgan 1962). Parker (1926) mentions that spacing the births of children was in the hands of the mother and there was greater delight at the birth of a daughter than at that of a son (Stites 1905). The mother often had the power to confer a name on her child (Goldenweiser 1912; 1914).

Crucial in consolidating the power of the women was the family long house. Traditionally this was a large structure of bark and wood containing many compartments and several fires all connected by a central aisle. Each family occupied a compartment and shared a fire with several other families (Bartram 1895: 40-41). Wright is quoted by Morgan (1965: 65-66) concerning the domestic arrangements of the tribe:

> As to their family system, when occupying the old long-houses, it is probable that some one clan predominated, the women taking husbands, however,

from the other clans; and sometimes, for a novelty, some of their sons bringing in their young wives until they felt brave enough to leave their mothers. Usually, the female portion ruled the house, and were doubtless clannish enough about it. The stores were in common; but woe to the luckless husband or lover who was too shiftless to do his share of the providing. No matter how many children, or whatever goods he might have in the house, he might at any time be ordered to pick up his blanket and budge; and after such an order it would not be healthful for him to disobey; the house would be too hot for him; and unless saved by the intercession of some aunt or grandmother, he must retreat to his own clan, or as was often done, go and start a new matrimonial alliance. . .

Two features of Iroquois domestic life deserve special mention. First, as noted by Murdock (1934), the authority over the household resided in the matron and not in one of her male relatives. Second, as Randle (1951) has pointed out, the long house was the analogy on which the League was built. The Iroquois referred to themselves as the people of the long house. The figurative long house of the League was divided into geographical compartments, each occupied by a tribe. It is probable that this analogy helped to consolidate the considerable political power of the Iroquois matrons.

In sum, Iroquois matrons enjoyed unusual authority in their society, perhaps more than women have ever enjoyed anywhere at any time. The position of matron was open to all women who qualified. The matrons were socially recognized and institutionalized powers behind the throne (though one can hardly term the supremely democratic Council of Elders as a "throne"). Women were able to serve as religious practitioners, and the matrons helped to select all "keepers of the faith." Finally, the matron ruled supreme within the long house, and domestic arrangements were such that all women had dominant power within the household.

THE POSITION OF WOMEN AMONG THE BEMBA

The Bemba, with whom the Iroquois will be compared, were the largest and the most highly organized tribe in North-Eastern Rhodesia at the time they were studied by Audrey Richards (1939). Unlike the Iroquois, they had a highly centralized government under an autocratic chief. However, they resembled the Iroquois in their strong military tradition, in their complex political organization, and in their relatively simple economic organization based on agriculture.

Among the Bemba, a few of the princesses (sisters and maternal nieces of the chiefs) enjoyed considerable political and religious power, as did the wives of senior chiefs and the mother of the supreme ruler. However, such roles were comparatively few, were ascribed and could not be aspired to by all Bemba women. Bemba women were free to contract their second marriages and were able to initiate divorce, unlike the women among their patrilineal neighbors.

However, in the domestic sphere, women were ultimately subservient to men, in spite of the considerable prestige a matron could acquire. Richards (1956: 50, 159) writes:

> Menfolk are dominant in Bemba society. Women used to greet men kneeling, and they still do so on formal occasions today. Men receive the best of the food and take precedence at beer drinks and on other social occasions. They speak first in family matters .... Girls are taught to please their husbands .... Women calmly accept the fact that their husbands will beat them ....
>
> ... Fathers are respected autocrats in the home, but are dethroned as their children grow up and realize that ultimate power lies with their mothers' brothers.

Thus although Bemba women enjoyed a higher status than women in many societies, it was not nearly as high as that of Iroquois women, in spite of the similarities in the rules of descent and marital residence between the two tribes.

Status has here been defined as power over basic resources and important decisions in the political, the religious and the domestic spheres. In agricultural societies such as the Iroquois and the Bemba such power does not exist independently from the control of food and the essential elements used in its production. It is to the economic organization of the subsistence activities of the two tribes that we now turn.

ECONOMIC ORGANIZATION OF SUBSISTENCE ACTIVITIES

Agricultural Activities

Both the Iroquois and the Bemba depended upon garden agriculture for the major portion of their food supply. Both tribes supplemented cultivated foods with foods gathered by the women, with meat hunted by the men and with fish obtained by both men and women. Among the Iroquois, women occasionally joined the hunting expeditions. Both tribes practiced shifting agriculture which consisted of four stages: clearing the ground, planting, cultivating and harvesting. Among the Iroquois, men were in charge of preparing the fields, although Waugh (1916) claims that the women helped. Trees were girdled and allowed to die. The following spring, the underbrush was burned off (Parker 1910). The remaining agricultural activities were conducted by the women in organized work groups. For men to do this work was considered demeaning. As Stites (1905) has pointed out, the warrior in the field was always an assistant, never an owner or director.

The economic organization of the Iroquois was remarkable (and far from unique) for the great separateness of the sexes which it fostered. Men were often away on war parties for years at a time. Although wives or temporary wives, appointed especially for the purpose, occasionally accompanied men on the hunt, it was more usual for this to be a male pursuit. Even at the daily meal, the sexes ate separately. It is no wonder that Morgan (1962: 323) wrote:

> Indian habits and modes of life divided the people socially into two great classes, male and female. The male sought the conversation and society of the male, and they went forth together for amusement, or for the severer duties of life. In the same manner the female sought the companionship of her own sex. Between the sexes there was but little sociality, as this term is understood in polished society.

This separateness of the sexes applied also to the child-rearing methods of the tribe. In the words of Morgan (1962: 325), "The care of their infancy and childhood was intrusted to the watchful affection of the mothers alone." This must have afforded the growing girl a reassuring continuity, but it contained inherent problems for the young boy. Eventually he would have to move from the agricultural world under female authority to the life of the hunter and warrior under the authority of older men.

Mary Jemison[4], a white woman adopted into the Seneca tribe, gave the following description of the women's work group and the tasks it performed:

> Our labor was not severe; and that of one year was exactly similar in almost every respect to that of the others .... Notwithstanding the Indian women have all the fuel and bread to procure, and the cooking to perform, their task is probably not harder than that of white women, who have those articles provided for them; and their cares certainly are not half as numerous, nor as great. In the summer season, we planted, tended, and harvested our corn, and generally had all of our children with us; but had no master to oversee or drive us, so that we could work as leisurely as we pleased. . . .
>
> We pursued our farming business according to the general custom of Indian women, which is as follows: In order to expedite their business, and at the same time enjoy each other's company, they all work together in one field, or at whatever job they may have on hand. In the spring, they choose an old active squaw to be their driver and overseer, when at labor, for the ensuing year. She accepts the honor, and they consider themselves bound to obey her.
>
> When the time for planting arrives, and the soil is prepared, the squaws are assembled in the morning, and conducted into a field, where each plants one row. [Note: The seeds were first soaked, and then planted in prepared hills.]
>
> They then go into the next field and plant once across, and so on till they have gone through the tribe. If any remains to be planted, they again commence where they did at first, (in the same field,) and so keep on till the whole is finished. By this rule, they perform their labor of every kind, and every jealousy of one having done more or less than another is effectually avoided (Seaver 1880: 69-71).

Loskiel (1794: part 1: 16) emphasized the toil of the women, adding "nothing but hunger and want can rouse the men from their drowsiness, and give them activity." Parker (1910) tends to agree with Mary Jemison that the work of the women was not hard.

The division of agricultural work by sex among the Bemba was essentially as follows: the land was cleared by the men with the help of the women, men and women planted, and women alone cultivated and harvested. Their method of clearing land was unique and is described by Richards (1939) as follows:

> The method of shearing the trees of their branches is exceedingly skilled. It is the man's task *par excellence* in the whole economic routine. The Bemba are daring climbers . . . (p. 289.) Every year two or three deaths occur during tree-cutting. Other men are disabled through falls (p. 290). It will be seen that in this form of cultivation the people's emotions seem entirely centered round one process – a particular method of tree-cutting which is their pride and delight, and closely associated with an elaborate form of ritual . . . (p. 300).
>
> Next comes the business of stacking the branches . . . . The aim of the native is plainly not to clear the bush of obstructions, but to collect the maximum amount of brushwood to burn. It is the ash which he considers valuable, and the burning of the soil. The woman who piles the branches carries them as high as possible from the ground, so that twigs and leaves should not snap off in transit, and thus waste valuable fuel.
>
> Piling the branches is the hardest work a Bemba woman does . . . . The women lift boughs, often fifteen or twenty feet long . . . (p. 293).

The millet seed was sown broadcast, usually by a man, while a woman walked behind him covering the seeds with earth. Richards (1939) considered the sowing a quick, light task, but one that required skill. The men also built fences for the gardens as they were needed. The little cultivation that was required was performed by the women. They also did the reaping.

In sum, the agricultural work of Iroquois women appears to have been lighter but more highly organized than that of the Bemba women. Although the work of the Bemba women was more arduous, their total contribution to economic activities was not as great. Furthermore, the pollarding of trees by Bemba men was unique to their tribe, a daring and celebrated enterprise which established the man as the owner of the fields he cleared. There was no cultural emphasis on the ground-clearing activities of the Iroquois men. Thus the actual agricultural activities reveal little that is relevant to the status of women in the two tribes.

Factors of Production

In agricultural production, land constitutes the natural resource; seeds constitute the raw materials; and agricultural implements constitute the tools. The ownership of these factors of production – the land, the seeds and the implements – among the Iroquois is difficult to establish from existing evidence. Goldenweiser (1912: 469) offers the following information: ". . . The husband, in ancient times, could regard as his own only his weapons, tools, and wearing apparel, his wife owned the objects of the household, the house itself, and the land."

It seems possible to infer that the women owned the seeds, and the rake, hoe and digging stick, the agricultural implements enumerated by Stites (1905). Possibly they were owned by the household or by the women's work group. Male ownership is nowhere recorded.

It is also not entirely clear who owned the land. The importance of the fields can be deduced from the fact that village sites were chosen largely for the fertility of the surrounding land. As Randle (1951) has pointed out, these sites were changed as land became depleted, and not when an area had been hunted out. The extent of the corn fields can be estimated from the various accounts of their destruction at the hands of white war parties. In one such foray mentioned by Stites (1905), it took the French forces about a week to destroy the fields of four Iroquois villages.

Morgan (1965) stressed that land was communally owned and that its individual ownership was unknown. Snyderman (1951) mentions the belief that land belonged to future generations as well as to the present generation. However, according to Randle (1951), land was often registered in female names. Hewitt (1933) states that women owned the lands, the village sites and the burial grounds. Nominal female ownership is indicated in the following statement by Red Jacket, speaker for the women at the Council of 1791: "You ought to hear and listen to what we women shall speak . . . for we are the owners of the land and it is ours . . ." (Snyderman 1951: 20).

In contrast, land ownership among the Bemba is described by Richards (1939) as follows:

> . . . Any chief will reply quite simply that the whole territory belongs to him, together with the food that is produced in it, its game and fish, and the labour of its people (p. 245).
>
> . . . Bemba rights to the use of land are a part of a reciprocal series of obligations between subject and chief. The former accepts the political status of subject and membership of a village group. He gives respect, labour, and tribute to his chief, and in return he is able to cultivate as much land as he pleases and to occupy it for as long as he needs. The latter prays to the tribal spirits in order to make the land productive, initiates economic effort, feeds the hungry, and maintains his court and tribal councillors . . . (p. 266).
>
> The millet garden is commonly spoken of as belonging to the man, because it is he who originally cleared the ground for it. But the married man is described as making a garden for his wife . . . (p. 189). Hence the millet garden is the man's, although the use of the crop is given to the wife. But her rights are not absolute. They depend strictly on the continuance of the marriage, and are forfeited by divorce or death, and are subject to the claims of the husband's relatives, who, since they live in another village, are constantly apprehensive lest they do not get their due (p. 190).

In short, the lands of the Iroquois appear to have been communally owned, but held by the women; whereas among the Bemba, all lands nominally belong to the chief, but were held by the men who cleared them.

The Food Produced

Among the Iroquois, a great variety of corn was raised. Speck (1945) estimates from 15 to 17 varieties, and it was prepared in numerous ways. Murdock (1934) suggests as many as 50. Even the husks, silk, cobs and leaves were used to make a number of useful articles (Parker 1910). Beans were also a popular food. Speck (1945) estimates there were 60 varieties, as were squashes, of which there were eight varieties according to Speck (1945). All three of these foods were provided by the women and held in high esteem by the Iroquois. The foods were represented in their pantheon as "The Three Sisters," "Our Life" and "Our Supporters" (Morgan 1962).

These staples were supplemented by goods gathered by the women: maple sugar, berries, wild fruit, nuts, roots, mushrooms, leaf foods and by other cultivated foods such as melons. Schoolcraft (1847) referred to the apple as "the Iroquois banana." The fruit was one of several introduced by the Dutch and the French. According to Parker (1910: 94), during the Revolutionary War "General Sullivan in his famous raid against the hostile Iroquois cut down a single orchard of 1500 trees." Thus an impressive commissariat was supplied by the women of the tribe. The diet of the Iroquois was ample, varied and nutritious. One is forced to agree with Morgan (1962) who considered the indigenous diet of the Iroquois far superior to that typical of the Europeans of pre-contact times.

The Bemba diet, like that of the Iroquois, contained one basic cereal staple: finger millet. Richards (1939: 37) writes:

> The bulk of each meal consists of a porridge made of this flour, and the subsidiary foods, meat or vegetable, are eaten with it in small quantities only (about half a pound of the latter to five pounds of the former). For their nutrition the Bemba depend almost entirely on the amount of millet they are able to get, and the seasonal variations from hunger and plenty consist in effect of the shortage or absence of this particular grain.

In distinct contrast to the Iroquois, the Bemba regularly experienced periods of food shortage. Richards (1939: 35) observes:

> The most pronounced feature of this dietary is its alternation between hunger and plenty. . . . In this territory the existence of a definite scarcity is noticed at once by the most casual observer. The Bemba constantly talk about "hunger months" as distinguished from food months.

A number of other foods besides the finger millet were available to the Bemba, but the list seems a short one indeed when compared with the foods available to the Iroquois. There were mushrooms and gourds, wild fruits, green leaves, cultivated groundnuts and assorted pulses. Game and fish were very scarce, but caterpillars and wood-lice were eaten.

The two societies present a distinct contrast. The Iroquois women provided a varied, nutritious and dependable diet. The Bemba women provided a monotonous, marginal diet which was interrupted by periods of near famine. These facts are significant for the way food was distributed, as will be shown below.

Distributing and Dispensing Food

The generous hospitality which was customary among the Iroquois was probably the most salient feature of their food distribution. The rule of hospitality was perpetuated and its protocol codified by Handsome Lake, the early nineteenth century prophet (Parker 1913). Hospitality was extended to all strangers, and the stranger was to be fed before he was questioned about his mission (Lafitau 1724). Hospitality was also extended to other members of the village, to the extent that no one went hungry (Parker 1910). It is of interest to note Morgan's (1962: 329) comment: "It [hospitality] rested chiefly upon the industry, and therefore upon the natural kindness of the Indian woman . . ." This statement demonstrates that the hospitality of the household reflected favorably on its women, not on its men. Furthermore, hospitality was motivated by generosity, which was valued in and of itself (Fenton 1957).

There is conflicting evidence concerning the distribution of the fruit of the chase. Beauchamp (1900) says that the meat was given to the hunter's wife. Carr (1887) claims it was given to the hunter's mother-in-law. Lafitau (1724) mentions that the legitimate wife had a prior claim to that of the temporary hunting wife. Although not a polygynous society like the Bemba, the Iroquois were not rigidly monogamous. Hunting expeditions often lasted as long as a year, and if the hunter's wife refused to go, a special temporary wife might accompany him instead.

Stites (1905) cites one *Jesuit Relation* to the effect that one of women's chief winter tasks was to go into the forest to bring home the deer their husbands had slain. However, citing a different *Jesuit Relation*, she states that women were sometimes not given a share of the meat at all.[5] Wright, quoted by Morgan (1965), seems to suggest that the meat was contributed by the hunter to his wife's household. Morgan (1965: 127) makes a similar statement himself, and this is probably the most correct description.

Thus the distribution of the food of the tribe, even the food procured by the men, appears to have been at the discretion of the matrons. By observing the rules of hospitality, the matrons made it possible for every member of the tribe and for visitors to obtain a share of the food supply.

The dispensing of food within the household also rested with the matrons. As Morgan (1962: 327) observed, "The care of the appetite was left entirely with the women, as the Indian never asked for food." No author mentions any specified obligations which the matron had to meet in performing this task.

The Iroquois had one meal a day, which was served in the morning. Lafitau (1724: III: 79-80) offers a description of this meal. Morgan's (1965: 65) later description is as follows:

> Every household was organized under a matron who supervised the domestic economy. After a single daily meal was cooked at the several fires the matron was summoned, and it was her duty to divide the food, from the kettle, to the several families according to their respective needs. What remained was placed in the custody of another person until it was required by the matron. . . . It shows that their domestic economy was not without method, and it displays the care and management of woman. . .

It was not only in the domestic realm that the matrons controlled the dispensing of food. By supplying the essential provisions for male activities – the hunt, the warpath and the Council – they were able to control these to some degree. Thus Randle (1951: 172) writes, "Indirectly, too, it is stated that the women could hinder or actually prevent a war party which lacked their approval by not giving the supplies of dried corn and the moccasins which the warriors required."

Stites (1905: 78) makes a similar assertion: "... They also had control of the cultivated land and its produce, and gave support to the warriors only in return for their military services ..."

This control was effected by the monopoly that the matrons exercised on the staple food used on both the hunt and the warpath. According to Morgan (1962), this food was prepared while the warriors performed their dance. He gives the recipe for the dried corn-maple syrup provision (see also Bartram 1895: 71) and concludes, "... The warrior could carry without inconvenience in his bear-skin pocket a sufficient supply for a long and perilous expedition" (Morgan 1962: 340). Further on he states, "This [the same recipe] was carried in the bear-skin pocket of the hunter, and upon it alone he subsisted for days together" (Morgan 1962: 373).

The importance of these provisions was also mentioned by Loskiel (1794), who observed that hunting was not possible on the warpath for fear of giving warning to the enemy. He also describes the importance of the food provided by the matrons for the Council. "Provisions must always be in plenty in the council-house; for eating and deliberating take their turns" (1794: part 1: 134; also see Bartram 1895: 58-63).

Iroquois women were in charge of the ingenious methods of preserving and storing the abundant food supplies. Corn, meat, fish, berries, squashes and even fats were preserved. Some of these foods were buried in specially constructed pits, and some were kept in the long house. Stored food constituted one of the major forms of wealth of the tribe. Stites (1905: 72) claims, "... It was the women's organization which controlled the surplus and represented the owning class." Hewitt (1933) describes a tribal public treasury which contained wampum belts, quill and feather work, furs and assorted stored foods. Its contents were scrupulously guarded by the matrons.

In sum, among the Iroquois, the distribution of food within the tribe was the responsibility of the matrons. They also controlled the provisions within the household, as well as those that made the major male activities possible. Some authors claim that the matrons controlled the wealth of the tribe (much of it in stored food) as well.

Like the Iroquois, the Bemba were hospitable and placed the dispensing of the daily meal in the hands of a few matrons. Here the similarity ends. The distribution of food followed a number of institutionalized rules, and far less was left to the discretion and generosity of the matrons. It is possible that these prescribed obligations stemmed from greater scarcity of food, just as it has only been in times of perceived scarcity that our own country has resorted to food rationing.

Concerning the distribution of Bemba grain Richards (1939: 188-189) writes:

> Control over the contents of the Bemba granary are governed by more complex rules. Roughly speaking, the labour given to the production of the crop gives a man ultimate right of disposal, but this is subject to the superior claims of certain older relatives and ultimately to that of the chief himself. That is to say, the owner may be the only person able to reap the grain and store it, but he may have to give portions of the crop to others on demand.

Furthermore, the dispensing of cooked food, although conducted by the matrons, reflected the prestige and power of the male household heads, and was analogous to the hospitality extended by the chief, which bestowed obligations on the recipients. Richards (1939: 135, 144, 150) observes:

> . . . The distribution of cooked food is an attribute of authority, and therefore prestige, and that its reception puts a man under an obligation to return respect, service, or reciprocal hospitality. . . It is on these reciprocal obligations to serve and to feed that the whole political and economic system of the tribe is based.
>
> The whole institution of the *kamitembo* (sacred kitchen and storehouse of the chief) illustrates to my mind that close association between authority and the power to distribute provisions on which the tribal organization depends. The chief owns the food and receives tribute, and the chief provides for his subjects and distributes cooked food to them.

Summary

The role of women in the economic organization of the Bemba and the Iroquois have been compared. Unlike Bemba women, Iroquois women controlled the factors of agricultural production, for they had rights in the land which they cultivated and in the implements and the seeds. Iroquois agricultural activities, which yielded bountiful harvests, were highly organized under elected female leadership. The male ground-clearing activities were not culturally emphasized unlike the pollarding of trees among the Bemba. Most important, Iroquois women maintained the right to distribute and to dispense all food, even that procured by the men. This was especially significant as stored food constituted one of the major forms of wealth for the tribe. Through their control of the economic organization of the tribe, Iroquois matrons were able to make available or to withhold food for meetings of the Council and for war parties, for the observance of religious festivals and for the daily meals of the household. These economic realities were institutionalized in the matrons' power to nominate Council Elders and to influence Council decisions. They had a voice in the conduct of war and the establishment of treaties. They elected "keepers of the faith" and served in that capacity. They controlled life in the long-house.

The unusual role of Iroquois women in politics, religion and domestic life cannot be dismissed simply as a historical curiosity. It cannot be explainted by Iroquois social structure, nor can it be attributed to the size of their contribution to the Iroquois economy. The high status of Iroquois women was the result of their control of the economic organization of their tribe.

NOTES

1. This study has been made possible by the generous support of the Radcliffe Institute. Hilda Kahne and Ying Ying Yuan have made numerous helpful comments on the manuscript.
2. Beauchamp (1900), Carr (1887) and Hewitt (1933) published their articles over a span of nearly fifty years, yet all describe Iroquois "matriarchy." Carr's article contains the most documentation. Hewitt's information is somewhat idiosyncratic and contains no documentation. He ends his article with a paraphrase of Lafitau's (1724) famous passage, but does not attribute it to its original source.
3. The letter was written in May, 1879, and appears in its entirety in Stern (1933). Another interpretation by Wright of the "knocking off of horns" appears in Fenton, *ed.* (1957).
4. *Life of Mary Jemison: Deh-he-wä-mis* was originally published in 1824 when Mary Jemison was about 80. The book, written by James Seaver, is supposed to present Mary Jemison's narrative, but it is written in a style that can hardly have been the idiom of a woman who spent most of her life as a Seneca. As it is the only source of its kind, it is quoted here.

   The edition used is that published in 1880 and contains chapters by a number of later authors. By 1924, the book had gone through 22 editions at the hands of four revisers, one of whom was Lewis Morgan. Any edition of the book is difficult to obtain today. Milliken (1924: 87) writes of the first edition:

   > Published before the day of the dime novel, at a time when tales of adventure and romance were much less common than now and the thrillers of the silver screen were entirely unknown, it was circulated and read almost to complete destruction.
5. This discrepancy demonstrates one of the difficulties in using the *Jesuit Relations*. The *Relations* cover an extended period of time and are anecdotal rather than descriptive. They are the work of many authors, whose prime purpose was to describe not the customs they found, but their own missionary activities.

REFERENCES

Aberle, David
1961 Matrilineal descent in cross-cultural perspective. In *Matrilineal kinship*, pp. 655-727. Edited by David M. Schneider and Kathleen Gough. Berkeley, University of California Press.

Bartram, John
1895 *Observations on the inhabitants, climate, soil, rivers, productions, animals, and other matters worthy of notice.* Geneva, New York, reprinted by W. F. Humphrey.

Beauchamp, William M.
1900 Iroquois women. *Journal of American Folk-Lore*, Vol. 13, no. 49 (April-June), pp. 81-91. Boston and New York, Houghton Mifflin & Company.

Carr, Lucien
1887 On the social and political position of woman among the Huron-Iroquois tribes. *Annual Report of the Trustees of the Peabody Museum of American Archaeology and Ethnology*, Vol. 3, pp. 207-232. Cambridge, The Trustees.

D'Andrade, Roy G.
1966 Sex differences and cultural institutions. *Stanford Studies in Psychology*, no. 5, pp. 174-204. Stanford, Stanford University Press.

Fenton, William N.
1957 Long-term trends of change among the Iroquois. *Proceedings of the 1957 Annual Spring Meetings of the American Ethnological Society*, pp. 30-35. Seattle, American Ethnological Society.

Fenton, William N., *ed.*
1957 Seneca Indians by Asher Wright (1859). *Ethnohistory*, Vol. 4, no. 3 (Summer), pp. 302-321. Bloomington, American Indian Ethnohistoric Conference.

Goldenweiser, Alexander A.
1912 On Iroquois work, 1912. *Summary Report of the Geological Survey of Canada, Anthropology Division*, sessional paper no. 26, pp. 464-475. Ottawa, Government Printing Bureau.
1914 On Iroquois work, 1913-1914. *Summary Report of the Geological Survey of Canada, Anthropology Division*, pp. 365-373. Ottawa, Government Printing Bureau.
Gough, Kathleen
1961 The modern disintegration of matrilineal descent groups. In *Matrilineal kinship*, pp. 631-652. Edited by David M. Schneider and Kathleen Gough. Berkeley, University of California Press.
Hewitt, John N. B.
1933 Status of woman in Iroquois polity before 1784. *Annual Report of the Board of Regents of the Smithsonian Institution for 1932*, pp. 475-488. Washington, United States Government Printing Office.
Jenness, Diamond
1932 The Indians of Canada. *Bulletin of the National Museum of Canada*, no. 65. Ottawa, F. A. Acland, Printer to the King.
Lafitau, Joseph F.
1724 *Moeurs des sauvages ameriquains, comparées aux moeurs des premiers temps*. Four volumes. Paris, Saugrain l'aîné [etc.].
Loskiel, George H.
1794 *History of the mission of the United Brethren among the Indians in North America*. Translated by Christian LaTrobe. London, The Brethren's Society for the Furtherance of the Gospel.
Lowie, Robert H.
1961 *Primitive society*. New York, Harper.
Malinowski, Bronislaw
1913 The family among the Australian aborigines. *Monographs on Sociology*, Vol. 1. London, University of London Press.
Milliken, Charles
1924 A biographical sketch of Mary Jemison, the white woman of the Genesee. *Researches and Transactions of the New York State Archeological Association, Lewis H. Morgan Chapter*, Vol. 4, no. 3, pp. 81-101. Rochester.
Morgan, Lewis H.
1962 *League of the Iroquois*. New York, Corinth Books.
1963 *Ancient society*. Edited by Eleanor B. Leacock. Cleveland, World Publishing Company.
1965 *Houses and house-life of the American aborigines*. Chicago, University of Chicago Press.
Murdock, George P.
1934 *Our primitive contemporaries*. New York, The Macmillan Co.
1967 Ethnographic atlas: a summary. *Ethnology*, Vol. 6, no. 2 (April), pp. 109-236. Pittsburgh, University of Pittsburgh.
Noon, John A.
1949 Law and government of the Grand River Iroquois. *Viking Fund Publications in Anthropology*, no. 12. New York, Viking Fund.
Parker, Arthur C.
1910 Iroquois uses of maize and other food plants. *New York State Museum Bulletin*, no. 144. Albany, University of the State of New York.
1913 The code of Handsome Lake, the Seneca prophet. *New York State Museum Bulletin*, no. 163. Albany, University of the State of New York.
1916 The constitution of the five nations. *New York State Museum Bulletin*, no. 184. Albany, The University of the State of New York.
1926 An analytical history of the Seneca Indians. *Researches and Transactions of the New York State Archeological Association, Lewis H. Morgan Chapter*, Vol. 6, nos. 1-4, pp. 1-162. Rochester.

Randle, Martha C.
1951 Iroquois women, then and now. *Bulletin of the Bureau of American Ethnology*, no. 149, pp. 167-180. Washington, United States Government Printing Office.

Richards, Audrey I.
1939 *Land, labour and diet in Northern Rhodesia.* London, New York [etc.], Oxford University Press.
1956 *Chisungu; a girls' initiation ceremony among the Bemba of Northern Rhodesia.* London, Faber and Faber.

Richards, Cara B.
1957 Matriarchy or mistake: the role of Iroquois women through time. *Proceedings of the 1957 Annual Spring Meeting of the American Ethnological Society*, pp. 36-45. Seattle, American Ethnological Society.

Schoolcraft, Henry R.
1847 *Notes on the Iroquois, or, contributions to American history, antiquities, and general ethnology.* Albany, Erastus H. Pease & Company.
1860 *Archives of aboriginal knowledge.* Six volumes. Philadelphia, J. B. Lippincott & Company.

Seaver, James E.
1880 *Life of Mary Jemison: Deh-he-wā-mis.* Buffalo, Matthews Brothers & Bryant.

Snyderman, George S.
1951 Concepts of land ownership among the Iroquois and their neighbors. *Bulletin of the Bureau of American Ethnology*, no. 149, pp. 13-34. Washington, United States Government Printing Office.

Speck, Frank G.
1945 The Iroquois, a study in cultural evolution. *Bulletin of the Cranbrook Institute of Science*, no. 23. Bloomfield Hills, Michigan.

Stern, Bernhard J., *ed.*
1933 The letters of Asher Wright to Lewis Henry Morgan. *American Anthropologist*, Vol. 35, no. 1 (January-March), pp. 138-145. Menasha, American Anthropological Association.

Stites, Sara H.
1905 Economics of the Iroquois. *Byrn Mawr College Monographs*, Vol. 1, no. 3 (April). Bryn Mawr.

Waugh, F. W.
1916 Iroquois foods and food preparation. *Memoir of the Canada Department of Mines, Geological Survey*, no. 86, *Anthropological Series*, no. 12. Ottawa, Government Printing Bureau.

ECONOMIC DEVELOPMENT AND NATIVE AMERICAN WOMEN IN THE EARLY NINETEENTH CENTURY

MARY C. WRIGHT

Rutgers University

ECONOMIC DEVELOPMENT AND PARTICIPATION IN THE EURO-AMERICAN market economy defines a common experience among women which transcends time, place, and culture.[1] Feminists and scholars of the Third World have pointed to the degradation of women's traditional economic and social power that accompanies western "modernization." American historians have similarly described the situation facing women in New England during the late eighteenth and early nineteenth centuries, as self-sufficiency gave way to agricultural production for sale, incipient industrialism, and a money economy. Native American women, as this ethnohistorical exploration attempts to show, suffered a comparable fate with the advent of the fur trade in the Pacific Northwest.[2]

For many Native Americans, the fur trade constituted the first contact with the Euro-American economic system, providing a beachhead for the subsequent conquest of the continent. As Francis Jennings has shown for the seventeenth century, the trade progressively weakened Indian societies by supplanting intertribal trade and undermining local craft production. Yet, paradoxically, the very success of the fur traders depended on Indian cooperation.[3] While every member of the Indian

[1] I am using the term "Euro-American" to signify a member of or an aspect of what has traditionally been called "western" culture. Europeans, Canadians, and citizens of the United States are included in the term.

[2] Ester Boserup, *Women's Role in Economic Development* (New York: St. Martin's Press, 1970); *Signs*, 3 (1977); Irene Tinker, Michele Bo Bramsen, and Mayra Buviniv, eds., *Women and World Development* (New York: Praeger, 1976). Nancy F. Cott, *The Bonds of Womanhood: 'Woman's Sphere' in New England, 1780–1835* (New Haven: Yale Univ. Press, 1977). Mona Etienne and Eleanor Leacock, eds., *Women and Colonization: Anthropological Perspectives* (New York: Praeger, 1980), covers Montagais, Seneca, mid-Atlantic Coast Algonkian, and Tlingit women, among others.

[3] Francis Jennings, *The Invasion of America: Indians, Colonialism, and the Cant of Conquest* (Chapel Hill: Univ. of North Carolina Press, 1975), 39–41, 85–103.

societies felt, on some level, the influence of the trade and contributed to its success, Native American women's involvement was pivotal. On the one hand and in the context of traditional practices, Indian women actively adapted to new opportunities offered by the traders. Through their participation, Euro-Americans gained access to local knowledge, skills, and resources. As liaisons between Indian and white culture, as intermediary traders, food gatherers, and crafts manufacturers, and as customers, employees, and service personnel, Native American women insured the success of the fur trade companies. On the other hand, the participation of Indian women contributed to the ultimate transformation of their societies' traditional subsistence economy—in which women played an important and often managerial role—into a dependent part of the Euro-American market economy.[4]

Since Indian women's subsistence activities faded and those with a cash value did not correspondingly grow, they gradually became trapped—just as had Euro-American women earlier and as Third World women would become later—into a sphere labeled domestic, with limited access to public arenas. Such limitation was tragic, for Indian societies until then had accorded women an honored place because of their crucial political and economic roles. Yet, according to definitions of gender held by white traders, women's assistance to the fur trade was informal and domestic. Thus, Indian women received neither recognition nor positions of power in keeping with the scope of their contributions; they remained nearly invisible. It has taken historians more than a century to discover the role Indian women played in the fur trade, but historical anonymity was the least of the consequences suffered by these women as a result of that trade. Denied power within the fur trading system so dependent on them, Indian women were unable to protect their societies' integrity in the face of further white expansion and economic development.[5]

[4] Sylvia Van Kirk, "The Role of Women in the Fur Trade Society of the Canadian West, 1700–1850," Diss. Queen Mary College, Univ. of London, 1975; Jennifer Brown, "Company Men and Native Families: Fur Trade Social and Domestic Relations in Canada's Old Northwest," Diss. Univ. of Chicago, 1976; Mary C. Wright, "The Role of Women and Family in Indian-White Relations in the Pacific Northwest, 1810–1850," Diss. Rutgers, The State Univ. of New Jersey (in progress).

[5] For an overview of Indian women's traditional powers, see Carolyn Niethammer, *Daughters of the Earth: The Lives and Legends of American Indian Women* (New York: Collier, 1977). The social position of Native American women is judged to be powerful by two surveys of the ethnographic literature. See, Valerie S. Mathes, "A New Look at the Role of Women in Indian Society," *American Indian Quarterly*, 2 (1975), 131–39; and, Clara Sue Kidwell, "The Power of Women in Three American Indian Societies," *The Journal of Ethnic Studies*, 6 (1978), 113–21. For Indian women's amenability to change, see Diane Rothenberg, "Mothers of the Nation: Seneca Resistance to Quaker Intervention" in Etienne and Leacock, eds., *Women and Colonization*, 63–87; and Laila Shukry Hamamsy, "The Role of Women in Changing Navaho Society," *American Anthropologist*, 59 (1957), 101–11.

The Pacific Northwest Seaboard regions were the focus of expanding fur trading activities in the early nineteenth century. With economic success as their goal, the first traders built upon existing native practices and patterns of trade and did not attempt to alter Indian culture except where it seriously interfered with their objectives. As the traders' substantial records make clear, Indian women of the Oregon Seaboard and Coast Salish societies played an important role in their enterprises.[6]

The Euro-American traders found that in that region's Indian cultures, women had high status and important roles. By lineage, wealth, and spiritual powers, a woman could lead her community politically, achieve prominence as a shaman, or be as active in trade as the men. "It is as common to see the wife . . . trading at the factory, as her husband," observed Alexander Ross, clerk of the North West Company.[7] Women spoke in council and their opinions were sought on all important matters, including trade bargains. Although the position of women was not uniformly high, for slavery existed, women had opportunities and respect equal to the men of their station in the Seaboard and Coast Salish Native American societies.[8]

In large part, the native women's power emanated from their role in the family and the importance of the kinship system to public issues. Indian society was not separated into distinct spheres; rather, functions of family were enmeshed with politics and economics. Intermarriage facilitated this merging. Exogamy was the rule and intermarriage occurred between families of high status in separate villages and language groups. Women maintained dual memberships, since descent was calculated on a bilateral basis. They thus remained fully recognized members of their own kin group and although they often resided with their husbands' people, they traveled, traded, and mediated between the two groups.[9]

[6] For a survey of traders' attitudes, see Lewis O. Saum, *The Fur Trader and the Indian* (Seattle: Univ. of Washington Press, 1965). Wright, "Role of Women and Family," chs. 2 and 3.

[7] Alexander Ross, *Adventures of the First Settlers on the Oregon or Columbia River* (1849; rpt. Reuben Gold Thwaites, ed., *Early Western Travels, 1748–1846* [Cleveland: Clark, 1904]), v. 7. 107, 110.

[8] George Simpson, *Fur Trade and Empire*, ed., Frederick Merk (Cambridge, Mass.: Belknap Press, 1968), 98, 104–05; Ross Cox, *The Columbia River*, eds., Edgar I. Steward and Jane R. Steward (Norman: Univ. of Oklahoma Press, 1957), 100–01; George Gibbs, "Tribes of Western Washington and Northwestern Oregon," *Contributions to North American Ethnology*, I (Washington: GPO, 1877), 185.

[9] Wayne Suttles, "Affinal Ties, Subsistence, and Prestige Among the Coast Salish," *American Anthropologist*, 62 (1960), 297–305. For ethnographic consideration of these people, see Verne F. Ray, "Lower Chinook Ethnographic Notes," *University of Washington Publications in Anthropology*, 7 (May 1938), 29–165; Hermann Haeberlin and Erna Gunther, *The Indians of Puget Sound* (Seattle: Univ. of Washington Press, 1952); David French, "Wasco-Wishram," *Perspectives in American Indian Culture Change*, ed., Edward H. Spicer, (Chicago: Univ. of Chicago Press. 1961), 337–430.

Indian women extended their role as mediators to the white traders. At times, they warned the fur traders of attack by groups to whom they owed no allegiance. When hostilities did erupt, their knowledge of diplomatic practices and their active intervention on the Euro-Americans' behalf often saved the companies. A representative incident, recorded by the North West Company, occurred in 1814 when the Wasco/Wishram peoples attacked a fur trade brigade and captured their trading goods and furs. The company's officers approached Lady Coalpo for assistance, daughter of the powerful Chinook Chief Concomly, sister-in-law to the important Kalapuya Chief Casino, and wife of the Oak Point Chief Coalpo. Drawing upon her kinship and tribal authority, she retrieved the company's goods and was amply rewarded. Impressed, Hudson's Bay Company leader George Simpson ranked her as the third most powerful Indian in the Columbia District.[10]

Among the Native American elite, observed Simpson, marriages were basically alliances "formed solely on political considerations."[11] Duncan McDougall, the first white trader to take an Indian wife in Oregon, apparently had the same end in mind when he espoused Illchee, Chinook Chief Concomly's daughter, in 1811. That the Indians continued to feel such unions advantageous was illustrated in 1833 by a Chehalis chief's offer of his kinswoman in marriage to trader William F. Tolmie. The traders followed Indian customs to the point of offering bridewealth to the women's families, receiving in return property of equal value. Good will, trading opportunities, and assistance with hostile tribes came to the Euro-Americans through marriage to Indian women.[12]

Intermarriage defined yet another influential role for Native American women, again to the benefit of trade. Women functioned as intermediary traders as they visited relatives and friends scattered throughout the region. One kinship obligation was the exchange of surplus food and goods for other forms of wealth possessed by affinal kin. Furs, *hiagua* (a type of shell circulated as currency), specialty items such as baskets or canoes, and slaves, as well as goods obtained from the Euro-Americans, circulated through the native women's distribution efforts.[13]

[10] Peter Corney, *Early Voyages in the North Pacific, 1813–1818* (Fairfield, Wash.: Ye Galleon Press, 1965), 100; Alexander Henry, *New Light on the Early History of the Greater Northwest: The Manuscript Journals of Alexander Henry and David Thompson, 1799–1814*, ed., Elliott Coues, (New York: Francis P. Harper, 1897), II, 783–810, 824; Simpson, *Fur Trade and Empire*, 104–05.

[11] Simpson, *Fur Trade and Empire*, 98.

[12] Washington Irving, *Astoria or Anecdotes of an Enterprise Beyond the Rocky Mountains*, ed., Richard D. Rust, (Boston: Twayne, 1976), 328–29; William F. Tolmie, *The Journals of William Fraser Tolmie: Physician and Fur Trader* (Vancouver, Canada: Mitchell Press, 1963), 219.

[13] Simpson, *Fur Trade and Empire*, 98; Gibbs, "Tribes," 197; Suttles, "Affinal Ties," 297–305.

The significance of women as intermediary traders probably increased with the arrival of sea-going fur traders in the late eighteenth century. By the 1810s, when white land-based trading operations began, this role was firmly entrenched. Profits to the intermediary—male or female—could be as high as fifty percent of the posts' price per pelt, so it was in the interest of the native traders to keep the Euro-Americans isolated from far-flung tribes. The fur trade companies soon recognized the ploy and attempted to counter it by sending trading parties throughout the territory and setting up small posts. To no avail—Indians still used the traditional networks of exchange and the strength of the native trade system continued, to the exasperation of the white traders. The Hudson's Bay Company admitted its "Great disadvantage" as Chinookan traders sought to monopolize contacts between Indians and whites into the 1820s.[14] As late as the 1840s, control of the trade had not been totally wrested from native hands because, as John McLoughlin complained, "in the lower parts of the Columbia, and along the Coast the Indians are so independent [and] the skins pass through so many hands."[15] The mutual obligations of kinship and the role of women as mobile traders enabled the Indians to withstand the considerable pressure to conform to the best interests of the Euro-American fur companies.[16]

Native American women along the Oregon Country's coast traditionally filled other economic functions beyond the exchange of goods. They gathered considerable quantities of food and produced many of the tools and utensils their people used. Modern scholars point to the centrality of such contributions to women's social status.[17] Several contemporary Euro-Americans also felt this productive work accounted for the women's high position. Thus in Seaboard societies, observed Clerk Ross Cox, women "assume an air of liberty and independence."[18] Throughout the

[14] George Simpson, *Part of a Dispatch from George Simpson, Esq. March 1, March 24, June 5, 1829*, ed., E. E. Rich (Toronto: The Champlain Society, 1947), 235; Corney, *First Voyages*, 154; Ross, *Adventures of the First Settlers*, 95; Dr. John Scouler, "Journals of a Voyage to Northwest America: Columbia, Vancouver and Nootka Sound," *Oregon Historical Quarterly*, 6 (1905), 195.

[15] John McLoughlin, *The Letters of John McLoughlin From Fort Vancouver to the Governor and Committee, Second Series, 1839–1844*, ed., E. E. Rich (Toronto: The Champlain Society, 1943), 70.

[16] Native market women in other areas have met with similar local trade stimulation and opportunities brought by economic development. The international market kept women's influence limited to the local scene, however. Sidney W. Mintz, "Men, Women and Trade," *Comparative Studies in Society and History*, 13 (1971), 247–269.

[17] Judith K. Brown, "Iroquois Women: An Ethnohistoric Note," *Toward an Anthropology of Women*, ed., Rayna R. Reiter (New York: Monthly Review Press, 1975), 235–251.

[18] Cox, *The Columbia River*, 266; Verne F. Ray, "The Chinook Indians in the Early 1800s," *The Western Shore*, ed. Thomas Vaughan (Portland: Durham and Downey, n.d.), 142.

Pacific Northwest, native women controlled the food they gathered and the meat or fish (brought in by the men), which they processed for long-term storage. Women's control over food was underscored by their exchange of surplus food products in the native trade system.

Initially, control of provisions gave Native American women a crucial bargaining power over white traders. Out of necessity, Euro-Americans depended on women for the foodstuffs needed to sustain their trading operations. Although supplies were sent from the East by ship and overland to these isolated posts, local produce supported the forts. The camas, wapato, and other roots, fresh vegetables, and dried and fresh fruits gathered by the women offset the traders' potential scurvy. Sturgeon, smelt, salmon, dried shellfish, and other meats processed by the women augmented company provisions. When out on expeditions, the Euro-American trappers repeatedly procured fresh provisions from women. Without this aid, the fur trade companies could not have expanded as they did in the Oregon Country.[19]

Efforts by the traders to supplant Indian sources with homegrown provisions had the reverse effect of opening up other opportunities which the women quickly seized. Potato cultivation was one of the most important adaptations. Gardens were planted around the fur trade posts beginning in 1811 in an effort to supplement imported and purchased supplies. Among the vegetables, potatoes were very successful. No records exist indicating that the whites purposefully undertook to teach their agricultural techniques to the Seaboard or Coast Salish people. Yet, by the 1840s, potato cultivation had spread throughout the region.[20]

Several factors, as ethnologist Wayne Suttles argues, were responsible for the quick integration of potatoes into the Indians' food supply. First, women already gathered roots similar to potatoes. They had the tools, harvesting techniques, and recipes applicable to this new food. Second, Indian women married to white fur traders had access to seed potatoes and were able to witness potato planting and harvesting about the forts. Third, as the women traveled throughout the territory they brought the new food to their kin and friends. Fourth, the crop needed little more care than was already given to clam beds, fishing sites, or root prairies under the stewardship of kin groups or particular individuals. The only men involved in the cultivation of potatoes, apparently, were slaves who helped

[19] Corney, *Early Voyages*, 112–13; Henry, *New Light*, II, 819–20, 851; Alexander Ross, *The Fur Hunters of the Far West*, ed. Kenneth A. Spaulding (Norman: Univ. of Oklahoma Press, 1956), 94.

[20] Gabriel Franchere, *Adventure of Astoria, 1810–1814*, ed. and trans. Hoyt C. Franchere (Norman: Univ. of Oklahoma Press, 1967), 105; Wayne Suttles, "The Early Diffusion of the Potato Among the Coast Salish," *Southwestern Journal of Anthropology*, 7 (1951), 272–88.

clear the natural prairies for planting. Otherwise, this whole new activity was a female endeavor.[21]

The utensils produced by women also filled an important role within native culture and in trade with the Euro-Americans. Each village or geographic group specialized in goods using resources available in the local area. Talent and techniques passed through families also added to a variety of specializations. Clatsop women, for instance, were famous for conical hats which kept off the ever-present Northwest rain. Decorated with woven designs of deer, fish, or dogs, the hats were in demand in the native trade system. Finely woven cedar bark mats, serving a multitude of uses from bedding to table settings, were also sought after. Baskets—some woven tightly enough to hold water, others large and sturdy enough for stored fish or berries—came from various groups. Euro-American traders used this roster of goods on their routes to fill the demands of native customers and to bring in the Indians' beaver pelts. In the mid-1820s, according to George Simpson, a first quality hat, for instance, was worth four cured beaver pelts.[22]

Although native handicrafts played a part in white-Indian exchange, the fur traders emphasized European goods. Metal, cloth, and some food items appeared superior to native crafts or were unknown to Indian culture. These imported goods, the traders hoped, would create "new wants and habitudes" among the Native Americans and thereby increase their trapping efforts. The women's acceptance and dissemination of these innovations contributed to the penetration of the Euro-American market economy into the region.[23] They, more than men, were trusted on the early trading vessels that visited the coast. In return for their assistance in mediating between the traders and the on-shore Indians, women often received "regales" of bread, molasses, and, to a lesser degree, rum. Thus established as prestige items, such foodstuffs by the 1820s had become the "prizes" of those natives "shrewd in trade," and they remained in high demand for decades.[24]

[21] Suttles, "Diffusion," 272–88.

[22] Scouler, "Journals," 165; Simpson, *Fur Trade and Empire*, 171, 174; Henry, *New Light*, II, 839, 854. The white traders also bartered from the further northern reaches of the coast *hiagua* shells, native blankets, and (reportedly) slaves, to fit in with local supplies and demands.

[23] John Dunn, *History of the Oregon Territory and the British North American Fur Trade* (London: Edwards and Hughes, 1844), 5.

[24] Corney, *Early Voyages*, 112–13; Robert Carlton Clark, *History of the Williamette Valley, Oregon* (Chicago: Clarke, 1927), III, 184; David Douglas, "Sketches of a Journey to the Northwestern Parts of the Continent of North America During the Years 1824–1827," *Oregon Historical Quarterly*, 5 (1904), 242.

Gifts of clothing to high-ranking women, as well as men, likewise served the interests of the traders. The physical appearance of the native women repulsed the traders. Women's breasts were left bare by their costume, a petticoat of twisted cedar bark (resembling a grass skirt), to which was added a cape of furs in the winter months. The paint, tatoos, feathers, brass anklets and bracelets, earrings, nose rings or plugs, and fish oil further contrasted Native American women to Euro-American fashion. The traders were only too happy to instigate new styles to replace these, for economic as well as moral reasons.[25]

Displays of material wealth counted high in Seaboard and Coast Salish culture. When a member of these societies exhibited a rare object or gave it away as potlatch wealth, others also sought it. Elite women fitted out in the traders' gifts and those Indian women married to whites initiated new patterns of consumption and provided models of newly appropriate fashions.[26]

New cloth was plentiful, reported Patrick Gass of the Lewis and Clark expedition, even before land-based fur trade operations began. In the 1810s, "ready-made clothes [were] in great demand," observed seagoing trader Peter Corney.[27] Only lack of the "means to buy the goods" kept the Indians from following Euro-American styles of dress, Clerk Gabriel Franchere claimed.[28]

The thorough infiltration made by the whites' trade goods is indicated by the "capeau, vest, pantaloons, and shirts" decorating the grave of an elite Wasco woman in 1832 for her use in the afterlife.[29] As the early ethnographer George Gibbs reported in the 1850s, "it is only in remote districts, or among old people too poor or too obstinately attached to the habits of their youth to change them, that one now sees . . . the petticoat" originally worn by all women of the Seaboard and Coast Salish regions. The nakedness so abhorred by the traders thus came to be covered and, more to the point, covered by goods obtainable only from Euro-American sources.[30]

Native American women, however, demanded practical goods from the fur trade companies. Prestige items such as food and clothing, as well as the bells, beads, vermilion, and other goods used for decoration of course had their place. But of greater importance were the various metal

[25] Cox, *The Columbia River*, 71; Franchere, *Adventure at Astoria*, 110–11.

[26] Henry, *New Light*, II, 914; Scouler, "Journals," 163.

[27] Sergeant Patrick Gass, *Gass' Journal of the Lewis and Clark Expedition*, (1811; rpt. Chicago: A. C. McClurg, 1904), 169; Corney, *Early Voyages*, 154.

[28] Franchere, *Adventure at Astoria*, 121.

[29] Nathaniel J. Wyeth, *The Correspondence and Journals of Captain Nathaniel J. Wyeth, 1831–1836*, ed. F. G. Young (Eugene: Univ. of Oregon Press, 1899), 175.

[30] Gibbs, "Tribes," 219.

goods offered by the whites. So alluring were their tools that theft was a continual problem for the Euro-Americans. Women sought new hatchets and knives to use in food gathering, awls, needles, and scissors for basketry and leather work, and brass, copper, or tin pots for cooking. Each of these standard trade goods carried by the fur trade companies eased the work traditionally done by the women and replaced tools or utensils they made from local resources.[31]

The disruption of native productive practices caused by such imported implements worked to the advantage of the Euro-American traders. "Homespun articles here, as elsewhere," observed Gibbs, "give place to 'store goods' with advancing civilization."[32] Subsistence activities of women, as well as men, were gradually replaced by the products, and thus demands, of a market economy replicating the patterns of work and consumption already apparent in the Euro-American culture of the northeastern United States.

As traditional productive practices gave way to exchange with white traders, Seaboard and Coast Salish women grasped opportunities for wage work in order to purchase these new goods. Most of this work, however, consisted of temporary projects or piece work, such as producing moccasins or doing laundry at the forts. Work as servants and agricultural laborers at the posts usually devolved upon those Indian women married to the white indentured servants of the fur trade companies. Instead of wages, they received provisions from fort supplies. Women served as partners to their spouses on the trapping expeditions begun by the companies to harvest furs in the 1810s through the 1830s. Aside from the "gifts" they received directly, the pay for their furs went under their husbands' names. Women, while doing labor for the fur trade, tended, therefore, to be invisible employees.[33]

Examination of Euro-American salmon fishing provides a further illustration of the loss in economic power experienced by women. Traditionally, fish caught during salmon runs were equally distributed to all community and kin members. Once the fish were up on the banks, the women cleaned and processed them for storage, and thereafter controlled their

[31] The sanctuary provided to a runaway white indentured blacksmith by one tribe, indicates the Indians were quite willing to incorporate the metal trades. Corney, *Early Voyages*, 98, 144, 173; On standard trade goods, see Simpson, *Fur Trade and Empire*, 171–73.

[32] Gibbs, "Tribes," 176.

[33] John K. Townsend, *Narrative of a Journey Across the Rocky Mountains to the Columbia River* (1839; rpt. Reuben Gold Thwaites, ed., *Early Western Travels, 1748–1846* [Cleveland: Clarke, 1905]), 11, 340; Tolmie, *Journals*, 251; Dunn, *History of the Oregon Territory*, 149; Peter Skene Ogden, *Peter Skene Ogden's Snake Country Journals, 1827–1828 and 1828–1829*, ed. Glyndwr Williams (London: Hudson's Bay Record Society, 1971), 166n. Also, see Van Kirk, "Role of Women in Fur Trade Society," 123–41.

allocation. But in the 1820s the Hudson's Bay Company began to cure salmon for its own use in the Pacific Northwest and to export small quantities to Britain. They employed Indian women to clean and pack the fish, and here the women worked for pay or gifts, losing control of the end product.[34]

Although traditional female productive functions were displaced by the use of imported goods during the fur trade, few new positions of economic opportunity replaced them. Prostitution became one "occupation" readily available to women. The early seagoing traders apparently instigated the institution, for by 1804, when Lewis and Clark spent several months wintering in Seaboard territory, the practice seemed firmly established.[35]

Several Indian customs of the Seaboard and Coast Salish people facilitated the emergence of prostitution, although it could not have developed without Euro-American customers. First, premarital sexual experimentation was permitted to adolescents, both male and female. Virginity at marriage apparently meant little, although fidelity to one's spouse was rigorously upheld. Girls in their experimental stage may have been open to sexual overtures from the whites. Second, women slaves were easily exploited as prostitutes by their owners. Since slaves were outside the kin group and could earn wealth to further the social standing of their owners, Seaboard elites soon organized their female slaves for "the trade."[36]

When a ship entered the Columbia River or a party of travelers entered the territory, a canoe of slaves, often headed by a high status woman, soon appeared to barter sexual service for Euro-American goods. Some elite women married to white traders provided prostitutes for the indentured servants at the forts, many of whom were not allowed to marry. When the Hudson's Bay Company forbade the practice in the mid-1820s, the women resolved, according to George Simpson, "they would not conform to this innovation as it deprived them of a very important source of Revenue."[37] The women were able to resist the reforms or at least to maintain their business outside the forts, for as late as the 1840s canoes or prostitutes under the supervision of elite Seaboard women still traversed the area for "the trade."[38]

The traders, in their written records, detested the sexual mores of the Seaboard women. They seemed "devoid of shame or decency"; their behavior "insupportably odious."[39] While the elite women who

[34] Dunn, *History of the Oregon Territory*, 163.
[35] Gass, *Journal*, 204; Ray, "The Chinook Indians," *The Western Shore*, 140, 142.
[36] Franchere, *Adventures at Astoria*, 117.
[37] Simpson, *Fur Trade and Empire*, 101.
[38] John Minto, "Number and Condition of the Native Race," *Oregon Historical Quarterly*, 1 (1900), 296–315.
[39] Henry, *New Light*, II, 754; Cox, *The Columbia River*, 71, 165.

organized prostitution perhaps saw it as another entrepreneurial undertaking consistent with their desire to increase their wealth and social standing, to the Euro-American traders it was depraved—despite their willingness to engage in it. Prostitution existed, of course, in white society, but usually involved only lower-class women. Middle- and upper-class women were expected to be innocent of such worldly goings-on. But in this Indian culture, one trader remarked with derision, "all classes from the highest to the lowest indulge in coarse sensuality and shameless profligacy."[40] The Euro-Americans considered it demeaning for elite Seaboard women to be involved, even on a managerial level, with prostitution.

For slave women, the trade in prostitution was not only demeaning, it was deadly. Veneral diseases—virtually incurable at this time (although some native herbal remedies alleviated its more obvious signs)—spread rapidly among their ranks. An epidemic of the diseases broke out among the white traders in 1814 and they sought to curtail contact with the prostitutes to bring it under control. While the Euro-American men received medical attention (such as it was) for the malady, veneral diseases resulting from prostitution brought death to many female slaves. Once illness rendered them useless, the slaves were often abandoned by their owners. In the case of death, they did not even merit burial.[41]

* * *

In sum, the fur trade brought mixed, but mostly detrimental, results to the Pacific Northwest Indians. It served as a transitory institution, eclipsed by later, more direct and relentless contact with Euro-American culture. In 1830, a recurring malarial epidemic broke out which decimated the Seaboard population; an estimated ninety percent died. A smallpox epidemic in 1836 seriously affected the Coast Salish villages. Protestant and Catholic missionaries began compaigns in the mid- to late 1830s to convert the Indians to the religion and ways of the whites. The incursion of farmers from the United States in the 1840s only sealed Euro-American dominance of the territory, begun in the economic realm by the fur trade.[42]

[40] Ross, *Adventures of the First Settlers*, 107.

[41] Henry, *New Light*, II, 826, 836, 890–911. The potential for a differential impact of contact upon women due to their class status was first brought to my attention by Elinor C. Burkett, "In Dubious Sisterhood: Race and Class in Spanish Colonial South America," *Latin American Perspectives*, 6 (1977), 18–26.

[42] S. F. Cook, "The Epidemic of 1830–1833 in California and Oregon," *University of California Publications in American Archaeology and Ethnology*, 43 (1955), 303–26; Robert T. Boyd, "Another Look at the 'Fever and Ague' of Western Oregon," *Ethnohistory*, 22 (1975), 135–54; Archibald McDonald to Edward Ermatinger, 9 Nov. 1848, Ermatinger Papers, Province Archives, Victoria, British Columbia.

Ironically, in light of the Native American cultural upheaval caused by Euro-American influences, Doctor John McLoughlin argued in 1843 that the fur trade fostered positive change in Seaboard and Coast Salish culture. Looking back over twenty years of Hudson's Bay Company control of the trade in the Pacific Northwest, he felt that the Company had "introduced order, and a respect for property, and moral obligation" among the Indians, had converted their hostility to respect, and "in short . . . reclaimed them from a state of barbarism to comparative civilization."[43]

One need not accept McLoughlin's ethnocentric idea of "civilization" to recognize that the earliest contacts between Indians and whites in the Pacific Northwest had turned on the active adaptation of Native Americans to the material goods and opportunities introduced by the traders. Native women, in particular, adapted their traditional economic and diplomatic roles to the new exigencies involved in exchange with the first white settlers. As mediators, customers, and support personnel, they insured the continued success of the trade. But in the long run, exchange with the whites proved a snare for Native Americans—both men and women.[44] Penetration of the Euro-American market, the introduction of European goods, the decline of native handicrafts, prostitution, and the ensuing decimation by disease shifted the balance of power in the Pacific Northwest from the civilization known for centuries by the native inhabitants, to a new "civilization," in which racial exclusion and subjugation would be paramount.*

[43] McLoughlin, *Letters, Second Series*, 185.

[44] For examples of several successful, long-range adaptations see Laura F. Kline, "Contending with Colonization: Tlingit Men and Women in Change," *Women and Colonization*, 88–108; or Vine Deloria, Jr., "The Tribe That Was Made to be Fishermen," *Northwest Mosaic: Minority Conflicts*, eds. James A. Halseth and Bruce A. Glosrud (Boulder: Pruett, 1977), 274–81.

* I would like to thank David Johnson, Rudolph Bell, and Judith Walkowitz for their comments on earlier drafts of this article.

the lady and the mill girl: changes in the status of women in the age of jackson

gerda lerner

The period 1800-1840 is one in which decisive changes occurred in the status of American women. It has remained surprisingly unexplored. With the exception of a recent, unpublished dissertation by Keith Melder and the distinctive work of Elisabeth Dexter, there is a dearth of descriptive material and an almost total absence of interpretation.[1] Yet the period offers essential clues to an understanding of later institutional developments, particularly the shape and nature of the women's rights movement. This analysis will consider the economic, political and social status of women and examine the changes in each area. It will also attempt an interpretation of the ideological shifts which occurred in American society concerning the "proper" role for women.

Periodization always offers difficulties. It seemed useful here, for purposes of comparison, to group women's status before 1800 roughly under the "colonial" heading and ignore the transitional and possibly atypical shifts which occurred during the American Revolution and the early period of nationhood. Also, regional differences were largely ignored. The South was left out of consideration entirely because its industrial development occurred later.

The status of colonial women has been well studied and described and can briefly be summarized for comparison with the later period. Throughout the colonial period there was a marked shortage of women, which varied with the regions and always was greatest in the frontier areas.[2] This (from the point of view of women) favorable sex ratio enhanced their status and position. The Puritan world view regarded idleness as sin; life in an underdeveloped country made it absolutely necessary that each member of the community perform an economic function. Thus work for women, married or single, was not only approved, it was regarded as a civic duty. Puritan town councils expected single girls, widows and unattached women to be self-supporting and for a long time provided needy spinsters with parcels of land. There was no social sanction against married women working; on the contrary, wives were expected to help their husbands in their trade and won social approval for doing extra work in or out of the home. Needy children, girls as well as boys, were indentured or apprenticed and were expected to work for their keep.

The vast majority of women worked within their homes, where their labor produced most articles needed for the family. The entire colonial production of cloth and clothing and partially that of shoes was in the hands of women. In addition to these occupations, women were found in many different kinds of employment. They were butchers, silversmiths, gunsmiths, upholsterers. They ran mills, plantations, tan yards, shipyards and every kind of shop, tavern and boarding house. They were gate keepers, jail keepers, sextons, journalists, printers, "doctoresses," apothecaries, midwives, nurses and teachers. Women acquired their skills the same way as did the men, through apprenticeship training, frequently within their own families.[3]

Absence of a dowry, ease of marriage and remarriage and a more lenient attitude of the law with regard to woman's property rights were manifestations of the improved position of wives in the colonies. Under British common law, marriage destroyed a woman's contractual capacity; she could not sign a contract even with the consent of her husband. But colonial authorities were more lenient toward the wife's property rights by protecting her dower rights in her husband's property, granting her personal clothing and upholding pre-nuptial contracts between husband and wife. In the absence of the husband, colonial courts granted women "femme sole" rights, which enabled them to conduct their husband's business, sign contracts and sue. The relative social freedom of women and the esteem in which they were held was commented upon by most early foreign travelers in America.[4]

But economic, legal and social status tell only part of the story. Colonial society as a whole was hierarchical, and rank and standing in society depended on the position of the men. Women did not play a determining role in the ranking pattern; they took their position in society through the men of their own family or the men they married. In other words, they participated in the hierarchy only as daughters and wives, not as individuals. Similarly, their occupations were, by and large, merely auxiliary, designed to contribute to family income, enhance their husbands' business or continue it in case of widowhood. The self-supporting spinsters were certainly the exception. The underlying assumption of colonial society was that women ought to occupy an inferior and subordinate position. The settlers had brought this assumption with them from Europe; it was reflected in their legal concepts, their willingness to exclude women from political life, their discriminatory educational practices. What is remarkable is the extent to which this felt inferiority of women was constantly challenged and modified under the impact of environment, frontier conditions and a favorable sex ratio.

By 1840 all of American society had changed. The Revolution had substituted an egalitarian ideology for the hierarchical concepts of colonial life. Privilege based on ability rather than inherited status, upward mobility for all groups of society and unlimited opportunities for individual self-fulfillment had become ideological goals, if not always realities. For men, that is; women were, by tacit consensus, excluded from the new democracy. Indeed their actual situation had in many respects deteriorated. While, as wives, they had benefitted from increasing wealth, urbanization and industrialization, their role as economic producers and as political members of society differed sharply from that of men. Women's work outside of the home no longer met with social approval; on the contrary, with two notable exceptions, it was condemned. Many business and professional occupations formerly open to women were now closed, many others restricted as to training and advancement. The entry of large numbers of women into low status, low pay and low skill industrial work had fixed such work by definition as "woman's work." Women's political status, while legally unchanged, had deteriorated relative to the advances made by men. At the same time the genteel lady of fashion had become a model of American femininity and the definition of "woman's proper sphere" seemed narrower and more confined than ever.

Within the scope of this article only a few of these changes can be more fully explained. The professionalization of medicine and its impact on women may serve as a typical example of what occurred in all the professions.

In colonial America there were no medical schools, no medical journals, few hospitals and few laws pertaining to the practice of the healing arts. Clergymen and governors, barbers, quacks, apprentices and women practiced medicine. Most practitioners acquired their credentials by reading Paracelsus and Galen and serving an apprenticeship with an established practitioner. Among the semi-trained "physics," surgeons and healers the occasional "doctoress" was fully accepted and frequently well rewarded. County records of all the colonies contain references to the work of the female physicians. There was even a female Army surgeon, a Mrs. Allyn, who served during King Philip's war. Plantation records mention by name several slave women who were granted special privileges because of their useful service as midwives and "doctoresses."[5]

The period of the professionalization of American medicine dates from 1765, when Dr. William Shippen began his lectures on midwifery in Philadelphia. The founding of medical faculties in several colleges, the standardization of training requirements and the proliferation of medical societies intensified during the last quarter of the eighteenth century. The American Revolution dramatized the need for trained medical personnel, afforded first hand battlefield experience to a number of surgeons and brought increasing numbers of semi-trained practitioners in contact with the handful of European-trained surgeons working in the military hospitals. This was an experience from which women were excluded. The resulting interest in improved medical training, the gradual appearance of graduates of medical colleges and the efforts of medical societies led to licensing legislation. In 1801 Maryland required all medical practitioners to be licensed; in 1806 New York enacted a similar law, providing for an examination before a commission. By the late 1820's all states except three had set up licensing requirements. Since most of these laws stipulated attendance at a medical college as one of the prerequisites for licensing, women were automatically excluded.[6] By the 1830's the few established female practitioners who might have continud their practice in the old ways had probably died out. Whatever vested interest they had had was too weak to assert itself against the new profession.

This process of pre-emption of knowledge, institutionalization of the profession and legitimation of its claims by law and public acceptance is standard for the professionalization of the sciences, as George Daniels has pointed out.[7] It inevitably results in the elimination of fringe elements from the profession. It is interesting to note that women had been pushed out of the medical profession in sixteenth-century Europe by a similar process.[8] Once the public had come to accept licensing and college training as guarantees of up-to-date practice the outsider, no matter how well qualified by years of experience, stood no chance in the competition. Women were the casualties of medical professionalization.

In the field of midwifery the results were similar, but the process was more complicated. Women had held a virtual monopoly in the profession in colonial America. In 1646 a man was prosecuted in Maine for practicing as a midwife.[9] There are many records of well trained midwives with diplomas from European institutions working in the colonies. In most of the colonies midwives were licensed, registered and required to pass an examination before a board. When Dr. Shippen announced his pioneering lectures on midwifery, he did it to "combat the widespread popular prejudice against the man-midwife" and because he considered most midwives ignorant and improperly trained.[10]

Yet he invited "those women who love virtue enough, to own their Ignorance, and apply for instruction" to attend his lectures, offering as an inducement the assurance that female pupils would be taught privately. It is not known if any midwives availed themselves of the opportunity.[11]

Technological advances, as well as scientific, worked against the interests of female midwives. In sixteenth-century Europe the invention and use of the obstetrical forceps had for three generations been the well-kept secret of the Chamberlen family and had greatly enhanced their medical practice. Hugh Chamberlen was forced by circumstances to sell the secret to the Medical College in Amsterdam, which in turn transmitted the precious knowledge to licensed physicians only. By the time the use of the instrument became widespread it had become associated with male physicians and midwives. Similarly in America, introduction of the obstetrical forceps was associated with the practice of male midwives and served to their advantage. By the end of the eighteenth century a number of male physicians advertised their practice of midwifery. Shortly thereafter female midwives also resorted to advertising, probably in an effort to met the competition. By the early nineteenth century male physicians had virtually monopolized the practice of midwifery on the Eastern seaboard. True to the generally delayed economic development in the Western frontier regions, female midwives continued to work on the frontier until a much later period. It is interesting to note that the concepts of "propriety" shifted with the prevalent practice. In seventeenth-century Maine the attempt of a man to act as a midwife was considered outrageous and illegal; in mid-nineteenth-century America the suggestion that women should train as midwives and physicians was considered equally outrageous and improper.[12]

Professionalization, similar to that in medicine with the elimination of women from the upgraded profession, occurred in the field of law. Before 1750, when law suits were commonly brought to the courts by the plaintiffs themselves or by deputies without specialized legal training, women as well as men could and did act as "attorneys-in-fact." When the law became a paid profession and trained lawyers took over litigation, women disappeared from the court scene for over a century.[13]

A similar process of shrinking opportunities for women developed in business and in the retail trades. There were fewer female storekeepers and business women in the 1830's than there had been in colonial days. There was also a noticeable shift in the kind of merchandise handled by them. Where previously women could be found running almost every kind of retail shop, after 1830 they were mostly found in businesses which served women only.[14]

The only fields in which professionalization did not result in the elimination of women from the upgraded profession were nursing and teaching. Both were characterized by a severe shortage of labor. Nursing lies outside the field of this inquiry since it did not become an organized profession until after the Civil War. Before then it was regarded peculiarly as a woman's occupation, although some of the hospitals and the Army during wars employed male nurses. These bore the stigma of low skill, low status and low pay. Generally, nursing was regarded as simply an extension of the unpaid services performed by the housewife—a characteristic attitude that haunts the profession to this day.

Education seems, at first glance, to offer an entirely opposite pattern from that of the other professions. In colonial days women had taught "Dame schools" and grade schools during summer sessions. Gradually, as educational opportunities for girls expanded, they advanced just a step ahead of their students. Professionalization of teaching occurred between 1820-1860, a period marked by a sharp increase in the number of women teachers. The spread of female seminaries, academies and normal schools provided new opportunities for the training and employment of female teachers.

This trend which runs counter to that found in the other professions can be accounted for by the fact that women filled a desperate need created by the challenge of the common schools, the ever-increasing size of the student body and the westward growth of the nation. America was committed to educating its children in public schools, but it was insistent on doing so as cheaply as possible. Women were available in great numbers and they were willing to work cheaply. The result was another ideological adaptation: in the very period when the gospel of the home as woman's only proper sphere was preached most loudly, it was discovered that women were the natural teachers of youth, could do the job better than men and were to be preferred for such employment. This was always provided, of course, that they would work at the proper wage differential—30-50% of the wages paid male teachers was considered appropriate. The result was that in 1888 in the country as a whole 63% of all teachers were women, while the figure for the cities only was 90.04%.[15]

It appeared in the teaching field, as it would in industry, that role expectations were adaptable provided the inferior status group filled a social need. The inconsistent and peculiar patterns of employment of black labor in the present-day market bear out the validity of this generalization.

There was another field in which the labor of women was appreciated and which they were urged to enter—industry. From Alexander Hamilton to Matthew Carey and Tench Coxe, advocates of industrialization sang the praises of the working girl and advanced arguments in favor of her employment. The social benefits of female labor particularly stressed were those bestowed upon her family, who now no longer had to support her. Working girls were "thus happily preserved from idleness and its attendant vices and crimes" and the whole community benefitted from their increased purchasing power.[16]

American industrialization, which occurred in an underdeveloped economy with a shortage of labor, depended on the labor of women and children. Men were occupied with agricultural work and were not available or willing to enter the factories. This accounts for the special features of the early development of the New England textile industry: the relatively high wages, the respectability of the job and relatively high status of the mill girls, the patriarchal character of the model factory towns and the temporary mobility of women workers from farm to factory and back again to farm. All this was characteristic only of a limited area and of a period of about two decades. By the late 1830's the romance had worn off; immigration had supplied a strongly competitive, permanent work force willing to work for subsistence wages; early efforts at trade union organization had been shattered and mechanization had turned semiskilled factory labor into unskilled labor. The process led to the replacement of the New England-born farm girls by immigrants in the mills and was accompanied by a loss of status and respectability for female workers.

The lack of organized social services during periods of depression drove ever greater numbers of women into the labor market. At first, inside the factories distinctions between men's and women's jobs were blurred. Men and women were assigned to machinery on the basis of local need. But as more women entered industry the limited number of occupations open to them tended to increase competition among them, thus lowering pay standards. Generally, women regarded their work as temporary and hesitated to invest in apprenticeship training, because they expected to marry and raise families. Thus they remained untrained, casual labor and were soon, by custom, relegated to the lowest paid, least skilled jobs. Long hours, overwork and poor working conditions would characterize women's work in industry for almost a century.[17]

Another result of industrialization was in increasing differences in life styles between women of different classes. When female occupations, such as carding, spinning and weaving, were transferred from home to factory, the poorer women followed their traditional work and became industrial workers. The women of the middle and upper classes could use their newly gained time for leisure pursuits: they became ladies. And a small but significant group among them chose to prepare themselves for professional careers by advanced education. This group would prove to be the most vocal and troublesome in the near future.

As class distinctions sharpened, social attitudes toward women became polarized. The image of "the lady" was elevated to the accepted ideal of femininity toward which all women would strive. In this formulation of values lower class women were simply ignored. The actual lady was, of course, nothing new on the American scene; she had been present ever since colonial days. What was new in the 1830's was the cult of the lady, her elevation to a status symbol. The advancing prosperity of the early nineteenth century made it possible for middle class women to aspire to the status formerly reserved for upper class women. The "cult of true womanhood" of the 1830's became a vehicle for such aspirations. Mass circulation newspapers and magazines made it possible to teach every woman how to elevate the status of her family by setting "proper" standards of behavior, dress and literary tastes. *Godey's Lady's Book* and innumerable gift books and tracts of the period all preach the same gospel of "true womanhood"—piety, purity, domesticity.[18] Those unable to reach the goal of becoming ladies were to be satisfied with the lesser goal—acceptance of their "proper place" in the home.

It is no accident that the slogan "woman's place is in the home" took on a certain aggressiveness and shrillness precisely at the time when increasing numbers of poorer women *left* their homes to become factory workers. Working women were not a fit subject for the concern of publishers and mass media writers. Idleness, once a disgrace in the eyes of society, had become a status symbol. Thorstein Veblen, one of the earliest and sharpest commentators on the subject, observed that it had become almost the sole social function of the lady "to put in evidence her economic unit's ability to pay." She was "a means of conspicuously unproductive expenditure," devoted to displaying her husband's wealth.[19] Just as the cult of white womanhood in the South served to preserve a labor and social system based on race distinctions, so did the cult of the lady in an egalitarian society serve as a means of preserving class distinctions. Where class distinctions were not so great, as on the frontier, the position of women was closer to what it had been in colonial days; their economic contribution was more highly valued, their opportunities were less restricted and their positive participation in community life was taken for granted.

In the urbanized and industrialized Northeast the life experience of middle class women was different in almost every respect from that of the lower class women. But there was one thing the society lady and the mill girl had in common—they were equally disfranchised and isolated from the vital centers of power. Yet the political status of women had not actually deteriorated. With very few exceptions women had neither voted nor stood for office during the colonial period. Yet the spread of the franchise to ever wider groups of white males during the Jacksonian age, the removal of property restrictions, the increasing numbers of immigrants who acquired access to the franchise, made the gap between these new enfranchised voters and the disfranchised women more obvious. Quite naturally, educated and propertied women felt this deprivation more keenly. Their own career expectations had been encouraged by widening educational opportunities; their consciousness of their own abilities and of their potential for power had been enhanced by their activities in the reform movements of the 1830's; the general spirit of upward mobility and venturesome entrepreneurship that pervaded the Jacksonian era was infectious. But in the late 1840's a sense of acute frustration enveloped these educated and highly spirited women. Their rising expectations had met with frustration, their hopes had been shattered; they were bitterly conscious of a relative lowering of status and a loss of position. This sense of frustration led them to action; it was one of the main factors in the rise of the woman's rights movement.[20]

The women, who in 1848 declared boldly and with considerable exaggeration that "the history of mankind is a history of repeated injuries and usurpations on the part of man toward woman, having in direct object the establishment of an absolute tyranny over her," did not speak for the truly exploited and abused working woman.[21] As a matter of fact, they were largely ignorant of her condition and, with the notable exception of Susan B. Anthony, indifferent to her fate. But they judged from the realities of their own life experience. Like most revolutionaries, they were not the most downtrodden but rather the most status-deprived group. Their frustrations and traditional isolation from political power funneled their discontent into fairly utopian declarations and immature organizational means. They would learn better in the long, hard decades of practical struggle. Yet it is their initial emphasis on the legal and political "disabilities" of women which has provided the framework for most of the historical work on women. For almost a hundred years sympathetic historians have told the story of women in America from the feminist viewpoint. Their tendency has been to reason from the position of middle class women to a generalization concerning all American women. This distortion has obscured the actual and continuous contributions of women to American life.[22] To avoid such a distortion, any valid generalization concerning American women after the 1830's should reflect a recognition of class stratification.

For lower class women the changes brought by industrialization were actually advantageous, offering income and advancement opportunities, however limited, and a chance for participation in the ranks of organized labor. They, by and large, tended to join men in their struggle for economic advancement and became increasingly concerned with economic gains and protective labor legislation. Middle and upperclass women, on the other hand, reacted to actual and fancied status deprivation by increasing militancy and the formation of organizations for women's rights, by which they meant especially legal and property rights.

The four decades preceding the Seneca Falls Convention were decisive in the history of American women. They brought an actual deterioration in the economic opportunities open to women, a relative deterioration in their political status and a rising level of expectation and subsequent frustration in a privileged elite group of educated women. The ideology still pervasive in our present-day society regarding woman's "proper" role was formed in those decades. Later, under the impact of feminist attacks this ideology would grow defensive and attempt to bolster its claims by appeals to universality and pretentions to a history dating back to antiquity or, at least, to *The Mayflower*. Women, we are told, have always played a restricted and subordinate role in American life. In fact, however, it was in mid-nineteenth-century America that the ideology of "woman's place is in the home" changed from being an accurate description of existing reality into a myth. It became the "feminine mystique"—a longing for a lost, archaic world of agrarian family self-sufficiency, updated by woman's consumer function and the misunderstood dicta of Freudian psychology.

The decades 1800-1840 also provide the clues to an understanding of the institutional shape of the later women's organizations. These would be led by middle class women whose self-image, life experience and ideology had largely been fashioned and influenced by these early, transitional years. The concerns of middle class women—property rights, the franchise and moral uplift—would dominate the women's rights movement. But side by side with it, and at times cooperating with it, would grow a number of organizations serving the needs of working women.

American women were the largest disfranchised group in the nation's history, and they retained this position longer than any other group. Although they found ways of making their influence felt continuously, not only as individuals but as organized groups, power eluded them. The mill girl and the lady, both born in the age of Jackson, would not gain access to power until they learned to cooperate, each for her own separate interests. It would take almost six decades before they would find common ground. The issue around which they finally would unite and push their movement to victory was the "impractical and utopian" demand raised at Seneca Falls—the means to power in American society—female suffrage.

SARAH LAWRENCE COLLEGE

footnotes

Research for this article was facilitated by a research grant provided by Long Island University, Brooklyn, N.Y., which is gratefully acknowledged.

The generalizations in this article are based on extensive research in primary sources, including letters and manuscripts of the following women: Elizabeth Cady Stanton, Susan B. Anthony, Abby Kelley, Lucretia Mott, Lucy Stone, Sarah and Angelina Grimke, Maria Weston Chapman, Lydia Maria Child and Betsey Cowles. Among the organizational records consulted were those of the Boston Female Anti-Slavery Society, the Philadelphia Female Anti-Slavery Society, Anti-Slavery Conventions of American Women, all the Woman's Rights Conventions prior to 1870 and the records of various female charitable organizations.

1. Keith E. Melder, "The Beginnings of the Women's Rights Movement in the United States: 1800-1840" (Diss. Yale, 1963).
Elisabeth A. Dexter, *Colonial Women of Affairs: Women in Business and Professions in America before 1776* (Boston, 1931).
———, *Career Women of America: 1776-1840* (Francestown, N.H., 1950).

2. Herbert Moller, "Sex Composition and Corresponding Culture Patterns of Colonial America," *William and Mary Quarterly*, Ser. 3, II (April, 1945), 113-153.

3. The summary of the status of colonial women is based on the following sources: Mary Benson, *Women in 18th Century America: A Study of Opinion and Social Usage* (New York, 1935); Arthur Calhoun, *A Social History of the American Family*, 3 vols. (Cleveland, 1918); Dexter, *Colonial Women;* Dexter, *Career Women;* Edmund S. Morgan, *Virginians at Home: Family Life in the 18th Century* (Williamsburg, 1952); Julia C. Spruill, *Women's Life and Work in the Southern Colonies* (Chapel Hill, 1938).

4. E. M. Boatwright, "The political and legal status of women in Georgia: 1783-1860," *Georgia Historical Quarterly*, XXV (April, 1941).
Richard B. Morris, *Studies in the History of American Law* (New York, 1930), Chap. 3.
A summary of travelers' comments on American women may be found in: Jane Mesick, *The English Traveler in America: 1785-1835* (New York, 1922), 83-99.

5. For facts on colonial medicine the following sources were consulted: Wyndham B. Blanton, *Medicine in Virginia*, 3 vols. (Richmond, 1930); N. S. Davis, M.D., *History of Medical Education and Institutions in the United States . . . .* (Chicago, 1851); Dexter, *Career Women;* K. C. Hurd-Mead, M.D., *A History of Women in Medicine: from the earliest Times to the Beginning of the 19th Century* (Haddam, Conn., 1938); Geo. W. Norris, *The Early History of Medicine in Philadelphia* (Philadelphia, 1886); Joseph M. Toner, *Contributions to the Annals of Medical Progress in the United States before and during the War of Independence* (Washington, D.C., 1874).
The citation regarding Mrs. Allyn is from Hurd-Mead, *Women in Medicine*, 487.

6. Fielding H. Garrison, M.D., *An Introduction to the History of Medicine* (Philadelphia, 1929).
For licensing legislation: Davis, 88-103.

7. George Daniels, "The Professionalization of American Science: the emergent period, 1820-1860," paper delivered at the joint session of the History of Science Society and the Society of the History of Technology, San Francisco, December 28, 1965.

8. Hurd-Mead, *Women in Medicine*, 391.

9. *Ibid.*, 486.

10. Betsy E. Corner, *William Shippen Jr.: Pioneer in American Medical Education* (Philadelphia, 1951), 103.

11. *Ibid.*

12. Benjamin Lee Gordon, *Medieval and Renaissance Medicine* (New York, 1959), 689-691.
Blanton, *Medicine*, II, 23-24; Hurd-Mead, *Women in Medicine*, 487-88; Annie Nathan Meyer, *Woman's Work in America* (New York, 1891).
Harriot K. Hunt, M.D., *Glances and Glimpses or Fifty Years Social including Twenty Years Professional Life* (Boston, 1856), 127-140.
Eleanor Flexner, *Century of Struggle: The Woman's Rights Movement in the United States* (Cambridge, Mass., 1959), 115-119.

13. Sophie H. Drinker, "Women Attorneys of Colonial Times," *Maryland Historical Society Bulletin*, LVI, No. 4 (Dec., 1961).

14. Dexter, *Colonial Women*, 34-35, 162-165.

15. Harriet W. Marr, *The Old New England Academies* (New York, 1959), Chap. 8; Thomas Woody, *A History of Women's Education in the United States*, 2 vols. (New York, 1929) *II*, 100-109, 458-460, 492-493.

16. Matthew Carey, *Essays on Political Economy . . . .* (Philadelphia, 1822), 459.

17. The statements on women industrial workers are based on the following sources: Edith Abbot, *Women in Industry* (New York, 1910), 66-80; Edith Abbot, "Harriet Martineau and the Employment of Women in 1836," *Journal of Political Economy*, XIV (Dec., 1906), 614-626; Matthew Carey, *Miscellaneous Essays* (Philadelphia, 1830), 153-203; Helen L. Sumner, *History of Women in Industry in the United States*, in *Report on Condition of Woman and Child Wage-Earners in the United States*, 19 vols. (Washington, D.C., 1910), IX.
Also: Elizabeth F. Baker, *Technology and Woman's Work* (New York, 1964), Chaps. 1-5.

18. Emily Putnam, *The Lady: Studies of certain significant Phases of her History* (New York, 1910), 319-320.
Barbara Welter, "The Cult of True Womanhood: 1820-1860," *American Quarterly*, XVIII, No. 2, Part 1 (Summer, 1966), 151-174.

19. Veblen generalized from his observations of the society of the Gilded Age and fell into the usual error of simply ignoring the lower class women, whom he dismissed as "drudges . . . fairly content with their lot," but his analysis of women's role in "conspicuous consumption" and of the function of women's fashions is unsurpassed.
For references see: Thorstein Veblen, *The Theory of the Leisure Class* (New York, 1962, first printing, 1899), 70-71, 231-232.
Thorstein Veblen, "The Economic Theory of Woman's Dress," *Essays in Our Changing Order* (New York, 1934), 65-77.

20. Like most groups fighting status oppression women formulated a compensatory ideology of female superiority. Norton Mezvinsky has postulated that this was clearly expressed only in 1874; in fact this formulation appeared in the earliest speeches of Elizabeth Cady Stanton and in the speeches and resolutions of the Seneca Falls Conventions and other pre-Civil War woman's rights conventions. Rather than a main motivating force, the idea was a tactical formulation, designed to take advantage of the popularly held male belief in woman's "moral" superiority and to convince reformers that they needed the votes of women. Those middle class feminists who believed in woman's "moral" superiority exploited the concept in order to win their major goal—female equality.
For references see: Norton Mezvinsky, "An Idea of Female Superiority," *Midcontinent American Studies Journal*, II, No. 1 (Spring, 1961), 17-26.
E. D. Stanton, S. B. Anthony and M. J. Gage, eds., *A History of Woman Suffrage*, 6 vols. (New York, 1881-1922), I, 72, 479, 522, 529 and *passim*.
Alan P. Grimes, *The Puritan Ethic and Woman Suffrage* (New York, 1967), Chaps. 2 and 3.

21. Stanton *et al*, *History of Woman Suffrage*, I, 70.

22. Mary R. Beard, *Woman as Force in History: A Study of Traditions and Realities* (New York, 1946).

REFLECTIONS ON THE BLACK WOMAN'S ROLE IN THE COMMUNITY OF SLAVES

BY ANGELA DAVIS

ANGELA DAVIS is presently being held, without bail, in the Marin County Jail in San Rafael, California facing three capital charges of murder, kidnapping, and conspiracy to commit both. The charges stem from an abortive escape by black prisoners from the Marin County Court House, Aug. 7, 1970. She has denied any involvement in the attempted escape. Prior to her arrest Sister Davis was teaching in the Philosophy Department at the University of California in Los Angeles. She was fired twice by the University's Regents: once because she is a member of the Communist Party and the second time for her speeches and other activities on behalf of the Soledad Brothers and all political prisoners. Her book, *If They Come in the Morning: Voices of Resistance*, edited by Angela Davis and Bettina Aptheker, was published October 1971 by Third Press, New York, New York. Containing a number of fundamental essays by Angela Davis, it includes articles by Bettina Aptheker, James Baldwin, Margaret Burnham, Ericka Huggins, Ruchell Magee, Howard Moore, Huey P. Newton, Bobby Seale and The Soledad Brothers.

INTRODUCTION

I was immensely pleased to learn of THE BLACK SCHOLAR's plans to devote an entire issue to the black woman.

The paucity of literature on the black woman is outrageous on its face. But we must also contend with the fact that too many of these rare studies must claim as their signal achievement the reinforcement of fictitious cliches. They have given credence to grossly distorted categories through which the black woman continues to be perceived. In the words of Nathan and Julia Hare, ". . . she has been labeled 'aggressive' or 'matriarchal' by white scholars and 'castrating female' by [some] blacks." (*Transaction*, Nov.-Dec., 1970) Many have recently sought to remedy this situation. But for the time being, at least, we are still confronted with these reified images of ourselves. And for now, we must still assume the responsibility of shattering them.

Initially, I did not envision this paper as strictly confined to the era of slavery. Yet, as I began to think through the issue of the black matriarch, I came to the conclusion that it had to be refuted at its presumed historical inception.

The chief problem I encountered stemmed from the conditions of my incarceration: opportunities for researching the issue I wanted to explore were extremely limited. I chose, therefore, to entitle this piece "Reflections . . ." It does not pretend to be more than a collection of ideas which would consitute a starting point — a framework within which to conduct a rigorous reinvestigation of the black woman as she interacted with her people and with her oppressive environment during slavery.

I would like to dedicate these reflections to one of the most admirable black leaders to emerge from the ranks of our liberation movement — to George Jackson, whom I loved and respected in every way. As I came to know and love him, I saw him developing an acute sensitivity to the real problems facing black women and thus refining his ability to distinguish these from their mythical transpositions. George was uniquely aware of the need to extricate himself and other black men from the remnants of divisive and destructive myths purporting to represent the black woman. If his life had not been so precipitously and savagely extinguished, he would have surely accomplished a task he had already outlined some time ago: a systematic critique of his past misconceptions about black women and of their roots in the ideology of the established order. He wanted to appeal to other black men, still similarly disoriented, to likewise correct themselves through self-criticism. George viewed this obligation as a revolutionary duty, but also, and equally important, as an expression of his boundless love for all black women.

THE MATRIARCHAL black woman has been repeatedly invoked as one of the fatal by-products of slavery. When the Moynihan Report consecrated this myth with Washington's stamp of approval, its spurious content and propagandistic mission should have become apparent. Yet even outside the established ideological apparatus, and also among black people, unfortunate references to the matriarchate can still be encountered. Occasionally, there is even acknowledgement of the "tangle of pathology" it supposedly engendered. (This black matriarchate, according to Moynihan *et. al.* defines the roots of our oppression as a people.) An accurate portrait of the African woman in bondage must debunk the myth of the matriarchate. Such a portrait must simultaneously attempt to illuminate the historical matrix of her oppression and must evoke her varied, often heroic, responses to the slaveholder's domination.

Lingering beneath the notion of the black matriarch is an unspoken indictment of our female forebears as having actively assented to slavery. The notorious cliche, the "emasculating female," has its roots in the fallacious inference that in playing a central part in the slave "family," the black woman related to the slaveholding class as collaborator. Nothing could be further from the truth. In the most fundamental sense, the slave system did not – and could not – engender and recognize a matriarchal family structure. Inherent in the very concept of the matriarchy is "power." It would have been exceedingly risky for the slaveholding class to openly acknowledge symbols of authority – female symbols no less than male. Such legitimized concentrations of authority might eventually unleash their "power" against the slave system itself.

THE AMERICAN brand of slavery strove toward a rigidified disorganization in family life, just as it had to proscribe all potential social structures within which black people might forge a collective and conscious existence.[1] Mothers and fathers were brutally separated; children, when they became of age, were branded and frequently severed from their mothers. That the mother was "the only legitimate parent of her child" did not therefore mean that she was even permitted to guide it to maturity.

Those who lived under a common roof were often unrelated through blood. Frederick Douglass, for instance, had no recollection of his father. He only vaguely recalled having seen his mother – and then on extremely rare occasions. Moreover, at the age of seven, he was forced to abandon the dwelling of his grandmother, of whom he would later say: "She was to me a mother and a father."[1a] The strong personal bonds between immediate family members which oftentimes persisted despite coerced separation bore witness to the remarkable capacity of black people for resisting the disorder so violently imposed on their lives.

WHERE FAMILIES were allowed to thrive, they were, for the most part, external fabrications serving the designs of an avaricious, profit-seeking slaveholder.

> The strong hand of the slave owner dominated the Negro family, which existed at his mercy and often at his own personal instigation. An ex-slave has told of getting married on one plantation: "When you married, you had to jump over a broom three times."[2]

---

1. It is interesting to note a parallel in Nazi Germany: with all its ranting and raving about motherhood and the family, Hitler's regime made a conscious attempt to strip the family of virtually all its social functions. The thrust of their unspoken program for the family was to reduce it to a biological unit and to force its members to relate in an unmediated fashion to the fascist bureaucracy. Clearly the Nazis endeavored to crush the family in order to ensure that it could not become a center from which oppositional activity might originate.

1a. Herbert Aptheker, ed., *A Documentary History of the Negro People in the United States*, New York: The Citadel Press, 1969 (1st ed., 1951), p. 272.

2. Andrew Billingsley, *Black Families in White America*, Englewood, New Jersey: Prentice-Hall, Inc., 1968, p. 61.

This slave went on to describe the various ways in which his master forcibly coupled men and women with the aim of producing the maximum number of healthy child-slaves. In the words of John Henrik Clarke,

> The family as a functional entity was outlawed and permitted to exist only when it benefited the slave-master. Maintenance of the slave family as a family unit benefited the slave owners only when, and to the extent that such unions created new slaves who could be exploited.[3]

The designation of the black woman as a matriarch is a cruel misnomer. It is a misnomer because it implies stable kinship structures within which the mother exercises decisive authority. It is cruel because it ignores the profound traumas the black woman must have experienced when she had to surrender her child-bearing to alien and predatory economic interests.

Even the broadest construction of the matriarch concept would not render it applicable to the black slave woman. But it should not be inferred that she therefore played no significant role in the community of slaves. Her indispensable efforts to ensure the survival of her people can hardly be contested. Even if she had done no more, her deeds would still be laudable. But her concern and struggles for physical survival, while clearly important, did not constitute her most outstanding contributions. It will be submitted that by virtue of the brutal force of circumstances, the black woman was assigned the mission of promoting the consciousness and practice of resistance. A great deal has been said about the black *man* and resistance, but very little about the unique relationship black women bore to the resistance struggles during slavery. To understand the part she played in developing and sharpening the thrust towards freedom, the broader meaning of slavery and of American slavery in particular must be explored.

SLAVERY IS AN ancient human institution. Of slave labor in its traditional form and of serfdom as well, Karl Marx had the following to say:

> The slave stands in absolutely no relation to the objective conditions of his labor; it is rather the *labor itself*, in the form of the slave as of the serf, which is placed in the category of *inorganic condition* of production alongside the other natural beings, *e.g.* cattle, or regarded as an appendage of the earth.[4]

The bondsman's existence as a natural condition of production is complemented and reinforced, according to Marx, by his membership in a social grouping which he perceives to be an extension of nature. Enmeshed in what appears to be a natural state of affairs, the attitude of the slave, to a greater or lesser degree, would be an acquiescence in his subjugation. Engels points out that in Athens, the state could depend on a police force consisting entirely of slaves.[5]

The fabric of American slavery differed significantly from ancient slavery and feudalism. True, black people were forced to act as if they were "inorganic conditions of production." For slavery was "personality swallowed up in the sordid idea of property – manhood lost in chattelhood."[6] But there were no pre-existent social structures or cultural dictates which might induce reconciliation to the circumstances of their bondage. On the contrary, Africans had been uprooted from their natural environment, their social relations, their culture. No legitimate socio-cultural surroundings would be permitted to develop and flourish, for, in all likelihood, they would be utterly incompatible with the demands of slavery.

---

3. John Henrik Clarke, "The Black Woman: A Figure in World History" Part III, *Essence*, New York: July, 1971.
4. Karl Marx, *Grundrisse der Kritik der Politischen Oekonomie*, Berlin: Dietz Verlag, 1953, p. 389.
5. Frederick Engels, *Origin of the Family, Private Property and The State*, New York: International Publishers, 1942, p. 107.
6. Frederick Douglass, *Life and Times of Frederick Douglass*, New York: Collier Books, 1962, p. 96.

Yet another fact would militate against harmony and equilibrium in the slave's relation to his bondage: slavery was enclosed in a society otherwise characterized by "free" wage-labor. Black men and women could always contrast their chains with the nominally free status of white working people. This was quite literally true in such cases where, like Frederick Douglass, they were contracted out as wage-laborers. Unlike the "free" white men alongside whom they worked, they had no right to the meager wages they earned. Such were some of the many contradictions unloosed by the effort to forcibly inject slavery into the early stages of American capitalism.

THE COMBINATION of a historically superceded slave labor system based almost exclusively on race and the drive to strip black people of all their social and cultural bonds would create a fateful rupture at the heart of the slave system itself. The slaves would not readily adopt fatalistic attitudes towards the conditions surrounding and ensnaring their lives. They were a people who had been violently thrust into a patently "unnatural" subjugation. If the slaveholders had not maintained an absolute monopoly of violence, if they had not been able to rely on large numbers of their fellow white men – indeed the entire ruling class as well as misled working people – to assist them in their terrorist machinations, slavery would have been far less feasible than it actually proved to be.

The magnitude and effects of the black people's defiant rejection of slavery has not yet been fully documented and illuminated. But there is more than ample evidence that they consistently refused to succumb to the all-encompassing dehumanization objectively demanded by the slave system. Comparatively recent studies have demonstrated that the few slave uprisings – too spectacular to be relegated to oblivion by the racism of ruling class historians – were not isolated occurrences, as the latter would have had us believe. The reality, we know now, was that these open rebellions erupted with such a frequency that they were as much a part of the texture of slavery as the conditions of servitude themselves. And these revolts were only the tip of an iceberg: resistance expressed itself in other grand modes and also in the seemingly trivial forms of feigned illness and studied indolence.

IF RESISTANCE was an organic ingredient of slave life, it had to be directly nurtured by the social organization which the slaves themselves improvised. The consciousness of their oppression, the conscious thrust towards its abolition could not have been sustained without impetus from the community they pulled together through the sheer force of their own strength. Of necessity, this community would revolve around the realm which was furthermost removed from the immediate arena of domination. It could only be located in and around the living quarters, the area where the basic needs of physical life were met.

In the area of production, the slaves – pressed into the mold of beasts of burden – were forcibly deprived of their humanity. (And a human being thoroughly dehumanized, has no desire for freedom.) But the community gravitating around the domestic quarters might possibly permit a retrieval of the man and the woman in their fundamental humanity. We can assume that in a very real material sense, it was only in domestic life – away from the eyes and whip of the overseer – that the slaves could attempt to assert the modicum of freedom they still retained. It was only there that they might be inspired to project techniques of expanding it further by leveling what few weapons they had against the slaveholding class whose unmitigated drive for profit was the source of their misery.

Via this path, we return to the African slave woman: in the living quarters, the major responsibilities "naturally" fell to her. It was the woman who was charged with keeping the "home" in order. This role was dictated by the male supremacist ideology of white society in America; it was also woven into the patriarchal traditions of Africa. As her biological destiny, the woman bore the fruits of procreation; as her social destiny, she cooked, sewed, washed, cleaned house, raised the children. Traditionally the labor of females, domestic work is supposed to complement and confirm their inferiority.

But with the black slave woman, there is a strange twist of affairs: in the infinite anguish of ministering to the needs of the men and children around her (who were not necessarily members of her immediate family), she was performing the *only* labor of the slave community which could not be directly and immediately claimed by the oppressor. There was no compensation for work in the fields; it served no useful purpose for the slaves. Domestic labor was the only meaningful labor for the slave community as a whole (discounting as negligible the exceptional situations where slaves received some pay for their work).

Precisely through performing the drudgery which has long been a central expression of the socially conditioned inferiority of women, the black woman in chains could help to lay the foundation for some degree of autonomy, both for herself and her men. Even as she was suffering under her unique oppression as female, she was thrust by the force of circumstances into the center of the slave community. She was, therefore, essential to the *survival* of the community. Not all people have survived enslavement; hence her survival-oriented activities were themselves a form of resistance. Survival, moreover, was the prerequisite of all higher levels of struggle.

But much more remains to be said of the black woman during slavery. The dialectics of her oppression will become far more complex. It is true that she was a victim of the myth that only the woman, with her diminished capacity for mental and physical labor, should do degrading household work. Yet, the alleged benefits of the ideology of feminity did not accrue to her. She was not sheltered or protected; she would not remain oblivious to the desperate struggle for existence unfolding outside the "home." She was also there in the fields, alongside the man, toiling under the lash from sun-up to sun-down.

This was one of the supreme ironies of slavery: in order to approach its strategic goal – to extract the greatest possible surplus from the labor of the slaves – the black woman had to be released from the chains of the myth of feminity. In the words of W.E.B. Du Bois, ". . . our women in black had freedom contemptuously thrust upon them."[7] In order to function as slave, the black woman had to be annulled as woman, that is, as woman in her historical stance of wardship under the entire male hierarchy. The sheer force of things rendered her equal to her man.

Excepting the woman's role as caretaker of the household, male supremacist structures could not become deeply embedded in the internal workings of the slave system. Though the ruling class was male and rabidly chauvinistic, the slave system could not confer upon the black man the appearance of a privileged position vis-a-vis the black woman. The man-slave could not be the unquestioned superior within the "family" or community, for there was no such thing as the "family provided" among the slaves. The attainment of slavery's intrinsic goals was contingent upon the fullest and most brutal utilization of the productive capacities of every man, woman and child. They all had to "provide" for the master. The black woman was therefore wholly integrated into the productive force.

> The bell rings at four o'clock in the morning and they have half an hour to get ready. Men and women start together, and the women must work as steadily as the men and perform the same tasks as the men.[8]

---

7. W.E.B. Du Bois, *Darkwater, Voices from Within the Veil*, New York: AMS Press, 1969, p. 185.
8. Lewis Clarke, *Narrative of the Sufferings of Lewis and Milton Clarke, Sons of a Soldier of the Revolution*, Boston: 1846, p. 127 [Quoted by E. Franklin Frazier, *The Negro Family in the United States*].

Even in the posture of motherhood – otherwise the occasion for hypocritical adoration – the black woman was treated with not greater compassion and with no less severity than her man. As one slave related in a narrative of his life:

> ... women who had sucking children suffered much from their breasts becoming full of milk, the infants being left at home; they therefore could not keep up with the other hands: I have seen the overseer beat them with raw hide so that the blood and the milk flew mingled from their breasts.[9]

Moses Grandy, ex-slave, continues his description with an account of a typical form of field punishment reserved for the black woman with child:

> She is compelled to lie down over a hole made to receive her corpulency, and is flogged with the whip, or beat with a paddle, which has holes in it; at every stroke comes a blister.[10]

The unbridled cruelty of this leveling process whereby the black woman was forced into equality with the black man requires no further explanation. She shared in the deformed equality of equal oppression.

But out of this deformed equality was forged quite undeliberately, yet inexorably, a state of affairs which could unharness an immense potential in the black woman. Expending indispensable labor for the enrichment of her oppressor, she could attain a practical awareness of the oppressor's utter dependence on her – for the master needs the slave far more than the slave needs the master. At the same time she could realize that while her productive activity was wholly subordinated to the will of the master, it was nevertheless proof of her ability to transform things. For "labor is the living, shaping fire; it represents the impermanence of thing, their temporality ..."[11]

The black woman's consciousness of the oppression suffered by her people was honed in the bestial realities of daily experience. It would not be the stunted awareness of a woman confined to the home. She would be prepared to ascend to the same levels of resistance which were accessible to her men. Even as she performed her housework, the black woman's role in the slave community could not be identical to the historically evolved female role. Stripped of the palliative feminine veneer which might have encouraged a passive performance of domestic tasks, she was now uniquely capable of weaving into the warp and woof of domestic life a profound consciousness of resistance.

With the contributions of strong black women, the slave community as a whole could achieve heights unscaleable within the families of the white oppressed or even within the patriarchal kinship groups of Africa. Latently or actively it was always a community of resistance. It frequently erupted in insurgency, but was daily animated by the minor acts of sabotage which harassed the slave master to no end. Had the black woman failed to rise to the occasion, the community of slaves could not have fully developed in this direction. The slave system would have to deal with the black woman as the custodian of a house of resistance.

The oppression of black women during the era of slavery, therefore, had to be buttressed by a level of overt ruling-class repression. Her routine oppression had to assume an unconcealed dimension of outright counter-insurgency.

• • • •

To say that the oppression of black slave women necessarily incorporated open forms of counter-insurgency is not as extravagant as it might initially appear. The penetration of counter-insurgency into the day to day routine of the slave master's domination will be considered towards the end of this paper. First, the participation of black

9. Moses Grandy, *Narrative of the Life of Moses Grandy; Late a Slave in the United States of America*, Boston: 1844, p. 18 [quoted by Frazier].
10. *Ibid.*
11. Marx, *Grundrisse*, p. 288.

women in the overt and explosive upheavals which constantly rocked the slave system must be confirmed. This will be an indication of the magnitude of her role as caretaker of a household of resistance – of the degree to which she could concretely encourage those around her to keep their eyes on freedom. It will also confirm the objective circumstances to which the slave master's counter-insurgency was a response.

With the sole exceptions of Harriet Tubman and Sojourner Truth, black women of the slave era remain more or less enshrouded in unrevealed history. And, as Earl Conrad has demonstrated, even "General Tubman's" role has been consistently and grossly minimized. She was a far greater warrior against slavery than is suggested by the prevalent misconception that her only outstanding contribution was to make nineteen trips into the South, bringing over 300 slaves to their freedom.

> [She] was head of the Intelligence Service in the Department of the South throughout the Civil War; she is the only American woman to lead troops black and white on the field of battle, as she did in the Department of the South . . . She was a compelling and stirring orator in the councils of the abolitionists and the anti-slavers, a favorite of the antislavery conferences. She was the fellow planner with Douglass, Martin Delany, Wendell Phillips, Gerrit Smith and other leaders of the anti-slavery movement.[12]

No extensive and systematic study of the role of black women in resisting slavery has come to my attention. It has been noted that large numbers of freed black women worked towards the purchase of their relatives' and friends' freedom. About the participation of women in both the well-known and more obscure slave revolts, only casual remarks have been made. It has been observed, for instance, that Gabriel's wife was active in planning the rebellion spearheaded by her husband, but little else has been said about her.

THE SKETCH which follows is based in its entirety on the works of Herbert Aptheker, the only resources available to me at the time of this writing.[13] These facts, gleaned from Aptheker's works on slave revolts and other forms of resistance, should signal the urgency to undertake a thorough study of the black woman as anti-slavery rebel. In 1971 this work is far overdue.

Aptheker's research has disclosed the widespread existence of communities of blacks who were neither free nor in bondage. Throughout the South (in South and North Carolina, Virginia, Louisiana, Florida, Georgia, Mississippi and Alabama), maroon communities consisting of fugitive slaves and their descendants were "an ever present feature" – from 1642 to 1864 – of slavery. They provided ". . . havens for fugitives, served as bases for marauding expeditions against nearby plantations and, at times, supplied leadership to planned uprisings."[14]

Every detail of these communities was invariably determined by and steeped in resistance, for their raison d'etre emanated from their perpetual assault on slavery. Only in a fighting stance could the maroons hope to secure their constantly imperiled freedom. As a matter of necessity, the women of those communities were compelled to define themselves – no less than the men – through their many acts of resistance. Hence, throughout this brief survey the counter-attacks and heroic efforts at defense assisted by maroon women will be a recurring motif.

As it will be seen, black women often poisoned the food and set fire to the houses of their masters. For those who were also employed as domestics these particular overt forms of resistance were especially available.

The vast majority of the incidents to be related involve either tactically unsuccess-

12. Earl Conrad, "I Bring You General Tubman," *The Black Scholar*, Vol. 1, No. 3-4, Jan.-Feb., 1970, p. 4.
13. In February, 1949, Herbert Aptheker published an essay in *Masses and Mainstream* entitled "The Negro Woman." As yet I have been unable to obtain it.
14. Herbert Aptheker, "Slave Guerrilla Warfare" in *To Be Free, Studies in American Negro History*, New York: International Publishers, 1969 (1st ed., 1948), p. 11.

ful assaults or eventually thwarted attempts at defense. In all likelihood, numerous successes were achieved, even against the formidable obstacles posed by the slave system. Many of these were probably unpublicized even at the time of their occurrence, lest they provide encouragement to the rebellious proclivities of other slaves and, for other slaveholders, an occasion for fear and despair.

During the early years of the slave era (1708) a rebellion broke out in New York. Among its participants were surely many women, for one, along with three men, was executed in retaliation for the killing of seven whites. It may not be entirely insignificant that while the men were hanged, she was heinously burned alive.[15] In the same colony, women played an active role in a 1712 uprising in the course of which slaves, with their guns, clubs and knives, killed members of the slaveholding class and managed to wound others. While some of the insurgents – among them a pregnant woman – were captured, others – including a woman – committed suicide rather than surrender.[16]

"In New Orleans one day in 1730 a woman slave received 'a violent blow from a French soldier for refusing to obey him' and in her anger shouted 'that the French should not long insult Negroes'."[17] As it was later disclosed, she and undoubtedly many other women, had joined in a vast plan to destroy slaveholders. Along with eight men, this dauntless woman was executed. Two years later, Louisiana pronounced a woman and four men leaders of a planned rebellion. They were all executed and, in a typically savage gesture, their heads publicly displayed on poles.[18]

Charleston, South Carolina condemned a black woman to die in 1740 for arson,[19] a form of sabotage, as earlier noted, frequently carried out by women. In Maryland, for instance, a slave woman was executed in 1776 for having destroyed by fire her master's house, his outhouses and tobacco house.[20]

In the thick of the Colonies' war with England, a group of defiant slave women and men were arrested in Saint Andrew's Parish, Georgia in 1774. But before they were captured, they had already brought a number of slave owners to their death.[21]

The maroon communities have been briefly described; from 1782 to 1784, Louisiana was a constant target of maroon attacks. When twenty-five of this community's members were finally taken prisoner, men and women alike were all severely punished.[22]

As can be inferred from previous example, the North did not escape the tremendous impact of fighting black women. In Albany, New York, two women were among three slaves executed for anti-slavery activities in 1794.[23] The respect and admiration accorded the black woman fighter by her people is strikingly illustrated by an incident which transpired in York, Pennsylvania: when, during the early months of 1803, Margaret Bradley was convicted of attempting to poison two white people, the black inhabitants of the area revolted en masse.

> They made several attempts to destroy the town by fire and succeeded, within a period of three weeks, in burning eleven buildings. Patrols were established, strong guards set up, the militia dispatched to the scene of the unrest . . . and a reward of three hundred dollars offered for the capture of the insurrectionists.[24]

A successful elimination by poisoning of several "of our respectable men" (said a letter to the governor of North Carolina) was met by the execution of four or five slaves. One was a woman who was burned

15. Herbert Aptheker, *American Negro Slave Revolts*, New York: International Publishers, 1970 (1st ed., 1943), p. 169.
16. *Ibid.*, p. 173.
17. *Ibid.*, p. 181.
18. *Ibid.*, p. 182.
19. *Ibid.*, p. 190.
20. *Ibid.*, p. 145.
21. *Ibid.*, p. 201.
22. *Ibid.*, p. 207.
23. *Ibid.*, p. 215.
24. *Ibid.*, p. 239.

alive.[25] In 1810, two women and a man were accused of arson in Virginia.[26]

In 1811 North Carolina was the scene of a confrontation between a maroon community and a slave-catching posse. Local newspapers reported that its members "had bid defiance to any force whatever and were resolved to stand their ground." Of the entire community, two were killed, one wounded and two – both women – were captured.[27]

APTHEKER'S *Documentary History of the Negro People in the United States* contains a portion of the transcript of an 1812 confession of a slave rebel in Virginia. The latter divulged the information that a black woman brought him into a plan to kill their master and that yet another black woman had been charged with concealing him after the killing occurred.[28]

In 1816 it was discovered that a community of three hundred escaped slaves – men, women, children – had occupied a fort in Florida. After the U.S. Army was dispatched with instructions to destroy the community, a ten day siege terminated with all but forty of the three hundred dead. All the slaves fought to the very end.[29] In the course of a similar, though smaller confrontation between maroons and a militia group (in South Carolina, 1826), a woman and a child were killed.[30] Still another maroon community was attacked in Mobile, Alabama in 1837. Its inhabitants, men and women alike, resisted fiercely – according to local newspapers, "fighting like Spartans."[31]

Convicted of having been among those who, in 1829, had been the cause of a devastating fire in Augusta, Georgia, a black woman was "executed, dissected, and exposed" (according to an English visitor). Moreover, the execution of yet another woman, about to give birth, was imminent.[32] During the same year, a group of slaves, being led from Maryland to be sold in the South, had apparently planned to kill the traders and make their way to freedom. One of the traders was successfully done away with, but eventually a posse captured all the slaves. Of the six leaders sentenced to death, one was a woman. She was first permitted, for reasons of economy, to give birth to her child.[33] Afterwards, she was publicly hanged.

THE SLAVE CLASS in Louisiana, as noted earlier, was not unaware of the formidable threat posed by the black woman who chose to fight. It responded accordingly: in 1846 a posse of slave owners ambushed a community of maroons, killing one woman and wounding two others. A black man was also assassinated.[34] Neither could the border states escape the recognition that slave women were eager to battle for their freedom. In 1850 in the state of Missouri, "about thirty slaves, men and women, of four different owners, had armed themselves with knives, clubs and three guns and set out for a free state." Their pursuers, who could unleash a far more powerful violence than they, eventually thwarted their plans.[35]

This factual survey of but a few of the open acts of resistance in which black women played major roles will close with two further events. When a maroon camp in Mississippi was destroyed in 1857, four of its members did not manage to elude capture, one of whom was a fugitive slave woman.[36] All of them, women as well as men, must have waged a valiant fight. Finally, there occurred in October, 1862 a skirmish between maroons and a scouting party of Confederate soldiers in the state of Virginia.[37] This time, however, the maroons were the victors and it may well have been that some of the many women helped to put the soldiers to death.

• • • •

25. *Ibid.*, pp. 241-242.
26. *Ibid.*, p. 247.
27. *Ibid.*, p. 251.
28. Aptheker, *Documentary History*, pp. 55-57.
29. Aptheker, *Slave Revolts*, p. 259.
30. *Ibid.*, p. 277.
31. *Ibid.*, p. 259.
32. *Ibid.*, p. 281.
33. *Ibid.*, p. 487.
34. Aptheker, "Guerrilla Warfare," p. 27.
35. Aptheker, *Slave Revolts*, p. 342.
36. Aptheker, "Guerrilla Warfare," p. 28.
37. *Ibid.*, p. 29.

The oppression of slave women had to assume dimensions of open counter-insurgency. Against the background of the facts presented above, it would be difficult indeed to refute this contention. As for those who engaged in open battle, they were no less ruthlessly punished than slave men. It would even appear that in many cases they may have suffered penalties which were more excessive than those meted out to the men. On occasion, when men were hanged, the women were burned alive. If such practices were widespread, their logic would be clear. They would be terrorist methods designed to dissuade other black women from following the examples of their fighting sisters. If all black women rose up alongside their men, the institution of slavery would be in difficult straits.

It is against the backdrop of her role as fighter that the routine oppression of the slave woman must be explored once more. If she was burned, hanged, broken on the wheel, her head paraded on poles before her oppressed brothers and sisters, she must have also felt the edge of this counter-insurgency as a fact of her daily existence. The slave system would not only have to make conscious efforts to stifle the tendencies towards acts of the kind described above; it would be no less necessary to stave off escape attempts (escapes to maroon country!) and all the various forms of sabotage within the system. Feigning illness was also resistance as were work slowdowns and actions destructive to the crops. The more extensive these acts, the more the slaveholder's profits would tend to diminish.

While a detailed study of the myriad modes in which this counter-insurgency was manifested can and should be conducted, the following reflections will focus on a single aspect of the slave woman's oppression, particularly prominent in its brutality.

Much has been said about the sexual abuses to which the black woman was forced to submit. They are generally explained as an outgrowth of the male supremacy of Southern culture: the purity of white womanhood could not be violated by the aggressive sexual activity desired by the white male. His instinctual urges would find expression in his relationships with his property — the black slave woman, who would have to become his unwilling concubine. No doubt there is an element of truth in these statements, but it is equally important to unearth the meaning of these sexual abuses from the vantage point of the woman who was assaulted.

In keeping with the theme of these reflections, it will be submitted that the slave master's sexual domination of the black woman contained an unveiled element of counter-insurgency. To understand the basis for this assertion, the dialectical moments of the slave woman's oppression must be restated and their movement recaptured. The prime factor, it has been said, was the total and violent expropriation of her labor with no compensation save the pittance necessary for bare existence.

Secondly, as female, she was the housekeeper of the living quarters. In this sense, she was already doubly oppressed. However, having been wrested from passive, "feminine" existence by the sheer force of things — literally by forced labor — confining domestic tasks were incommensurable with what she had become. That is to say, by virtue of her participation in production, she would not act the part of the passive female, but could experience the same need as her men to challenge the conditions of her subjugation. As the center of domestic life, the only life at all removed from the arena of exploitation, and thus as an important source of survival, the black woman could play a pivotal role in nurturing the thrust towards freedom.

The slave master would attempt to thwart this process. He knew that as female, this slave woman could be particularly vulnerable in her sexual existence. Although he would not pet her and deck her out in frills, the white master could endeavor to reestablish her femaleness by reducing her to the level of her *biological* being. Aspiring with his sexual assaults to establish her as a female *animal*, he would be striving to destroy her proclivities towards resistance. Of the sexual relations of animals, taken at their abstract biological level (and not in terms of their quite different social potential for human beings), Simone de Beauvoir says the following:

> It is unquestionably the male who *takes* the female – she is *taken*. Often the word applies literally, for whether by means of special organs or through superior strength, the male seizes her and holds her in place; he performs the copulatory movements; and, among insects, birds, and mammals, he penetrates . . . Her body becomes a resistance to be broken through . . .[38]

The act of copulation, reduced by the white man to an animal-like act, would be symbolic of the effort to conquer the resistance the black woman could unloose.

In confronting the black woman as adversary in a sexual contest, the master would be subjecting her to the most elemental form of terrorism distinctively suited for the female: rape. Given the already terroristic texture of plantation life, it would be as potential victim of rape that the slave woman would be most unguarded. Further, she might be most conveniently manipulable if the master contrived a ransom system of sorts, forcing her to pay with her body for food, diminished severity in treatment, the safety of her children, etc.

The integration of rape into the sparsely furnished legitimate social life of the slaves harks back to the feudal "right of the first night," the *jus primae noctis*. The feudal lord manifested and reinforced his domination over the serfs by asserting his authority to have sexual intercourse with all the females. The right itself referred specifically to all freshly married women. But while the right to the first night eventually evolved into the institutionalized "virgin tax,"[39] the American slaveholder's sexual domination never lost its openly terroristic character.

As a direct attack on the black female as potential insurgent, this sexual repression finds its parallels in virtually every historical situation where the woman actively challenges oppression. Thus, Franz Fanon could say of the Algerian woman: "A woman led away by soldiers who comes back a week later – it is not necessary to question her to understand that she has been violated dozens of times."[40]

In its political contours, the rape of the black woman was not exclusively an attack upon her. Indirectly, its target was also the slave community as a whole. In launching the sexual war on the woman, the master would not only assert his sovereignty over a critically important figure of the slave community, he would also be aiming a blow against the black man. The latter's instinct to protect his female relations and comrades (now stripped of its male supremacist implications) would be frustrated and violated to the extreme. Placing the white male's sexual barbarity in bold relief, Du Bois cries out in a rhetorical vein:

> I shall forgive the South much in its final judgement day: I shall forgive its slavery, for slavery is a world-old habit; I shall forgive its fighting for a well-lost cause, and for remembering that struggle with tender tears; I shall forgive its so-called 'pride of race,' the passion of its hot blood, and even its dear, old, laughable strutting and posing; but one thing I shall never forgive, neither in this world nor the world to come: its wanton and continued and persistent insulting of the black womanhood which it sought and seeks to prostitute to its lust.[41]

The retaliatory import of the rape for the black man would be entrapment in an untenable situation. Clearly the master hoped that once the black man was struck by his manifest inability to rescue his women from sexual assaults of the master, he would begin to experience deep-seated doubts about his ability to resist at all.

38. Simone de Beauvoir, *The Second Sex*, New York: Bantam Books, 1961, pp. 18-19.
39. August Bebel, *Women and Socialism*, New York: Socialist Literature Co., 1910, p. 66-69.
40. Franz Fanon, *A Dying Colonialism*, New York: Grove Press, 1967, p. 119.
41. Du Bois, *Darkwater*, p. 172.

Certainly the wholesale rape of slave women must have had a profound impact on the slave community. Yet it could not succeed in its intrinsic aim of stifling the impetus towards struggle. Countless black women did not passively submit to these abuses, as the slaves in general refused to passively accept their bondage. The struggles of the slave woman in the sexual realm were a continuation of the resistance interlaced in the slave's daily existence. As such, this was yet another form of insurgency, a response to a politically tinged sexual repression.

Even E. Franklin Frazier (who goes out of his way to defend the thesis that "the master in his mansion and his colored mistress in her special house nearby represented the final triumph of social ritual in the presence of the deepest feelings of human solidarity"[42]) could not entirely ignore the black woman who fought back. He notes: "That physical compulsion was necessary at times to secure submission on the part of black women . . . is supported by historical evidence and has been preserved in the tradition of Negro families."[43]

The sexual contest was one of many arenas in which the black woman had to prove herself as a warrior against oppression. What Frazier unwillingly concedes would mean that countless children brutally fathered by whites were conceived in the thick of battle. Frazier himself cites the story of a black woman whose great grandmother, a former slave, would describe with great zest the battles behind all her numerous scars – that is, all save one. In response to questions concerning the unexplained scar, she had always simply said: "White men are as low as dogs, child, stay away from them." The mystery was not unveiled until after the death of this brave woman: "She received that scar at the hands of her master's youngest son, a boy of about eighteen years at the time she conceived their child, my grandmother Ellen."[44]

• • • •

An intricate and savage web of oppression intruded at every moment into the black woman's life during slavery. Yet a single theme appears at every juncture: the woman transcending, refusing, fighting back, asserting herself over and against terrifying obstacles. It was not her comrade brother against whom her incredible strength was directed. She fought alongside her man, accepting or providing guidance according to her talents and the nature of their tasks. She was in no sense an authoritarian figure; neither her domestic role nor her acts of resistance could relegate the man to the shadows. On the contrary, she herself had just been forced to leave behind the shadowy realm of female passitivity in order to assume her rightful place beside the insurgent male.

This portrait cannot, of course, presume to represent every individual slave woman. It is rather a portrait of the potentials and possibilities inherent in the situation to which slave women were anchored. Invariably there were those who did not realize this potential. There were those who were indifferent and a few who were outright traitors. But certainly they were not the vast majority. The image of black women enchaining their men, cultivating relationships with the oppressor is a cruel fabrication which must be called by its right name. It is a dastardly ideological weapon designed to impair our capacity for resistance today by foisting upon us the ideal of male supremacy.

According to a time-honored principle, advanced by Marx, Lenin, Fanon and numerous other theorists, the status of women in any given society is a barometer measuring the overall level of social development. As Fanon has masterfully shown, the strength and efficacy of social

---

42. E. Franklin Frazier, *The Negro Family in the United States*, Chicago: U. of Chicago Press, 1966 (1st ed., 1939), p. 69.
43. *Ibid.*, p. 53.
44. *Ibid.*, pp. 53-54.

struggles – and especially revolutionary movements – bear an immediate relationship to the range and quality of female participation.

THE MEANING of this principle is strikingly illustrated by the role of the black woman during slavery. Attendant to the indiscriminant brutal pursuit of profit, the slave woman attained a correspondingly brutal status of equality. But in practice, she could work up a fresh content for this deformed equality by inspiring and participating in acts of resistance of every form and color. She could turn the weapon of equality in struggle against the avaricious slave system which had engendered the mere caricature of equality in oppression. The black woman's activities increased the total incidence of anti-slavery assaults. But most important, without consciously rebellious black women, the theme of resistance could not have become so thoroughly intertwined in the fabric of daily existence. The status of black women within the community of slaves was definitely a barometer indicating the overall potential for resistance.

THIS PROCESS did not end with the formal dissolution of slavery. Under the impact of racism, the black woman has been continually constrained to inject herself into the desperate struggle for existence. She – like her man – has been compelled to work for wages, providing for her family as she was previously forced to provide for the slaveholding class. The infinitely onerous nature of this equality should never be overlooked. For the black woman has always also remained harnessed to the chores of the household. Yet, she could never be exhaustively defined by her uniquely "female" responsibilities.

As a result, black women have made significant contributions to struggles against the racism and the dehumanizing exploitation of a wrongly organized society. In fact, it would appear that the intense levels of resistance historically maintained by black people and thus the historical function of the Black Liberation Struggle as harbinger of change throughout the society are due in part to the greater *objective* equality between the black man and the black woman. Du Bois put it this way:

> In the great rank and file of our five million women, we have the up-working of new revolutionary ideals, which must in time have vast influence on the thought and action of this land.[45]

Official and unofficial attempts to blunt the effects of the egalitarian tendencies as between the black man and woman should come as no surprise. The matriarch concept, embracing the cliched "female castrator," is, in the last instance, an open weapon of ideological warfare. Black men and women alike remain its potential victims – men unconsciously lunging at the woman, equating her with the myth; women sinking back into the shadows, lest an aggressive posture resurrect the myth in themselves.

THE MYTH MUST be consciously repudiated as myth and the black woman in her true historical contours must be resurrected. We, the black women of today, must accept the full weight of a legacy wrought in blood by our mothers in chains. Our fight, while identical in spirit, reflects different conditions and thus implies different paths of struggle. But as heirs to a tradition of supreme perserverance and heroic resistance, we must hasten to take our place wherever our people are forging on towards freedom.

45. Du Bois, *Darkwater*, p. 185.

"MY MOTHER WAS MUCH OF A WOMAN": BLACK WOMEN, WORK, AND THE FAMILY UNDER SLAVERY

JACQUELINE JONES

"Ah was born back due in slavery," says Nanny to her granddaughter in Zora Neale Hurston's novel, *Their Eyes Were Watching God,* "so it wasn't for me to fulfill my dreams of whut a woman oughta be and to do." Nanny had never confused the degrading regimen of slavery with her own desires as they related to work, love, and motherhood: "Ah didn't want to be used for a work-ox and a brood-sow and Ah didn't want mah daughter used dat way neither. It sho wasn't mah will for things to happen lak they did." Throughout her life, she had sustained a silent faith in herself and her sisters that was permitted no expression within the spiritual void of bondage: "Ah wanted to preach a great sermon about colored women sittin' on high, but they wasn't no pulpit for me," she grieved.[1]

Nanny's lament offers a challenge to the historian who seeks to understand American slave women — their unfulfilled dreams as well as their day-in, day-out experiences. Despite recent scholarly interest in the relationship between women's work and family life on the one hand and Afro-American culture on the other, a systematic analysis of the roles of slave women is lacking. In her pioneering article entitled "Reflections on the Black Woman's Role in the Community of Slaves" (published over a decade ago), Angela Davis made a crucial distinction between the work that women were forced to perform for a master and the domestic labor that they provided for their own families. But her emphasis on the political implications of nurturing under slavery has not received the in-depth consideration it deserves.[2]

For example, a few scholars have explored the roles of the bondwoman as devoted wife and mother, physically powerful

Feminist Studies 8, no. 2 (Summer 1982).

fieldworker, and rebellious servant. Herbert G. Gutman has illuminated the strength of kin ties within the slave community, and Eugene D. Genovese has furthered our understanding of black-white, male-female relations on the antebellum plantation. However, most historians continue to rely on the gender-neutral term "slave" — which invariably connotes "male" — and race supersedes sex as the focal point of their discussions. Consequently, questions related to the sexual division of labor under slavery and the way in which task assignments in the fields, the "Big House," and the slave quarters shaped the experiences of black women have largely gone unanswered — and unasked.[3]

Moreover, historians primarily concerned with the status of American women have examined the effects of patriarchy on various classes and ethnic groups over time; in the process they have highlighted variations on the theme of women's distinctive work patterns as determined by changing economic conditions, combined with traditional cultural assumptions about women's domestic responsibilities. Yet within the context of current feminist scholarship, slave women as a group remain for the most part neglected, perhaps because they existed outside the mainstream of the industrial revolution and (together with their menfolk) had few opportunities to put into practice their own ideas about appropriate work for women and men. According to this view, slave women were something of a historical aberration, a "special case" that has little relevance to current theoretical and methodological perspectives on women's work.[4]

The purpose of this article is to suggest that the burdens shouldered by slave women actually represented in extreme form the dual nature of all women's labor within a patriarchal, capitalist society: the production of goods and services and the reproduction and care of members of a future work force. The antebellum plantation brought into focus the interaction between notions of women *qua* "equal" workers and women *qua* unequal reproducers; hence a slaveowner just as "naturally" put his bondwomen to work chopping cotton as washing, ironing, or cooking. Furthermore, in seeking to maximize the productivity of his entire labor force while reserving certain domestic tasks for women exclusively, the master demonstrated how patriarchal and capitalist assumptions concerning women's work could reinforce one another. The "peculiar institution" thus involved forms of oppression against women that were unique manifestations of a more universal condition. The following discussion focuses on female slaves in the American rural South between 1830 and 1860 — cotton boom years that laid bare the economic and social underpinnings of slavery and indeed all of American society.[5]

Under slavery, blacks' attempts to maintain the integrity of family life amounted to a political act of protest, and herein lies a central irony in the history of slave women. In defiance of their owners' tendencies to ignore gender differences in making work assignments in the fields, the slaves whenever possible adhered to a strict division of labor within their own households and communities. This impulse was exhibited most dramatically in patterns of black family and economic life after emancipation. Consequently, the family, often considered by feminists to be a source (or at least a vehicle) of women's subservience, played a key role in the freed people's struggle to resist racial and gender oppression, for black women's full attention to the duties of motherhood deprived whites of their power over these women as field laborers and domestic servants.[6]

Interviewed by a Federal Writers Project (FWP) worker in 1937, Hannah Davidson spoke reluctantly of her experiences as a slave in Kentucky: "The things that my sister May and I suffered were so terrible . . . . It is best not to have such things in our memory." During the course of the interview, she stressed that unremitting toil had been the hallmark of her life under bondage. "Work, work, work," she said; it had consumed all her days (from dawn until midnight) and all her years (she was only eight when she began minding her master's children and helping the older women with their spinning). "I been so exhausted working, I was like an inchworm crawling along a roof. I worked till I thought another lick would kill me." On Sundays, "the only time they had to themselves," women washed clothes, and some of the men tended their small tobacco patches. As a child she loved to play in the haystack, but that was possible only on "Sunday evening, after work."[7]

American slavery was an economic and political system by which a group of whites extracted as much labor as possible from blacks through the use or threat of force. A slaveowner thus replaced any traditional division of labor that might have existed among blacks before enslavement with a work structure of his own choosing. All slaves were barred by law from owning property or acquiring literacy skills, and although the system played favorites with a few, black females and males were equal in the sense that neither sex wielded economic power over the other. Hence property relations — "the basic determinant of the sexual division of labor and of the sexual order" within most societies[8] — did not affect male-female interaction among the slaves themselves. To a considerable extent, the types of jobs slaves did, and the amount and regularity of labor they were forced to devote to such jobs, were all dictated by the master.

For these reasons the definition of slave women's work is problematical. If work is any activity that leads either directly or indirectly to the production of marketable goods, then slave women did nothing *but* work.[9] Even their efforts to care for themselves and their families helped to maintain the owner's work force, and to enhance its overall productivity. Tasks performed within the family context — childcare, cooking, and washing clothes, for example — were distinct from labor carried out under the lash in the field or under the mistress's watchful eye in the Big House. Still, these forms of nurture contributed to the health and welfare of the slave population, thereby increasing the actual value of the master's property (that is, slaves as both strong workers and "marketable commodities"). White men warned prospective mothers that they wanted neither "runts" nor girls born on their plantations, and slave women understood that their owner's economic self-interest affected even the most intimate family ties. Of the pregnant bondwomen on her husband's expansive Butlers Island (Georgia) rice plantation, Fanny Kemble observed, "they have all of them a most distinct and perfect knowledge of their value to their owners as property," and she recoiled at their obsequious profession obviously intended to delight her: "Missus, tho' we no able to work, we make little niggers for Massa." One North Carolina slave woman, the mother of fifteen children, used to carry her youngest with her to the field each day, and "when it get hungry she just slip it around in front and feed it and go right on picking or hoeing. . . ," symbolizing in one deft motion the equal significance of the productive and reproductive functions to her owner.[10]

It is possible to divide the daily work routine of slave women into three discrete types of activity. These involved the production of goods and services for different groups and individuals, and included women's labor that directly benefited first, their families, second, other members of the slave community, and third, their owners. Although the master served as the ultimate regulator of all three types of work, he did not subject certain duties related to personal sustenance (that is, those carried out in the slave quarters) to the same scrutiny that characterized fieldwork or domestic service.

The rhythm of the planting-weeding-harvesting cycle shaped the lives of almost all American slaves, 95 percent of whom lived in rural areas. This cycle dictated a common work routine for slaves throughout the South, though the staple crop varied from tobacco in the Upper South to rice on the Georgia and South Carolina Sea Islands, sugar in Louisiana, and the "king" of all agricultural products, cotton, in the broad swath of "Black Belt" that dominated the whole region. Of almost four million slaves, about one-half labored on farms with holdings of twenty slaves or more; one-quarter endured bondage with at least fifty other people on the same plantation. In its most basic form, a life of slavery meant working the soil with other blacks at a pace calculated to reap the largest harvest for a white master.[11]

In his efforts to wrench as much field labor as possible from female slaves without injuring their capacity to bear children, the master made "a noble admission of female equality," observed one abolitionist sympathizer with bitter irony. Slaveholders had little use for sentimental platitudes about the delicacy of the female constitution when it came to grading their "hands" according to physical strength and endurance. Judged on the basis of a standard set by a healthy adult man, most women probably ranked as three-quarter hands; yet there were enough women like Susan Mabry of Virginia, who could pick four or five hundred pounds of cotton a day (one hundred and fifty to two hundred pounds was considered respectable for an average worker), to remove from a master's mind all doubts about the ability of a strong, healthy, woman fieldworker. As a result, he conveniently discarded his time-honored Anglo-Saxon notions about the types of work best suited for women, thereby producing many "dreary scenes" like the one described by northern journalist Frederick Law Olmsted: during winter preparation of rice fields on a Sea Island plantation, a group of black women, "armed with axes, shovels and hoes . . . all slopping about in the black, unctuous mire at the bottom of the ditches." Although pregnant and nursing women suffered from temporary lapses in productivity, most slaveholders apparently agreed with the (in Olmsted's words) "well-known, intelligent, and benevolent" Mississippi planter who declared that "labor is conducive to health; a healthy woman will rear most children." In essence, the quest for an "efficient" agricultural work force led slaveowners to downplay gender differences in assigning adults to field labor.[12]

Dressed in coarse osnaburg gowns; their skirts "reefed up with a cord drawn tightly around the body, a little above the hips" (the traditional "second belt"); long sleeves pushed above the elbows and kerchiefs on their heads, female field hands were a common sight throughout the antebellum South. Together with their fathers, husbands, brothers, and sons, black women were roused at four A.M. and spent up to fourteen hours a day toiling out of doors, often under a blazing sun. In the cotton belt they plowed fields; dropped seed; and hoed, picked, ginned, and sorted cotton. On farms in Virginia, North Carolina, Kentucky, and Tennessee, women hoed tobacco; laid worm fences; and threshed, raked, and bound wheat. For those on the Sea Islands and in coastal areas, rice culture included raking and burning the stubble from the previous year's crop; ditching; sowing seed; plowing, listing, and hoeing fields; and harvesting, stacking, and threshing the rice. In the bayou region of Louisiana, women planted sugarcane cuttings, plowed, and helped to harvest and gin the cane. During the winter, they performed a myriad of tasks necessary on nineteenth-century farms of all kinds: repairing roads, pitching hay, burning brush, and setting up post and rail fences. Like Sara Colquitt of Alabama, most adult females "worked in de fields every day from 'fore daylight to almost plumb dark." During the busy harvest season, everyone was forced to labor up to sixteen hours at a time — after sunset by the light of candles or burning pine knots. Miscellaneous chores occupied women and men around outbuildings regularly and indoors on rainy days. Slaves of both sexes watered the horses, fed the chickens, and slopped the hogs. Together they ginned cotton, ground hominy, shelled corn and peas, and milled flour.[13]

Work assignments for women and men differed according to the size of a plantation and its degree of specialization. For example, on one Virginia wheat farm, the men scythed and cradled the grain, women raked and bound it into sheaves which children then gathered and stacked. Thomas Couper, a wealthy Sea Island planter, divided his slaves according to sex and employed men exclusively in ditching and women in moting and sorting cotton. Within the two gender groups, he further classified hands according to individual strength so that during the sugarcane harvest three "gangs" of women stripped blades (medium-level task), cut them (hardest), and bound and carried them (easiest). However, because cotton served as the basis of the southern agricultural system, distinct patterns of female work usually transcended local and regional differences in labor-force management. Stated simply, most women spent a good deal of their lives plowing, hoeing, and picking cotton. In the fields, the notion of a distinctive "women's work" vanished as slaveholders realized that "women can do plowing very well and full well with the hoes and equal to men at picking."[14]

To harness a double team of mules or oxen and steer a heavy wooden plow was no mean feat for any person, and yet a "substantial minority" of slave women mastered these rigorous activities. White women and men from the North and South marvelled at the skill and strength of female plow hands. Emily Burke of eastern Georgia saw women and men "promiscuously run their ploughs side by side, and day after day. . . and as far as I was able to learn, the part the women sustained in this masculine employment, was quite as efficient as that of the more athletic sex." In his travels through Mississippi, Olmsted watched as women "twitched their plows around on the headland, jerking their reins, and yelling to their mules, with apparent ease, energy, and rapidity." He saw no indication that "their sex unfitted them for the occupation."[15]

On another estate in the Mississippi Valley, Olmsted observed forty of the "largest and strongest" women he had ever seen; they "carried themselves loftily, each having a hoe over the shoulder, and walking with a free, powerful swing, like *chasseurs* on the march." In preparing fields for planting, and in keeping grass from strangling the crop, women as well as men blistered their hands with the clumsy hoe characteristic of southern agriculture. "Hammered out of pig iron, broad like a shovel," these "slave-time hoes" withstood most forms of abuse (destruction of farm implements constituted an integral part of resistance to forced labor). Recalled one former slave of the tool that also served as pick, spade, and gravedigger: "Dey make 'em heavy so dey fall hard, but de bigges' trouble was liftin' dem up." Hoeing was backbreaking labor, but the versatility of the tool and its importance to cotton cultivation meant that the majority of female hands used it a good part of the year.[16]

The cotton-picking season usually began in late July or early August and continued without interruption until the end of

December. Thus for up to five months annually, every available man, woman, and child was engaged in a type of work that was strenuous and "tedious from its sameness." Each picker carried a bag fastened by a strap around her neck and deposited the cotton in it as she made her way down the row, at the end of which she emptied the bag's contents into a basket. Picking cotton required endurance and agility as much as physical strength, and women frequently won regional and interfarm competitions conducted during the year. Pregnant and nursing women usually ranked as half-hands and were required to pick an amount less than the "average" one hundred and fifty or so pounds per day.[17]

Slaveholders often reserved the tasks that demanded sheer muscle power for men exclusively. These included clearing the land of trees, rolling logs, and chopping and hauling wood. However, plantation exigencies sometimes mandated women's labor in this area, too; in general, the smaller the farm, the more arduous and varied was women's fieldwork. Lizzie Atkins, who lived on a twenty-five-acre Texas plantation with only three other slaves, remembered working "until slam dark every day"; she helped to clear land, cut wood, and tend the livestock in addition to her other duties of hoeing corn, spinning thread, sewing clothes, cooking, washing dishes, and grinding corn. One Texas farmer, who had his female slaves haul logs and plow with oxen, even made them wear breeches, thus minimizing outward differences between the sexes. Still, FWP interviews with former slaves indicate that blacks considered certain jobs uncharacteristic of bondwomen. Recalled Louise Terrell of her days on a farm near Jackson, Mississippi: "The women had to split rails all day long, just like the men." Nancy Boudry of Georgia said she used to "split wood jus' like a man." Elderly women reminisced about their mothers and grandmothers with a mixture of pride and wonder. Mary Frances Webb declared of her slave grandmother, "in the winter she sawed and cut cord wood just like a man. She said it didn't hurt her as she was strong as an ox." Janie Scott's description of her mother implied the extent of the older woman's emotional as well as physical strength: she was "strong and could roll and cut logs like a man, and was much of a woman."[18]

Very few women served as skilled artisans or mechanics; on large estates, men invariably filled the positions of carpenter, cooper, wheelwright, tanner, blacksmith, and shoemaker. At first it seems ironic that masters would utilize women fully as field laborers, but reserve most of the skilled occupations that required manual dexterity for men. Here the high cost of specialized and extensive training proved crucial in determining the division of labor; although women were capable of learning these skills, their work lives were frequently interrupted by childbearing and nursing; a female blacksmith might not be able to provide the regular service required on a plantation. Too, masters frequently "hired out" mechanics and artisans to work for other employers during the winter, and women's domestic responsibilities were deemed too important to permit protracted absences from the quarters. However, many young girls learned to spin thread and weave cloth because these tasks could occupy them during confinement.[19]

The drive for cotton profits induced slaveowners to squeeze every bit of strength from black women as a group. According to the estimates of Roger L. Ransom and Richard Sutch, in the 1850s at least 90 percent of all female slaves over sixteen years of age labored more than 261 days per year, eleven to thirteen hours each day. Few overseers or masters had any patience with women whose movements in the field were persistently "clumsy, awkward, gross, [and] elephantine" for whatever reasons — malnutrition, exhaustion, recalcitrance. As Hannah Davidson said: "If you had something to do, you did it or got whipped." The enforced pace of work more nearly resembled that of a factory than a farm; Kemble referred to female field hands as "human hoeing machines." The bitter memories of former slaves merely suggest the extent to which the physical strength of women was exploited. Eliza Scantling of South Carolina, only sixteen years old at the end of the Civil War, plowed with a mule during the coldest months of the year: "Sometimes me hands get so cold I jes' cry." Matilda Perry of Virginia "Use to wuk fum sun to sun in dat ole terbaccy field. Wuk till my back felt lak it ready to pop in two."[20]

At times a woman would rebel in a manner commensurate with the work demands imposed upon her. "She'd git stubborn like a mule and quit." Or she took her hoe and knocked the overseer "plum down" and "chopped him right across his head." When masters and drivers "got rough on her, she got rough on them, and ran away in the woods." She cursed the man who insisted he "owned" her so that he beat her "till she fell" and left her broken body to serve as a warning to the others: "Dat's what you git effen you sass me." Indeed, in the severity of punishment meted out to slaves, little distinction was made between the sexes: "Beat women! Why sure he [master] beat women. Beat women jes' lak men." A systematic survey of the FWP slave narrative collection reveals that women were more likely than men to engage in "verbal confrontations and striking the master but not running away," probably because of their family and childcare responsibilities.[21]

Family members who perceived their mothers or sisters as particularly weak and vulnerable in the fields conspired to lessen their work load. Frank Bell and his four brothers, slaves on a Virginia wheat farm, followed his parents down the long rows of grain during the harvest season. "In dat way one could help de other when dey got behind. All of us would pitch in and help Momma who warn't very strong." The overseer discouraged families from working together because he believed "dey ain't gonna work as fast as when dey all mixed up," but the black driver, Bell's uncle, "always looked out for his kinfolk, especially my mother." James Taliaferro told of his father, who counted the corn rows marked out for Aunt Rebecca ("a short-talking woman that ole Marsa didn't like") and told her that her assignment was almost double that given to the other women. Rebecca indignantly confronted the master, who relented by reducing her task, but not before he threatened to sell James's father for his meddling. On another plantation, the hands surreptitiously added handfuls of cotton to the basket of a young woman who "was small and just couldn't get her proper amount."[22]

No slave women exercised authority over slave men as part of their work routine, but it is uncertain whether this practice reflected the sensibilities of the slaveowners or of the slaves themselves. Women were assigned to teach children simple tasks in the house and field and to supervise other women in various facets of household industry. A master might "let [a woman] off fo' de buryings 'cause she know how to manage de other niggahs and keep dem quiet at de funerls," but he would not install her as a driver over people in the field. Many strong-willed women demonstrated that they commanded respect among males as well as females, but more often than not masters perceived this as a negative quality to be suppressed. One Louisiana slaveholder complained bitterly about a particularly "rascally set of old negroes" — "the better you treat them the worst they are." He had no difficulty pinpointing the cause of the trouble, for "Big Lucy, the leader, corrupts every young negro in her power." On other plantations, women were held responsible for instigating all sorts of undesirable behavior among their husbands and brothers and sisters. On Charles Colcock Jones's Georgia plantation, the slave Cash gave up going to prayer meeting and started swearing as soon as he married Phoebe, well-known for her truculence. Apparently few masters attempted to co-opt high-spirited women by offering them positions of formal power over black men.[23]

In terms of labor-force management, southern slaveowners walked a fine line between making use of the physical strength of women as productive workers and protecting their investment in women as childbearers. These two objectives — one focused on immediate profit returns and the other on long-term economic considerations — at times clashed, because women who spent long hours picking cotton, toiling in the fields with heavy iron hoes, and walking several miles a day sustained damage to their reproductive systems immediately before and after giving birth. For financial reasons, slaveholders might have "regarded pregnancy as almost holy," in the words of one medical historian. But they frequently suspected their bondwomen (like "the most insufferable liar" Nora) of shamming illness — "play [ing] the lady at your expense," as one Virginia planter put it. These fears help to account for the reckless brutality with which owners forced women to work in the fields during and after pregnancy.[24]

Work in the soil thus represented the chief lot of all slaves, female and male. In the Big House, a division of labor based on both gender and age became more apparent, reflecting slaveowners' assumptions about the nature of domestic service. Although women predominated as household workers, few devoted their energies full time to this kind of labor; the size of the plantation determined the degree to which the tasks of cleaning, laundering, caring for the master's children, cooking, and ironing were specialized. According to Eugene Genovese, as few as 5 percent of all antebellum adult slaves served in the elite corps of house servants trained for specific duties. Of course, during the harvest season all slaves, including those in the house, went to the fields to make obeisance to King Cotton. Thus the lines between domestic service and fieldwork blurred during the day and during the lives of slave women. Many continued to live in the slave quarters, but rose early in the morning to perform various chores for the mistress — "up wid de fust light to draw water and help as a house girl" — before heading for the field. James Claiborne's mother "wuked in de fiel' some, an' aroun' de house sometimes .

. . ." Young girls tended babies and waited on tables until they were sent outside — "mos' soon's" they could work — and returned to the house years later, too frail to hoe weeds, but still able to cook and sew. The circle of women's domestic work went unbroken from day to day and from generation to generation.[25]

Just as southern white men scorned manual labor as the proper sphere of slaves, so their wives strove (often unsuccessfully) to lead a life of leisure within their own homes. Those duties necessary to maintain the health, comfort, and daily welfare of white slaveholders were considered less women's work than black women's and black children's work. Slave mistresses supervised the whole operation, but the sheer magnitude of labor involved in keeping all slaves and whites fed and clothed (with different standards set according to race, of course) meant that black women had to supply the elbow grease. For most slaves, housework involved hard, steady, often strenuous labor as they juggled the demands made by the mistress and other members of the master's family. Mingo White of Alabama never forgot that his slave mother had shouldered a work load "too heavy for any one person." She served as personal maid to the master's daughter, cooked for all the hands on the plantation, carded cotton, spun a daily quota of thread, wove and dyed cloth. Every Wednesday she carried the white family's laundry three-quarters of a mile to a creek, where she beat each garment with a wooden paddle. Ironing consumed the rest of her day. Like the lowliest field hand, she felt the lash if any tasks went undone.[26]

Although mistresses found that their husbands commandeered most bondwomen for fieldwork during the better part of the day, they discovered in black children an acceptable alternative source of labor. Girls were favored for domestic service, but a child's sex played only a secondary role in determining household assignments. On smaller holdings especially, the demands of housework, like cotton cultivation, admitted of no finely honed division of labor. Indeed, until puberty, girls and boys shared a great deal in terms of dress and work. All children wore a "split-tail shirt," a knee-length smock slit up the sides: "Boys and gals all dress jes' alike . . . . They call it a shirt iffen a boy wear it and call it a dress iffen the gal wear it." At the age of six or so, many received assignments around the barnyard or in the Big House from one or more members of the master's family. Mr. and Mrs. Alex Smith, who grew up together, remembered performing different tasks. As a girl she helped to spin thread and pick seeds from cotton and cockle burrs from wool. He chopped wood, carried water, hoed weeds, tended the cows, and picked bugs from tobacco plants. However, slave narratives contain descriptions of both girls and boys elsewhere doing each of these things.[27]

Between the ages of six and twelve, black girls and boys followed the mistress's directions in filling woodboxes with kindling, lighting fires in chilly bedrooms in the morning and evening, making beds, washing and ironing clothes, parching coffee, polishing shoes, and stoking fires while the white family slept at night. They fetched water and milk from the springhouse and meat from the smokehouse. Three times a day they set the table, helped to prepare and serve meals, "minded flies" with peacock feather brushes, passed the salt and pepper on command and washed the dishes. They swept, polished, and dusted, served drinks and fanned overheated visitors. Mistresses entrusted to the care of those who were little more than babies themselves the bathing, diapering, dressing, grooming, and entertaining of white infants. In the barnyard black children gathered eggs, plucked chickens, drove cows to and from the stable and "tended the gaps" (opened and closed gates). (In the fields they acted as human scarecrows, toted water to the hands, and hauled shocks of corn together.) It was no wonder that Mary Ella Grandberry, a slave child grown old, "disremember[ed] ever playin' lack chilluns do today."[28]

In only a few tasks did a sexual division of labor exist among children. Masters always chose boys to accompany them on hunting trips and to serve as their personal valets. Little girls learned how to sew, to milk cows and churn butter, and to attend to the personal needs of their mistresses. As tiny ladies-in-waiting, they did the bidding of fastidious white women and of girls not much older than they. Cicely Cawthon, age six when the Civil War began, called herself the mistress's "little keeper"; "I stayed around, and waited on her, handed her water, fanned her, kept the flies off her, pulled up her pillow, and done anything she'd tell me to do." Martha Showvely recounted a nightly ritual with her Virginia mistress. After she finished her regular work around the house, the young girl would go to the woman's bedroom, bow to her, wait for acknowledgment, and then scurry around as ordered, lowering the shades, filling the water pitcher, arranging towels on the washstand, or "anything else" that struck the woman's fancy. Mary Woodward, only eleven in 1865, was taught to comb her mistress's hair, lace her corset, and arrange her hoop skirts. At the end of the toilet Mary was supposed to say, "You is served, mistress!" Recalled the former slave, "Her lak them little words at de last."[29]

Sexual exploitation of female servants of all ages (described in graphic detail by Harriet Jacobs in Lydia Maria Child's *Incidents in the Life of a Slave Girl*) predictably antagonized white women. Jealousy over their husbands' real or suspected infidelities resulted in a propensity for spontaneous violence among many. Husbands who flaunted their adventures in the slave quarters increased the chance that their wives would attack a specific woman or her offspring. Sarah Wilson remembered being "picked on" by the mistress, who chafed under her husband's taunts; he would say, '"Let her alone, she got big, big blood in her,' and then laugh."[30]

A divorce petition filed with the Virginia legislature in 1848 included a witness's testimony that the master in question one morning told his slave favorite to sit down at the breakfast table "to which Mrs. N [his wife] objected, saying. . . that she (Mrs. N.) would have her severely punished." Her husband replied "that in that event he would visit her (Mrs. N.) with a like punishment. Mrs. N. then burst into tears and asked if it was not too much for her to stand." This husband went to extreme lengths to remind his spouse of slave-mistress Mary Chesnut's observation that "there is no slave, after all, like a wife." In the black woman the mistress saw not only the source of her own degradation, she saw herself — a woman without rights, subject to the impulses of an arrogant husband-master.[31]

To punish black women for minor offenses, mistresses were likely to attack with any weapon available — a fork, butcher knife, knitting needle, pan of boiling water. Some of the most barbaric forms of punishment resulting in the mutilation and permanent scarring of female servants were devised by white mistresses in the heat of passion. As a group they received well-deserved notoriety for the "veritable terror" they unleashed upon black women in the Big House.[32]

Interviews with former slaves suggest that the advantages of domestic service (over fieldwork) for women have been exaggerated in accounts written by whites. Carrying wood and water, preparing three full meals a day over a smoky fireplace or pressing damp clothes with a hot iron rivaled cotton picking as backbreaking labor. Always "on call," women servants often had to snatch a bite to eat whenever they could, remain standing in the presence of whites, and sleep on the floor at the foot of their mistress's bed (increasing the chances that they would sooner or later be bribed, seduced, or forced into sexual relations with the master). To peel potatoes with a sharp knife, build a fire, or carry a heavy load of laundry down a steep flight of stairs required skills and dexterity not always possessed by little girls and boys, and injuries were common. Chastisement for minor infractions came with swift severity; cooks who burned the bread and children who stole cookies or fell asleep while singing to the baby suffered every conceivable form of physical abuse, from jabs with pins to beatings that left them disfigured for life. The master's house offered no shelter from the most brutal manifestations of slavery.[33]

For any one or all of these reasons, black women might prefer fieldwork to housework. During his visit to a rice plantation in 1853, Olmsted noted that hands "accustomed to the comparatively unconstrained life of the negro-settlement detest the close control and careful movements required of the house servants." Marriage could be both a means and an incentive to escape a willful mistress. Jessie Sparrow's mother wed at age thirteen in order "to go outer de big house. Dat how come she to marry so soon. . . ." Claude Wilson recalled many years later that "his mother was very rebellious toward her duties and constantly harassed the 'Missus' about letting her work in the fields with her husband until finally she was permitted to make the change from the house to the fields to be near her man." Other women, denied an alternative, explored the range of their own emotional resources in attempting to resist petty tyranny; their "sassiness" rubbed raw the nerves of mistresses already harried and high-strung. A few servants simply withdrew into a shell of "melancholy and timidity."[34]

The dual status of a bondwoman — a slave and a female — afforded her master a certain degree of flexibility in formulating her work assignments. When he needed a field hand, her status as an able-bodied slave took precedence over gender considerations, and she was forced to toil alongside her menfolk. At the same time, the master's belief that most forms of domestic service required the attentions of a female reinforced among slave women the traditional role of woman as household worker.

The authority of the master in enforcing a sexual division of labor was absolute, but at times individual women could influence his decisions to some extent. In certain cases, a woman's preferences for either fieldwork or domestic service worked to her advantage. For example, the rebelliousness of Claude Wilson's mother prompted her removal from the Big House to the field, a change she desired. Similarly, masters might promise a woman an opportunity to do a kind of work she preferred as a reward for her cooperation and diligence. On the other hand, a slave's misbehavior might cause her to lose a position she had come to value; more than one prized cook or maid was exiled to the fields for "sassing" the mistress or stealing. A system of rewards and punishments thus depended on the preferences of individual slaves, and a servant determined to make life miserable for the family in the Big House might get her way in any case.[35]

In the field and Big House, black women worked under the close supervision of whites (the master, overseer, or mistress) at a forced pace. The slaves derived few, if any, tangible benefits from their labor to increase staple-crop profits and to render the white family comfortable (at least in physical terms). However, their efforts to provide for their own health and welfare often took place apart from whites, with a rhythm more in tune with community and family life. For slave women, these responsibilities, although physically arduous, offered a degree of personal fulfillment. As Martha Colquitt remarked of her slave grandmother and mother who stayed up late to knit and sew clothes "for us chillun": "Dey done it 'cause dey wanted to. Dey wuz workin' for deyselves den." Slave women deprived of the ability to cook for their own kinfolk or discipline their own children felt a keen sense of loss; family responsibilities revealed the limited extent to which black women (and men) could control their own lives. Furthermore, a strict sexual division of labor in the quarters openly challenged the master's opportunistic approach to slave women's work.[36]

A number of activities were carried out either communally or centrally for the whole plantation by older women. On smaller farms, for example, a cook and her assistants might prepare one or all of the meals for the other slaves each day except Sunday. Similarly, an elderly woman, with the help of children too young to work in the fields, often was assigned charge of a nursery in the quarters, where mothers left their babies during the day. To keep any number of little ones happy and out of trouble for up to twelve to fourteen hours at a time taxed the patience of the most kindly souls. Slave children grew up with a mixture of affection and fear for the "grandmothers" who had dished out the licks along with the cornbread and clabber. Other grannies usurped the position of the white physician (he rarely appeared in any case); they "brewed medicines for every ailment," gave cloves and whiskey to ease the pain of childbirth, and prescribed potions for the lovesick. Even a child forced to partake of "Stinkin' Jacob tea" or a concoction of "turpentine an' castor oil an' Jerusalem oak" (for worms) would assert years later that "Gran'mammy was a great doctor," surely a testimony to her respected position within the slave community, if not to the delectability of her remedies.[37]

On many plantations, it was the custom to release adult women from fieldwork early on Saturday so that they could do their week's washing. Whether laundering was done in old wooden tubs, iron pots, or a nearby creek with batten sticks, wooden paddles, or washboards, it was a time-consuming and difficult chore. Yet this ancient form of women's work provided opportunities for socializing "whilst de 'omans leaned over de tubs washin' and a-singin' dem old songs." Mary Frances Webb remembered wash day — "a regular picnic" — with some fondness; it was a time for women "to spend the day together," out of the sight and earshot of whites.[38]

Much of the work black women did for the slave community resembled the colonial system of household industry. Well into the nineteenth century throughout the South, slave women continued to spin thread, weave and dye cloth, sew clothes, make soap and candles, prepare and preserve foods, churn butter, and grow food for the family table. Slave women mastered all these tasks with the aid of primitive equipment and skills passed on from grandmothers. Many years later, blacks of both sexes exclaimed over their slave mothers' ability to prepare clothing dye from various combinations of tree bark and leaves, soil and berries; make soap out of ashes and animal skins; and fashion bottle lamps from string and tallow. Because of their lack of time and materials, black women only rarely found in these activities an outlet for creative expression, but they did take pride in their resourcefulness and produced articles of value to the community as a whole.[39]

Black women's work in home textile production illustrates the ironies of community labor under slavery, for the threads of cotton and wool bound them together in both bondage and sisterhood. Masters (or mistresses) imposed rigid spinning and weaving quotas on women who worked in the fields all day. For example, many were forced to spin one "cut" (about three hundred yards) of thread nightly, or four to five cuts during rainy days or in the winter. Women of all ages worked together and children of both sexes helped to tease and card wool, pick up the loom shuttles, and knit. In the flickering candlelight, the whirr of the spinning wheel and the clackety-clack of the loom played a seductive lullabye, drawing those who were already "mighty tired" away from their assigned tasks.[40]

As the "head spinner" on a Virginia plantation, Bob Ellis's mother was often sent home from fieldwork early to prepare materials for the night's work; "She had to portion out de cotton dey was gonna spin an' see dat each got a fair share." Later that evening, after supper, as she moved around the dusty loom room to check on the progress of the other women, she would sing:

> Keep yo' eye on de sun,
> See how she run
> Don't let her catch you with you work undone,
> I'm a trouble, I'm a trouble,
> Trouble don' las' always.

With her song of urgency and promise she coaxed her sisters to finish their work so they could return home by sundown: "Dat made de women all speed up so dey could finish fo' dark catch 'em, 'cause it mighty hard handlin' dat cotton thread by fire-light."[41]

In the quarters, group work melded into family responsibilities, for the communal spirit was but a manifestation of primary kin relationships. Here it is possible only to outline the social dynamics of the slave household. The significance of the family in relation to the sexual division of labor under slavery cannot be overestimated; out of the mother-father, wife-husband nexus sprang the slaves' beliefs about what women and men should be and do. Ultimately, the practical application of those beliefs (in the words of Genovese) "provided a weapon for joint resistance to dehumanization."[42]

The two-parent, nuclear family was the typical form of slave cohabitation regardless of the location, size, or economy of a plantation; the nature of its ownership; or the age of its slave community. Because of the omnipresent threat of forced separation by sale, gift, or bequest, this family was not "stable." Yet, in the absence of such separations, unions between husbands and wives and parents and children often endured for many years. Marital customs, particularly exogamy, and the practice of naming children after the mother's or father's relatives (the most common pattern was to name a boy after a male relative) revealed the strong sense of kinship among slaves. Households tended to be large; Herbert G. Gutman found families with eight living children to be quite common. Out of economic considerations, a master would encourage his work force to reproduce itself, but the slaves welcomed each new birth primarily as "a social and familial fact." A web of human emotions spun by close family ties — affection, dignity, love — brought slaves together in a world apart from whites.[43]

In their own cabins, the blacks maintained a traditional division of labor between the sexes. Like women in almost all cultures, slave women had both a biological and a social "destiny." As part of their childbearing role, they assumed primary responsibility for childcare (when a husband and wife lived on separate plantations, the children remained with their mother and belonged to her master). Women also performed operations related to daily household maintenance — cooking, cleaning, tending fires, sewing and patching clothes.[44]

Fathers shared the obligations of family life with their wives. In denying slaves the right to own property, make a living for themselves, participate in public life, or protect their children, the institution of bondage deprived black men of access to the patriarchy in the larger economic and political sense. But at home women and men worked together to support the father's role as provider and protector. In the evenings and on Sundays, men collected firewood; made shoes; wove baskets; constructed beds, tables, and chairs; and carved butter paddles, ax handles, and animal traps. Other family members appreciated a father's skills; recalled Molly Ammonds, "My pappy make all de funiture dat went in our house an' it were might' good funiture too," and Pauline Johnson echoed, "De furn'chure was ho-mek, but my daddy mek it good an' stout." Husbands provided necessary supplements to the family diet by hunting and trapping quails, possums, turkeys, rabbits, squirrels, and raccoons, and by fishing. They often assumed responsibility for cultivating the tiny household garden plots allotted to families by the master. Some craftsmen, like Bill Austin's father, received goods or small sums of money in return for their work on nearby estates; Jack Austin, "regarded as a fairly good carpenter, mason, and bricklayer," was paid in " hams, bits of cornmeal, cloth for dresses for his wife and children, and other small gifts; these he either used for his small family or bartered with other slaves."[45]

These familial duties also applied to men who lived apart from their wives and children even though they were usually allowed to visit only on Saturday night and Sunday. Lucinda Miller's family "never had any sugar, and only got coffee when her father would bring it to her mother" during his visits. The father of Hannah Chapman was sold to a nearby planter when she was very small. Because "he missed us and us longed for him," she said many years later, he tried to visit his family under the cover of darkness whenever possible. She noted, "Us would gather 'round him an' crawl up in his lap, tickled slap to death, but he give us dese pleasures at painful risk." If the master should happen to discover him, "Us could track him de nex' day by de blood stains," she remembered.[46]

Hannah McFarland of South Carolina well remembered the time when the local slave patrol attempted to whip her mother, "but my papa sho' stopped dat," she said proudly. Whether or not he was made to suffer for his courage is unknown; however, the primary literature of slavery is replete with accounts of slave husbands who intervened, at the risk of their own lives, to save wives and children from violence at the hands of white men. More often, however, fathers had to show their compassion in less dramatic (though no less revealing) ways. On a Florida plantation, the Minus children often rose in the morning to find still warm in the fireplace the potatoes "which their father had thoughtfully roasted and which [they] readily consumed." Margrett Nickerson recalled how her father would tenderly bind up the wounds inflicted on her by a maniacal overseer; in later years, her crippled legs preserved the memory of a father's sorrow intermingled with her own suffering.[47]

The more freedom the slaves had in determining their own activities the more clearly emerged a distinct division of labor between the sexes. During community festivities like log rollings, rail splittings, wood choppings, and corn shuckings, men performed the prescribed labor while women cooked the meals. At times, male participants willingly "worked all night," for, in the words of one former slave, "we had the 'Heavenly Banners' (women and whiskey) by us." A limited amount of primary evidence indicates that men actively scorned women's work, especially cooking, housecleaning, sewing, washing clothes, and intimate forms of childcare (like bathing children and picking lice out of their hair). Some slaveholders devised forms of public humiliation that capitalized on men's attempts to avoid these tasks. One Louisiana cotton planter punished slave men by forcing them to wash clothes (he also made chronic offenders wear women's dresses). In *This Species of Property*, Leslie Howard Owens remarks of men so treated, "So great was their shame before their fellows that many ran off and suffered the lash on their backs rather than submit to the discipline. Men clearly viewed certain chores as women's tasks, and female slaves largely respected the distinction."[48]

The values and customs of the slave community played a predominant role in structuring work patterns among women and men within the quarters in general and the family in particular. Yet slaveholders affected the division of labor in the quarters in several ways; for example, they took women and girls out of the fields early on Saturdays to wash the clothes, and they enforced certain task assignments related to the production of household goods. An understanding of the social significance of the sexual division of labor requires at least brief mention of West African cultural preferences and the ways in which the American system of slavery disrupted or sustained traditional (African) patterns of women's work. Here it is important to keep in mind two points. First, cotton did not emerge as the South's primary staple crop until the late eighteenth century (the first slaves on the North American continent toiled in tobacco, rice, indigo, and corn fields); and second, regardless of the system of task assignments imposed upon antebellum blacks, the grueling pace of forced labor represented a cruel break from the past for people who had followed age-old customs related to subsistence agriculture.[49]

Though dimmed by time and necessity, the outlines of African work patterns endured among the slaves. As members of traditional agricultural societies, African women played a major role in producing the family's food as well as in providing basic household services. The sexual division of labor was more often determined by a woman's childcare and domestic reponsibilities than by any presumed physical weakness. She might engage in heavy, monotonous fieldwork (in some tribes) as long as she could make provisions for nursing her baby; that often meant keeping an infant with her in the field. She cultivated a kitchen garden that yielded a variety of vegetables consumed by the family or sold at market, and she usually milked the cows and churned butter.[50]

West Africans in general brought with them competencies and

knowledge that slaveowners readily exploited. Certain tribes were familiar with rice, cotton, and indigo cultivation. Many black women had had experience spinning thread, weaving cloth, and sewing clothes. Moreover, slaves often used techniques and tools handed down from their ancestors — in the method of planting, hoeing, and pounding rice, for example. Whites frequently commented on the ability of slave women to balance heavy and unwieldy loads on their heads, an African trait.[51]

The primary difficulty in generalizing about African women's part in agriculture stems from the fact that members of West African tribes captured for the North American slave trade came from different hoe-culture economies. Within the geographically limited Niger Delta region, for example, women and men of the Ibo tribe worked together in planting, weeding, and harvesting, but female members of another prominent group, the Yoruba, helped only with harvest. In general, throughout most of sub-Saharan Africa (and particularly on the west coast) women had primary responsibility for tilling (though not clearing) the soil and cultivating the crops; perhaps this tradition, combined with work patterns established by white masters in this country, reinforced the blacks' beliefs that cutting trees and rolling logs was "men's work." In any case it is clear that African women often did fieldwork. But because the sexual division of labor varied according to tribe, it is impossible to state with any precision the effect of the African heritage on the slaves' perceptions of women's agricultural work.[52]

The West African tradition of respect for one's elders found new meaning among American slaves; for most women, old age brought increased influence within the slave community even as their economic value to the master declined. Owners, fearful lest women escape from "earning their salt" once they became too infirm to go to the field, set them to work at other tasks — knitting, cooking, spinning, weaving, dairying, washing, ironing, caring for the children. (Elderly men worked as gardeners, wagoners, carters, and stocktenders.) But the imperatives of the southern economic system sometimes compelled slaveowners to extract from feeble women what field labor they could. In other cases they reduced the material provisions of the elderly — housing and allowances of food and clothing — in proportion to their decreased productivity.[53]

The overwhelming youth of the general slave population between 1830 and 1860 (more than one-half of all slaves were under twenty years of age) meant that most plantations had only a few old persons — the 10 percent over fifty years of age considered elderly. These slaves served as a repository of history and folklore for the others. Harriet Ware, a northern teacher assigned to the South Carolina Sea Islands, reported in 1862, "'Learning' with these people I find means a knowledge of medicine, and a person is valued accordingly." Many older women practiced "medicine" in the broadest sense in their combined role of midwife, root doctor, healer, and conjurer. They guarded ancient secrets about herbs and other forms of plant life. In their interpretation of dreams and strange occurrences, they brought the real world closer to the supernatural realm and offered spiritual guidance to the ill, the troubled, and the lovelorn.[54]

For slaves in the late antebellum period, these revered (and sometimes feared) women served as a tangible link with the African past. Interviewed by an FWP worker in 1937, a Mississippi-born former slave, James Brittian, recalled his own "grandma Aunt Mary" who had lived for 110 years. A "Molly Gasca [Madagascar?] negro," she was plagued by a jealous mistress because of her striking physical appearance; "Her hair it was fine as silk and hung down below her waist." Ned Chaney's African-born Granny Silla (she was the oldest person anyone knew, he thought) commanded respect among the other slaves by virtue of her advanced age and her remarkable healing powers: "Ever'body set a heap of sto' by her. I reckon, because she done 'cumullated so much knowledge an' because her head were so white." When Granny Silla died, her "little bags" of mysterious substances were buried with her because no one else knew how to use them. Yet Chaney's description of his own mother, a midwife and herb doctor, indicates that she too eventually assumed a position of at least informal authority within the community.[55]

As a little girl in Georgia, Mary Colbert adored her grandmother, a strong field hand, "smart as a whip." "I used to tell my mother that I wished I was named Hannah for her, and so Mother called me Mary Hannah," she recalled. Amanda Harris, interviewed in Virginia when she was ninety years old, looked back to the decade before the war when her grandmother was still alive: "Used to see her puffin' on dat ole pipe o' her'n, an' one day I ast her what fun she got outen it. 'Tain't no fun, chile,' she tole me. 'But it's a pow'ful lot o' easment. Smoke away trouble, darter. Blow ole trouble an' worry 'way in smoke.'" Amanda started smoking a pipe shortly before her grandmother died, and in 1937 she declared, "Now dat I'm ole as she was I know what she mean." In the quiet dignity of their own lives, these grandmothers preserved the past for future generations of Afro-American women.[56]

Within well-defined limits, the slaves created — or preserved — an explicit sexual division of labor based on their own preferences. Wives and husbands and mothers and fathers had reciprocal obligations toward one another. Together they worked to preserve the integrity of the family. Having laid to rest once and for all the myth of the slave matriarchy, some historians suggest that relations between the sexes approximated "a healthy sexual equality."[57] Without private property, slave men lacked the means to achieve economic superiority over their wives, one of the major sources of inequality in the ("free") sexual order. But if female and male slaves shared duties related to household maintenance and community survival, they were nonetheless reduced to a state of powerlessness that rendered virtually meaningless the concept of equality as it applies to marital relations.

Developments during the turbulent postwar years, when the chains of bondage were loosened but not destroyed, made clear the significance of black women's work in supporting the southern staple-crop economy. They also revealed the connection between patterns of women's work and black family life — a connection that had, at least to some degree, remained latent under slavery. Black women did their part in helping to provide for their families after the war. Female household heads had a particularly difficult time, for under the "free labor" system, a mother working alone rarely earned enough to support small children who were themselves too little to make any money. Relatives in a better financial situation often "adopted" these children, or took the whole family under their care.[58]

After the war, black women continued to serve as domestic servants, but large numbers stopped going to the fields altogether, or agreed to work only in harvest time. Indeed, from all over the South came reports that "the negro women are now almost wholly withdrawn from field labor." Ransom and Sutch, in their study of the economic consequences of emancipation, estimate that between one-third and one-half of all the women who worked in the fields under slavery provided proportionately less agricultural labor in the 1870s. This decline in overall female productivity was the result of two factors: many wives stayed home, and the ones who did continue to labor in the fields (like black men) put in shorter hours and fewer days each year than they had as slaves.

Crop output in many locales dropped accordingly, and white landowners lamented their loss, "for women were as efficient as men in working and picking cotton."[59]

In their speculation about the sources of this "evil of female loaferism," whites offered a number of theories, from the pernicious influence of northern schoolteachers to the inherent laziness of the black race. Actually, black women and men responded to freedom in a manner consistent with preferences that had been thwarted during slavery. Husbands sought to protect their wives from the sexual abuse and physical punishment that continued to prevail under the wage system of agricultural labor. Wives wanted to remain at home with their children, as befitted free and freed women; many continued to contribute to the family welfare by taking in washing or raising chickens.[60]

By 1867, freed people who wanted to assert control over their own productive energies had reached what some historians term a "compromise" with white landowners anxious to duplicate antebellum crop levels. This "compromise" came in the form of the sharecropping system, a family organization of labor that represented both a radical departure from collective or "gang" work characteristic of slavery and a rejection of the wage economy so integral to the (North's) fledgling industrial revolution. Freed families moved out of the old slave quarters into cabins scattered around a white man's plantation; they received "furnishings" (tools and seed) and agreed to pay the landlord a share of the crop — usually one-half of all the cotton they produced — in return for the use of the land and modest dwelling. Under this arrangement, black husbands assumed primary responsibility for crop management, and their wives devoted as much attention as possible to their roles as mothers and homemakers. During the particularly busy planting or harvesting seasons, a woman would join her husband and children at work in the field. In this way she could keep an eye on her offspring and still put to use her considerable strength and skills unmolested by white men.[61]

The Reconstruction South was not the best of all worlds in which to foster a new order between the races — or the sexes. Faced with persistent economic exploitation and political subservience within white-dominated society, black men sought to assert their authority as protectors of their communities and families. Outwardly, they placed a premium on closing ranks at home. This impulse was institutionalized in the freed people's churches ("Wives submit yourselves to your husbands" was the text of more than one postbellum sermon) and political organizations. One searches in vain for evidence of female participants in the many black conventions and meetings during this period, although this was perhaps in part attributable to the fact that women did not have the right to vote. Black women remained militantly outspoken in defense of their families and property rights, but they lacked a formal power base within their own communities. And in an atmosphere fraught with sexual violence, where freedwomen remained at the mercy of white men and where "the mere suggestion" that a black man was attracted to a white woman was "enough to hang him," a black husband's resentment might continue to manifest itself in his relations with those closest to him. A Sea Island slave folktale offered the lesson that "God had nebber made a woman for the head of a man." In the struggle against white racism this often meant that black women were denied the equality with their men to which their labor — not to mention justice — entitled them.[62]

The sexual division of labor under slavery actually assumed two forms — one system of work forced upon slaves by masters who valued women only as work-oxen and brood-sows, and the other initiated by the slaves themselves in the quarters. Only the profit motive accorded a measure of consistency to the slaveholder's decisions concerning female work assignments; he sought to exploit his "hands" efficiently, and either invoked or repudiated traditional notions of women's work to suit his own purposes. In this respect, his decision-making process represented in microcosm the shifting priorities of the larger society, wherein different groups of women were alternately defined primarily as producers or as reproducers according to the fluctuating labor demands of the capitalist economy.[63]

Within their own communities, the slaves attempted to make work choices based on their African heritage as it applied to the American experience. Their well-defined sexual division of labor contrasted with the calculated self-interest of slaveowners. Slave women were allowed to fulfill their duties as wives and mothers only insofar as these responsibilities did not conflict with their masters' demands for field or domestic labor. As sharecroppers, freed people sought to institutionalize their resistance to the whites' conviction that black women should be servants or cotton pickers first, and family members only incidentally. In working together as a unit, black parents and children made an explicit political statement to the effect that their own priorities were inimical to those of white landowners.

To a considerable extent, the freed family's own patriarchal tendencies — fathers took care of "public" negotiations with the white landlord while mothers assumed primary responsibility for childcare — resulted from the black man's desire to protect his household in the midst of a violently racist society. The postbellum black nuclear family never duplicated exactly the functions of the white middle-class model, which (beginning in the late eighteenth century) drew an increasingly rigid distinction between masculine and feminine spheres of activity characteristic of commercial-industrial capitalism. Clearly, the peculiar southern way of life suggests that an analysis of black women's oppression should focus not so much on the family as on the dynamics of racial prejudice. However, black women and men in the long run paid a high price for their allegiance to a patriarchal family structure, and it is important not to romanticize this arrangement as it affected the status and opportunities of women, even within the confines of black community life. Women continued to wield informal influence in their roles as herb doctors and "grannies," but men held all positions of formal political and religious authority. Ultimately, black people's "preferences" in the postwar period took shape within two overlapping caste systems — one based on race, the other on gender. Former slaves were "free" only in the sense that they created their own forms of masculine authority as a counter to poverty and racism.

The story of slave women's work encapsulates an important part of American history. For here in naked form, stripped free of the pieties often used in describing white women and free workers at the time, were the forces that shaped patriarchal capitalism — exploitation of the most vulnerable members of society, and a contempt for women that knew no ethical or physical bounds. And yet, slave women demonstrated "true womanhood" in its truest sense. Like Janie Scott's mother who was "much of a woman," they revealed a physical and emotional strength that transcended gender and preached a great sermon about the human spirit.

NOTES

The author would like to acknowledge the helpful suggestions and comments provided by Rosalind Petchesky and other members of the *Feminist Studies* editorial board and by Michael P. Johnson. Research for this project (part of a full-length study of black women, work, and the family in America, 1830-1980) was funded by a grant from the National Endowment for the Humanities.

[1]Zora N. Hurston, *Their Eyes Were Watching God* (London: J.M. Dent and Sons, 1938), pp. 31-32. Novelist, folklorist, and anthropologist, Hurston (born 1901, died 1960) had collected a massive amount of primary data on the culture and folklore of Afro-Americans before she began work on *Their Eyes Were Watching God*. In 1938 she served as supervisor of the Negro Unit of the Florida Federal Writers Project which compiled interviews with former slaves. Her various writings are finally receiving long-overdue literary attention and critical acclaim. See Robert E. Hemenway, *Zora Neale Hurston: A Literary Biography* (Urbana: University of Illinois Press, 1977); and a recent anthology: Zora N. Hurston, *I Love Myself When I Am Laughing. . . And Then Again When I Am Looking Mean And Impressive*, ed. Alice Walker (Old Westbury, N.Y.: Feminist Press, 1980).

[2]Angela Davis, "Reflections on the Black Woman's Role in the Community of Slaves," *The Black Scholar* 3 (December 1971): 3-15. For other works that focus on slave women, see Mary Ellen Obitko, "'Custodians of a House of Resistance': Black Women Respond to Slavery," in *Women and Men: The Consequences of Power*, ed. Dana V. Hiller and Robin Ann Sheets (Cincinnati: Office of Women's Studies, University of Cincinnati, 1977), pp. 256-59; Deborah G. White, "Ain't I A Woman? Female Slaves in the Antebellum South" (Ph.D. dissertation, University of Illinois-Chicago Circle, 1979). White's work examines several important themes related to slave women's work and family life, but her study lacks a coherent theoretical framework. She asserts that slave women gained considerable "self-confidence" because they achieved "equality" with men of their race, and even suggests that emancipation resulted in a "loss" of women's "equality"; freedom amounted to "a decline in the status of black women" (p. 51). When used in this context, the concepts of equality and status lose all meaning and relevance to the complex issues involved; White's argument obscures the subtleties of black female-male relations under bondage and after emancipation.

The volume edited by Gerda Lerner, *Black Women in White America: A Documentary History* (New York: Randam House, 1972), includes material on the history of slave women.

[3]Herbert G. Gutman, *The Black Family in Slavery and Freedom, 1750-1925* (New York: Pantheon Books, 1976); Eugene D. Genovese, *Roll, Jordan, Roll: The World the Slaves Made* (New York: Randam House, 1974); Leslie Howard Owens, *This Species of Property: Slave Life and Culture in the Old South* (New York: Oxford University Press, 1976); John D. Blassingame, *The Slave Community: Plantation Life in the Old South* (New York: Oxford University Press, 1972); Paul A. David et al., *Reckoning With Slavery: A Critical Study in the Quantitative History of American Negro Slavery* (New York: Oxford University Press, 1976); Paul D. Escott, *Slavery Remembered: A Record of Twentieth-Century Slave Narratives* (Chapel Hill: University of North Carolina Press, 1978).

In some specialized studies, women are largely excluded from the general analysis and discussed only in brief sections under the heading "Women and Children." See, for example, Robert S. Starobin, *Industrial Slavery in the Old South* (New York: Oxford University Press, 1970); and Todd L. Savitt, *Medicine and Slavery: The Diseases and*

Health Care of Blacks in Antebellum Virginia (Urbana: University of Illinois Press, 1978).

[4]For examples of studies of specific groups of women and the relationship between their work and family life, see Nancy F. Cott, *The Bonds of Womanhood: 'Woman's Sphere' in New England, 1780-1835* (New Haven: Yale University Press, 1977); Thomas Dublin, *Women at Work: The Transformation of Work and Community in Lowell, Massachusetts, 1826-1860* (New York: Columbia University Press, 1979); Milton Cantor and Bruce Laurie, eds., *Class, Sex, and the Woman Worker* (Westport, Conn.: Greenwood Press, 1977); Virginia Yans McLaughlin, "Patterns of Work and Family Organization: Buffalo's Italians," *Journal of Interdisciplinary History* 2 (Autumn 1971): 297-314; Leslie Woodcock Tentler, *Wage-Earning Women: Industrial Work and Family Life in the United States, 1900-1930* (New York: Oxford University Press, 1979).

General overviews and theoretical formulations that fail to take into account the experiences of slave women include Patricia Branca, "A New Perspective on Women's Work: A Comparative Typology," *Journal of Social History* 9 (Winter 1975): 129-53; W. Elliot Brownlee, "Household Values, Women's Work, and Economic Growth, 1800-1930," *Journal of Economic History* 39 (March 1979): 199-209; Maurine Weiner Greenwald, "Historians and the Working-Class Woman in America," *International Labor and Working-Class History*, no. 14/15 (Spring 1979): 23-32; Alice Kessler-Harris, "Women, Work, and the Social Order," in *Liberating Women's History: Theoretical and Critical Essays*, ed. Berenice A. Carroll (Urbana: University of Illinois Press, 1976), pp. 330-43.

[5]On women's "productive-reproductive" functions and the relationship between patriarchy and capitalism, see Joan Kelly, "The Doubled Vision of Feminist Theory: A Postcript to the 'Women and Power' Conference," *Feminist Studies* 5 (Spring 1979): 216-27; Heidi Hartmann, "Capitalism, Patriarchy, and Job Segregation by Sex," and Zillah Eisenstein, "Developing a Theory of Capitalist Patriarchy and Socialist Feminism," and "Some Notes on the Relations of Capitalist Patriarchy," in *Capitalist Patriarchy and the Case for Socialist Feminism*, ed. Zillah R. Eisenstein (New York: Monthly Review Press, 1979); Annette Kuhn and AnnMarie Wolpe, "Feminism and Materialism" and Veronica Beechey, "Women and Production: A Critical Analysis of Some Sociological Theories of Women's Work," both in *Feminism and Materialism: Women and Modes of Production*, ed. Annette Kuhn and AnnMarie Wolpe (London: Routledge and Kegan Paul, 1978).

Several scholars argue that the last three decades of the antebellum period constituted a distinct phase in the history of slavery. Improved textile machinery and a rise in world demand for cotton led to a tremendous growth in the American slave economy, especially in the Lower South. A marked increase in slave mortality rates and family breakups (a consequence of forced migration from Upper to Lower South), and a slight decline in female fertility rates indicate the heightened demands made upon slave labor during the years 1830-60. See David, et al., *Reckoning With Slavery*, pp. 99, 356-57; Jack Erickson Eblen, "New Estimates of the Vital Rates of the United States Black Population During the Nineteenth Century," *Demography* 11 (May 1974): 307-13.

[6]For example, see Kelly, "Doubled Vision," pp. 217-18, and Eisenstein, "Relations of Capitalist Patriarchy," pp. 48-52, on the regressive implications of family life for women. But Davis notes that the slave woman's "survival-oriented activities were themselves a form of resistance" ("Reflections on the Black Woman's Role," p.7).

[7]Interviews with former slaves have been published in various forms, including George P. Rawick, ed., *The American Slave: A Composite Autobiography*, 41 vols., Series 1 and 2, supp. Series 1 and 2 (Westport Conn.: Greenwood Press, 1972, 1978, 1979); Social Science Institute, Fisk University, *Unwritten History of Slavery:*

Autobiographical Accounts of Negro Ex-Slaves (Washington, D.C.: Microcards Editions, 1968); Charles L. Perdue, Jr., Thomas E. Borden, and Robert K. Phillips, *Weevils in the Wheat: Interviews with Virginia Ex-Slaves* (Charlottesville: University Press of Virginia, 1976); John B. Cade, "Out of the Mouths of Ex-Slaves," *Journal of Negro History* 20 (July 1935): 294-337.

The narratives as a historical source are evaluated in Escott, *Slavery Remembered*, pp. 3-18 ("the slave narratives offer the best evidence we will ever have on the feelings and attitudes of America's slaves . . ."); Martia Graham Goodson, "An Introductory Essay and Subject Index to Selected Interviews from the Slave Narrative Collection" (Ph.D. dissertation, Union Graduate School, 1977); and C. Vann Woodward, "History from Slave Sources," *American Historical Review* 79 (April 1974): 470-81.

The Davidson quotation is from Rawick, ed., *American Slave*, Ohio Narrs., Series 1, vol. 16, pp. 26-29. Hereafter, all references to this collection will include the name of the state, series number, volume, and page numbers. The other major source of slave interview material taken from the FWP collection for this paper — Perdue, et al. — will be referred to as *Weevils in the Wheat*.

[8]Joan Kelly-Gadol, "The Social Relations of the Sexes: Methodological Implications of Women's History," *Signs* 1 (Summer 1976): 809-10, 819.

[9]For discussions of women's work and the inadequacy of male-biased economic and social-scientific theory to define and analyze it, see Joan Acker, "Issues in the Sociological Study of Women's Work," in *Working Women: Theories and Facts in Perspective*, ed., Ann H. Stromberg and Shirley Harkess (Palo Alto, Calif.: Mayfield Publishing Co. 1978), pp. 134-61; and Judith K. Brown, "A Note on the Division of Labor by Sex," *American Anthropologist* 72 (October 1970): 1073-78.

[10]Miss. Narrs., supp. Series 1, pt. 2, vol. 7, p. 350; Okla. Narrs., supp. Series 1, vol. 12, p. 110; Davis, "Reflections on the Black Woman's Role," p. 8; Frances Anne Kemble, *Journal of A Residence on a Georgian Plantation in 1838-1839* (London: Longman, Green, 1863), pp. 60, 92.

[11]Owens, *This Species of Property*, pp. 8-20.

[12]Kemble, *Journal of a Residence*, p. 28; Lewis Cecil Gray, *History of Agriculture in the Southern United States*, vol. 1 (Washington, D.C.: Carnegie Institution, 1933), pp. 533-548; *Weevils in the Wheat*, p. 199; Fla. Narrs., Series 1, vol. 17, p. 305; Charles S. Sydnor, *Slavery in Mississippi* (Gloucester, Mass.: P. Smith, 1965), p. 20; Frederick Law Olmsted, *A Journey in the Seaboard Slave States* (New York: Dix and Edwards, 1856), p. 470; Frederick Law Olmsted, *A Journey in the Back Country* (New York: Mason Brothers, 1860), p.59.

[13]Olmsted, *A Journey in the Seaboard Slave States*, p. 387; Ala. Narrs., Series 1, vol. 6, p. 87. Work descriptions were gleaned from the FWP slave narrative collection (*American Slave* and *Weevils in the Wheat*) and Gray, *History of Agriculture*. Goodson ("Introductory Essay") has indexed a sample of the interviews with women by subject (for example, "candlemaking," "carding wool," "field work," "splitting rails.").

For pictures of early twentieth-century black women of St. Helena's Islands, South Carolina, wearing the second belt, see photographs in Edith M. Dabbs, *Face of an Island: Leigh Richmond Miner's Photographs of St. Helena's Island* (New York: Grossman, 1971). The caption of one photo entitled "Woman with Hoe" reads: "Adelaide Washington sets off for her day's work in the field. The second belt or cord tied around the hips lifted all her garments a little and protected the long skirts from both early morning dew and contact with the dirt . . . . [according to] an African superstition . . . the second cord also gave the wearer extra strength" (no pp.). Olmsted, *Slave States*, p. 387, includes a sketch of this form of dress.

[14]*Weevils in the Wheat,* p. 26; Gary, *History of Agriculture,* p. 251; planter quoted in Owens, *This Species of Property,* p. 39.

[15]Genovese, *Roll, Jordan, Roll,* p. 495; Burke quoted in Gray, *History of Agriculture,* p. 549; Olmsted, *A Journey in the Back Country,* p. 81. For former slaves' descriptions of women who plowed, see Okla. Narrs., Series 1, vol. 7, p. 314; Fla. Narrs., Series 1, vol. 17, p. 33.

[16]Olmsted quoted in Sydnor, *Slavery in Mississippi,* p. 68; *Weevils in the Wheat,* p. 77. Of the women who worked in the South Carolina Sea Islands cotton fields, Harriet Ware (a northern teacher) wrote, "they walk off with their heavy hoes on their shoulders, as free, strong, and graceful as possible." Elizabeth Ware Pearson, ed., *Letters from Port Royal Written at the Time of the Civil War* (Boston: W.B. Clarke, 1906), p. 52.

[17]Stuart Bruchey, ed., *Cotton and the Growth of the American Economy: 1790-1860* (New York: Harcourt, Brace & World, 1967), p. 174. See the documents under the heading "Making Cotton" and "The Routine of the Cotton Year," pp. 171-80. For examples of outstanding female pickers see Ala. Narrs., Series 1, vol 6, p. 275 ("Oncet I won a contest wid a man an' made 480 pounds."); *Weevils in the Wheat,* p. 199.

[18]Texas Narrs., supp. Series 2, pt. 1, vol. 2, pp. 93-94; Miss. Narrs., supp. Series 1, pt. 1, vol. 6, pp. 235-36, and pt. 2, vol. 7, p. 404; Tex. Narrs., Series 1, pt. 3, vol. 5, p. 231; Ind. Narrs., Series 1, vol. 6, p. 25; Ga. Narrs., Series 1, pt. 1, vol. 12, p. 113; Okla. Narrs., Series 1, vol. 7, p. 314; Ala. Narrs., Series 1, vol. 6, p. 338.

[19]For a general discussion of slave artisans in the South see Gray, *History of Agriculture,* pp. 548, 565-67; Sydnor, *Slavery in Mississippi,* p. 9. Roger L. Ransom and Richard Sutch, in *One Kind of Freedom: The Economic Consequences of Emancipation* (Cambridge: Cambridge University Press, 1977), discuss "Occupational Distribution of Southern Blacks: 1860, 1870, 1890" in app. B, pp. 220-31. The works of Starobin *(Industrial Slavery),* and James H. Brewer, *The Confederate Negro: Virginia's Craftsmen and Military Laborers, 1861-1865* (Durham: Duke University Press, 1969), focus almost exclusively on male slaves. See also Herbert Gutman and Richard Sutch, "Victorians All? The Sexual Mores and Conduct of Slaves and their Masters," in David, et al., *Reckoning With Slavery,* p. 160; Gutman, *Black Family,* pp. 599-600. The "hiring out" of men and children frequently disrupted family life.

[20]Ransom and Sutch, *One Kind of Freedom,* p. 233; Olmsted, *Slave States,* p. 388; Ohio Narrs., Series 1, vol. 16, p. 28; Kemble, *Journal,* p. 121; S.C. Narrs., Series 1, pt. 4, vol. 3, p. 78; *Weevils in the Wheat,* pp. 223-24. Genovese describes the plantation system as a "halfway house between peasant and factory cultures" *(Roll, Jordan, Roll,* p. 286). For further discussion of the grueling pace of fieldwork see Herbert G. Gutman and Richard Sutch, "Sambo Makes Good, or Were Slaves Imbued with the Protestant Work Ethic?" in David, et al., *Reckoning With Slavery,* pp. 55-93.

[21]Ala. Narrs., Series 1, vol. 6, p. 46; Fla. Narrs., Series 1, vol. 17, p. 185; *Weevils in the Wheat,* pp. 259, 216; Va. Narrs., Series 1, vol. 16, p. 51; Escott, *Slavery Remembered,* pp. 86-93. Escott includes an extensive discussion of resistance as revealed in the FWP slave narrative collection and provides data on the age, sex, and marital status of resisters and the purposes and forms of resistance. Gutman argues that the "typical runaway" was a male, aged sixteen to thirty-five years (*Black Family,* pp. 264-65). See also Obitko, "Custodians of a House of Resistance,"; Owens, *This Species of Property,* pp. 38, 88, 95.

[22]*Weevils in the Wheat,* pp. 26, 282, 157. According to Gutman, plantation work patterns "apparently failed to take into account enlarged slave kin groups, and further study may show that a central tension between slaves and their owners had its origins

in the separation of work and kinship obligations" *(Black Family*, p. 209.).

[23]Fla. Narrs., Series 1, vol. 17, p. 191; Bennet H. Barrow quoted in Gutman, *Black Family*, p.263; Robert S. Starobin, ed., *Blacks in Bondage: Letters of American Slaves* (New York: New Viewpoints, 1974), p. 54.

In his recent study, *The Slave Drivers: Black Agricultural Labor Supervisors in the Antebellum South* (Westport, Conn.: Greenwood Press, 1979), William L. Van DeBurg examines the anomalous position of black (male) drivers in relation to the rest of the slave community.

[24]Savitt, *Medicine and Slavery*, pp. 115-20; planter quoted in Owens, *This Species of Property*, pp. 38-40; planter quoted in Olmsted, *A Journey in the Seaboard Slave States*, p. 190; Kemble, *Journal of a Residence*, p. 121. Cf. White, "Ain't I A Woman?" pp. 77-86, 101, 155-60.

[25]Genovese, *Roll, Jordan, Roll*, pp. 328, 340; Ala. Narrs., Series 1, vol. 6, p. 273; Miss. Narrs., supp. Series 1, pt. 2, vol. 7, p. 400; Tex. Narrs., Series 1, pt. 3, vol. 5, p. 45. Recent historians have emphasized that the distinction between housework and fieldwork was not always meaningful in terms of shaping a slave's personality and self-perception or defining her or his status. See Owens, *This Species of Property*, p. 113; Escott, *Slavery Remembered*, pp. 59-60.

[26]Ala. Narrs., Series 1, vol. 6, pp. 416-17. In her study of slave mistresses, Anne Firor Scott gives an accurate description of their numerous supervisory duties, but she ignores that most of the actual manual labor was performed by slave women. See *The Southern Lady: From Pedestal to Politics, 1830-1930* (Chicago: University of Chicago Press, 1970), p.31.

[27]Tex. Narrs., Series 1, pt. 4, vol. 5, p. 11; Ind. Narrs., Series 1, vol. 6, p. 83. See also Miss. Narrs., supp. Series 1, pt. 1, vol. 6, pp. 54-55, 216, 257, 365, 380-81.

[28]The FWP slave narrative collection provides these examples of children's work, and many more. Ala. Narrs., Series 1, vol. 6, p. 157; Genovese, *Roll, Jordan, Roll*, pp. 502-19; Owens, *This Species of Property*, p. 202.

In early adolescence (ages ten to fourteen), a child would normally join the regular work force as a half-hand. At that time (or perhaps before), she or he received adult clothing. This *rite de passage* apparently made more of an impression on boys than girls, probably because pants offered more of a contrast to the infant's smock than did a dress. Willis Cofer attested to the significance of the change: "Boys jes' wore shirts what looked lak dresses 'til dey wuz 12 years old and big enough to wuk in de field . . . and all de boys wuz mighty proud when dey got big enough to wear pants and go to wuk in de fields wid grown folkses. When a boy got to be man enough to wear pants, he drawed rations and quit eatin' out of de trough [in the nursery]." Ga. Narrs., Series 1, pt. 1, vol. 12, p. 203. For other examples of the significance of change from adults' to children's clothing, see Tex. Narrs., Series 1, pt. 3, vol. 5, pp. 211, 275; p. 4, pp. 109-110; Ga. Narrs., Series 1, pt. 1, vol. 12, p. 277; Genovese, *Roll, Jordan, Roll*, p. 505.

[29]Ga. Narrs., supp. Series 1, pt. 1, vol. 3, p. 185; *Weevils in the Wheat*, pp. 264-65; S.C. Narrs., Series 1, pt. 4, vol. 3, p. 257.

[30]Okla. Narrs., Series 1, vol. 7, p. 347; White "Ain't I A Woman?" pp. 210-15; L. Maria Child, ed., *Incidents in the Life of a Slave Girl, Written By Herself* (Boston: L. Maria Child, 1861).

[31]James Hugo Johnston, *Race Relations in Virginia and Miscegenation in the South, 1776-1860* (Amherst: University of Massachusetts Press, 1970), p. 247; Mary Boykin Chesnut, *A Diary From Dixie*, ed. Ben Ames Williams (Cambridge, Mass.: Harvard University Press, 1980), p. 49.

[32]Fla. Narrs., Series 1, vol. 17, p. 35. For specific incidents illustrating these points, see *Weevils in the Wheat*, pp. 63, 199; Okla. Narrs., Series 1, vol. 7, pp. 135, 165-66; Tenn. Narrs., Series 1, vol. 16, p. 14. Slave punishment in general is discussed in Escott, *Slavery Remembered*, pp. 42-46; Owens, *This Species of Property*, p. 88; Savitt, *Slavery and Medicine*, pp. 65-69; Gutman and Sutch, "Sambo Makes Good," pp. 55-93; Frederick Douglass, *Narrative of the Life of Frederick Douglass, An American Slave* (Cambridge: Harvard University Press, 1960), pp. 60-61. These examples indicate that Anne Firor Scott is a bit sanguine in suggesting that although southern women were sensitive to the "depravity" of their husbands, "It may be significant that they did not blame black women, who might have provided convenient scapegoats. The blame was squarely placed on men." See Anne Firor Scott, "Women's Perspectives on the Patriarchy in the 1850s," *Journal of American History* 61 (June 1974): 52-64.

[33]Genovese, *Roll, Jordan, Roll*, pp. 333-38. See, for example, the document entitled "A Seamstress is Punished" in Lerner, ed., *Black Women in White America*, pp. 18-19.

[34]Olmsted, *A Journey in the Seaboard Slave States*, p. 421; S.C. Narrs., Series 1, pt. 4, vol. 3, p. 126; Fla. Narrs., Series 1, vol. 14, p. 356; Escott, *Slavery Remembered*, p. 64; Kemble, *Journal of a Residence*, p. 98; Genovese, *Roll, Jordan, Roll*, pp. 346-47.

[35]Fla. Narrs., Series 1, vol. 17, p. 356; Gutman and Sutch, "Sambo Makes Good," p. 74; Kemble, *Journal of a Residence*, p. 153; Gray, *History of Agriculture*, p. 553; Owens, *This Species of Property*, p. 113.

[36]Ga. Narrs., Series 1, pt. 1, vol. 12, p. 243; Davis, "Reflections on the Black Woman's Role," pp. 4-7. For general discussions of women's work as it related to slave communal life see also Owens, *This Species of Property*, pp. 23, 225; and White, "Ain't I A Woman?." Polly Cancer recalled that, when she was growing up on a Mississippi plantation, the master "wudn't let de mammies whip dey own chillun [or "do dey own cookin"] . . . , ef he cum 'cross a 'ooman whuppin' her chile he'd say, 'Git 'way 'ooman; dats my bizness . . . ." Miss. Narrs., supp. Series 1, pt. 2, vol. 7, pp. 340-41.

[37]Gray, *History of Agriculture*, p. 563; Olmsted, *A Journey in the Seaboard Slave States*, pp. 424-25, 697-98; Owens, *This Species of Property*, p. 47; Fla. Narrs., Series 1, vol. 17, p. 175; Ala. Narrs., Series 1, vol. 6, p. 216; Miss. Narrs., supp. Series 1, pt. 1, vol. 6, pp. 10, 23, 25, 123; Ga. Narrs., supp. Series 1, pt. 1, vol. 3, p. 27. Savitt (*Slavery and Medicine*) includes a section on "Black Medicine" (pp. 171-84) and confirms Rebecca Hook's recollection that "on the plantation, the doctor was not nearly as popular as the 'granny' or midwife." Fla. Narrs., Series 1, vol. 17, p. 175.

[38]Ga. Narrs., Series 1, pt. 1, vol. 12, p. 70; Okla. Narrs., Series 1, vol. 7, pp. 314-15; White, "Ain't I A Woman?" pp. 22-23; Tex. Narrs., Series 2, pt. 1, vol. 2, p. 98.

[39]The FWP slave narrative collection contains many descriptions of slaves engaged in household industry. Alice Morse Earle details comparable techniques used by white women in colonial New England in *Home Life in Colonial Days* (New York: MacMillan Co., 1935).

[40]See, for example, S.C. Narrs., Series 1, pt. 3, vol. 3, pp. 15, 218, 236; Tex. Narrs., Series 1, pt. 3, vol. 5, pp. 20, 89, 108, 114, 171, 188, 220; Miss. Narrs., supp. Series 1, pt. 1, vol. 6, p. 36.

[41]*Weevils in the Wheat*, pp. 88-89. George White of Lynchburg reported that his mother sang a similar version of this song to women while they were spinning (p. 309).

[42]Genovese, *Roll, Jordan, Roll*, p. 319.

[43]Gutman, *Black Family*, p. 75. Escott points out that masters and slaves lived in "different worlds" (*Slavery Remembered*, p. 20). This paragraph briefly summarizes Gutman's pioneering work.

[44]Davis, "Reflections on the Black Woman's Role," p. 7.

[45]Ala. Narrs., Series 1, vol. 6, p. 9; Tex. Narrs., supp. Series 2, pt. 5, vol. 6, pp. 2036-37; Fla. Narrs., Series 1, vol. 17, pp. 22-23; White, "Ain't I A Woman?," pp. 30-31, 65.

[46]Gutman, *Black Family*, pp. 142, 67-68, 267-78; Genovese, *Roll, Jordan, Roll*, pp. 318, 482-94; S.C. Narrs., Series 1, pt. 3, vol. 3, p. 192; Miss. Nars., supp. Series 1, pt. 2, vol. 7, pp. 380-81.

[47]Okla. Narrs., Series 1, vol. 7, p. 210; Escott, *Slavery Remembered*, pp. 49-57, 87; Owens, *This Species of Property*, p. 201.

[48]Gutman and Sutch, "Sambo Makes Good," p. 63; Owens, *This Species of Property*, p. 195; Miss. Narrs., supp. Series 1, pt. 1, vol. 6, pp. 59-60. For mention of corn shuckings in particular, see Genovese, *Roll, Jordan, Roll*, p. 318; Miss. Narrs., Series 1, vol. 7, p. 6; Okla. Narrs., Series 1, vol. 7, p. 230. In the context of traditional female-male roles, what Genovese calls the "curious sexual division of labor" that marked these festivities was not "curious" at all (p. 318).

[49]Unfortunately, much of the data about pre colonial African work patterns must be extrapolated from recent findings of anthropologists. The author benefited from conversations with Dr. M. Jean Hay of the Boston University African Studies Center concerning women's work in precolonial Africa and methodological problems in studying this subject.

[50]For a theoretical formulation of the sexual division of labor in preindustrial societies, see Brown, "A Note on the Division of Labor By Sex."

[51]Peter Wood, *Black Majority: Negroes in Colonial South Carolina From 1670 Through the Stono Rebellion* (New York: Alfred A. Knopf, 1974), pp 59-62; P.C. Lloyd, "Osi fakunde of Ijebu," in *Africa Remembered: Narratives by West Africans from the Era of the Slave Trade*, ed. Philip D. Curtin (Madison: University of Wisconsin Press, 1967), p. 263; Marguerite Dupire, "The Position of Women in a Pastoral Society," in *Women of Tropical Africa*, ed. Denise Paulme (Berkeley: University of California Press, 1963), pp. 76-80; Olaudah Equiano, "The Life of Olaudah Equiano or Gustavus Vassa the African Written By Himself," in *Great Slave Narratives*, ed. Arna Bontemps (Boston: Beacon Press, 1969), pp. 7-10; Kemble, *Journal of a Residence*, p. 42; Pearson, ed., *Letters from Port Royal*, pp. 58, 106.

[52]Melville J. Herskovits, *The Myth of the Negro Past* (New York: Harper & Bros., 1941), pp. 33-85; Wood, *Black Majority*, pp. 179, 250; Hermann Baumann, "The Division of Work According to Sex in African Hoe Culture," *Africa* 1 (July 1928): 289-319.

On the role of women in hoe agriculture, see also Leith Mullings, "Women and Economic Change in Africa," in *Women in Africa: Studies in Social and Economic Change*, ed. Nancy J. Hafkin and Edna G. Bay (Stanford: Stanford University Press, 1976), pp. 239-64; Sylvia Leith-Ross, *African Women: A Study of the Ibo of Nigeria* (New York: Frederick A. Praeger, 1965), pp. 84-91; Ester Boserup, *Woman's Role in Economic Development* (New York: St. Martin's Press, 1970), pp. 156-36; Jack Goody and Joan Buckley, "Inheritance and Women's Labour in Africa," *Africa* 63 (April 1973): 108-21. No tribes in precolonial Africa used the plow.

[53]Olmsted, *A Journey in the Seaboard Slave States*, p. 433; Gray, *History of Agriculture*, p. 548; Kemble, *Journal of a Residence*, pp. 164, 247; Douglass, *Narrative*, pp. 76-78. According to Genovese, the ability of these elderly slaves "to live decently and with self-respect depended primarily on the support of their younger fellow slaves" *(Roll, Jordan, Roll*, p. 523); White "Ain't I A Woman?" p. 49; Miss. Narrs., supp. Series 1, pt. 1, vol. 6, p. 242.

[54]Eblen, "New Estimates," p. 306; Pearson, ed. *Letters from Port Royal*, p. 25;

Genovese, *Roll, Jordan, Roll,* pp. 522-23; Eliza F. Andrews, *The War-Time Journal of a Georgia Girl, 1864-1865* (New York: D. Appleton & Co., 1908), p. 101; Escott, *Slavery Remembered,* pp., 108-09; Owens, *This Species of Property,* p. 140; Gutman, *Black Family,* p. 218. For specific examples, see Ala. Narrs., supp. Series 1, pt. 1, vol. 6, p. 217; pt. 2, vol. 7, pp. 369-73. See also White, "Ain't I A Woman?" pp. 107-112.

[55]Miss. Narrs., Supp. Series 1, pt. 1, Vol. 6, p. 217; pt. 2, Vol. 7, pp. 369-73. See also White, "Ain't I A Woman?" pp. 107-112.

[56]Ga. Narrs., Series 1, pt. 1, vol. 12, p. 214; *Weevils in the Wheat,* p. 128

[57]Genovese, *Roll, Jordan, Roll,* p. 500. See also White, "Ain't I A Woman?" pp. 3-20, 51-54; and Davis, "Reflections on the Black Woman's Role," p. 7.

[58]This section summarizes material in an essay by the author entitled "Freed Women?: Black Women, Work, and the Family During the Civil War and Reconstruction," Wellesley Center for Research on Women Working Paper No. 61 (Wellesley, Mass., 1980). "'My Mother'" and "Freed Women" constitute the first two chapters of a book on Afro-American women, work, and the family, 1830-1980 (forthcoming).

[59]Robert Somers, *The Southern States Since the War, 1870-1* (London: MacMillan & Co., 1871), p. 59; Ransom and Sutch, *One Kind of Freedom,* p. 233; Francis W. Loring and C.F. Atkinson, *Cotton Culture and the South Considered with Reference to Emigration* (Boston: A. Williams, 1869), pp. 4-23. Other primary works that include relevant information are Frances Butler Leigh, *Ten Years on a Georgia Plantation Since the War* (London: R. Bentley, 1883); Charles Nordhoff, *The Cotton States in the Spring and Summer of 1875* (New York: D. Appleton & Co., 1876); George Campbell, *White and Black: The Outcome of a Visit to the United States* (London: Chatto and Windus, 1879).

[60]Freedmen's Bureau official quoted in Gutman, *Black Family,* p. 167.

[61]The transition from wage labor to the sharecropping system is examined in Ralph Shlomowitz, "The Origins of Southern Sharecropping," *Agricultural History* 53 (July 1979): 557-75, and his "The Transition From Slave to Freedman Labor Arrangements in Southern Agriculture, 1865-1870," *Journal of Economic History* 39 (March 1979): 333-36; Jay R. Mandle, *The Roots of Black Poverty: The Southern Plantation Economy After the Civil War* (Durham, N.C.,: Duke University Press, 1978); Joseph D. Reid, Jr., "White Land, Black Labor, and Agricultural Stagnation: The Causes and Effects of Sharecropping in the Postbellum South," *Explorations in Economic History* 16 (January 1979): 31-55; Ransom and Sutch, *One Kind of Freedom.*

Jonathan Wiener suggests that blacks' rejection of gang labor and preference for family share units "represented a move away from classic capitalist organizations." See "Class Structure and Economic Development in the American South, 1865-1955," *American Historical Review* 84 (October 1979): 984.

[62]Elizabeth Hyde Botume, *First Days Amongst the Contrabands* (Boston: Lee & Shepard, 1893), p. 166; Campbell, *White and Black,* pp. 172, 344, 364; tale entitled "De Tiger an' de Nyung Lady" quoted in Owens, *This Species of Property,* p. 144. See Leon Litwack, *Been in the Storm So Long: The Aftermath of Slavery* (New York: Alfred A. Knopf, 1979), pp. 502-56, for a detailed discussion of various freedmen's conventions held throughout the South.

[63]For an analysis of the ways in which the household responsibilities of women are defined and redefined to alter the supply of available wage-earners, see Louise A. Tilly and Joan Scott, *Women, Work, and Family* (New York: Holt, Rinehart & Winston, 1978).

FREE BLACK WOMEN AND THE QUESTION OF MATRIARCHY: PETERSBURG, VIRGINIA, 1784-1820

SUZANNE LEBSOCK

In 1853, Eliza Gallie, a middle-aged, free black woman of Petersburg, Virginia, was arrested and charged with stealing cabbages from the patch of Alexander Stevens, a white man. She was tried in Mayor's Court and sentenced to thirty-nine lashes. There was nothing unusual in this; free black women were frequently accused of petty crimes, and for free blacks, as for slaves, whipping was the punishment prescribed by law. What made the case a minor spectacle was that Eliza Gallie had resources, and she fought back. She filed an appeal immediately, and two weeks later she hired three of Petersburg's most eminent attorneys and one from Richmond as well. "If the Commonwealth, God bless her, has not met her match in Miss Liza," a local newspaper commented, "it won't be for lack of lawyers." The case came up in Hustings Court in March 1854. Gallie's lawyers argued first of all that her ancestors were of white and Indian blood and that she should therefore be tried as a white person. The court was unconvinced. On the trial's second day, her counsel argued that she was innocent of the theft. The court was again unconvinced. Gallie was pronounced guilty and sentenced to "twenty lashes on her bare back at the public whipping post . . . ." At first she set another appeal in motion, but deciding that the case was hopeless, Eliza Gallie dismissed her lawyers and took her punishment.[1]

Gallie's case was in many ways an unusual one, and yet her story cuts straight to the central contradiction in our common image of the historic black woman. Eliza Gallie was, relatively speaking, a powerful woman, propertied, autonomous (divorced, actually), and assertive. But she was helpless in the end, the victim of the kind of deliberate humiliation that for most of us is past im-

Feminist Studies 8, no. 2 (Summer 1982). © 1982 by Feminist Studies, Inc.

agining. So it is with our perception of the history of black women as a group. On the one hand, we have been told that black women, in slavery and afterward, were formidable people, "matriarchs" in fact. On the other hand, we know that all along, black women were dreadfully exploited. Rarely has so much power been attributed to so vulnerable a group.

The contradiction can be ironed out, with sufficient attention to definition and evidence. All the evidence used here comes from Petersburg, Virginia, and it comes mainly from the Petersburg of Eliza Gallie's youth, when the first generation out of slavery, the women emancipated in the wake of the American Revolution, established a pattern of female responsibility radically different from that prevailing among whites. Petersburg had fewer than seven thousand residents in 1820, but for its time and region, it was a city of some consequence. Flour milling, tobacco manufacture, and the commerce generated by the farmers of Southside Virginia sustained Petersburg's growth, while the horse races and the theater gave it touches of urban glitter. Only two cities in Virginia had larger populations, and no other Virginia town had a higher proportion of free blacks among its people. Before the statute of 1806 brought manumissions to a near standstill, Petersburg's free black population grew at a prodigious pace, its size swelled by a high rate of emancipation in the town itself and by the hundreds of migrants from the countryside who came in search of kin, work, and community. By 1810, there were over one thousand free blacks in Petersburg; nearly one-third of Petersburg's free people (31.2 percent) were black.[2]

Some definitions are called for. The term "matriarch" has been used in so many different ways that it has become almost useless as a descriptive term. But it should be understood that the word "matriarch" would never have been applied to black women in the first place were it not for our culture's touchiness over reduced male authority within the family. It is a telling fact that "matriarchy" has most often been used as a relative term. That is, women are called matriarchs when the power they exercise relative to men of their own group is in some respect greater than that defined as appropriate by the dominant culture. Given this standard, women need not be the equals of men, much less men's superiors, in order to qualify as matriarchs. The acquisition by women of just one commonly masculine prerogative will do, and hence it becomes possible to attribute matriarchal power to some of society's most disadvantaged people. The woman who had no vote, no money, and no protection under the law was nonetheless a "matriarch," so long as she also had no husband present to compete with her for authority over her children.

Concern over the reduction of male authority has also been the touchstone of scholarship on black family life (relatively little has been written on the history of black women per se). For all the disagreements among scholars on the character of the historic black family, it has been assumed on almost all sides that female-headed families are, and were, pathological. There were two key assertions in the classic thesis advanced by E. Franklin Frazier four decades ago and revived in 1965 in the Moynihan Report. First, as a result of slavery and continued discrimination, an alarming proportion of black families were "matriarchal," that is, the husband/father was either absent or (Frazier added) he was present, but of negligible influence. Second, the woman-dominant family was unstable and disorganized, at once the symptom and cause of severe social pathology among black people.[3] The Frazier-Moynihan thesis came under heavy fire in the 1970s when scholars began to check the matriarchy image for historical accuracy. And yet the historians, too, reinforced the prevailing prejudice against female-headed households. Working for the most part with census data from the second half of the nineteenth century, several historians found that female-headed households were outnumbered by two-parent households. This, along with additional evidence of the statistical insignificance of the woman-headed household, was offered in defense of the Afro-American family: Black families were not generally matriarchal/matrifocal/female-headed (the term varies), therefore they were not disorganized, unstable, or otherwise pathological after all.[4]

This is a dangerous line of defense, and its problems are highlighted when we encounter evidence like that for early Petersburg. Here was a town in which well over half of the free black households were headed by women. Shall we therefore label it a nest of social sickness? It would make better sense to disentangle our evidence from conventional, androcentric value judgments on what is healthy and what is not.

For the time being, it would seem wise to set aside the issue of the integrity of black family life (by what standard, after all, are we to judge it?) and to concentrate instead on the impact of racial oppression on the status of women and on the distribution of power between the sexes. When we do this for Petersburg, we are confronted once again with the dual image of strength and exploitation. Women were prominent among Petersburg's free blacks. They outnumbered the men three to two, they headed more than half of the town's free black households, and they constituted a large segment of the paid labor force of free blacks. Yet this was for the most part the product of wretched poverty and persistent discrimination. The "matriarch" and the victim, it turns out, were usually the same woman.

Still, the fact remains that among free blacks there was less inequality between the sexes than there was among whites; when black women of the present say they have always been liberated, they have a point. Among those free blacks who managed to accumulate property in early Petersburg, a high proportion — about 40 percent — were women. And because they were more likely than their white counterparts to refrain from legal marriage, free black women were more likely to retain legal control over whatever property they did acquire. It may well have been that free black women valued their relative equality and did their best to maintain it.

How all this came to be is not entirely clear, for census data are sketchy, measures of wealth are crude, evidence on the occupational structure is thin, and vital records do not exist. It seems likely, however, that the preponderance of women in the free black population began with the cumulative decisions of emancipators: Women slaves stood the better chance. Before the Virginia legislature tied the hands of would-be emancipators in 1806, 173 slaves were manumitted in Petersburg.[5] Ninety-four of them (54.3 percent) were female. Of the manumitted adults, meanwhile, 59.3 percent (54 of 91) were female. Sexual intimacy, antislavery principle, and economic calculation could all have been responsible for women's easier access to emancipation.

That a number of manumissions resulted from sexual unions would seem to be a good bet for a town full of well-to-do bachelors, many of whom were a long way from home. Documentable cases, however, are few. Only one white emancipator was known to have acknowledged his kinship with his former slaves, and in only two instances is there strong circumstantial evidence of a sexual connection. In 1814, Mary Moore, a "great, large, fat, bouncing-looking" Irish woman, manumitted Sylvia Jeffers, as she was authorized to do by the will of her late brother John Jeffers. Sylvia was apparently John's daughter; in any case, in 1853 she talked the local court into escorting her across the color line, claiming descent from Indians and whites only.[6] Betsy Atkinson, too, won the special affection of her owner. A week after James Gibbon freed her, he wrote his last will. To Atkinson, he left a slave and furniture already in her possession, some livestock, and three hundred dollars.[7]

Anti-slavery principle may also have accounted for the women's edge in emancipation. Under Virginia law, the child inherited the status of the mother. To free a man, therefore, was to guarantee the freedom of but one person. The emancipation of a woman in her childbearing years might secure the freedom of generations.[8]

In the short run, meanwhile, the emancipation of a woman meant a lesser loss of income for the owner. Women suffered a distinct disadvantage in earning power, a disadvantage that began in slavery and that showed in the inability of slave women to purchase themselves. Hiring oneself out was illegal, but both women and men did it, and most of them got away with it.[9] The women who hired themselves out did not, however, command wages equivalent to those of men, or so it appears from the incidence of self-purchase. Self-purchase was uncommon in this period; from 1784 to 1820, just nine of the two hundred slaves emancipated bought themselves. Amy Jackson, who paid her master $410 in 1819, was the sole woman among them.[10]

The same disparity in earning power limited the numbers of slaves whom emancipated women managed to free in turn. Altogether, free blacks themselves were responsible for thirty-three manumissions (one-sixth of the total to 1820), and although about one-half of the black emancipators were women (7 of 15), no woman was able to liberate more than one slave. Graham Bell showed what could be done with a remunerative skill (shoemaking), hard work, and business sense. In 1792, Bell set free his wife, or possibly his daughter, and five sons. From 1801 to 1805, he emancipated his brother, two women, one of whom he had purchased "for the express purpose of manumitting or emancipating her," and a child.[11] No one else came near Bell's record, but four of the other men did manumit at least two slaves. In the years after 1820, several women would join the ranks of the multiple emancipators. Meantime, one apiece was the best they could do.[12]

Emancipation was itself a step up on the economic ladder; the woman at last owned her person and her labor. In Petersburg, she was not likely to own anything else, not in the beginning anyhow. White emancipators expected their former slaves to fend for themselves. James Campbell made it explicit in 1802 when he freed forty-two-year-old Sally, "whom I have reason to believe is an honest woman, and one that will earn by her labour a proper support for herself."[13] A few emancipators may have granted their former slaves some kind of economic assistance, but in only one deed was something promised in writing. Persons manumitted by will did not fare much better. Of the twenty-seven slaves whose freedom was directed by will, only four were staked by their masters, and three of the four were men.[14]

The emancipators no doubt believed they were giving their former slaves an even chance. Given the circumstances under which many of the women were freed, however, making a living would be an uphill struggle. Some emancipators freed the children with the mother, and while this spared the women from trying to save to buy their children (and from the pain of being unable to save enough), it did mean extra mouths to be fed. Most of these women had one child or two, but three or four or five was not unusual.[15] Age was important as well. The emancipators who stipulated the ages of the persons they freed were too few to provide a reliable sample, but the ages that were recorded suggest that relative to the men, the women were disproportionately middle-aged. A large proportion of the women set free were, or would soon be, past their best wage-earning years.

TABLE 1. AGE AT EMANCIPATION

Age	Women	Men
18-30	9	4
31-40	1	4
41-50	8	2
51 and up	0	1

The most significant handicap, however, was the near absence of occupational options. The vast majority of free black women engaged in domestic employment of one kind or another. This was not a matter of choice, and it was more a matter of sex than of race. Nothing made the women's occupational bind plainer than the apprenticeship orders issued by the court for free black children. Among the masters who took on free black boys as apprentices were a carpenter, a cabinetmaker, a painter, a cooper, a barber, a blacksmith, a hatter, a boatman, and a baker. So limited were the girls' options that the clerk hardly ever wasted ink on specifying the trade. The few specific orders contained no surprises. In 1801, Lucy Cook was ordered bound "to learn the business of a Seamstress & Washer." On the same day Polly Flood was "bound to Abby Cook, to learn to Sew & Wash &c untill of lawful age — being now about 9 years of age." Polly was bound to a second master "to learn Household business" five years later. And Polly White, an orphan just five years old, was apprenticed "to Mrs. Brewer to learn the duties of a House Servant."[16]

There were some women who broke the mold and engaged, at least part time, in more specialized occupations. Betty Morris and Aggy Jackson were nurses, Judy Denby and Judy Darvels were midwives. A few engaged in legitimate commerce. Amelia Gallé ran a bath house, Lurany Butler operated a dray, Nelly White was a baker, and Elizabeth Allerque and Sarah Elliott were licensed storekeepers.[17] As with white women, just as many pursued illegitimate commerce. At least five black women were nabbed by the Petersburg Grand Jury for keeping a "tippling house" or for selling liquor without a license.[18] The fact that specific occupations can be identified for only a dozen black women is testimony to the predominance of domestics among them. Cooks, cleaning women, washerwomen, seamstresses, and child-nurturers did not advertise, nor were they likely to surface in any of the public records.[19]

If the gentlemen of the Grand Jury had been asked, they would probably have identified prostitution as a major enterprise of free black women. In 1804, the Grand Jury registered a grievance against the invasion of free black "strangers," many of whom "come only for the purpose of Prostitution . . . ."[20] There is no telling whether or how often free black women in fact resorted to prostitution, but the Grand Jury was right about the invasion. Dismal as economic opportunities were in Petersburg, they were apparently worse in the countryside, particularly for women. Black migration from the country was thus spearheaded by women. By 1820, the sex ratio among free blacks aged fourteen and above was 85.0 (males per 100 females) for eastern Virginia as a whole. In Petersburg it was 64.5.[21]

Petersburg was, relatively speaking, a land of opportunity, and a few of the women emancipated there did register gains. Betty Call was freed on Independence Day, 1786, and within four years she managed to buy her grown son, London, from an Amelia County owner. After ten years, she set him free. Betty Call never did own any real estate, but she was taxed on a female slave (evidently hired) for years, and when she died in 1815, the sale of her household goods netted just over seventy dollars.[22] Emancipated on the same day as her mother, Teresa Call saved for nine years. In 1795, she purchased a small lot and continued to live there for decades.[23] Dolly Clark acquired a female slave five years after her manumission. On the other hand, women like Nancy Hall and Sally Steward accumulated no traceable property. Emancipated in 1799 and 1805, respectively, their continued residence in Petersburg was confirmed by entries in various public record books, but neither of them owned the land or slaves or horses or carriages that would have resulted in their appearance on the tax lists.[24]

New arrivals fared worse than the natives. Only nine free black women were among the town's taxpayers in 1810, and most of them were old-timers. All but one had lived in Petersburg as free women for at least six years. Betty and Teresa Call had both been free for twenty-four years, while Sarah Vaughan held the record for longevity on the tax lists. Vaughan owned real estate when Petersburg's first land tax book was assembled in 1788, and thirty years later she still held, and presumably rented out, her "4 small tenements."[25] On the average, the nine women had been paying taxes for almost nine years, and they held on to what they had. In the decade after 1810 three of them died, but the remaining six, all landowners, were still paying real estate taxes in 1820.

By that time they had more company. In 1820, there were thirty-eight free black women among the taxpayers. However one chooses to measure it, this was an impressive relative increase. In 1810, black women constituted but 2.2 percent of (9 of 413) of the town's taxpayers. In 1820, their proportion was 5.5 percent (38 of 687). The increase is not attributable to any relative growth in the free black female population. A count of the percentage of taxpayers among heads of families does help control for possible population shifts; similarly, it indicates a doubling of property holding among free black women. In 1810, 5.1 percent (7 of 138) of the black women designated as heads of families in the census schedules were also listed in the tax books; by 1820, the proportion had risen to 10.1 percent (17 of 168). All in all, blacks were gaining on whites, women were gaining on men, and black women were gaining on black men.[26]

At least three developments accounted for the sudden economic ascent of a portion of the free black female population. With the deaths of propertied men, a few black women claimed their inheritances. More important were the hard-won savings of the women themselves. And third, it looks very much as though the Panic of 1819 forced slaveholders to put their slaves on the market at prices more women could afford.

Among the black female taxpayers of 1810, only Molly James had acquired her property by inheritance. James was the heir to the house and lot her husband had owned at his death in 1804. By 1820, two more legacies marked the passing of the first generation of prosperous black men. Graham Bell in 1817 left to his wife, Mary, a life estate in one of his town lots, while Elizabeth Graves was daughter and one of two surviving heirs of Richmond Graves, a livery stable operator.[27] Mary Ann Vizonneau and Amelia Gallé, meanwhile, were heirs of white merchants. Vizonneau's Scottish father, John Stewart, had threatened to disown her when she married Andre Thomas Vizonneau. But moments before his death in 1813, Stewart relented and directed that Mary Ann be given "all the money he then had in the Bank and the house & Lot he then lived on," on the condition "that her husband . . . might have no manner of Controul over, or right, to the same." This was a considerable bequest, worth over eighteen thousand dollars, and it made Mary Ann Vizonneau one of the wealthiest women in Petersburg.[28]

Amelia Gallé was also the heir of a white merchant. She had earned her inheritance. Amelia Gallé was still a slave when she first arrived in Petersburg, and she was known by a slave name, Milly Cassurier. In 1800, French merchant Jean Gallé bought her for eighty pounds, and he emancipated her four years later, after she had borne him a son. Jean Gallé died in 1819, and while in his will he termed Milly "my housekeeper," it was clear from the provisions of the will that she had been his wife in every sense but the legal one. He acknowledged her son Joseph as his natural son. He left to the two of them the greater part of his estate. And he enjoined Milly to act as mother to his "mulatto Girl slave" Catherine Gregory, charging her "to support the said Catherine and bring her up to lead a moral and religious life.[29]

Jean Gallé also left to Milly Cassurier his bathhouse, a business she had apparently been running for years. When she assumed sole management of the bathhouse in the spring of 1820, she became the first black businesswoman in Petersburg to exploit the full possibilities of newspaper advertising. At first she settled for a two-sentence announcement that the bathing season had arrived. By midsummer, however, her appeal was more effusive.

> The character of this bath, is so well known that it needs no comment. The subscriber is resolved if possible to improve it, by consulting the comfort and convenience of the visitants — and to enable her to do so more effectually, she humbly solicits a continuation of that patronage which has so liberally supported the institution till this time. Having had several years experience in this business, the subscriber believes she will generally succeed in pleasing — and therefore, with stronger confidence humbly solicits a portion of the public support . . . .

For several years thereafter, she opened the season with just a brief announcement. Two or three months later, as the heat of the Virginia summer grew tediously oppressive, she would follow with greater fanfare. "She has the pleasure of tendering to her patrons," came the notice of May 1823, "her most grateful thanks for their former encouragement, and begs a continuance of the same." August brought the harder sell.

> HEALTH
>
> Purchased Cheap!
>
> In consequence of *Small Change* being scarce, and wishing to contribute towards the health of the ladies and gentlemen, the subscriber has the pleasure to inform her patrons and the public, that she has reduced the price of her baths to 25 CENTS for a single one. She will make no comments on the necessity of Bathing in warm weather: — suffice it to say, that with Mr. Rambaut's FAMILY MEDICINES, and some Cold or Warm BATHS, the health of her friends will keep at a proper degree of the thermometer, without the aid of Calomel or any other mineral Medicines.[30]

These advertisements were not just a means of drumming up business. They were also the means by which a free black claimed for herself the respect due a propertied widow. In her first advertisement, she signed herself "Milly Cassurier." In the second, she was "Milly Galle." She signed the third "Amelia Galle." In the fourth, she was "Amelia Galle, widow." How far others accorded her the respect she asked for is an open question. She made some progress with the census taker, who listed her as "Milly Gallie," but to the tax collector she was still Cassurier, "col^{d} at Galle's."[31]

Amelia Gallé, Mary Ann Vizonneau, Elizabeth Graves, and Mary Bell were the only black female taxpayers of 1820 whose property was (documentably) acquired by inheritance. More significant was the economic maturation of the women themselves, and here the foremost success story belonged to Elizabeth Allerque. "Madame Betsy," she was called, "a French colored woman" who was probably a refugee from St. Dominigue She was, in any case, well connected with Petersburg's French immigrant community, and the connections in combination with her commercial talent spelled steady financial progress. Allerque first opened a store in 1801. At some point she added a partnership with French merchant André Vizonneau (Mary Ann Vizonneau's father-in-law), who in 1809 made sure that Allerque would be paid her full share of the proceeds when the firm was dissolved by his death: "I declare that the partnership which I had entered into with Elizabeth Alergues was joint and equal both as to capital and profit . . . ." Five years later, French physician L. J. Hoisnard wrote his will, charging Allerque with the care and legal guardianship of his daughter. Moreover, "in consideration of her good attention to me during the latter part of my life," Hoisnard left to Allerque and her two children a legacy of a thousand dollars.[32] Even without this bequest, Elizabeth Allerque would have done well for herself. She first invested in real estate in 1806 and improved it several times thereafter. In 1806, too, she became a slaveholder for the first time. Allerque was one of Petersburg's few black commercial slaveholders; in 1806 she advertised in the Richmond and Norfolk newspapers for the return of her runaway woman Charlotte. Madame Betsy died in 1824, free of debt and the owner of land and six slaves.[33]

Most free black women had neither the skills nor the connections of an Elizabeth Allerque, but a few had enough savings to take advantage of the Panic of 1819. While the general economic dislocation that surrounded the Panic must have caused great suffering among many black women, it also afforded the better-placed the opportunity to hire or purchase slaves for the first time. (The tax lists, unhappily, do not indicate whether the taxpayer owned or hired the slave.)[34] As more and more whites scrambled to find the money to pay their debts, more and more slaves were put up for hire or sale, and probably at bargain prices. There is no estimating just how many slaves changed hands during the Panic years. In 1819 and 1820 alone, however, Petersburg owners mortgaged over 240 slaves; these slaves would be sold at auction for whatever they would bring if the owners failed to pay their creditors on schedule.[35]

For the master class the time was unnerving, for the slaves it was potentially disastrous, but for the free black woman with some savings, here was a rare opportunity, a chance to acquire a loved one or a laborer. Three-quarters of the black women taxed in 1820 (27 of 38) made their debuts on the tax lists in 1819 or 1820. And all but two of the newcomers were taxed on one or more slaves.

It was in slaveholding that black women registered their greatest gains by 1820 and in slaveholding that they came closest to economic parity with black men. In 1820, forty-six slaves were held by black men, forty-five by the women. Women were farther from equality in other measures of the black sex ratio of wealth, but they were gaining on the men. Two-fifths (13 of 32) of the black landowners of 1820 were women, a somewhat larger fraction than in 1810.[36] Two-fifths of the black taxpayers of 1820 were women, up from one-fourth in 1810. And two-fifths of the tax collected from free blacks in 1820 was collected from women, again, up from one-fourth in 1810.

Measured against comparable figures for whites, these were stunning proportions. In 1820 women were but 12.8 percent of the white taxpayers (76 of 593), and they accounted for only 3.5 percent of the tax money collected from whites.

This glaring disparity in the status of black and white women relative to men of the same race fades somewhat when sex ratios are taken into consideration. It should also be said that free black women were more likely than were white women to maintain their legal eligibility to control property. Virginia was a common-law state, and the common law made razor-sharp distinctions between single and married women. Single women and widows had the same property rights and obligations as men. But the instant a woman married, she surrendered both her rights and her obligations to her husband; if she had owned taxable property, the surrender was manifested in her summary disappearance from the tax lists.[37]

It is impossible to estimate how many of Petersburg's free black women shunned lawful matrimony, but the qualitative evidence suggests that the proportion was high, higher than among whites. The sex ratio, the law, poverty, and preference conspired to keep a great many free black women single, and to the extent that women remained single, they remained free agents in the economic realm.

The sex ratio and the law together dictated the single life for one-third of Petersburg's free black women. Because blacks were not permitted to marry whites, and slaves were not permitted to marry anyone, the pool of marriageable men was restricted to free blacks, and there were simply not enough of them to go around.

A few black women did take up with whites, and more, apparently, were coupled with slaves. These matches yielded some interesting economic arrangements. Milly Cassurier, when she was still known by that name, acquired property in her own right while she was living with Jean Gallé, something she could not have done had the two of them been married.[38] When a free woman cohabited with a slave, meanwhile, here were the legal materials for a complete sex-role reversal, for the woman assumed all legal rights and responsibilities for the pair. In 1800, a slave named David White was jailed for going at large and trading as a free person. The fine for White's misdeeds fell on his wife, Polly Spruce, a free woman who had hired White for the year and who was therefore legally answerable for his behavior. Nearing her death years later, Jane Cook found it necessary to make special provision for her slave husband, Peter Matthews. Cook had purchased two small boats, "the Democrat and the experiment," as her husband's agent and with his money. These she bequeathed to Matthews, appointing a free black man to act as his agent and to stand guardian to her daughter, to whom she left her own property.[39]

The women whose mates were white or enslaved had no choice but to remain technically single, but it is by no means certain that all of them would have married had they been given the chance. When free black women entered into partnerships with men who were also black and free, legal wedlock was not the inevitable result. For one thing, marrying did cost money. Ministers were authorized to charge one dollar for their services, and the clerk's fee was a quarter. If a poor couple found that amount an obstacle, they likely found it well-nigh impossible to locate a third party willing to post the $150 bond required to obtain the license.[40]

Nonmarriage among free blacks, however, was evidently as much a matter of ethics as of expenses, for even the propertied showed no consistent tendency to make their conjugal ties legal ties. Christian Scott was hardly well-to-do, but he did own some animals and a goodly stock of household furniture; "having for some time past lived with Charlotte Cook by whom I have a son called Jesse Mitchell . . . ," Scott explained, "And being desirous from the friendship & Regard I bear to the said Charlotte Cook & affection to my said Son, to convey the property aforesaid to them," Scott deeded them the property, dividing it exactly as it would have been divided had Scott married Cook and then died intestate (without a will). James Vaughan was far wealthier than Scott. He was also in trouble. In 1806 Vaughan was tried for the murder of "his supposed wife," Milly Johnston. After his conviction, a contrite Vaughan was permitted to write a will to direct the distribution of an estate that included cash and bonds worth over two thousand dollars, a town lot, three horses, and four slaves. Vaughan gave half of his estate to Sarah Vaughan, his daughter by Polly Hull. The other half went to John Vaughan, his son by Ann Stephens. Whether James Vaughan's relationships with Johnston, Hull, and Stephens were simultaneous or sequential is both unclear and beside the point. The point is that he did not marry any of them.[41]

So much the better for the women's control over their property and wages. Polly Hull, for example, bought a town lot a few months before James Vaughan wrote his will and was taxed on it for more than a decade thereafter.[42] There were other free black women in roughly similar circumstances. Charlotte Rollins was part of an uneasy triangle that included a free black named Captain Billy Ash and a slave named Julius. Ash was tried for "shooting and wounding" Julius in 1802, and Rollins's sister and brother-in-law were examined in the case: "On their being asked if Charlotte was wife of the prisoner, it was answered, that they both, the prisoner & Julius, resorted where she was." It is unclear what became of Billy Ash, but Charlotte Rollins never married him or anyone else. In 1810, she was listed as the head of a three-person family, and in 1817, she disposed of her household furniture and kitchen utensils by deed of gift, a probable substitute for the writing of a will.[43] Nelly White, unhappily, was unable to enjoy the property she had acquired in her baking business. In 1811, White was examined on suspicion of knifing a free man named Tom, and a witness described their relationship. "Tom & the Prisoner had lived in the same House, in different apartments — and been considered as man & wife but lived badly together after wrangling." White was convicted in District Court and sent to the penitentiary. She left behind "some property & Estate," and the town sergeant was ordered to look after it while she served her sentence.[44]

A member of one of Petersburg's most prominent free black families, Molly Brander married once, but opted for cohabitation the second time around. The first time, she married Nathan James. After his death in 1804, Molly began a new family, taking James Butler "as her husband tho not lawfully married," and adopting her orphaned niece. Because she did not marry Butler, Molly James retained her rights to the house and lot she had inherited from her first husband, and when she died intestate in 1812, her mother and brothers inherited the property in turn. Before her death, however, Molly James had told her family that she wanted the lot to pass to James Butler and her adoptive daughter; the family complied in 1815 by means of a deed of gift.[45]

Just how commonly black women acquired some kind of property and retained legal control over it by not marrying the men in their lives is a mystery, for evidence surfaces only sporadically in trial reports (hence the prevalence of violent crime in the preceding paragraphs) and in a very occasional deed. Moreover, these few documents give no clues as to whether the women deliberately refused marriage for the sake of maintaining their property rights. The legacy and continued presence of slavery no doubt provided cause enough. Slave marriages were necessarily based on mutual consent; for a good many black couples, consent was sufficient in freedom as well, an attitude that the black churches would combat with mixed success in the decades that followed.[46] Still, it may have been that women so recently emancipated, and women accustomed to providing for themselves, did not give up their legal autonomy lightly.[47] Certainly free black women had unique incentive for staying single. For the woman who hoped to buy an enslaved relative, legal wedlock meant that her plan could be sabotaged at any time by her husband or by her husband's impatient creditors. The common-law disabilities of married women added an ironic twist to chattel slavery's strange fusion of persons and property: Matrimony could pose a threat to the integrity of the free black woman's family.

Whether by necessity, deliberation, or default, sufficient numbers of free black women avoided legal marriage to constitute a major departure from the white norm. The contrast with the experience of white women was sharper still in the extent to which black women shouldered the burden of supporting their families. If most of the women listed by the census taker as "heads of families" were primary breadwinners, then the magnitude of economic responsibility borne by free black women was truly staggering. In 1810, 56.3 percent (138 of 245) of the free black households of Petersburg were headed by women. For 1820, the figure was 58.1 percent (168 of 289). In 1820, these female-headed households sheltered over one-half (52.3 percent) of all free black persons living in black households and an even larger proportion (57.3 percent) of free black children under fourteen.

So uninformative are these early census returns, and so suspect the given numbers, that no satisfactory reconstruction of household composition is possible.[48] From the unembellished hashmarks that made up the 1820 schedules, the one safe conclusion is that there was no typical free black household structure. The most commonplace household type (87 of 289) was, it appears, the female-headed family containing one woman and her (?) children. Further guesswork suggests that the second most frequent arrangement was the male-headed household containing an adult couple and their children (51 of 289).[49] Thirty-seven households were composed of but one person, twenty-nine of them female, and there were apparently twenty-four childless couples. The remaining households, about one-third of the total, contained persons of ages and sexes that defy categorization. Worth noting, however, is the incidence of extended or augmented families. One-fifth of all free black households contained at least one "surplus" person over the age of twenty-five.[50]

It should be emphasized that there was no typical household structure among whites either.[51] The difference was that Petersburg's multiform white households were overwhelmingly male-headed. The proportion of white households headed by women was 15.7 percent in 1810 and 17.0 percent ten years after. In addition, a disproportionately small number of whites lived in these female-headed households. The census taker of 1820 found only 13.3 percent of white children under sixteen resident in female-headed households, while 12.8 percent of all white persons lived in households headed by women.[52]

Nineteenth-century census data usually raise more questions than they answer, and this is particularly true of the early returns. It is impossible to discern the precise family structure within households, much less assess the meaning of familial roles played by neighbors and nonresident kin. This last blind spot is especially troublesome given the probability that for numerous free blacks, spouses and close kin remained the slaves of white owners. Least of all does the census tell us anything about love, commitment, giving children a chance in life — those qualities that despite our disclaimers usually lurk behind our reading of the numbers.

These problems only begin the list of the source limitations that frustrate any attempts to recapture the experience of the mass of free black women. We do know that there was a flourishing free black Baptist church in Petersburg before 1820 and that in 1820 a Sunday school run by free blacks had girls as well as boys among its two hundred students.[53] But there are no records for the church in this period and none at all for the Sunday school. Newspapers reported next to no local news. The whites whose correspondence is preserved wrote of their own kind; only rarely did they discuss their slaves, and free blacks were never mentioned. While the local public records are surprisingly rich, they are decidedly slanted toward the property owners. The majority of free black women thus appear to us only as names — or worse, as numbers — on the census schedules.

The conclusion nevertheless stands. In a slave society of the early nineteenth century, there developed among free blacks a relatively high degree of equality between the sexes. There is not much material here for romanticizing. For free black women, the high rate of gainful employment and the high incidence of female-headed households were symptoms of oppression. Neither was chosen from a position of strength; both were products of a shortage of men and of chronic economic deprivation. The high incidence of female property holding, meanwhile, was largely the consequence of a system that limited the achievement of black men.

Yet there was autonomy of a kind, and the fact that its origins lay in racial subordination should not detract from its significance. The autonomy experienced by the free black women of Petersburg was relative freedom from day-to-day domination by black men. We cannot say for certain how free black people looked on this. The fact that so many couples refrained from legal marriage, however, at least suggests that the women valued their autonomy and that one way or another the men learned to live with it. The tragedy for the nineteenth century — or one of many tragedies — was that white people were unable to use the free black example to call their own gender arrangements into question, that no one outside the free black community took anything positive from the free black experience. Perhaps we can do better.

NOTES

The author wishes to thank the Colonial Williamsburg Foundation and the Woodrow Wilson National Fellowship Foundation Program in Women's Studies for their support of the research on which this article is based. She would also like to thank Sharon Harley for her comments on an earlier version of the article.

[1]*South-Side Democrat*, 29 November, 12 December 1853 (first quotation), 17 March, 18 March, 20 March 1854; Minutes, 15 December 1853, 16 March, 17 March 1854 (second quotation).

All references to minutes, deeds, wills, accounts, and marriages are to the records of the Petersburg Hustings Court, on microfilm in the Virginia State Library, Richmond, Va. References to land books, personal property books, and legislative petitions are to the original manuscripts in the Virginia State Library.

[2]Calculated from *Aggregate Amount of Persons Within the United States in the Year 1810* (Washington, 1811), p. 55a. According to this census, Petersburg contained 1,089 free blacks, 2,173 slaves, and 2,404 whites. The town's free black population grew to only 1,165 by 1820. In reading these figures, allowance shou'd be made for probable undercounting.

[3]E. Franklin Frazier, *The Negro Family in the United States* (Chicago: University of Chicago Press, 1939); U.S. Department of Labor, Office of Policy Planning and Research, *The Negro Family: The Case for National Action* by Daniel P. Moynihan (Washington, D.C.: U.S. Government Printing Office, 1965.) More detailed summaries of these works may be found in the articles by Gutman, Lammermeier, and Shifflett, cited in note 4.

[4]John W. Blassingame, *Black New Orleans 1860-1880* (Chicago and London: University of Chicago Press, 1973), pp. 79-105; Frank F. Furstenberg Jr., Theodore Hershberg, and John Modell, "The Origins of the Female-Headed Black Family: The Impact of the Urban Experience," pp. 211-33; Herbert G. Gutman, "Persistent Myths About the Afro-American Family," pp. 181-210; Crandall A. Shifflett, "The Household Composition of Rural Black Families: Louisa County, Virginia, 1880," pp. 235-60, all in *Journal of Interdisciplinary History* 6 (Autumn 1975); Herbert G. Gutman, *The Black Family in Slavery and Freedom, 1750-1925* (New York: Pantheon Books, 1976), pp. 432-60; Paul J. Lammermeier, "The Urban Black Family of the Nineteenth Century: A Study of Black Family Stucture in the Ohio Valley, 1850-1880," *Journal of Marriage and the Family* 35 (August 1973): 440-56; Elizabeth H. Pleck, "The Two-Parent Household: Black Family Structure in Late Nineteenth-Century Boston," *Journal of Social History* 5 (Fall 1971): 3-31. Pleck, however, does point out the value-laden nature of terms like "family disorganization," and in *Black Migration and Poverty: Boston 1865-1900* (New York: Academic Press, 1979), has reevaluated the significance of two-parent households.

[5]This may be a slight overcount; of the two dozen slaves directed freed by will, some may have remained in slavery due to owners' indebtedness or to litigation. The law of 1806 discouraged manumission by requiring all newly freed persons to leave the state within one year of emancipation, and for a time it was extremely effective. There were no emancipations in Petersburg from 1807 to 1810. Emancipations began again in 1811, but from 1811 to 1820 were granted at less than half their pre-1807 rate, even though a new statute of 1816 made it easier for the manumitted to obtain permission to remain in Virginia.

The female advantage in emancipation seems to have been more than a reflection of the sex ratio among slaves; calculations from the Personal Property Book for 1790 show that females constituted only a 51.5 percent majority of slave adults.

[6]Mary Cumming to Margaret Craig, December 1811, Margaret and Mary Craig Letters, Virginia Colonial Records Project, Alderman Library, University of Virginia, Charlottesville, Virginia (quotation); Wills I, 238 (1796); Deeds IV, 304 (1815); Luther P. Jackson, "Manumission in Certain Virginia Cities," *Journal of Negro History* 15 (July 1930): 310. John Jeffers's will also authorized the emancipation of Sylvia's mother.

[7]Deeds V, 324 (1818); Wills II, 163 (1819).

[8]Luther P. Jackson counted the deeds of emancipation recorded in Petersburg and Richmond from 1784 to 1806 and found more in Petersburg, even though it was the smaller city. This he attributed to the early presence in Petersburg of antislavery Methodists. See Jackson, "Manumission," pp. 281-82. By my count, six Methodists accounted for almost one-fifth of Petersburg emancipations to 1806.

[9]Six women were apprehended and jailed for hiring themselves out. The court had the choice of selling them or fining their masters; two of the six were ordered sold. Minutes, 5 April 1802, 5 September 1803, 2 January, 9 February, 4 April 1809, 6 May 1811. See William Waller Hening, *The New Virginia Justice, Comprising the Office and Authority of a Justice of the Peace in the Commonwealth of Virginia* . . . 2nd. ed. (Richmond: Johnson & Warner, 1810), p. 549.

[10]Deeds VI, 51 (1819).

[11]Deeds II, 157 (1792), III, 58 (quotation), 74 (1802), 236 (1805).

[12]Two of the women freed their sons; no relationship was stated by the others. Deeds II, 174 (1792), 581 (1799), 701 (1800), 737 (1801), Deeds III, 75 (1802), 116 (1803), Deeds V, 325 (1818).

[13]Deeds III, 78 (1802).

[14]Deeds III, 267 (1805); Wills II, 69 (1812), 114 (1815), 139 (1817), 161 (1819).

[15]At least sixteen women were manumitted with their children (this does not include those freed by husbands or other kin from whom they could expect financial assistance). Six had a single child, five had two children, and five had three or more.

[16]Minutes, 1 June 1801, 6 January 1806, 7 August 1809.

[17]Accounts I, 31, 55 (1808), 37 (1809), Accounts II, 189 (1821); Luther Porter Jackson, *Free Negro Labor and Property Holding in Virginia, 1830-1860* (New York and London: D. Appleton-Century Co., 1942), p. 221; Personal Property Books, 1801-1820.

[18]Minutes, 2 November 1790, 5 August 1799, 2 March 1812.

[19]There were probably more gainfully employed women among free blacks than among whites, but because the whites were more likely to escape (paid) domestic service, they are far more visible; specific occupations can be identified for more than 150 white women. These women, with a few exceptions, were milliners, dressmakers, midwives, teachers, and keepers of taverns, boardinghouses, and stores. Meanwhile, the only female occupations in which no free black women were found were teaching and millinery.

[20]Minutes, 4 November 1804.

[21]Calculated from the United States *Census for 1820* (Washington, D.C.: Gales and Seaton, 1821). The imbalance may also have been due to a higher rate of male migration to the free states. It does not appear to have been due to higher mortality rates among men, because the sex ratio was higher (71.3) among free blacks aged forty-five and above.

[22]Deeds I, 270 (1786), Deeds II, 116 (1800); Personal Property Books, 1795-1804; Accounts I, 75 (1817).

[23]Deeds I, 303 (1787), Deeds II, 379 (1795); Land Books, 1795-1820.

[24]Deeds II, 205 (1792), 593 (1799), Deeds III, 237 (1805); Personal Property Books, 1797-1802; Wills II, 69 (1812); Minutes, 5 October 1812, 8 August 1815, 5 March 1816, 17 July, 16 October 1818.

Few of the persons emancipated in Petersburg can be traced. Emancipators stated last names for fewer than one-third of the slaves freed (black emancipators were more prone than whites to state surnames), and because ex-slaves hardly ever took the name of the last owner, inference is of little help.

[25]Land Book, 1820.

[26]Taxable property consisted of land (taxed according to its annual rental value), slaves over twelve years of age (taxed by the head), horses, carriages, and exports from the tobacco warehouses. My calculations include all taxes paid by living individuals, except those paid on tobacco exports, there being no comparable taxes on other businesses.

It should be emphasized that all along, white men controlled the lion's share of the taxable wealth, ranging from 85 percent in 1790, when town matriarch Mary Marshall Bolling was in her heyday, to 94 percent in 1820. The best way to characterize the trend for the decade after 1810 is that more white women and blacks of both sexes were acquiring small pieces of an expanding pie. The following table shows the proportion, in percent, of the persons listed in the census schedules as heads of families who also paid taxes:

	1810	1820
White men	60.1	61.8
Black men	21.5	24.8
White women	14.8	30.3
Black women	5.1	10.1

[27]Deeds III, 300 (1806), Deeds IV, 351 (1815); Wills II, 141 (1817).

[28]Legislative Petitions, 23 December 1839; Wills II, 94 (1814).

[29]Deeds III, 156 (1804); Wills II, 161 (1819). Amelia Gallé's son Joseph later on became the husband of Eliza Gallie.

[30]Petersburg *Republican*, 18 April, 7 July 1820, 23 May, 22 August 1823.

[31]United States Manuscript Census Schedule, 1820; Personal Property Books, 1819, 1820.

[32]Accounts I, 91 (1814) (first quotation); Deeds IV, 332 (1815) (second quotation); Wills II, 40 (1809) (third quotation), 95 (1814) (fourth quotation).

[33]Accounts II, 68 (1824-1826); Deeds III, 279 (1806); Land Books, 1806-1820; Personal Property Books, 1801-1820; *Republican*, 29 October 1816.

[34]Slave sales were not usually publicly recorded, and this adds to the difficulty of determining the extent of slave ownership.

[35]The number of slaves mortgaged was calculated from the deed books. During the same two years, Petersburg newspapers advertised the sale of about eighty slaves "according to a deed of trust," in other words, for owners' indebtedness. Both figures given here are lower than the actual totals, because the advertisements and deeds of trust did not always stipulate the precise numbers of slaves involved. Anyone prone to discount the significance of the threat of forced sale would do well to sample some deed books. In 1819 and 1820 alone, at least one-tenth of Petersburg's slaves were put up as collateral for owners' debts.

[36]In 1810, eight of twenty-three black landowners were women.

[37]By using the legal loopholes provided by the equity tradition of jurisprudence, a few married women were able to exempt their property from the control of husbands and husbands' creditors. Mary Ann Vizonneau provides one example. Her father's

stipulation that her inheritance was not to be controlled by her husband set up a "separate estate," which was formalized in 1818 by a separation agreement executed by Vizonneau and her estranged husband. Deeds V, 284 (1818). In this period, however, separate estates were still very rare.

[38]In his will, Jean Gallé apprised his executors that the woman slave Faith and all but two of the beds in his house belonged to Cassurier and not to his estate. Wills II, 161 (1819).

[39]Minutes, 3 September 1800; Wills II, 192 (1822).

[40]Joseph Tate, *A Digest of the Laws of Virginia, which are of a Permanent Character and General Operation; Illustrated by Judicial Decisions: To which is Added, An Index of the Names of Cases in the Virginia Reporters* (Richmond: Shepherd and Pollard, 1823), pp. 415-18, secs. 1, 11, 13. Because the Marriage Register did not stipulate race, not even a rough estimate of black marriage rates can be made.

[41]Deeds V, 124 (1817); Minutes, 21 November 1806; Wills II, 182 (1821). Vaughan was born free and the son of the Sarah Vaughan who appeared year after year on the tax lists.

[42]Deeds III, 376 (1807); Land Books, 1809-1820.

[43]Minutes, 27 January 1802; Deeds V, 197 (1817).

[44]Minutes, 6 April 1811 (first quotation), 6 May 1812 (second quotation).

[45]Land Books, 1806-1812; Deeds IV, 330 (1815) (quotation).

[46]Records of the Gillfield Baptist Church suggest that as late as 1860, there was still ambivalence on the marriage issue. An entry of 29 January 1860, for example, reads: "It was moved & 2nd that the Past Action of the church be reconsidered of mutual concent being considered Man & Wife Carried — non considered Man & Wife But those joined together By Matrimony." Gillfield Baptist Church Record Book, Alderman Library.

[47]Two cases suggest that some free black women were aware of the law and concerned about its consequences. Two days before she married Jacob Brander, Nancy Curtis deeded her furniture and livestock to her teenaged children, a clear attempt to protect the rights of her own heirs. Lydia Thomas maintained her property rights in a slave and some furniture, despite her marriage to John Stewart, by entering into a prenuptial contract with him. This gave her a separate estate, much like that of Mary Ann Vizonneau. Deeds IV, 335 (1815), Deeds V, 288 (1818); Marriages, 1814, 1817.

[48]The 1810 census listed the names of free black heads of households, but the only further information given was the total number of free blacks (with a separate total for slaves) living in each household. The census for 1820 is somewhat more informative, supplying the number of persons of each sex in each of four age categories (under fourteen, fourteen to twenty-five, twenty-six to forty-four, and forty-five and above).

[49]The first figure is the total of all households in which one female from fourteen to twenty-five was listed along with one or more children under age fourteen, and in which one female of twenty-six or above was listed along with one or more persons under age twenty-six. The same age categories were used for the second figure.

[50]For female-headed households, surplus adult is defined as anyone over twenty-five listed in addition to the head. For male-headed households, surplus adults are those listed in addition to one man and one woman. There were twenty-one surplus women and six men in male-headed households, thirty surplus women and twenty-three men in female-headed households.

[51]Even counting resident slaves and free blacks out of the analysis, fewer than one-third of the households headed by whites can be reasonably classified as nuclear, that is, as being composed of an adult couple or an adult couple with their children with no surplus persons.

One-tenth of Petersburg's free blacks were listed as residing in households headed by whites. Three-fifths of these free blacks were males, and they outnumbered females resident in white households in every age group except the over-forty-four category.

[52]The incidence of female-headedness among poorer white households was considerably higher, as might be expected. In 1820, 27.1 percent of the households of nontaxpaying whites were female headed. Comparison of white and black households is complicated by the fact that different age categories were used for the two groups.

[53]Luther P. Jackson, *A Short History of the Gillfield Baptist Church of Petersburg, Virginia* (Petersburg: Virginia Printing Co., 1937); *Republican*, 17 October 1820.

Elizabeth H. Pleck

TWO WORLDS IN ONE: WORK AND FAMILY

Nowhere is the subdivision of topics into areas of specialized inquiry more troubling than in social history. Beyond the divisions by national boundaries and time periods, new "specialties" have emerged (the cynical would suggest as a means of securing employment in a declining labor market). Someone who has used the manuscript census schedules to study the family and religious life among Irish Catholic mill girls in Lawrence can be considered a historian of labor, women, family, immigrants, the city, religion, or a quantitative methodologist – seven types of social history in a single study! Whether the motives for this compartmentalization are laudatory or predatory, the fact is that social history has become locked into narrow areas of specialization. Periodically, social historians call for a new synthesis of these specialities, but without any palpable explanation of how this reconciliation can be achieved; it is easy to decry the "balkanizing thrust in social history,"[1] but harder to overcome it.

Efforts to mesh two important specialities, labor history and the history of the family, seem particularly worthwhile because in their concern for work and family these topics embrace two of the more fundamental areas of human activity and emotional investment. Some developments in labor and family history make it possible to examine the link between the two in some detail. Historians of labor, once concerned amost exclusively with the organization of labor unions, are now analyzing the significance of work itself.[2] In the meantime, historians of the family, who initially focused on changes in household composition, have become increasingly interested in family norms, especially the changing emotional climate of the family.[3] Ironically, these two rather similar trends (the shift in interest from organizational membership to changes in norms) have developed separately, as if families existed without workers and workers were devoid of families. One sociologist, in fact, has argued that modern industrial society and the corporation helped to propagate the "myth of separate worlds," the division between the spheres of work and of the family.[4] Whatever the reasons for this inattention to the intersection of the two worlds, it seems obvious that the description of relationships between work and family makes for a richer and more complex social history.

A single sociological theory has informed most of the historical study of the relationship between work and family – this is that industrialization led to the separation of home and work. The most dramatic case of this separation was the English textile industry in the nineteenth century. Neil Smelser in *Social Change and the Industrial Revolution* points to the gradual shift (through a series of technological changes) from home to factory production.[5] No longer a productive unit, the family would come to specialize in other largely neglected functions – emotional satisfaction, the socialization of children, and consumption.

For industrial society this separation of the worlds of work and family was necessary for the stability of each institution and for the society as a whole.[6] According to Talcott Parsons, the most esteemed "functionalist" theorist:

> The family has become a more specialized agency than before; probably more specialized than in any previous known society . . . but not in any general sense less important, because the society is dependent more exclusively on it for the performance of certain of its vital functions.[7]

The functionalists argue that the institutions of the family and workplace – divided into geographical and emotional units – specialized in their separate activities without mutual interference. According to this theory, human emotions were split between the two worlds – particularistic, ascriptive norms governing the family and universalistic, achieved norms dominating the world of work.

All of this specialization and differentiation in family function has been attributed to industrialization, specifically, technological change and the organization of work outside the household. Functionalist theory assumes that industrialization fundamentally altered the balance between the family and other social institutions. Although the consequences arising from this separation of work and family were many, only one – the family's loss of its role in production – has been isolated as the crucial factor. A long list of other results has been attributed to the loss of the family's production function, including the decline of kinship as the basis of work organization, the loss of power for mothers and children, the revolt of youth against their parents, the emergence of adolescence as a separate life stage, and greater sexual freedom for young women. Some historians have minimized the extent of these social changes, or attributed them to causes other than the loss of the family's economic function. Not enough attention, however, has been paid to specifying the nature and scope of the family's loss of productive function – indeed, to whether such a loss of function occurred at all.

Historians of the family generally follow the functionalist scheme.[8] In most cases, of course, they adopt this interpretation without necessarily subscribing to the larger functionalist world view. Still, the history of the family has been concerned largely with the way institutional changes affect family functions. John Demos, for example, writes that "the history of the family has been the history of contraction and withdrawal; its central theme is the gradual surrender to other institutions of functions that once lay very much within the realm of family responsibility."[9] In studying English family structure between 1500 and 1700, Lawrence Stone concluded that "the economic functions of the family as a distributive mechanism for goods and services declined."[10] Or consider this highly Parsonian statement by a Marxist historian, E. P. Thompson, describing the changes wrought by English industrialization:

> Women became more dependent upon the employer of the labour market, and they looked back to a golden period in which home earnings from spinning, poultry, and

> the like could be gained around their own door. In good times, the domestic economy, like the peasant economy, supported a way of life centered upon the home, in which inner whims and compulsions were more obvious than external discipline. Each stage in industrial differentiation and specialization struck also at the family economy, disturbing customary relations between man and wife, parents and children, and differentiating more sharply between "work" and "life." It was to be a full hundred years before this differentiation was to bring returns, in the form of labour-saving devices, back into the working woman's home. Meanwhile, the family was roughly torn apart each morning by the factory bell.[11]

There are several reasons why this theoretical perspective is "dysfunctional" to the history of work-family relationships. First, since a function can be defined either as a classification of activities of an evaluation of them, there has been a serious confusion between norms and behavior. To argue, for example, that the Victorian family "functioned" as an emotional retreat from the world of work is a normative judgment, not a description of behavior, although it has been taken as both. According to Arlene Skolnick, "what people actually do may have little relation to what they think they are doing and what they think they should be doing."[12] But this is a confusion in much social history, not simply in this specialty. A second objection is that such history emphasizes the evolution of functions, the search for the origins of declining functions, their stubborn persistence, or their greater differentiation. The difficulty with this is the same as in Whig or Progressive history – where the historian, assuming a model of decay or progress, searches for proof, often wrenching evidence out of its historical context. Anachronistic interpretation is the most serious problem with this evolutionary approach. A third limitation of functionalist history is its emphasis on how institutions fit together rather than how people cross institutional boundaries. Sociologist Rosabeth Kanter has argued that with "few exceptions, the traditional emphasis [in the functionalist theory of the family] was almost totally on the roles and positions and forms or outcomes for the individual with relatively little conceptualizing until recently on the family as an *interacting system.*"[13] Functionalist theory presents a structural model for the evolution of institutions, perhaps a worthy enterprise in itself, but ill-suited to studying the process of interaction between work and family.

Did industrialization cause the separation of home and work? Historians have modified or limited this interpretation without fundamentally challenging it. In this paper, I will first examine the recent historical work that partly refutes this interpretation, and then describe briefly two alternative emphases, also derived from contemporary work which present more promising lines of inquiry. Since issues in the history of work and family cross national boundaries, I have drawn on research in American and European social history. I have ordered the evidence from historical research, largely designed for purposes other than addressing this argument, into four different categories of arguments against the notion that industrialization created two distinct worlds for work and family.

1. Until recent times, separation of home and work characterized only the middle-class.

Historians of the Victorian family, as a case in point, have closely followed the functionalist emphasis on differentiation between family and work roles.

Their descriptions of the Victorian middle-class family merely restates much of the sociological argument: the home was a place of repose where the breadwinner recuperated from the world of work.[14] Only the husband earned an income and he alone moved between the two worlds. As family and work became increasingly separated, the Victorian home became more privatized,[15] with separation of physical space for mothers and children and the division of the house between the more public and more private areas.

In this greater differentiation of function, a new role emerged for women: the glorification of motherhood.[16] Mothers devoted increased hours of attention to their children. Removed from wage-earning, children became dependents in the family and took years preparing to enter the world of work.[17] Husbands and wives increasingly inhabited two different emotional worlds – the task-preoccupied husband taking only a leisure time interest in the family, his expressive wife providing all the love and nurturance.

This argument points out the class dimension of a process – that work and family life first became separated among the middle classes where only one breadwinner was required to maintain the family. All the consequences of this new style of life – the glorification of motherhood, the new stages of childhood and adolescence, the segregation of fathers from their families – were attributed to the prosperity of these families and the loss of the productive role from the home. In this argument, the home, devoid of economic activity, served as a retreat from the world of work.

2. **Contrary to the functionalist assumption, production in the home declined gradually.**

Two systems of work, production on the farm or in the household and production in the factory coexisted for at least a century. The major form of home production was farming; as late as 1900, nearly two-thirds of all American families earned their living from the land. Nor did the development of industry simply end family enterprise. In the United States, France, England or Italy during the nineteenth century, daughters from farm families worked in the textile mills and returned home with wages and money for a dowry (or, at least in the United States, for their brother's education). Working sons and daughters often left the farm only to return with money which helped purchase capital improvements, thereby increasing the value of their inheritance.[18]

Even with the organization of production in factories, many commodities were still produced at home. Everything from shoes, cigars and matchboxes to artificial flowers and buttons was made there. Even printing presses were located originally in shops next to the family living quarters. Some technological changes outside the home actually increased work within it.[19] The sewing machine, located in a small corner of the family's apartment, made it possible to produce more garments at home, and as late as the 1880's, most apparel for American women, with the exception of cloaks, was made by families sewing in their apartments. With the introduction of new shears, for example, garments were cut at factories and parcelled out to sewing families. In fact, the lower wages of family workers at home led to a decline in craft shops and a rise in sweated labor.[20]

Such commodity production, of course, gradually ended; however, the demise of the early handloom weavers in England has often been interpreted as the abrupt end of the family workshop.[21] Actually, as noted by Patricia Branca, home production declined much less rapidly in Western Europe than in England or the United States, and when handloom weaving finally disappeared in Europe, it was replaced by dressmaking in France, silk manufacturing in Italy and linen cloth making in Belgium.[22] By the end of the nineteenth century the home economy still generated income and employment. In the cities, filled with migrants, taking boarders was a major wage-earning occupation of women, especially among childless married women with no outside employment.[23] Around the turn of the century between 20% and 30% of American families accepted boarders.[24] The persistence of all these forms of home production and services indicates considerable economic activity within the household.

Another development in the home economy was the rise of service industries. In some cases, wage-earners took work into their own homes (for example, laundresses[25]), but such labor was performed mostly in the employer's home.[26] While the most common category of female employment in the United States or in Western Europe around the turn of the century was domestic service, it was only one of a large list of home service occupations which included home repairs (plumbing, carpentry, repair and gardening) along with services outside the home (laundry and restaurants). Since homes purchased the services of workers, they continued to be centers of economic exchange, if not of commodity production.

The modifications of the functionalist interpretation accept the basic definitions of terms; they merely argue for a more precise dating of the decline in home production. The family workshop declined gradually – far more slowly in some European countries than in England or in America. Along with the organization of industry, home production grew and even prospered as it absorbed certain technological improvements. The two modes of work organization actually developed simultaneously for almost a century.

3. Market work moved outside the home but nonmarket work remained.

A new group of "home economists," that is, econometricians interested in the household as an economic unit, have challenged the old distinction between production and consumption.[27] They point out that production and consumption are both merely allocations of time between monetized and nonmonetized activities. It takes time and purchased raw material to produce commodities – whether steel in a rolling mill or dinner at home. The steelworker receives wages for doing his labor while the housewife does not. The dinner is immediately "used" while the steel is exchanged for cash or credit. This perspective on work deemphasizes wage-earning, suggesting a much broader definition of "work" which includes nonmarket labor, most of which was (and is) performed by women.

Marxist historians also have emphasized the role of women in production;[28] in maintaining and servicing the worker – the wife, according to Engels, "became the first domestic servant."[29] For families only slightly above subsistence, these kinds of economic activities were the margin of survival. In Pittsburgh, for example, where around the turn of the century there were few municipal services in working-class districts, a steelworker who wanted clean clothes, water to bathe in or drink, or a cooked meal, required the services of a wife.[30] Most unmarried male workers lived in boarding houses where there was at least one woman who performed this work. Beyond this direct form of maintenance, wives and children denied themselves food, garments, and heat in order to sustain and clothe the breadwinner.[31] With increasing prosperity, wifely services were directed less toward family survival than toward maintaining high standards of cleanliness, child care, nutrition and leisure, all of which required greater time investments, and modern studies of housework (between 1920 and 1970) show no substantial change in the number of hours devoted to household tasks despite rising real wages and the introduction of more technology in the home.[32] Even in the Victorian period, middle-class women – far from idle – devoted a full week's work to housecare. The typical middle-class housewife hired a servant for the heavier tasks, but still performed most of her own cleaning.[33] The one major change during this period was the increasing allocation of time to child care, an investment of the mother's hours occasioned as much by changing job requirements in middle-class work as by new sentiments towards children.

In connection with the pursuit of particular strategies of family fertility, it can be argued that reproduction was, in fact, a continuation of home production. In the view of some Marxists, children were commodities made in the home; that is, in a strictly economic sense, children were produced by time and labor and when mature, they repaid their parents' initial investment with either wages or free labor.[34] Whether from farm or factory families they were needed as workers and as investments for their parents' old age. Parents purposely kept their daughters from marrying early in order to retain the extra wages.[35] In so doing, they raised their daughters' marriage age, thereby lowering the number of future grandchildren. Thus these family strategies manipulated the production of labor power in the household.

Thus, to these two groups of economists, the family's functions at home and at work form part of the larger economic program, that is productive activities within the home include the unpaid labor of a housewife along with her reproduction of children. By defining "work" in this manner, these groups of economists have revised the view of housework and also its relationship to paid employment. Still, these arguments only limit but do not contradict the functionalist interpretation. If one amended the argument to read, "industrialization caused a decline in the home production *of goods and services for exchange*," there would be no apparent objection from these theorists.

4. To a great extent, home and work were separated prior to industrialization.

Some historians are prone to argue that the separation of home and work occurred prior to factory production. Work in pre-industrial society was, of course, organized on a far smaller scale; it was often performed in households, on farms, or in craft shops. But if the question is one of whether families worked together in such settings, there is abundant evidence that they did not. To demonstrate that home and work were separated in pre-industrial society, one would begin by pointing out that the family in that period was *never integrated* as a work force. The level of population mobility was extremely high; between one and two-thirds of the inhabitants in English and colonial American villages moved away in less than a decade.[36] These migrants were adults, landless workers looking for jobs, or men impressed into the armies – or adolescents employed away from home as servants, apprentices, or live-in laborers.[37] In colonial America the putting out of children with neighboring families was common. Even among children who lived at home, many worked as hired hands and servants for neighbors. Sometimes these child laborers wanted to retain control over their own wages rather than contribute to the family economy.[38] Where families worked the land together, death was so common that the family was often forced to employ outside workers. Such evidence contradicts the simplistic sociological notion that "in the earlier household economy, the members of the family daily worked together at home to produce their livelihood . . ."[39]

One might even argue that for a short interval economic and technological change created working families of this pure sociological model. Introduction of new machinery indeed led to the specialization of labor, thereby creating cottage industries where whole families produced commodities within the household.[40] Family togetherness was even more usual among households in factory towns than in rural areas. However, the common residence of teenagers with the family was more frequent in industrial cities than in rural areas simply because adolescent children could find work in the mills.[41] Thus, if the argument for the preindustrial integration of work and family is based solely on the fact of common residence in the family, then one cannot prove that work and family were integrated.

More substantially, one can argue that it was the subdivision of land rather than factory production that destroyed the functional unity of the family. Only because land was controlled by parents and economic opportunity was restricted was it possible for children to remain as family workers. Philip Greven's study of farmers in colonial Massachusetts traces the dissolution of the family work unit.[42] In 17th century Andover adult children remained on these small farms, even postponing marriage, in return for their eventual inheritance of the property. As a result of the continued division of the land into smaller parcels, these Andover sons finally became less interested in inheriting the property and began to settle new farms far from their parents' residences.

As much or more unity of work and family was to be found in industrial settings as in farming areas. Some industries, like textile production in England, France, or the United States, employed the whole family.[43] Sometimes English spinners hired their own sons as assistants.[44] William Reddy estimates that over 50% of the workers in the textile mills of Armentièrs in 1906 were related to at least one other person in the mill.[45] In a similar American situation during the same period, Tamara Hareven reports that families recruited the laborers for the textile mills of Manchester, New Hampshire and even controlled their placement within the factory's workrooms.[46] Glassblowers, file makers and miners in France, England and the United States worked alongside their relatives.[47] The extent of family control over conditions of work varied among industries; it is conceivable that families held greater sway in the textile industry, where women and children were often employed in the work force, than in heavy industries such as steel or machine production.[48]

The argument concerning family cohesion in pre-industrial society proposes causes other than industrialization for the declining economic function of the family. Patterns of land inheritance largely determined the composition of the family work force. Landless wage laborers were as separated from their homes as modern proletarians. In fact, cottage industry and the employment of whole families in factories actually increased the unity of the family work force. The family's economic function was beginning to decline prior to industrialization, and in certain respects, it achieved a new unity as a result of industrial development.

In effect, the first three refutations amount only to slight modifications of functionalist theory; they try to show that the family lost its productive role only gradually, with rapid change occurring first for the bourgeoisie and subsequently for the working class, and with production for use continuing within the household. This fourth more drastic refutation of functionalist argument – that the family workplace was breaking down prior to industrialization – questions the cause of the decline but not the decline itself. Yet these backward or forward oscillations do little to advance the study of work and family. Christopher Lasch has pointed out that historians of the family "have suggested how the sociological model of family history might be modified in detail, but they have not questioned the validity of its broader assumptions."[49]

Beyond functionalist theory, two alternative perspectives apply to the study of the relationship between work and family.[50] One, exchange theory, invokes a specific theoretical perspective to explain how changes in control over economic resources altered the family economy; a second emphasizes changes in the structures and norms in the workplace.

Exchange theory analyzes the relationship between work and family by examining the process of bargaining between family members. In this model, relatives with varying resources engage in any number of exchanges with each other. The outcomes – changes in family power, psychic rewards, or the psychological climate within the family – result from differential control of resources, that is, what holds the family (or any other social system) together is the norm of reciprocity,[51] the assumption that one will receive payment in exchange for goods and/or services. According to this argument, one possible resource, although not the only one, is the income of family wage-earners. In studying the textile workers in Preston, England, Michael Anderson found a shift from normative kinship to calculative kinship, as the weight of community opinion, religion and tradition decreased, and the rational appraisal of mutual needs increased. Human needs – for housing, jobs, child care, nursing during sickness and assistance in old age – were met by family members, whose alternatives were largely determined by two factors: their relative possession of resources and the number of available partners. These structural conditions determined the whole content of kin relationships, even the pattern of household composition in Preston.[52]

For all its analytic power in explaining the persistence of kinship in industrial society, certain objections may be made to exchange theory. Empirical studies in this perspective often define resources and rewards only in economic terms, forgetting that physical attractiveness, level of social skills, educational backgrounds and the potential for violence are resources as well. Exchange theory takes a highly instrumental view of interpersonal relations, assuming that "people engage in a kind of mental bookkeeping before they enter into relations and that they perform a periodic audit of the ones they have."[53] Behavior is sometimes motivated by rational calculations but it is also influenced by personality needs, irrational factors, and the desire to emulate norms. Yet despite these weaknesses exchange theory has several advantages over functionalism. It shifts emphasis from the description of family functions to the interactive process (bargaining), between family members. And, it portrays the family as a potential arena of conflict rather than consensus between relatives with differing resources and needs.

From a second, less rigorously analytic perspective, one can examine how family norms determine one's position and perspective toward work. Specifically, this perspective describes the relationships between family life and changes in the salience, culture and scheduling of work. In their studies of women workers in nineteenth-century Europe, Joan Scott and Louise Tilly argue that despite new economic roles, women workers still defined themselves as members of the family enterprise. Even though changes in work and values eventually led to a decline in familialism, premodern values continued to persist in new environments and, in turn, determined behavior in these new locations. Under this analysis "behavior is less the product of new ideas than of the effects of old ideas operating in new or changing contexts."[54] A diametrically opposite point of view is presented by Edward Shorter in *The Making of the Modern Family* where he argues that capitalism created rather immediate consequences, especially for young women working far from their familial homes.[55] Removed from social controls and economic independent for the first time, these women sought and found sexual freedom, as reflected in the higher rate of legitimate and illegitimate births between 1750 and 1800.[56] If women workers under capitalism achieved "economic independence" and thereby increased their sexual activity, one would have to show that 1) women's wages were high enough to insure independence, and 2) that women workers controlled their earnings. On both counts, the evidence goes against Shorter. Women's wages were less than men's (one-half of men's in the nineteenth century English garment industry, for example),[57] too low to allow for residence separate from the family. The wages were often set lower, in fact, because employers assumed that women were living at home.[58] A working woman was far less likely to control her own wages than her male counterpart; in 19th century France employers often gave the entire paycheck to the family of the working girl.[59] As late as the 1920's most American working daughters living at home turned over their entire paycheck to their families and the ones living away from home donated at least half of their wages.

It is an odd commentary on the study of work and family that issues about changing commitment to work are posed only for women workers – who presumably experienced conflict between the two worlds, which male employees did not. The real issue is not whether capitalism altered or did not alter women's fundamental attitudes towards work and the family but that historians (like Anderson or Scott and Tilly) have gone beyond functionalist theory to examine changing behavior in the workplace as well as in the family. The next stage, then, is to examine these changes within the context of *specific occupational cultures,* rather than to refer to the "capitalist marketplace" or to the general conditions of poverty.[60]

How did the physical and emotional demands of work alter family life? In many unskilled occupations, demands outside of working hours were minimal (thereby successfully dividing work and family into separate entities), but in as many others, time demands intruded on the worker's leisure and on the life of other family members. Most of the "absorptive" occupations were careers,[61] whose characteristics sociologists have defined as a series of "age-graded," upwarded occupational changes.[62] Some of these highly absorptive occupations were structured as "two-person" careers,[63] involving the paid efforts of the husband and also the unpaid assistance of a wife (and sometimes of other family members). For some such careers, as noted by Rosabeth Kanter, work residence was combined with family living arrangements, such as the rectory, the embassy, the apartment above the family store of even the White House.

We know very little about the history of this category of occupations, which emerged in the 18th and 19th centuries,[64] even though such careers reordered relationships in middle-class family life. What has been described as the "cult of domesticity" might be better understood as the family response to the emergence of the male career. For middle-class wives membership in charity organizations or social clubs or home entertaining was actually designed to advance a husband in his work. The emergence of the career may have had other consequences as well, perhaps delayed age at marriage or postponement of child-bearing. Possibly the fertility decline among the middle class in the 19th century was much a response to the new male career as to changes in the level of prosperity, in middle-class values or in the wife's power.[65]

Aside from the absorptiveness of any occupation, the additional characteristics of work – its structure, emotions, and norms – have transformed family life. Particular jobs reshaped the individual's personality by presenting a set of learning experiences that socialized his or her view of the world. Pessimism, insecurity, physical fatigue were often the consequences of menial work, just as self-esteem, control and autonomy were often psychological traits derived from bureaucratic tasks. New work experiences not only changed workers' perceptions but also introduced them to heretofore unavailable skills, such as when domestic servants in 19th-century France learned to read and write while at work.[66] At the same time the experience in work coincided with altered levels of fertility. We know very little about this important connection, even though there is abundant information about the effects of occupational level on fertility. Yet it is clear that even within the same occupational stratum, only certain work was coincident with high fertility. Michael Haines has analyzed the reasons for high fertility among miners' families in England, Wales, Prussia and the United States around the turn of the century, arguing that in mining villages isolated from urban influences, premodern values towards the importance of children persisted. This, along with other factors – the absence of work opportunities for women, the men's relatively high wages and short period of peak earnings – contributed to high fertility.[67]

Finally, the cultural milieu of work shaped leisure and family styles. Gareth Stedman Jones shows that by the end of the 19th century, the decline in the work day had increased the extent of working-class leisure for the whole family; he documents the rise of the new sex-segregated institutions among the working class – the pub, the men's clubs and sporting activities.[68]

Changes in the scheduling of work also altered family life.[69] Many labor historians have argued that despite the imposition of new scheduling, some workers continued to favor preindustrial habits of work, family, and leisure.[70] As late as the middle- to late-19th century, industrial workers celebrated "St. Monday," a non-scheduled day of leisure from work.[71] Margaret Hewitt, in studying married women mill operatives in 19th-century Lancashire, notes how new scheduling changed family patterns:

> On Saturday the mills closed at midday and the men and single women make real holiday . . . The married women, who seem the slaves of Lancashire society, are obliged then, however, to set to work harder than ever. They have only this day to clean their houses, provide for the week, bake for the family, mend clothes, besides doing any washing that was not put out and attend the market to purchase the Sunday's dinner . . . The market is kept open very late at night for this purpose . . .[72]

Despite considerable scattered evidence about the effect of changes in scheduling on "family time," we need to know more about how the introduction of scheduled working hours and work days (or, for that matter night shifts), or the adoption of scheduled time in the schools changed family life.[73] In addition to reducing the work hours during the day, the declining number of workdays and the sequencing of days or weeks away from work (that is, "holidays" or vacations), may have created more opportunities for family leisure. Any single change in the time or timing of school or work reverberated throughout the two worlds. Another aspect of scheduling change was the sequencing of the family life cycle with the world of work. The investigation of changes in these life cycle events[74] (age at leaving home, marriage, birth of first and last child, widowhood) has occupied so much scholarly effort that little attention has been given to how the changing life cycle redounded on the world of work, although it is clear that an increase in family poverty – due to the absence of a mother's or child's labor – or more sexual freedom that often resulted from leaving the parental home can be understood as the changing intersection between the family's needs and the world of work.

To understand the history of work and family, historians must begin by rejecting theories based on "the myth of separate worlds," the separation of home and work under industrialization. They have raised objections and offered modifications of this argument without questioning its assumptions. One cannot study the relationship between work and family if it is assumed that the connections are only tangential. Functionalist analysis must be replaced by perspectives which examine how people reconciled the two worlds. I have suggested two possible approaches, although even in these alternative perspectives, there are difficulties and limitations. There is the danger for one thing of describing only one part of the process – how work affects family, or how family affects work. It will be necessary not only to follow the worker home from the job, but also to observe activity within the home and to study the influence of the family on the worker's participation in and involvement with work. If work and family form a larger whole, the social historian must specify how people move between the domains and demands of both worlds.

FOOTNOTES

The author acknowledges the thoughtful criticisms of this paper by Miriam Cohen, Joseph Pleck, and Louise Tilly.

1. Herbert G. Gutman, *Work, Culture and Society in Industrializing America* (New York, 1976) 211.

2. Paul Faler, "Working-Class Historiography," *Radical America*, 3 (1969), 56-68; Robert H. Zieger, "Workers and Scholars: Recent Trends in American Labor Historiography," *Labor History*, 12 (1972), 245-266; Thomas Krueger, "American Labor Historiography: Old and New – A Review," *Journal of Social History*, 4 (1971), 277-285.

3. Tamara K. Hareven, "The History of the Family as an Interdisciplinary Field," *Journal of Interdisciplinary History*, II (1971), 399-414; John Demos, "The American Family in Past Time," *American Scholar*, 43 (1974), 422-446: Jonathan Prude, "The Family in Context," *Labor History*, XVII, 3 (1976), 422-436; Christopher Lasch, "The Family and History," (November 13, 1975), 33-38; and "The Emotions of Family Life," *ibid.* (November 27, 1975), 37-42; "What the Doctor Ordered," (December 11, 1975); *New York Review of Books*, Barbara J. Harris, "Recent Work on the History of the Family: A Review Article," *Feminist Studies* (1976), 159-172. Additional reasons for joining labor history with family study can be found in John Modell, "Economic Dimensions of Family History," *The Family in Historical Perspective*, 6 (1974), 7-12.

4. Rosabeth Moss Kanter, *Work and Family in the United States: A Critical Review and Agenda for Research and Policy*, (forthcoming, New York, 1976).

5. Neil J. Smelser, *Social Change in the Industrial Revolution* (Chicago, 1959); Neil J. Smelser, "The Industrial Revolution and the British Working-Class Family," *Journal of Social History*, 1 (1967), 17-35. See also Peter Laslett, *The World We Have Lost* (New York, 1965), 1-21 and Frances Collier, *The Family Economy of the Working Classes in the Cotton Industry, 1784-1833* (Manchester, 1965). For a necessary corrective to Smelser see also M. M. Edwards and R. Lloyd-Jones, "N. J. Smelser and the Cotton Factory Family: A Reassessment," in N. B. Harte and K. G. Ponting, ed., *Textile History and Economic History: Essays in Honour of Miss Julia de Lacy Mann* (Manchester, 1973), 304-319.

6. Talcott Parsons and R. F. Bales, *Family Socialization and Process* (Glencoe, Illinois, 1955); W. F. Ogburn and N. B. Nimkoff, *Technology and the Changing Family* (Boston, 1955); Fred Weinstein and Gerald M. Platt, *The Wish to be Free: Society, Psyche and Value Change* (Berkeley, 1971); Normal W. Bell and Ezra J. Vogel, "Introductory Essays: Toward a Framework for Functional Analysis of Family Behavior," in Norman W. Bell and Ezra J. Vogel, eds., *The Family* (Glencoe, Illinois, 1960), 1-36; Talcott Parsons, "The Social Structure of the Family," in R. N. Anshen, ed., *The Family: its Function and Destiny* (New York, 1949), 173-201.

7. Talcott Parsons and R. F. Bales, *Family, Socialization and Interaction Process*, 3-9.

8. The functionalist perspective also dominates the social history of education. See Bernard Bailyn, *Education in the Forming of American Society* (New York, 1960); Phyllis Vine,

"Parents and Students: The Social Function of Eighteenth-Century Higher Education," *History of Education Quarterly* (forthcoming); and Frank Musgrove, *The Family, Education and Society* (London, 1966).

9. John Demos, *A Little Commonwealth: Family Life in Plymouth Colony* (New York, 1970), 183.

10. Lawrence Stone, "The Rise of the Nuclear Family in Early Modern England: The Patriarchal Stage," in Charles Rosenberg, ed., *The Family in History* (Philadelphia, 1975), 13.

11. E. P. Thompson, *The Making of the English Working Class* (New York, 1963), 416.

12. Arlene Skolnick, "The Family Revisited: Themes in Recent Social Science Research," *Journal of Interdisciplinary History*, V, 4 (1975), 703-719.

13. Rosabeth Moss Kanter, *Work and Family*, 23.

14. Barbara Laslett, "The Family as a Public and Private Institution: An Historical Perspective," *Journal of Marriage and the Family*, XXIV, 3 (August, 1973), 480-494; Clifford E. Clark, Jr., Domestic Architecture as an Index to Social History: The Romantic Revival and the Cult of Domesticity in America, 1840-1870," *Journal of Interdisciplinary History*, VII, 1 (1976), 33-56.

15. A similar argument has also been used for the London working-class between 1870 and 1900. See Gareth Stedman Jones, "Working-Class Culture and Working-Class Politics in London, 1870-1900: Notes on the Remaking of a Working Class," *Journal of Social History*, VII, 4 (1974), 460-508. One can also argue that increasing emphasis on scientific management in the home paralleled such developments in the world of work. On the growth of efficiency movement among housewives, consult Emma Seifrit Weigley, "It Might Have Been Euthenics: The Lake Placid Conferences and the Home Economics Movement," *American Quarterly*, 26 (1974), 79-96; David Handlin, "Efficiency and the American Home," *Architectural Association Quarterly*, 5 (1973), 50-54.

16. Phillipe Aries, *Centuries of Childhood* (New York, 1960); Bernard Wishy, *The Child and the Republic* (Philadelphia, 1968).

17. Barbara Welter, "The Cult of True Womanhood: 1820-1860," *American Quarterly*, XVIII (Summer, 1966), 151-174; Gerda Lerner, "The Lady and the Mill Girl: Changes in the Status of Women in the Age of Jackson," *Midcontinent American Studies Journal*, 10 (1969), 5-15; Phillida Bunkle, "Sentimental Womanhood and Domestic Education, 1830-1870," *History of Education Quarterly*, 14 (1974), 13-20.

18. Joan W. Scott and Louise Tilly, "Women's Work and the Family in Nineteenth Century Europe," *Comparative Studies in Society and History* (1975), 36-64; Alice Kessler Harris, "Women, Work and the Social Order," in Berenice A. Carroll, ed., *Liberating Women's History: Theoretical and Critical Essays* (Urbana, 1976), 330-344; Thomas Dublin, "Women, Work, and Protest in the Early Lowell Mills: "The Oppressing Hand of Avarice Would Enslave Us," *Labor History*, 16, 1 (1976), 99-116.

19. Gareth Stedman Jones, "Working-Class Culture," 484-485.

20. *Ibid.*

21. Neil Smelser, *Social Change and the Industrial Revolution.*

22. Patricia Branca, "A New Perspective on Women's Work: A Comparative Typology," *Journal of Social History*, 9, 2 (Winter, 1975), 126. Louise Tilly argues that autonomy in work declined and the pace of home production quickened toward the end of the nineteenth century. Personal Communication from Louise Tilly, September 11, 1976. See also Peter N. Stearns, *The Lives of Labour* (London, 1975), 195 and Heidi Hartmann, "Capitalism, Patriarchy and Job Segregation by Sex," *Signs*, 1, 3 (1976), 159-167

23. John Modell, "The Fruits of Their Toil: The Family Economy of the American

Workingmen in the Late Nineteenth Century," in Tamara K. Hareven and Maris A. Vinovskis, eds., *Demographic Processes and Family Organization in Nineteenth Century American Society* (forthcoming).

24. John Modell and Tamara K. Hareven, "Urbanization and the Malleable Household: An Examination of Boarding and Lodging in American Families," *Journal of Marriage and the Family*, 35 (1973), 467-479.

25. Elizabeth H. Pleck, "A Mother's Wages: A Comparison of Income-Earning Among Urban Black and Italian Married Women, 1896-1911," *Signs* (forthcoming, Winter, 1977).

26. For a comparison of these roles among paid domestics and working-class housewives, see Leonore Davidoff, "Mastered for Life: Servant and Wife in Victorian and Edwardian England," *Journal of Social History*, 7, 4 (1974), 406-428.

27. Cynthia B. Lloyd, ed., *Sex, Discrimination and the Division of Labor* (New York, 1975); Marc Nerlove, "Towards a New Theory of Population and Economic Growth," in Theodore W. Schultz, ed., *Economics of the Family: Marriage, Children and Human Capital* (Chicago, 1970), 527-545; Gary Becker, "A Theory of the Allocation of Time," *Economic Journal*, 75 (1965), 493-517. An intelligent guide to this and other new literature on nonmarket labor is Nona Glazer-Malbin's review essay on "Housework," *Signs*, 1, 4 (1976), 905-922.

28. Lisa Vogel, "The Earthly Family," *Radical America*, VII, 4-5 (1975), 9-50; Ira Gerstein, "Domestic Work and Capitalism," *Ibid.*, 101-120; Eli Zaretsky, "Capitalism, the Family and Personal Life," *Socialist Revolution*, III 3, 2-3 (1975), 69-126; Dorothy Smith, "Women, the Family and Corporate Capitalism," *Berkeley Journal of Sociology*, (1976), 55-90; Juliet Mitchell, "Women: The Longest Revolution," *New Left Review*, 40 (December, 1966), 11-37; Margaret Benston, "The Political Economy of Women's Liberation," *Monthly Review*, XXI, 4 (1969), 13-27; Mariarosa Dalla Costa, "Women and the Subversion of Community," *Radical America*, 6 (1972), 67-102; Wally Secombe, "The Housewife and Her Labour Under Capitalism," *New Left Review*, 83 (1974), 3-24.

29. Frederick Engels, *The Origin of the Family, Private Property and the State* (Moscow, 1968), 73.

30. Susan J. Kleinberg, "Technology and Women's Work: The Lives of Working-Class Women in Pittsburgh, 1870-1900," *Labor History*, XVII, 1 (1976), 58-72; Margaret F. Byington, *Homestead: The Household of a Mill Town* (New York, 1910; Pittsburgh, 1974).

31. Joan Scott and Louise Tilly, "Women's Work," 48; Olwen Hufton, "Women in Revolution, 1789-1796," *Past and Present*, 53 (1971), 91-93; Michael Anderson, *Family Structure in Nineteenth Century Lancashire* (Cambridge, England, 1971), 77; Laura Oren, "The Welfare of Women in Laboring Families: England, 1860-1950," *Feminist Studies*, 1 (1972), 107-125; Peter Stearns, "Working Class Women in Britain, 1890-1914," in Martha Vicinus, ed., *Suffer and Be Still: Women in the Victorian Age* (Bloomington, 1972), 116.

32. Joann Vanek, "Time Spent in Housework," *Scientific American* (November, 1974), 116-120; Ruth Schwartz Cowan, "The Industrial Revolution in the Home: Household Technology and Social Change in the United States," *Technology and Culture*, 17 (1976), 1-26.

33. Patricia Branca, "Image and Reality: The Myth of the Idle Victorian Woman," in Mary Hartman and Lois W. Banner, eds. *Clio's Consciousness Raised: New Perspectives on the History of Women* (New York, 1974), 179-191.

34. Charles Tilly, "Population and Pedagogy in France," *History of Education Quarterly* (Summer, 1973), 113-128; David Stern, Sandra Smith and Fred Doolittle, "How Children Used to Work," *Law and Contemporary Problems*, LXXXIX, 3 (Summer, 1975), 93-117; Starns, *Lives of Labour*, 279.

35. Janet Salaff, "Working Daughters in the Hong Kong Chinese Family: Female Filial Piety or a Transformation in the Family Power Structure," *Journal of Social History*, IX, 4

(1976), 439-465; Tamara K. Hareven, "Family Time and Industrial Time: Family and Work in a Planned Corporation Town, 1900-1924," *Journal of Urban History*, I, 3 (1975), 365-389; U. S Senate, *Report on Conditions of Woman and Child Wage-Earners in the United States*, 1, as quoted in Salaff, "Working Daughters in the Hong Kong Chinese Family," 439-465.

36. Peter Laslett, "Clayworth and Cogenhoe," in H. E. Bell and R. L. Ollard, eds., *Historical Essays*, 1600-1750 (London, 1963), 77; Lawrence Stone, "Social Mobility in England," *Past and Present*, 38 (1966), 29-30; R. S. Schofield, "Age-Specific Mobility in an Eighteenth Century Rural England Parish," *Annales de Demographic Historique* (1970), 261; Douglas Lamar Jones, "The Strolling Poor: Transiency in Eighteenth Century Massachusetts," *Journal of Social History* (1975), 28-54. Edward Shorter argues that the rate of geographic mobility in pre-industrial France was less than in England. Edward Shorter, *The Making of the Modern Family* (New York, 1976), 27.

37. For illustrative materials, see Alan Macfarlane, *The Family Life of Ralph Josselin, A Seventeenth Century Clergyman: An Essay in Historical Anthropology* (Cambridge, 1970), 205-210 and Douglas Lamar Jones, "Female Vagabonds in Eighteenth-Century Massachusetts," unpublished paper presented at the George Washington University Conference on Women and the American Revolution, July, 1975. Lutz Berkner argues that Austrian peasants hired laborers only when their children were too young to till the land. Lutz K. Berkner, "The Stem Family and the developmental cycle of the peasant household: an eighteenth century Austrian example," *American Historical Review*, 77 (1972), 98-118.

38. Michael Anderson, *Family Structure in Nineteenth Century Lancashire*, 87.

39. Meyer F. Nimkoff, *Marriage and the Family* (Cambridge, 1947), 91-92.

40. In a refutation of this argument, Gareth Stedman Jones points out that craftsmen, living in cramped rooms, preferred to spend their waking hours in the workshop. Stedman Jones, "Working-Class Culture," 485.

41. Anderson, *Family Structure*, Table 27, 85.

42. Philip Greven, *Four Generations: Population, Land, and Family in Colonial, Andover, Massachusetts* (Ithaca, New York, 1970), but see also Maris Vinovskis, "The Field of Early American Family History: A Methodological Critique," in *The Family in Historical Perspective: An International Newsletter*, 7 (1974), 1-8; Maris Vinovskis, "American Historical Demography: A Review Essay," *Historical Methods Newsletter*, 14 (September, 1971), 141-148. For the impact of declining availability of land on the Dutch family, see William Peterson, "The demographic transition in the Netherlands," *American Sociological Review*, 25 (1960), 334-347.

43. Rudolf Braun makes a similar argument for European society. He points out that the development of cottage industry – young sons and daughters establishing separate residences – led to the eventual dissolution of the unity of work and family among Swiss peasants. Rudolf Braun, "The Impact of Cottage Industry on an Agricultural Population," in David S. Landes, ed., *The Rise of Capitalism* (New York, 1966), 53-64.

44. Neil Smelser, *Social Change and the Industrial Revolution*, 189. Actually in Preston factories for 1816, parents were the employers of only 10% of the child laborers. See M. M. Edwards and R. Lloyd-Jones, "N. J. Smelser and the Cotton Factory Family," 304-319.

45. William M. Reedy, "Family and Factory: French Linen Weavers in the Belle Èpoque," *Journal of Social History*, VIII, 2 (1975), 102-112.

46. Tamara K. Hareven, "The Laborers of Manchester, New Hampshire, 1912-1922: The Role of Family and Ethnicity in Adjustment to Industrial Life," *Labor History*, XIV, 2 (1975), 249-265; Tamara K. Hareven, "The Dynamics of Kin in Industrial Communities: The Historical Perspective," forthcoming, *American Journal of Sociology* (Winter, 1976).

47. Michael Hanagan, "Artisans and Industrial Workers: Strikes in Three French Towns, 1870-1914," unpublished Ph.D. dissertation, University of Michigan, 1976; Louise A. Tilly,

"Occupational Structure and Demographic Change in Roubaix and Anzin," unpublished paper presented at the Social Science History Conference, October, 1976.

48. Daniel Nelson argues that one of the consequences of new developments in scientific management around the turn of the century was the declining family basis of work organization. Daniel Nelson, *Managers and Workers: Origins of the New Factory System in the United States, 1880-1920* (Madison, 1975); Rosabeth Moss Kanter, *Work and Family*, 13; Margaret F. Byington, "The Family in a typical mill town," *American Journal of Sociology*, 4 (March, 1909), 648-659.

49. Christopher Lasch, "The Family and History," 4.

50. My outline of these issues follows closely the interpretive perspectives in three works by social scientists. They include Rosabeth Moss Kanter, *Work and Family;* Rhona and Robert Rapaport, "Work and Family in Modern Society," *American Sociological Review*, 20 (1965), 381-394 and Joseph H. Pleck, "The Work-Family Role System," *Social Problems*, forthcoming.

51. Alvin Gouldner, "The Norm of Reciprocity: A Preliminary Statement," *American Sociological Review*, 25 (1960), 162-178.

52. For some suggestions on applying exchange theory to migration, see Edwards and Lloyd-Jones, "N. J. Smelser and the Cotton Factory Family," 218-219.

53. Michael B. Katz, "Essay Review," *Journal of Social History*, VII, 1, (1973), 86-92.

54. Scott and Tilly, "Women's Work," 4; Miriam Cohen, "Italian-American Women in New York City, 1900-1950: Work and School," in Milton Cantor, ed., *Class, Sex and the Woman Worker* (forthcoming, Westport, Connecticut, 1977); Anderson, *Family Structure;* Hareven, "Family Time and Industrial Time," Virginia Yans-McLaughlin, "Patterns of Work and Family Organization: Buffalo's Italians," in Theodore K. Rabb and Robert I. Rotberg, eds., *The Family in History: Interdisciplinary Essays* (New York, 1971), 111-126; Virginia Yans-McLaughlin. "A Flexible Tradition: South Italian Immigrants Confront a New Work Experience," *Journal of Social History*, VII, 4 (1974), 429-445; Carol Groneman, "Working-Class Immigrant Women in Mid-Nineteenth Century New York: The Irish Woman's Experience," unpublished paper delivered at the annual meeting of the American Studies Association, November, 1975; Elizabeth H. Pleck, "The Two-Parent Household: Black Family Structure in Late-Nineteenth Century Boston," *Journal of Social History*, VI, 2 (1972), 3-36; Barbara Klaczynska, "Why Women Work: A Comparison of Various Groups – Philadelphia, 1910-1930," *Labor History*, XVII, 1 (1976), 73-87; Judith R. Walkowitz and Daniel J. Walkowitz, "We are Not Beasts of the Field: Prostitution and the Poor in Plymouth and Southampton under the Contagious Diseases Acts," in Mary Hartmann and Lois W. Banner, ed., *Clio's Consciousness Raised: New Perspectives on the History of Women* (New York, 1974), 119-126.

55. According to Scott and Tilly, these changes include "the location of job opportunities, increased exposure to and adherence to bourgeois standards as chances for mobility into the bourgeoisie increased, ethnic variations in work patterns and family organization and different rates of development in different regions and different countries." Scott and Tilly, "Women's Work," 69.

56. Shorter, *Modern Family*, 79-119; Edward Shorter, "Illegitimacy, sexual revolution, and social change in modern Europe," *Journal of Interdisciplinary History*, 2 (1971), 237-273; Edward Shorter, "Sexual change and illegitimacy: The European experience," in Robert Bezucha, ed., *Modern European Social History* (Lexington, Massachusetts, 1972), 231-269; Robert P. Neuman, "Industrialization and sexual behavior: some aspects of working class life in Imperial Germany," in *Ibid.*, 270-298; John Knodel, "Law, marriage and illegitimacy in nineteenth century Germany," *Population Studies*, 20 (1967), 279-294. Louise Tilly, Joan Scott and Miriam Cohen argue that despite increasing illegitimacy, the sexual attitudes of young working women were far from liberated. When young men were removed from familial controls and placed in uncertain circumstances, they no longer felt compelled to marry pregnant girlfriends. Louise Tilly, Joan Scott, and Miriam Cohen, "Women's Work and European Fertility Patterns," *Journal of Interdisciplinary History*, VI, 8 (1976), 447-476.

57. Leslie Woodcock Tentler, "Women and Work: Industrial Employment and Sex Roles, 1900-1929," unpublished Ph.D. dissertation, University of Michigan, 1975, chapter I.

58. *Ibid.* Scott and Tilly, "Women's Work," 56; U. S. Department of Labor, Women's Bureau, *The Share of Wage-Earning Women in Family Support, Bulletin No. 40* (Washington, D.C., 1923), 137-140.

59. Scott and Tilly, "Women's Work," 54.

60. These relationships have been explored in detail only for one category of workers, domestic servants. The servants' age at marriage, choice of marital partners, even style of dress was altered by the experience of work. See Theresa McBride, "Social Mobility for the Lower Class: Domestic Servants in France," *Journal of Social History*, VIII, 1 (1974), 62-78.

61. For an excellent survey of the rise of professionalism within American society, consult Robert H. Wiebe, *The Search for Order, 1877-1920* (New York, 1967), 111-132 along with William R. Johnson, "Education and Professional Life Styles: Law and Medicine in the Nineteenth Century," *History of Education Quarterly* (1974), 188-208.

62. Harold Wilensky, "Work, careers and social integration," *International Social Science Journal*, 12 (1960), 54-560; James D. Thompson, Robert W. Avery and Richard Carlson, *Occupations, Personnel and Careers* (Pittsburgh, 1962); Wilbert E. Moore, *Conduct of the Corporation* (New York, 1962); Curt Tausky and Robert Dubin, "Career Anchorage: Managerial Mobility Aspirations," *American Sociological Review*, 20 (1965), 725-735.

63. Hanna Papenek, "Men, Women and Work: Reflections on the Two-Person Career," *American Journal of Sociology*, 78 (1973), 852-872.

64. For some suggestive evidence about the emergence of the female career, see Peter Filene, *Himherself: Sex Roles in Modern America* (New York, 1974), 121-168; Janis Calvo, "Quaker Women Ministers in Nineteenth Century America," *Quaker History*, 62 (1974), 75-92.

65. For these last three arguments, see J. A. Banks, *Prosperity and Parenthood: A Study of Family Planning Among the Victorian Middle Classes* (London, 1954); J. A. and Olive Banks, *Feminism and Family Planning in Victorian England* (New York, 1964); Daniel Scott Smith, "Family Limitation, Sexual Control and Domestic Feminism in Victorian America," in Mary Hartman and Lois W. Banner, eds., *Clio's Consciousness Raised: New Perspectives on the History of Women* (New York, 1974), 119-126; Linda Gordon, "Voluntary Motherhood: The Beginnings of the Feminist Birth Control Ideas in the United States," in *Ibid.*, pp 54-72.

66. Theresa McBride, "Social Mobility for the Lower Classes," 62-78.

67. Michael R. Haines, *Fertility and Occupation: Coal Mining Populations in the Nineteenth and Early Twentieth Centuries in Europe and America* (Princeton, 1975). Additional studies which relate specific occupations to fertility include Peter N. Stearns, "Adaptation to Industrialization: German Workers and a Test Case," *Central European History*, III, 4 (1970), 303-331; Peter N. Stearns, "The Lives of Labour, 271-272; John W. Innes, *Class Fertility Trends in England and Wales, 1876-1934* (Princeton, 1938); John Knodel, *The Fertility Decline in Germany, 1871-1939* (Princeton, 1974). I am indebted to Louise Tilly for calling these studies to my attention. Modern sociological reports on British workers indicate that even among men at the same occupational level, there were major differences in family size. Miners and truck drivers had large families, while garment workers and fishermen had small ones. These differences were attributed to the husband's work – his physical separation from his wife, insecurity in employment, and the extent of community among fellow workers. See Geoffrey Hawthorn and Michael Paddon, "Work, Family and Fertility," *Human Relations*, XXIV, 61 (1971), 611-628.

68. Jones, "Working-Class Culture," 471-500.

69. For a general survey of the changing pace of work in nineteenth century Europe, see Stearns, *Lives of Labour*, 192-228.

70. Keith Thomas, "Work and Leisure in Pre-Industrial Societies," Past and Present, 29 (1962), 50-62; E. P. Thompson, "Time, Work-Discipline and Industrial Capitalism," *Past and Present*, 28 (1967), 56-97; Alasdair Clayre, *Work and Play: Ideas and Experience of Work and Leisure* (New York, 1976); Herbert G. Gutman, "Work, Culture and Society in Industrializing America, 1815-1918," *American Historical Review*, LXXVIII, 2 (June, 1973), 581-588; Sidney Pollard, "Factory Discipline in the Industrial Revolution," *Economic History Review*, 16 (1968), 254-271; Sebastian de Grazia, *Of Time, Work and Leisure* (Garden City, New York, 1964). Michael Marrus also suggests that leisure activities were purged from the workplace in the nineteenth century because employers, speeding up the pace of work, became less tolerant of drunken workers. Michael P. Marrus, "Social Drinking in the Belle Époque," *Journal of Social History*, VII, 2 (1974), 115-141. See also Bruce Laurie, "Nothing on Impulse:" Life Styles of Philadelphia Artisans, 1820-1850," *Labor History*, XV, 3 (1974), 327-366 and Paul Faler, "Cultural Aspects of the Industrial Revolution: Lynn, Massachusetts Shoemakers and Industrial Morality, 1826-1860," *Labor History*, XV, 3 (1974), 367-394.

71. Douglas A. Reid, "The Decline of Saint Monday, 1766-1876," *Past and Present*, 71 (1976), 76-101.

72. Margaret Hewitt, *Wives and Mothers in Victorian Industry* (London, 1958), 62-84; see also Ivy Pinchbeck, *Women Workers in the Industrial Revolution, 1750-1850* (London, 1930), 280.

73. Samuel Bowles and Herbert Gintis, *Schooling in Capitalist America* (New York, 1976); Leonore Davidoff, "Mastered for Life," 406-428.

74. Laurence A. Glasco, "The Life Cycle and Household Structure of American Ethnic Groups: Irish, Germans and Native-Born Whites in Buffalo, New York, 1855," *Journal of Urban History*, 1 (1975), 339-364; John Modell, Frank F. Furstenberg, Jr., Douglas Strong, "The Timing of Marriage in the Transition to Adulthood: Continuity and Change, 1860-1975," forthcoming, *American Journal of Sociology* (1976); John and Virginia Demos, "Adolescence in Historical Perspective," *Journal of Marriage and the Family*, 81 (1969), 632-638; Frank Musgrove, *Youth and the Social Order* (Bloomington, 1965); John Modell, Frank F. Furstenberg, Jr., and Theodore Hershberg, "Social Change and Life Course Development in Historical Perspective," forthcoming, *Journal of Family History*; Paul C. Glick and Robert Parke, Jr., "New Approaches in Studying the Life Cycle of the Family," *Demography*, 2 (1965), 187-202; Joseph F. Kett, "Adolescence and Youth in Nineteenth Century America," *Journal of Interdisciplinary History*, II (1971), 283-298.

THE LIFE CYCLES AND HOUSEHOLD STRUCTURE OF AMERICAN ETHNIC GROUPS

Irish, Germans, and Native-born Whites in Buffalo, New York, 1855

LAURENCE A. GLASCO
University of Pittsburgh

Despite increased interest in the ethnic dimension of American history, we still know relatively little about the social and economic characteristics of the immigrants themselves, especially their family patterns. And most of what we do know centers primarily around those who were both adult and male.[1] An understanding of ethnic groups—or of any population for that matter—should be based on all the component age and sex groupings: women as well as men; children and adolescents as well as adults.

Life-cycle analysis offers a useful method for doing this. The systematic age-related analysis of a population enables us to observe and compare the social characteristics of all its members as they pass through the age stations of childhood, adolescence, adulthood, and old age.[2]

The technique has other advantages as well. A division of the life cycle into separate stages can deepen our understanding of the two major themes of ethnic study: work and acculturation. If we relate stages of the life cycle to economic behavior and household organization, we can delineate patterns of "economic" and household cycles. Most of what we know in this area is based on the experiences of adult males. It is their occupation and income which is investigated in studies of ethnic stratification; it is they who are pictured as agents of change or acculturation, and the women as bastions of conservatism. In the present case, we have used life-cycle analysis to examine these issues, and have compared the age-related household and work experiences of men and women for each of three ethnic groups–Irish, Germans, and native-born whites–in a mid-nineteenth-century American city. The procedure helps to clarify how age and sex were related to the processes of ethnic stratification and acculturation.

Few studies have employed the method of life-cycle analysis because the sources are difficult to locate and utilize. The present study, using Buffalo, New York as an example, takes the city's three major ethnic groups at one point in time, 1855, and describes their changing life situations in relation to age. It was possible to do this because the New York State manuscript census of 1855 provides not only the usual information on each person's age, sex, race, birthplace, and occupation, but also his or her marital condition and relationship to the head of the household. This material, transcribed and machine encoded for the city's entire population, enabled us to compare ethnic differences in the timed sequence by which both men and women passed through the various stages of childhood, adolescence, marriage, childbearing, and retirement, as well as corresponding household statuses of husband, wife, child, boarder, servant, and relative. Finally, it enabled us to trace and describe the age-related patterns of work and property ownership.

Such a description of the life cycle at one point in time cannot tell us whether any particular age cohort had previously followed, or in the future would follow, such patterns. That is, young children would not necessarily follow the example of their older brothers in regard to the timing or the sequence in which they left home, married, and established their own households. In fact, given the rapidly modernizing society of mid-nineteenth-century America, there is every chance that they would not. The complete answer to that question can be found only in cohort analysis, tracing the life cycles of specific age groups back in time and forward into the future. The form of analysis employed here, however, does tell us the age and age-related life patterns prevailing in a given period and provides a baseline from which to measure future deviations.

By the mid-nineteenth century, nationality virtually defined Buffalo's population and social structure. Like many northern cities at that time, Buffalo had a large, rapidly growing immigrant population jostling alongside a native-born, in-migrant population drawn mainly from New England and the eastern part of New York State. Between 1845 and 1855 the city's population more than doubled, to over 70,000 residents, about one-fourth of whom were native-born, one-fifth Irish and forty percent German, the latter coming mainly from Bavaria and other southern principalities.

These residents had been attracted by the city's booming economy, based on the commerce of the Erie Canal and a rapidly growing manufacturing sector, especially of iron. Occupations tended to divide along ethnic lines, with Irish men holding many of the unskilled jobs along the docks, German men dominating the construction crafts, and native-born men controlling the finances, professions, and trade of the city.[3]

Ethnic differences of occupation and income were reflected in the life experiences of all members of society. As we will see, they extended through the entire life span, and included both the household and work cycles. Finally, as revealed by an examination of the household and work cycles, first of the men and then of the women, ethnic differences were as pronounced among young women as they were among adult men.

NATIVE-BORN MEN

The life cycle of native-born men reveals a rather prolonged childhood and adolescence. They did not begin to leave home until late adolescence, around age 19, and it was not until age

29 that virtually all had left the shelter of their parents' home. Many who left home, particularly if they were new to the city, became boarders. The practice of boarding, which has been associated generally with immigrants, involved one-third of all native-born men between the ages of 19 and 29, and over half of those present less than one year in the city. Most of these boarders—about four-fifths—were single, and less than one-half had a permanent occupation listed by the census. The longer they remained in the city, the less likely they were to board out. After residing in the city for five years, only about one-third of those in their early or late twenties and a fifth of those in their early thirties boarded out; among eight-year residents this was true of only 8% to 13% (Figure 1).

The typical native-born boarder lived with a family, almost always a native-born family, along with perhaps one or two other boarders who were also native-born. He was, in short, only semi-independent since in this situation his comings and

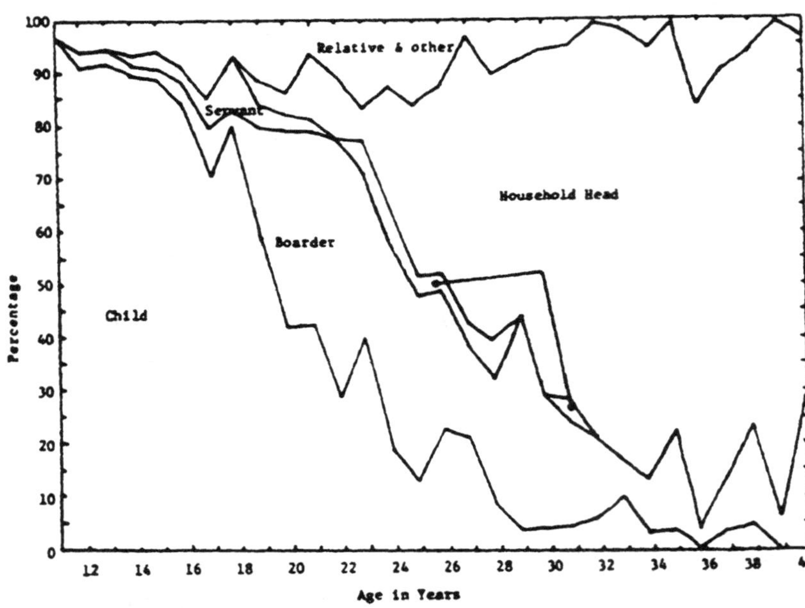

Figure 1: NATIVE-BORN MALES: HOUSEHOLD STATUS BY AGE

goings were subject to supervision by the family with which he lived. The large, impersonal boarding house which characterized seaport towns housed less than half of the city's boarders. For the majority of young boarders, this practice was structured to provide a moderate amount of adult supervision, in a family setting, and to insulate the young men from intimate, unsupervised contact with the wider world.[4]

Native-born men who had been in the city a few years seldom became boarders. Instead, they got married as soon as they left home and quickly established their own household. For this reason there was great variation in the average age at which native-born men got married. Marriage began as early as age 20 for about 10% of native-born men and did not include half of any age group until age 26.[5] Thereafter, the process speeded up and by age 28 three-fourths of that age group were married. Those who married early tended to delay the establishment of a separate household. Less than half the married men under age 24 had their own household. From age 25 on, however, three-fourths or more of married native-born men had their own household.

Once established, the native-born household was quite resistant to structural change. Half of the households consisted of husband and wife (with or without children); a fourth had one or more relatives; and a fifth had one or more boarders and roomers.[6] With only two exceptions, this distribution remained relatively unchanged as the household head grew older. When the household head was in his twenties he was slightly more likely to take in boarders: about a third took in boarders at that age, compared to a fourth of those in their thirties, forties, and fifties. When the household head reached old age, he was less likely to take boarders into his household, and more likely to take in relatives; about a fourth of household heads in their sixties took in boarders, compared to only 14% of those in their seventies. For the same age groups the proportion taking in relatives increased from 19% to 32%. Over the large middle range of age, however—the thirties, forties, fifties, and sixties—the native-born household was remarkably stable in form, with consistently close to half being nuclear, a fifth being extended, and a fourth being augmented.[7]

Although the native-born household head did not significantly alter the composition of his household with advancing age, he did change his status within that household by purchasing his own home. Almost a fourth of native-born family heads in their twenties owned real property. This proportion increased with age, and included two-fifths of those in their thirties, half of those in their forties and fifties, and three-fifths of those over sixty years of age.

Aiding him in the acquisition of his home was a clear occupational advantage. Native-born men dominated the white-collar, professional, and entrepreneurial positions in the city, and made up at least their share of the painters and mechanics. Moreover, they enjoyed these advantages over the entire course of their working years. There were not substantial age-related differences in their occupational chances. In their twenties, thirties, or forties, native-born men were likely to be clerks; when older, in their fifties and sixties, they tended to be entrepreneurs. Regardless of age, almost all native-born men were able to avoid the low-paying, unskilled position of day laborer. Moreover, the work career of native-born men extended over forty years. They began work fairly early, about age 16; by age 19 one-fourth were employed and by age 24 over half. As they aged, an increasing proportion of native-born men retired from the work force. Retirement began in their early sixties, when the percentage of men listed with an occupation decreased from 58% of those in their late fifties to 48% of those in their early sixties. For men in their late sixties the figure dropped to 40% and decreased still further among those in their seventies.

As they retired from the labor force, an increasing proportion ceased to head their own household. About one-third of native-born men over the age of sixty were living outside their own household, compared to about a tenth of those in their forties and fifties. Of those who did not maintain their own household, only a fifth went to live among possible strangers as a roomer or boarder. The great majority went to live with relatives. In over half of the cases, they lived with one of their children, while about 15% lived with an in-law.

This, then, briefly summarizes the age-related life experiences of native-born white men in a mid-nineteenth-century American city. Their household cycle was typically characterized by a prolonged childhood and adolescence, followed by a brief, relatively sheltered boarding experience, designed especially for those who were single, young, and new to the city. They generally married in their mid to late twenties and began a family. During middle age their household consisted of a wife, two or three children and, for about half, either a relative or boarder, plus a servant. Increasing age brought its economic satisfactions. An examination of the economic cycle shows that they dominated the white-collar, professional, and entrepreneurial occupations, as well as certain of the skilled trades—especially metal working—and avoided the unskilled, day-laboring positions. This preferential occupational standing was enjoyed throughout the native-born man's occupational career. It paid off over the years. By the time they were in their sixties, about two-thirds continued to head their own household, and almost all of those who did so owned their own home. Most of the rest went to live with one of their children, such that only a few were left to live alone or to board out among strangers. All in all, the patterns suggest a fairly stable life experience.

IRISH MEN

To a remarkable degree the household cycle of Irish men resembled that of the native-born.[8] Like their native-born counterparts, Irish men began leaving home relatively late in adolescence, around age 19, although they completed the leaving process somewhat earlier, around age 25. As with the native-born, this amounted to just under a third of Irish men aged 19 to 29 and 40% of those aged 20 to 24 became boarders (Figure 2). Nearly all of these boarders were single and most

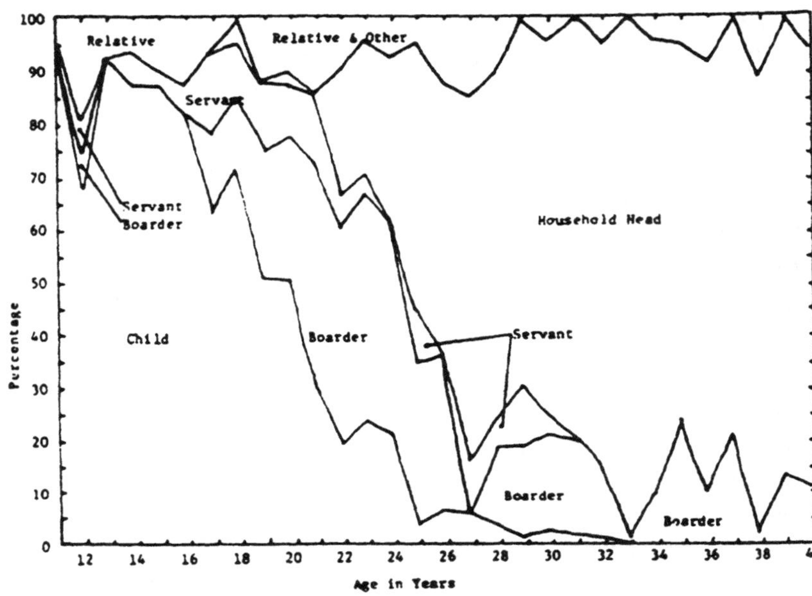

Figure 2: IRISH MALES: HOUSEHOLD STATUS BY AGE

were new to the city as well. Of Irish men aged 20 to 24 years, 70% of those present for less than one year were boarders, compared to a third among those present five years, and just over a tenth of those present eight years. Among those in their late twenties the corresponding decline was from 58% to between 7% and 12%. Again, as with the native-born most Irish boarders lived with families of their own ethnic background, with perhaps one other boarder.

Irish men passed from a dependent to an independent status somewhat more quickly than native-born men. First, the process of leaving home was more accelerated, being virtually completed by age 25, compared to age 29 for the native-born. Second, the Irish boarding experience was somewhat shorter. Impressions to the contrary of boarding being primarily an immigrant phenomenon, boarding for Irish males was virtually over by the age of 27, whereas there were still a moderate number of native-born boarders in their early thirties.

The Irish marriage experience was similar too, but somewhat more compressed than that of native-born men. It began two years later (age 22) and was completed at about the same age—28 or 29. Irish married men achieved independence somewhat earlier, however, in that there was not a notable delay between marriage and the establishment of a separate household. Whereas only half the native-born men through age 23 headed their own household, two-thirds or more of Irish married men from age 22 (when they began marrying in substantial numbers) headed their own households.

In contrast to the native-born household, the Irish household was more likely to be nuclear in composition. Only 15% took in relatives and 13% took in roomers and boarders, compared to 25% and 20% respectively, for the native-born. The practice of taking in boarders did not vary with the age of the household head, and in this regard, too, the Irish pattern resembled the native-born.

The similarities between native-born and Irish break down in regard to the presence of relatives, however. The likelihood of an Irish household including relatives was clearly articulated to the life cycle. The proportion of Irish households containing extended kin declined from about 20% of those in their twenties to only about 10% of those in their forties; thereafter the trend reversed, such that older household heads were more likely to have relatives—about 15% of those in their sixties and 30% of those in their seventies. The causes of this inverted, or U-shaped, pattern are not clear. Possibly it is related to particular Irish migration patterns, in which young unmarried brothers and sisters came to America and set up a sibling household when young, which was followed by marriage in middle age and the establishment of independent households. This possibility, however, has not been tested.

The difference in the experience of Irish and native-born was also reflected in property ownership. Native-born household heads, as they grew older, were increasingly successful in buying their own home. This was not true for Irish men. Those owning real estate increased from 16% of those in their twenties to 26%

of those in their thirties. The trend then stabilized, and ownership actually decreased among those over sixty years of age.

The reason for such a relatively low proportion of Irish home owners was their unfavorable occupational structure. Irish men dominated no specific occupation, but were overrepresented among teamsters, sailors, ship carpenters, and especially among unskilled day laborers. As a result, two-thirds of Irish family heads either were unskilled or—especially older men—had no occupation listed. Examination of this aspect of the economic cycle, furthermore, reveals that this maldistribution of occupational skills did not significantly vary with age; at no point in their working lives did a majority of Irish men have a chance for stable, well-paying work. The impact of this occupational pattern can be gauged by the fact that semi-skilled and skilled Irish workers were as successful as their native-born counterparts in acquiring property. This was not true for unskilled Irish laborers, suggesting the operation of cultural values as well in the matter of property acquisition.

To maintain even this position, many Irish men had to work past what was a normal retirement age for native-born men. Irish boys began working at about age 17, one year later than native-born boys. One fourth were employed by the age 19, and the proportion rose to one half by the time they reached age 22. They worked substantially longer, however. By the early seventies, when only 14% of native-born men had a listed occupation, this was the case of one third of Irish men.

In old age, the household status of Irish men came once again to resemble that of native-born men. Most were able to maintain their position as household heads. Indeed, the proportion who did so (three-fourths) exceeded that for native-born household heads (two-thirds). Of those who did not remain household heads, only about a fifth boarded out, and an insignificant number went to live with collateral kin. Almost half went to live with a child, and a third went to live with an in-law. In this way, their pattern resembled that of the native-born.

This, then, summarizes the age-related life experiences of Irish men. The greatest differences emerged in their economic cycle, specifically in the type of jobs held and the amount of property acquired over a lifetime. In certain respects there were striking, unexpected parallels in regard to their household cycles. They left home at about the same age, became boarders at about the same age and in about the same proportions, and in a similarly structured situation that provided adult supervision in a family setting and reduced contact with peers outside the ethnic group. Their households differed somewhat in composition, since fewer Irish families took in boarders or relatives. Yet the differences seem more one of degree than of kind.

There were similarities in the aging process as well. About the same proportion of Irish and native-born men headed their own households in old age, although a greater proportion of native-born men owned the dwelling in which they lived. Finally, the experience of those who left their households was similar: few of either group had to live among possible strangers in a boarding situation; a majority of both went to live with their children or, less frequently, with their in-laws.

GERMAN MEN

At first glance, the life cycle of German men differed from that of native-born and Irish men. German men began leaving home at a substantially earlier age—16 years, compared to 19 years for the other two groups. Moreover, they practiced apprenticeship as an additional intermediate step between childhood and boarding or marriage. This practice was brought over from Germany and continued in Buffalo because of German domination of the city's crafts. It was most pronounced among young men between the ages of 18 and 22, when about one-fourth of German young men lived with a master craftsman (Figure 3).

Except for apprenticeship, the household cycle of German men broadly resembled that of the other two groups. About

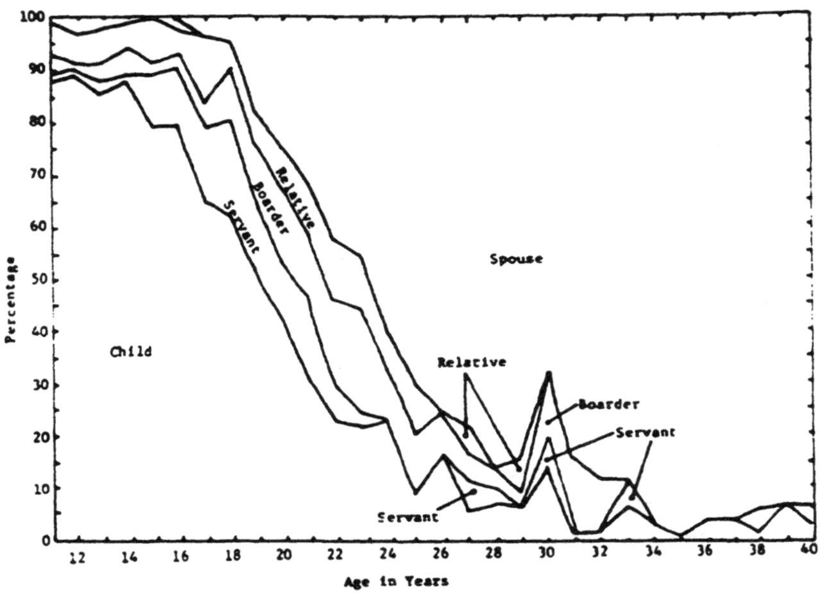

Figure 3: GERMAN MALES: HOUSEHOLD STATUS BY AGE

one-third of German young men between the ages of 21 and 24, and as many as 10% up to age 31 were boarders. The corresponding figures for those in their late teens and twenties were substantially lower (by about half) and were insignificant for most other age groups.

The marriage pattern for German men was compressed like that for Irish men, although it began and concluded about a year earlier, at ages 21 and 27, respectively.[9] Also like the Irish, German men experienced no delay in establishing their own household once they married.

Of the three ethnic groups, Germans had the most intensely nuclear household pattern. There existed few German boarding houses; boarders lived primarily with a German family. Once established, the German household was only moderately subject to modification as the household head grew older. Only 8% of German families took in a roomer or boarder, and the figure varied very slightly over the life cycle of the household head.

The percentage of family heads taking in relatives fell slowly, but steadily, from 11% of those in their twenties to 5% of those in their fifties; thereafter, the trend reversed, as 11% among those in their sixties headed extended households and 20% of those in their seventies. German households taking in boarders and roomers declined very slightly, but noticeably, among older members, from 12% of those in their twenties to 6% of those in their seventies.

German men experienced a fairly stable economic cycle and were substantially more successful than their Irish counterparts in buying a home. During their early adult years—the twenties and thirties—their patterns of home ownership were similar to those of natives, with about one-fourth and two-fifths of the family heads in those age categories owning their own homes. Thereafter, the German percentage stabilized while that of the native-born advanced, such that by the time they were sixty years or older, less than half of German family heads owned their own homes, compared to almost three-fifths of native-born family heads. If one allows for length of residence in the city (German family heads had been present eight years on the average, compared to thirteen years for the native-born), the differences disappear entirely. Finally, although home ownership among the Germans did not advance with old age as did that for the native-born, neither did it decline, as was the case for the Irish.

Part of the German success in acquiring a home, of course, can be attributed to their occupational patterns. Although they lacked any significant number of white-collar, professional, or entrepreneurial occupations, and over half of their family heads were unskilled or without occupation, they had a firm grip on the city's crafts and dominated many of the lucrative building trades. As a result, over a third of their family heads were skilled workers, compared to only a fifth of the native-born and a sixth of the Irish. There were proportionately more young skilled workers than older ones. Moreover, German men stayed longer in the labor force than either of the other two groups. At age 16, when native-born men were just entering the labor force and a year before Irish young men began to work, one-fourth of German boys were already employed. By age 20, almost half were listed with an occupation, a level not reached by the native-born and Irish until age 22. They also retired from the labor force at a later age than either of the other two groups. Whereas half of the native-born and Irish men retired in their early sixties, less than 40% of German men had retired before their late sixties.

Despite the undoubted significance of work, occupational patterns accounted for only part of the German success in acquiring property. Cultural preferences undoubtedly operated as well, for if one allows for differences in age and length of residence in the city, German family heads not only equaled, but often exceeded, their native-born and Irish counterparts in the proportion owning real property. It was particularly among unskilled workers that German family heads bested their ethnic competitors.

As with the Irish and native-born men, advanced age brought relatively few unsettling changes in their life patterns. About one German man in three past the age of sixty was not the head of his own household. The great majority (three-fifths) of those who were not household heads lived with a child or grandchild; somewhat over one-tenth lived with an in-law, and somewhat fewer than one in ten lived with a nephew or niece. Only 12% lived as a boarder or roomer.

The notable aspect of this comparison of age-related life experiences of native-born, Irish, and German men is that alongside the not unexpected socioeconomic differences—occupation and property ownership—there existed such remarkable similarities in the timing and form of their respective family cycles. As we will now see, it was the women who demonstrated the most striking and pervasive ethnic differences in their family and economic cycles.

NATIVE-BORN WOMEN

Native-born women began leaving home at age 16—several years before their brothers. Few left, however, to take a job; at no age did more than 5% of native-born women have an occupation listed in the census other than that of domestic servant. Few became servants. Only 12% to 17% of native-born women aged 16 to 19 were classified as domestic servants. By age 24, virtually none were domestics. Boarding was an equally rare experience, occurring primarily between the ages of 22 and 23 and even then involving less than one-fifth of the native-born women. Thus, except for a very brief period in their late teens, these women never lived in a household other than that of their parents (Figure 4).

Beginning at age 19 native-born women began to marry. By age 21 over half were listed as wives and by age 25 over three-fourths.[10] Most established their own household shortly

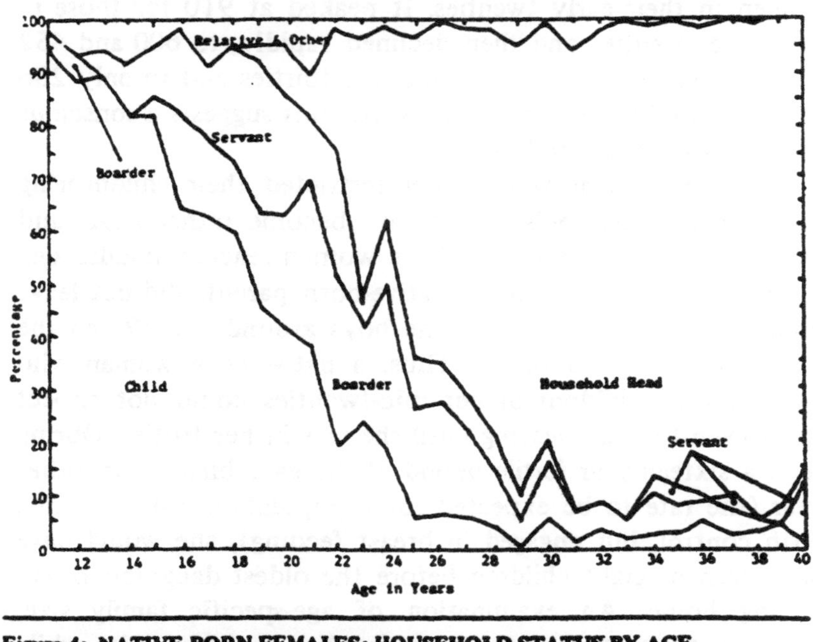

Figure 4: NATIVE-BORN FEMALES: HOUSEHOLD STATUS BY AGE

after marrying. Three-fifths had done so between the ages of 19 and 22, and by age 27 virtually all had married. Native-born women delayed bearing children until a household was established. This conclusion in based on the following evidence: first, some 69% of native-born married women aged 20 to 24, and 89% of those aged 25 to 29 had their own households; second, there were 69 children aged 0-4 years per 100 married native-born women aged 20-24, and 91 children per 100 women aged 25-29 years. If the assumption is that most of these women had only one child under five years of age, this would mean that most of those without their own household had no children.

Even after they began to bear children, native-born women restricted their family size. They had a very low fertility ratio, only 585 children aged 0-4 years per 100 married women of childbearing years, 15-44.[11] They achieved this low rate by having most of their children before age 35. The fertility rate was 188 for native-born women in their late teens, 685 for women in their early twenties. It peaked at 910 for those in their late twenties and then declined rapidly, to 600 and 452 among women in their early and late thirties and to only 286 among those in their early forties. All this suggests a conscious pattern of limited childbearing.

Had native-born women not restricted their childbearing years, their households would have become rather large, and would have remained so, until the women reached middle age. As noted above, children of native-born parents did not leave home until late adolescence–the boys around age 19 and the girls around age 16 or 17. Thus, a native-born woman who began raising children in her mid-twenties could not expect them even to begin leaving until she was in her forties. During such a sixteen-year fertile period, if she gave birth every other year (the rate to be expected for a population not practicing birth control, but engaged in breast feeding), she would have had seven or eight children before the oldest daughters began leaving home. An examination of age-specific family size, however, shows that native-born families peaked in size while the family head was in his late thirties, with two to three children—2.56 on the average. Such a low figure reveals the extent to which most native-born women limited their family size.

As they aged, the death of the husband and/or financial pressures meant that fewer women were able to maintain their previous status as wife in an independent household. The first major decline in the proportion listed as "spouse" of their own household occurred among those in their early fifties. Prior to that, over two-thirds of any particular age group were so listed; after age sixty only about a fifth. What happened to the others? Of the women over sixty years of age who were not living with their husbands in their own households, only a few (16%) became household heads in their own right, half went to live with one of their children, and slightly less than a fifth went to live with in-laws. As with the men, a negligible percentage lived as boarders or with collateral kin.

IRISH WOMEN

While the life cycles of Irish and native-born men converged at several points, the pattern for Irish and native-born women was one of sharp and persistent differences. The divergence began in early adolescence. At age 17, when native-born women were just beginning to leave home, over half of the Irish girls had already left theirs to take on domestic work, starting as early as 11 years of age; and by age 21 virtually all of them were living apart from their parents. This was not true of native-born women until age 25. Whereas only a few native-born women ever lived outside the household of either their parents or of their husbands, live-in domestic service claimed the energies of more than one-fourth of Irish girls between the ages of 13 and 25, and from half to two-thirds of those aged 18 to 21 years. (Figure 5).

Domestic service was closely related to at least two demographic factors—age and length of residence in the city.

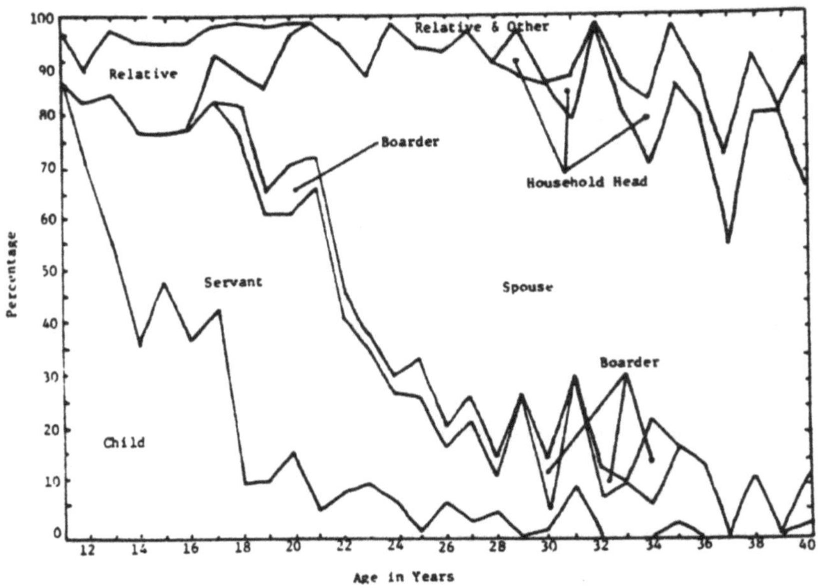

Figure 5: IRISH FEMALES: HOUSEHOLD STATUS BY AGE

Undoubtedly, Irish parents did not want their daughters to work as live-in domestics. These girls typically lived and worked among native-born families who themselves had adolescent sons living at home. Those who were new to the city, however, were unable to keep even their very young daughters out of domestic service. One-fourth of Irish girls aged 10 to 14 who were present in the city for one year or less worked as live-in domestics, compared to less than 15% of those present more than three years. The corresponding drop among those aged 15 to 19 was equally dramatic, from 75% to 32%. Among older girls, however, those in their early twenties, the decline was only from 52% to 39%; among those in their late twenties the decline was from about 30% to about 15%. Domestic service was the female counterpart of boarding out for the men and was much more widely practiced. Regardless of how long they had been in the city, however, domestic service was not a permanent feature of Irish women's lives. Beginning at age 21 Irish girls rapidly left such work and by age 26 virtually none were so employed.

Irish girls left domestic service in their late teens in order to get married. One fourth were married by age 19, half by age 21, and three-fourths by age 25. Despite domestic service (or perhaps financially because of it), Irish women caught up with their native-born counterparts in terms of age at marriage. As with the native-born women, about half of those who married early set up their own household. By age 22 over four-fifths of married Irish women had their own, independent household.

By contrast to the severely restricted overall fertility rate of native women, Irish women had a fertility rate high enough to suggest virtually unregulated childbearing. The Irish figure was 100, for married women 15-44, almost double that of native-born women. Inspection of the age-specific fertility rates for Irish women in comparison to their native-born counterparts reinforces this impression. Thus, among married Irish women aged 15 to 19 the fertility rate was 313, or about two-thirds higher than that for native-born women of the same age. Among Irish women in their twenties and early thirties the fertility rate was much higher, 1,130 among those aged 25 to 29, and 1,290 among those aged 30 to 34 years. The latter figure was over twice as high as that for native-born women of the same age. Not until their late thirties did the Irish rate decline. It fell to 927 among the 35 to 39 age group and to 446 among the 40 to 44 age group. By the late thirties, however, simple biological restraints would have been operating, as many women drew toward the end of their fertile period.

Despite higher fertility rates and longer periods of childbearing, Irish families were not substantially larger than native-born families. Irish families had an average of 2.37 children, not significantly higher than the figure of 2.06 for native-born families. Moreover, native-born families peaked in the average number of children living at home with 2.56; Irish families peaked (at age 50) with 3.43. The maximum average differences between the two, then, were just one child. The only plausible explanation of this small divergence in family size in light of such major differences in fertility is related to the household cycle, by which native-born families kept their children home until late adolescence, whereas Irish families sent their children, particularly their young girls, out for a prolonged period of domestic service. Domestic service, then, served as an important regulator of Irish family size.

In describing the transition to old age for men, whether native-born or Irish, we focused on the age group over sixty because that was the period of major shifts in household status. The same was true for native-born women. For Irish women, however, shifts in household status began much earlier—in the age group 41 to 60. Beginning in their forties, the Irish woman's household began to break up. Only half of Irish women in their forties and fifties were wives living in their own households compared to three-fifths of native-born women. Similarly, one-fourth of all Irish women in that age bracket headed their own household, compared to less than 15% of native-born women. The reasons for this unusually high number of female-headed households among the Irish is not clear. It is possible that Irish men had a higher death rate than Irish women, but in the 41 to 60 age group there were 604 men compared to 565 women, suggesting that mortality alone is not a sufficient cause. Whatever the cause—death, separation, or divorce—it is clear that many middle-aged Irish women did not remarry.

Among older women, those over sixty years of age, Irish women continued to head a disproportionate number of households. About a fourth of those not living with a husband headed their own household (compared to 16% among the native-born). Half had gone to live with children, another 15% had gone to live with other in-laws, and an insignificant proportion boarded.

The life cycle of Irish women, therefore, diverged substantially from that of native-born women. The differences emerged in early adolescence, as most Irish girls went to live and work as servants in native-born households. This prolonged period of domestic service, however, was not a permanent part of their lives. Between the ages of 20 and 24, most Irish girls left that service in order to get married. At that point their age-related life experiences diverged again from the native-born pattern. Irish mothers had a much higher rate of childbearing, lasting over a longer period of time. While native-born mothers kept their daughters home until the time for them to marry, this was not possible for most Irish mothers. Perhaps out of both economic necessity and considerations of space in the house, their daughters spent most of their adolescence living with, and working for, those native-born families. During much of the middle and later years, Irish women were more likely than native-born women to head their own households, a type of independence which they probably did not relish. An insignificant number of Irish women were listed in the census with an occupation, reflecting the fact that Buffalo was not a city with an industry which could provide outside sources of income for working women. We may assume, however, that these women heading households did work; it probably only consisted of such poorly remunerative work as taking in other people's laundry.

GERMAN WOMEN

Like Irish girls, German girls left home at a very early age. The transition began at the age of 11 years, but was more gradual. Not until age 23, two years after almost all Irish girls had left home, was it completed (Figure 6).

As with the Irish, nearly all German girls at some point during their adolescence served as live-in domestics, almost invariably for native-born families. For the Germans, however, the length of service was shorter. Only between the ages of 17 and 18 did as many as two-thirds work in such a capacity, a figure which characterized Irish women in the age group from 18 to 21. Finally, German girls married and helped to establish a household earlier than either Irish or native-born girls. They began at age 17 (two or three years before the Irish), and by age 25 over 80% were listed as wives of household heads, compared

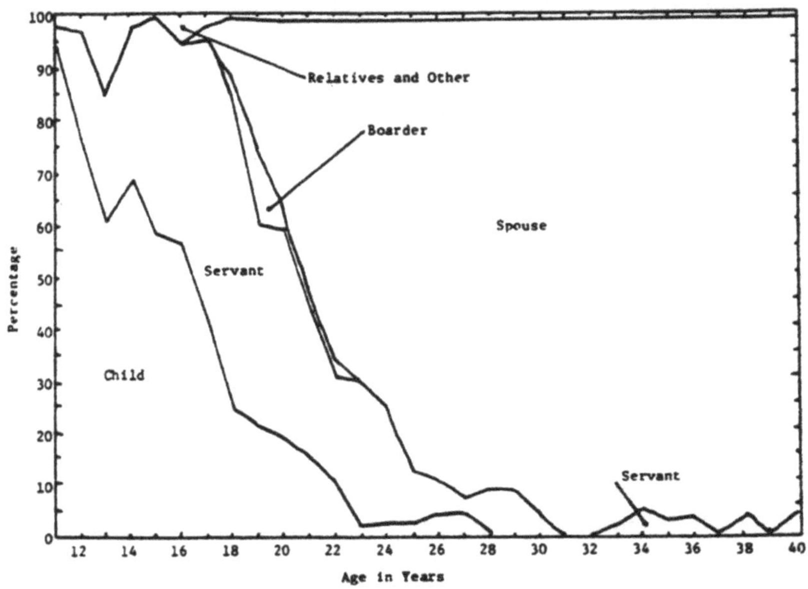

Figure 6: GERMAN FEMALES: HOUSEHOLD STATUS BY AGE

to only 60% of Irish women and 70% of native-born women. After marriage, never more than 5% were listed with an occupation.

As with the Irish, once German women married, they experienced little or no delay in setting up a household. Nor was there any delay in beginning a family. German women aged 15 to 44 had the same overall fertility rate as Irish women, but a review of age-specific fertility shows that among the young and the old, German women had a higher rate than the Irish, and among the middle childbearing years, a rate only slightly under that of the Irish. As with the Irish, the suggestion is that their childbearing was regulated primarily by biological consideration.

Despite their high, prolonged fertility, the German family averaged just over two children (2.13), somewhat more than native-born families (2.06), and less than Irish families (2.37). The explanation is not related to age differences between the groups, for the average number of children present in German families peaked among family heads 45 years old at just over three children (3.08), again not substantially higher than the peak for native-born families at 2.56 and below the Irish figure of 3.43. As with the Irish, family size was regulated by sending children out of the household. German girls went into domestic service among the native-born; German boys became apprentices for German master craftsmen. Among the Germans, then, both domestic service and apprenticeship served as important regulators of effective family size.

As they aged, German women were more fortunate than either native-born or Irish women in remaining spouses in their own households. Among those over sixty years of age, over a third had that status, compared to a fifth or less among the native-born and Irish. Of those whose position changed, about a fifth became household heads in their own right, half went to live with their children and 14% went to live with in-laws. Thus, as with the other ethnic groups, boarding or living with collateral kin was seldom resorted to by the elderly.

CONCLUSION

Irish, Germans, and native-born whites, then, had distinctive life cycles. This was true for both the men and the women, but the men's patterns differed primarily in their economic cycles, while the women's patterns differed in terms of both the economic and the household cycles.

Among the men the household cycle was more notable for similarities than for differences among the ethnic groups. The most impressive differences among the men involved not the timing, but the content, of their life cycles. Thus, throughout their working lives, native-born men dominated the white-collar and entrepreneurial occupations, virtually to the exclusion of immigrant men; the ranks of the unskilled were composed largely of immigrant men, and most of the crafts, especially in the construction industry, were dominated by Germans. Occupational differences among them were largely independent of age.

Age-related patterns, and ethnic differences in those patterns, were also pronounced for the men in terms of property ownership. A substantial proportion of each group owned their own homes, but the differences were nonetheless substantial—one-fourth of the Irish, two-fifths of the Germans, and over two-fifths of the native-born. Moreover, the differences became even greater as the household head aged, reflecting presumably age-related differences in the earning potential among the types of occupations.

It was among the women that there existed the most consistent ethnic differences in life cycles. The years of "adolescence" for immigrant girls were strikingly different, not only from their native-born counterparts, but also from their brothers. For an extended period of time they lived and worked with native-born families. Their brothers, however, were never exposed to an intimate living situation with persons of another ethnic group. They remained home until late adolescence, boarded among families of the same nationality, married a girl also of the same nationality, and established a household usually in an ethnically homogeneous neighborhood. Their only chance for contact with the native-born occurred in the work situation, but, given the degree of occupational specialization along ethnic lines, this was probably neither extensive nor significant.

This early departure of girls from their parents' household was functional, both in terms of their later marriage prospects being increased from the earnings and especially as a regulator of the household size. In this way, although Irish and German fertility rates were almost double that for the native-born, and although the childbearing period for them extended ten years longer, immigrant families were not substantially larger than those of the native-born population.

The implications of these age-related sex differences are enormous, especially for the question of acculturation. The contact of immigrant girls with native-born families occurred at an impressionable age, when patterns of behavior, dress, language, and cultural values were still being learned. For foreign-language groups like the Germans, in particular, the girls probably learned English before their brothers. For the second generation it would be they who taught and translated such behavior to their children, years before the schools did their work. For working-class populations of immigrant background, the institution of domestic service was probably as important a force for acculturation as the more widely known institutions of work and schooling. These are only some of the perspectives that a comparative life-cycle analysis can offer for all of a community's members, young and old, male and female.

NOTES

1. Earlier historical studies of immigration give scant treatment to family composition or to age-related aspects of immigrant adjustment. A partial exception would be Oscar Handlin, *Boston's Immigrants: A Study in Acculturation* (Cambridge, Mass., 1941, 1959), which describes a wide range of social characteristics of Boston's Irish immigrants. The focus of much subsequent history, particularly the "new" urban history, has been on occupation and geographic mobility. Only lately has attention shifted to studies of the family and household. See Tamara K. Hareven, "The History of the Family as an Interdisciplinary Field," Journal of Interdisciplinary History, 2 (1970); Journal of Marriage and the Family, 35 (1973); Michael Gordon, ed., *The American Family in Social-Historical Perspective* (New York, 1973); Peter Laslett and Richard Wall, eds., *The Household and Family in Past Time* (Cambridge, England, 1972).

2. Paul C. Glick and Robert Parke, Jr., "New Approaches in Studying the Life Cycle of the Family," Demography, 2 (1965), 187-202, summarizes much of the sociological literature on the life cycle applied to the family. Tamara K. Hareven, "The Family as Process: The Historical Study of the Family Cycle," Journal of Social History (March 1974), 322-329, urges historians to adapt, in a creative fashion, this analytical tool for their own purposes. There are no studies comparing the life cycles of ethnic groups in nineteenth-century America, but see Robert V. Wells, "Demographic Change and the Life Cycle of American Families," Journal of Interdisciplinary History, 2 (1971), 273-282; Howard P. Chudacoff, "The Non-Private Newlyweds: Familial Extension in the First Stage of the Family Cycle, Providence, Rhode Island, 1864-1865 and 1879-1880," paper submitted to the MSSB Conference on Family History, Williams College, July 1974. Because of lack of space, not all the tables were included in this paper. For tables see Laurence A. Glasco, "Ethnicity and Social Structure: Irish, Germans and Native-Born of Buffalo, N.Y.,

1850-1860," Ph.D. dissertation, State University of New York at Buffalo, 1973; esp. ch. 3, "Household and Family Structure."

3. Laurence A. Glasco, "Ethnicity and Occupation in the Mid-19th Century: Irish, Germans and Native-born Whites in Buffalo, N.Y.," paper delivered at the Conference on Immigrants in Industrial America, Eleutherian Mills Historical Library and the Balch Institute, November 1973; Theodore Hershberg et al., "Occupation and Ethnicity in Five Nineteenth-Century Cities: A Collaborative Inquiry," Historical Methods Newsletter, 7 (1974), 174-216.

4. Michael Anderson found that in mid-nineteenth-century Preston, England about half of the lodgers were single and between the ages of 15 and 24. Only one-fifth lived in a household containing more than five lodgers. Anderson, *Family Structure in Nineteenth Century Lancashire* (Cambridge, England, 1971), 47. Compare with John Modell and Tamara K. Hareven, "Urbanization and the Malleable Household: An Examination of Boarding and Lodging in American Families," Journal of Marriage and the Family, 35 (1973) 478-479.

5. The same as in 1890 for all white males in the United States. See Paul C. Glick and Robert Parke, Jr., "New Approaches in Studying the Life Cycle of the Family," Demography, 2 (1965), 189.

6. These figures for relatives and lodgers are almost identical to those for Preston, England. Anderson, *Family Structure in Nineteenth Century Lancashire*, 46.

7. The distribution of households with relatives and boarders–one fourth and one-fifth, respectively–does not quite agree with the distribution of extended and augmented household–one-fifth and one-fourth, respectively–because the classification "augmented" includes households which contained both relatives and boarders.

8. Unfortunately, the printed U.S. census does not provide information of the family and household characteristics of immigrants. For information on the Irish, see K. H. Connell, *The Population of Ireland, 1750-1845* (Oxford, England, 1950).

9. John Knodel, "Law, Marriage and Illegitimacy in Nineteenth-Century Germany," Population Studies, 20 (1966-1967), 279-294, deals with the effects on marriage age and illegitimacy of marriage restriction by various German states.

10. From the late eighteenth century onward, this has been the median age at marriage for American women. Wells, "Demographic Change and the Life Cycle of American Families," 280 ff. Cf. Tamara K. Hareven and Maris A. Vinovskis, "Marital Fertility, Ethnicity and Occupation in Urban Families: An Analysis of South Boston and the South End in 1880," paper presented at the MSSB Conference on Family History, Williams College, July 1974.

11. A rate only moderately below that for other cities of its size in the mid-nineteenth century. Warren S. Thompson and P. K. Whelpton, *Population Trends in the U.S.* (New York, 1933), 263, 279.

Fertility and Marriage in a Nineteenth-Century Industrial City: Philadelphia, 1850–1880

MICHAEL R. HAINES

This paper examines age-specific and differential fertility, both marital and total, and nuptiality for census samples of white Philadelphia families headed by native white Americans, Germans, and Irish for 1850–1880. Using Philadelphia Social History Project data, own-children techniques are employed to construct age-standardized child-woman ratios and age-specific total and marital fertility rates. Conclusions are that the low fertility among native whites was due to both low marital fertility and later marriage; that rapid declines in marital fertility occurred among second generation migrants; and that variations existed in marital fertility across occupational groupings within ethnic groups.

A central part of the evolution of the nineteenth century was the progressive urbanization and industrialization of the society. Accompanying this massive relocation and restructuring of economic activity and population was a demographic transition from high to lower levels of fertility and mortality, and substantial international and internal migration. This paper provides a summary of some findings on demographic differentials and change in nineteenth-century Philadelphia, one of America's largest cities and premier industrial centers by 1850. The research is part of a continuing effort to study the historic social, economic, and demographic dynamics of Philadelphia by the Philadelphia Social History Project.

Fertility change and differentials within nineteenth-century urban and industrial areas recently have been receiving more attention. Part of the reason is the availability of the U.S. census enumerators' manuscripts prior to 1900, which provides the opportunity to make detailed studies of differentials for groups and for smaller areas. In those studies, it has been found that generally fertility of urban areas fell below that for rural areas, of native-born whites below that of foreign-born whites, of more educated women below that of less educated women, and of wives of professional, proprietary, and white collar workers below that of blue collar workers. It

The Journal of Economic History, Vol. XL, No. 1 (March 1980). ISSN 0022–0507.

The author is Research Associate Professor, School of Public and Urban Policy, and Research Associate, Philadelphia Social History Project (PSHP), University of Pennsylvania. Support is acknowledged from the PSHP and its director, Theodore Hershberg, and from the following agencies: NIMH (MH16621), NSF (SOC 76–20069), NEH (RO32485–78–1612), and NICHHD (RO1–HO–12413). Most of the footnotes in this paper have been eliminated to conserve space. A full version is available from the author upon request.

is useful to establish whether these and other differentials existed for Philadelphia and also to observe the pattern of change over time.

The data consist of samples of approximately 2000 households, each headed by Irish-born, German-born, and native white Americans from the U.S. census manuscripts of 1850, 1860, 1870, and 1880. Also employed were tabulations of the census populations for small geographic units, called "grid-units," into which the city was divided. The household samples were not suitable for fertility analysis as they stood. In particular, a sub-family structure had to be imposed and, in addition, for 1850, 1860, and 1870, marital status and relationship to head of household had to be inferred. The nuclear family thus inferred was taken as the unit for fertility analysis. An important part of this process was the assignment of children to their mothers within families, which is basic to the "own-children" methods currently used extensively in demography. Once this was completed, age-specific marital child-woman ratios (defined as children 0-4 per married woman by age) are calculated. These either can be presented directly, or they can be standardized to some uniform age structure in order to present a single number that is free of variation because of differences in age structures between groups or across time. The latter is the way the results are presented in Table 2.

A further extension was to compute more standard demographic measures such as age-specific overall and marital fertility rates, total fertility rates, net reproduction rates, and so on. For this purpose various corrections to the age-specific child-woman ratios were needed, including those for mortality of young children and women in the previous five years, for children missing from their mothers for reasons other than mortality, and for relative underenumeration of children and adult women. These calculations were performed and some of the summary measures are given in the first table.

Some basic data are presented in Table 1. The upper panel provides a capsule description of the demographic situation of the city between 1850 and 1880, with the total population increasing from 408,762 in 1850 to 847,170 in 1880, an average growth rate of 2.43 percent per year. Combined with this rapid demographic growth was a considerable influx of foreign born, who ranged from 24 percent of the population in 1880 to 30 percent in 1860. This actually understates the population in the foreign-born community since many of the children of the foreign born were first generation native born. Most of the foreign born were, as may be seen, Irish and German. Thus the samples of native white, Irish, and German households represented about 94 percent of the total white population. Philadelphia also had a small but important black population (3–5 percent of the total) that will be the subject of subsequent study.

In terms of overall fertility for the white population, child-woman ratios (children 0–4 per 1000 women aged 15–49) are presented in the second panel of Table 1. Fertility among Philadelphia whites was about 20–

TABLE 1
SELECTED DATA ON POPULATION, FERTILITY, AND MARRIAGE: PHILADELPHIA, PENNSYLVANIA AND THE UNITED STATES, 1850–1880

Variable	Year 1850	1860	1870	1880
Population				
Total Population[a]	408,762	565,529	674,022	847,170
Percent Non-White	4.8	3.9	3.3	3.8
Percent Foreign Born	28.9	30.0	27.2	24.1
Percent of White Population				
Native White	69.6	69.2	71.9	74.9
Irish Born	18.5	17.4	14.9	12.3
German Born	5.9	7.8	7.6	6.9
Fertility (White Population)				
Child-Woman Ratios[b]				
United States	613.3	627.0	589.7	537.4
Pennsylvania	610.7	612.7	556.0	506.7
Philadelphia County	456.0	485.3	401.2	368.2
Philadelphia Samples				
Irish Sample	522.9	688.2	500.0	385.9
German Sample	602.8	761.9	585.4	406.6
Native White Sample	393.4	358.5	340.4	325.3
Total Fertility Rates[c]				
Irish Sample	4,350	4,997	4,434	3,510
German Sample	5,016	5,896	5,202	3,883
Native White Sample	3,450	2,958	2,788	2,492
Total Marital Fertility Rates[d]				
Irish Sample	6,306	7,560	7,441	7,341
German Sample	6,366	7,076	6,822	7,225
Native White Sample	6,194	5,420	4,884	4,115
Marriage (White Population)				
Estimated Proportions Married at Ages 20–24: Females				
Irish Sample	.432	.471	.329	.192
German Sample	.551	.577	.462	.261
Native White Sample	.352	.347	.378	.399

[a] Philadelphia County.
[b] Children 0–4 per 1000 women aged 15–49.
[c] The summation of the age-specific fertility rates, per 1000 total women. The rates refer to the five-year period prior to the census.
[d] The summation of the age-specific marital fertility rates, excluding women aged 15–19, per 1000 married women. The rates refer to the five-year period prior to the census.
Source: Published census volumes and samples of census enumerators' manuscripts for Philadelphia.

30 percent below that for the United States as a whole or for Pennsylvania. Fertility also declined over time in all areas from 1860 to 1880. Philadelphia, however, showed a more rapid decrease (24.1 percent) relative both to Pennsylvania (17.3 percent) and to the United States as a whole (14.3 percent) over this period. Actually, the decline was consistent throughout the nineteenth century for all areas with the exception of the 1850s. As is clear from Table 1, however, the modest increase in the child-woman ratio in Philadelphia in the 1850s was caused by increases in fer-

tility among the Irish and German born (if not the other foreign born), whereas fertility continued to decline among the native born. It is interesting to speculate whether the same was true for the country as a whole and, more importantly, whether this change was some sort of adjustment from the extremely disturbed social and economic conditions in Europe in the late 1840s to the better conditions in the United States in the late 1850s. This speculation awaits further investigation.

The total fertility rates (the sum of age-specific birth rates) also reflected the same pattern as the child-woman ratios, which perhaps is not surprising. Marital fertility (as measured by the total marital fertility rate) showed a pattern of decline only for the native white population and not for the Irish and German samples. The bottom panel of Table 1 presents the estimated proportions of married females aged 20–24,[1] which is a good indicator of age at marriage and hence of exposure to risk of childbearing. A glance at these data reveals that the downward movement of overall fertility among the native white population was an adjustment of fertility within marriage, whereas the changes in overall fertility among the Germans and Irish was a mixture of changes in marital fertility and nuptiality. Between 1850 and 1860, nuptiality changed relatively little, whereas marital fertility rose. Thereafter, the decline in overall fertility was produced almost entirely by a rising age at marriage among Irish and German females; marital fertility remained relatively constant.

The explanation for these patterns, and changes in patterns, of nuptiality is not immediately apparent. It appears that the native white population adhered more closely to the "European marriage pattern" of late marriage ages and high proportions of permanently celibate. German and Irish immigrant females did not exhibit this pattern in 1850, but moved closer to it later. By 1880, the proportion of native white females married at ages 20-24 actually increased, whereas that of German- and Irish-born females declined. In 1880, when data were available for the calculation of the singulate mean age at marriage (SMAM), Irish females had the highest SMAM (26.4 years); German females had the lowest SMAM (23.9 years); and native white females occupied an intermediate ranking (25.4 years). Males had a similar ranking with higher marriage ages that were typical of the "European marriage pattern" (29.1 years for Irish males, 25.9 years for Germans, and 28.0 years for native whites). These differentials were attributable partly to sex ratios (males per 100 females) that were considerably more favorable to early female marriage among the German population than among the native whites or the Irish. In the Irish population, the immigration of large numbers of young, single, female domestic servants helped reduce female marriage probabilities considerably. This obviously explains the situation only partially, however, since the

[1] The proportions married are the actual numbers for 1880. They were estimated for 1850–70 from the proportion of spouses and adjusted upward for the proportion of total married women to spouses in 1880.

German male age at marriage was also the lowest in 1880 despite a high sex ratio (that is, well above 100).

The fertility differentials exhibited in Table 1 have been noted previously but deserve further discussion. Ethnicity apparently did make a considerable difference in fertility. For overall fertility, German-headed families showed the highest fertility; the Irish were usually close; and native white-headed families were well below the Germans and Irish. For marital fertility, some results are given in Table 2 in the form of age-standardized child-woman ratios (children 0-4 per 1000 married women aged 15-49 with husband present).[2] As was apparent from the total marital fertility rates in Table 1, the differentials were much smaller than for overall fertility in 1850; thereafter the differentials widened considerably. It was frequently true that families with both spouses foreign born had higher fertility than families in which the wife was native born. For 1870 and 1880, at least, native-born white husbands with foreign-born wives had higher fertility than native white husbands with native spouses. The reverse was true in 1850, and the ratios were very close in 1860. Finally, for 1880, when data on nativity of parents were available, fertility of families where both parents of the head were native white was below that for families in which one parent was foreign born, which, in turn, was below that for families in which both parents were foreign born. Thus first generation native born were intermediate in fertility between the foreign born and native whites of native parents. The fertility of the first generation native born was somewhat closer to that of the native population, but more definite statements must await analysis of precise ethnic differences across generations.

Thus, levels of fertility clearly differed across ethnic groups in predictable ways. Within ethnic groups, differentials also exhibited expected patterns. Literate wives usually had lower fertility than illiterate wives, and employed wives (who were noticeably few in number) had fertility lower than that of non-employed wives. Differentials by occupation of husband also were calculated. Frequently the professional and higher white collar groups had fertility below that of the proprietary and lower white collar groups and that of manual workers (that is, skilled manual workers, unskilled workers with specified occupations, and laborers). The pattern was far from uniform, however, as was differential fertility among the manual worker groups. The main point, then, should be that fertility gradients by occupation of husband existed within the ethnic groups, although the composition of those groups varied considerably. The native white husbands were much more heavily represented in the professional, proprietary, white collar, and skilled manual categories. Larger proportions of Irish husbands were in unskilled manual jobs, whereas the German male

[2] From this point, the discussion treats marital and overall child-women ratios as fertility, although they are net of mortality. In general, the differentials are present even after correction for mortality.

TABLE 2
STANDARDIZED TOTAL AND MARITAL CHILD-WOMAN RATIOS,* BY ETHNICITY, OCCUPATION OF HUSBAND, LITERACY AND EMPLOYMENT OF SPOUSE, AND WEALTH OF FAMILY, WHITE POPULATION, PHILADELPHIA, 1850–1880
(children 0–4 per 1000 women 15–49)

	Year							
Variable	*1850*	*(N)*	*1860*	*(N)*	*1870*	*(N)*	*1880*	*(N)*
Total Women								
Irish	511.8	(2750)	576.9	(2479)	493.3	(3012)	473.2	(3211)
German	571.8	(3074)	695.3	(2839)	590.8	(3090)	447.1	(3281)
Native White	407.3	(4141)	450.2	(3643)	335.9	(4568)	303.7	(3809)
Married Women with Husband Present								
Total								
Irish	823.1	(1483)	970.8	(1445)	899.4	(1460)	844.5	(1440)
German	841.4	(1868)	995.0	(1886)	896.9	(1892)	840.8	(1612)
Native White	813.3	(1685)	755.6	(1516)	676.2	(1984)	606.3	(1771)
Literacy of Spouse								
Irish								
Literate	819.1	(1289)	969.5	(1321)	888.4	(1104)	848.5	(1209)
Illiterate	845.0	(185)	1002.1	(124)	952.5	(356)	785.6	(231)
German								
Literate	832.8	(1805)	1040.6	(1871)	898.3	(1805)	842.6	(1575)
Illiterate	1078.2	(63)	1064.3	(15)	982.6	(87)	816.0	(37)
Native White								
Literate	811.8	(1642)	750.2	(1501)	674.2	(1888)	596.9	(1722)
Illiterate	836.3	(43)	970.7	(15)	687.2	(96)	934.7	(49)
Nativity of Spouse								
Irish								
Native	827.1	(193)	880.2	(163)	801.3	(222)	898.4	(298)
Foreign	821.5	(1290)	982.6	(1279)	901.8	(1238)	830.9	(1142)
German								
Native	880.1	(308)	924.1	(242)	838.7	(298)	731.7	(454)
Foreign	834.3	(1559)	992.3	(1628)	903.7	(1593)	867.2	(1158)
Native White								
Native	820.5	(1579)	757.3	(1369)	691.6	(1789)	593.9	(1574)
Foreign	718.6	(104)	756.5	(138)	824.2	(194)	700.7	(197)
Nativity of Head's Parents								
Native White								
Both Native	—	—	—	—	—	—	571.6	(1181)
One Foreign	—	—	—	—	—	—	621.7	(135)
Both Foreign	—	—	—	—	—	—	678.5	(418)
Unknown	—	—	—	—	—	—	858.1	(37)
Employment of Spouse								
Irish								
Employed	—	—	675.0	(71)	511.8	(76)	639.4	(65)
Not Employed	—	—	991.4	(1374)	921.4	(1384)	859.0	(1375)
German								
Employed	—	—	1033.3	(66)	602.8	(69)	588.6	(91)
Not Employed	—	—	995.6	(1820)	905.6	(1823)	860.6	(1521)
Native White								
Employed	—	—	407.5	(50)	424.1	(165)	392.5	(190)
Not Employed	—	—	767.8	(1466)	685.0	(1911)	632.0	(1581)
Occupation of Head								
Irish								
Professional and High White Collar	585.9	(24)	817.8	(21)	645.5	(21)	678.0	(11)

TABLE 2 CONT.

Variable	Year 1850	(N)	1860	(N)	1870	(N)	1880	(N)
Proprietary and Low White Collar	855.1	(169)	926.2	(214)	837.0	(212)	867.9	(266)
Skilled Manual	785.2	(591)	950.3	(497)	856.9	(483)	880.3	(449)
Specified Unskilled	808.9	(186)	997.8	(199)	1033.8	(257)	812.0	(271)
Laborer	881.8	(458)	1011.5	(477)	967.0	(457)	803.5	(419)
German								
Professional and High White Collar	769.7	(41)	1081.3	(29)	965.4	(36)	628.1	(25)
Proprietary and Low White Collar	805.2	(249)	1033.2	(330)	943.1	(451)	757.0	(396)
Skilled Manual	864.7	(1208)	1007.4	(1190)	875.3	(1039)	864.5	(917)
Specified Unskilled	790.9	(82)	687.8	(100)	931.6	(219)	884.6	(175)
Laborer	821.6	(204)	1047.0	(186)	862.2	(31)	965.3	(86)
Native White								
Professional and High White Collar	802.7	(139)	755.0	(102)	624.5	(113)	579.0	(80)
Proprietary and Low White Collar	852.4	(363)	729.9	(403)	638.6	(583)	524.1	(545)
Skilled Manual	821.3	(907)	795.6	(745)	693.3	(922)	615.6	(788)
Specified Unskilled	728.0	(104)	689.9	(107)	748.0	(218)	761.0	(228)
Laborer	760.3	(90)	845.3	(74)	807.4	(97)	709.2	(89)
Family Wealth								
Irish								
None stated	827.7	(1350)	919.8	(739)	882.9	(791)	—	—
$1-500 }	880.9	(48)	1052.7	(470)	919.4	(315)	—	—
$501-1000 }			1114.3	(68)	967.2	(77)	—	—
$1001-2000 }			1083.0	(61)	1052.2	(89)	—	—
$2001-5000 }	713.3	(85)	1001.2	(56)	884.1	(104)	—	—
$5001 and over }			548.2	(51)	788.5	(84)	—	—
German								
None stated	827.3	(1672)	949.1	(928)	841.7	(675)	—	—
$1-500 }	926.8	(48)	1036.6	(565)	981.6	(523)	—	—
$501-1000 }			977.9	(97)	807.4	(153)		
$1001-2000 }			1046.6	(90)	913.5	(135)	—	—
$2001-5000 }	982.8	(148)	1029.8	(118)	944.6	(195)	—	—
$5001 and over }			1249.0	(88)	980.7	(211)	—	—
Native White								
None stated	804.3	(1407)	713.4	(540)	647.1	(782)	—	—
$1-500 }	851.2	(32)	812.2	(488)	671.5	(519)	—	—
$501-1000 }			742.0	(99)	794.2	(125)	—	—
$1001-2000 }			677.6	(69)	734.4	(83)	—	—
$2001-5000 }	898.9	(246)	638.0	(114)	718.6	(182)	—	—
$5001 and over }			789.5	(206)	731.2	(293)	—	—

[a] Standardization for the overall ratios was to the age distribution of all white women in Philadelphia in 1870. Standardization for the marital child-woman ratios was to the age distribution of married women in the Pennsylvania anthracite mining region in 1880.

Source: Samples of census enumerators' manuscripts of approximately 2000 households headed by Irish, 2000 households headed by Germans, and 2000 households headed by native white Americans.

heads of family were heavily involved in skilled manual trades. This, of course, accords with the image one has of the social and economic characteristics of these ethnic groups in nineteenth-century America.

Finally, the pattern of fertility by wealth holding was irregular. Usually families with no stated wealth had lower fertility than those with some modest amount. Sometimes families with the largest amount of wealth had fertility higher than that of the intermediate groups. Some positive effect of economic constraints on fertility is indicated, but the results are far from uniform. The only distinctive relationship was that of a curvilinear pattern among the Irish.

In conclusion, much of what has been found thus far has not been unexpected. The overall ethnic fertility differentials were predictable but the marital fertility differentials were not nearly as wide as overall fertility differentials, especially in 1850, which indicates an important role for nuptiality differentials. Within ethnic groups, differentials in marital fertility according to mixed ethnicity of spouses, literacy and employment of wives, occupation of husband, and wealth of family were usually either consistent with prior findings or consistently irregular. Changes over time were quite different across groups, with the families headed by native whites experiencing a consistent decline in both overall and marital fertility, whereas both the Irish- and German-headed families had dramatic increases in marital fertility between the late 1840s and the late 1850s. Further work is under way that will include comparisons of the various white ethnic groups to the black population, extension of the study to 1900, and application of multivariate analysis to micro data using community-level variables from the grid unit files of the PSHP data base.

Reconceptualizing Family, Work and Labor Organizing: Working Women in Troy, 1860–1890

CAROLE TURBIN

ABSTRACT: This study of women collar workers in Troy, New York (1860–1890) examines the impact of the relationship between work and family life on labor organizing. It poses a neglected question: under what conditions did women form successful unions, become aware of shared interests and develop alliances with men, despite obstacles to permanent organization? By analyzing collar women's employment patterns, family and ethnic networks, as well as work-related factors such as level of expertise and status within the occupation and community, the popular view that working women were a homogeneous group characterized by temporary labor force participation, lack of identification with their work, passivity, and isolation from each other and male workers is challenged. Distinctions between women in different collar occupations shed additional light on levels and characteristics of women's labor activism and group consciousness. The relationship between ethnic and family ties and Troy's industrial structure fostered cooperation between women and men unionists and contributed to the high level of labor activism in Troy. An important conclusion is that a factor formerly viewed as suited to understanding women, the family, is also key for understanding an area thought of as men's domain, labor activity, and indeed the labor militancy of an entire community.

INTRODUCTION

In the past decade the argument that work and family life are systematically related and overlapping dimensions of existence has become an important framework for the study of working women and the family. This view, which has displaced the earlier concept of work and family as distinct and mutually exclusive spheres, is a part of the growing literature on links between private life (women's world of family and household) and public life (men's world of business, industry, politics, and professions). Scholars have argued that family life and workplace experience are interconnected and that the relationship between them is dynamic (Tilly and Scott 1978; Kelly 1979). Shifts in the work process related to industrialization changed the family, but family ties also influenced the organization of work, work rhythms and who worked with whom and where (Hareven 1977; Dublin 1979). More recently researchers have questioned the idea that women's work was transferred from home to factory in a unilinear manner; they have developed a new analysis of how industrialization transformed household production and consequently the rela-

Empire State College, State University of New York, Old Westbury, New York.
Portions of this essay and some of the ideas on which it is based originally appeared in Turbin (1979). I wish to thank Houghton Mifflin Company for graciously allowing me to use previously published material. The National Endowment for the Humanities and the Research Foundation of the State University of New York provided generous funding for further research. I am indebted to Harold Benenson for his insights and to the collective and individual contributions of the women and work study group (Chris Bose, Carol Brown, Peggy Crull, Roslyn Feldberg, Nadine Felton, Myra Marx Ferree, Evelyn Nakano Glenn, Amy Kesselman, Susan Lehrer, Natalie Sokoloff, and Amy Gilman Srebnick). Thanks also to Mary Blewett and the *RRPE* editors, Susan Himmelweit, Laurie Nisonoff, and especially to Sandy Schilen for her detailed and valuable criticisms.

tionship between family life and work experience (Dublin 1981; Blewett 1980,[1] 1983).

This essay on women collar workers in Troy, New York (1860–1890) examines a neglected aspect of the relationship between work and family life: the bearing of these relationships on women's labor militancy.[1] Troy offers a good opportunity to study these relationships. The mid-nineteenth century was not only a period of rapid industrialization, but also a time when the nation was debating the rights of Blacks and women, and the right of wage-earners to organize. At the same time as Suffragists were organizing, the labor movement was developing a national organization. Troy played an important part in these developments. The city was the home of the Emma Willard School, the first women's secondary school which provided a traditional men's curriculum. As a major industrial center with a strong labor movement, the city led the movement to establish producer's cooperatives. Two industries dominated Troy: the iron industry which was a major producer of the region's iron products such as stoves, bells, and nails, and the shirt, collar, and cuff industry. Troy earned its current nickname, "Collar City," because it produced ninety percent of the nation's detachable collars. In 1860 the industry employed over 3,000 women, largely of Irish background; by 1880 the number grew to over 8,000. Collar women included factory operatives who stitched men's detachable collars and laundresses who washed, starched, and ironed newly-manufactured goods before they were sold to retailers. In addition, uncounted numbers of women from Troy and surrounding communities did finishing work at home.[2] Although both factory operatives and laundresses went on strike at various times it was the laundresses, particularly the ironers, whose organization was so impressive. In 1864 collar ironers formed a union of about 500 members which lasted until the end of their major three-month strike in 1869. In 1886 laundresses and collar sewers formed the Joan of Arc Assembly of the Knights of Labor and again, led by the ironers, engaged in a major strike.

In this well-organized labor community, the Iron Molders' Union No. 2 was the collar women's close ally. The local was one of the strongest in the Iron Molders' International Union, which was one of the nation's most prominent unions. Several events highlight this alliance. In 1864 iron molders helped collar laundresses organize a union and in subsequent years they continued to offer support. In 1866, during the molders' Great Lockout the laundresses reciprocated (and demonstrated their own financial solvency) by donating the immense sum of $500.00 to the molders' strike fund. Molders again provided crucial support during the collar ironers' spring 1869 strike. Partly because this strike concerned workers' right to organize, a central issue in the molders' 1866 strike and in the labor movement in general, the collar ironers' struggle became a *cause célèbre* for New York State's labor movement. Seventeen years later the 1886 lockout involved a similar issue. Molders and collar women were again linked, but the Knights of Labor in general, rather than molders in particular, were the women's special allies.[3]

Most studies of women's unions explore the question of why a smaller proportion of women formed sustained labor organizations than men.[4] Links between family life and work experience are examined in order to shed light on an important part of the picture: how women's family roles discouraged them from forming permanent organizations.[5] However, too often this analysis is presented not as a partial explanation, but as a framework for understanding all of women's labor activity. This is misleading not only because it fails to explain organizations like the collar laundry union, but also because it does not contribute to an accurate, comprehensive understanding of women's labor activism and women's consciousness of their shared interests as workers. A full analysis of women's unions must ask a question few researchers have explored: considering the barriers to permanent organization for women, under what conditions were some women able to form relatively successful, permanent unions, develop an awareness of shared interests, and form strong alliances with male workers?[6]

Studies which focus on the question of what factors discouraged women's organization tend to over-emphasize contrasts between women and men wage-earners. This approach tends to view women workers as a homogeneous group and to stress specifically female characteristics such as passivity. In previous work I have argued that analyses of women's unions must take into account factors similar to those considered in studies of men's labor movements, including status in the labor force and the community, level of skill and earnings, and identification with occupation (Turbin 1979). This essay will summarize these points and discuss further implications. It will also take the analysis a step further by considering a dimension which has been suggested by studies of women and which only recently has been considered in analyses of men: the relationship among family and community ties, household economy, industrial structure, and workplace experience. These relationships have a bearing on the consciousness and labor activity of both women and men, and indeed an entire labor community.

RETHINKING WOMEN'S WORK PATTERNS AND CONSCIOUSNESS

Viewing women workers as a homogeneous group tends to lump women together on the lowest level of the working class and to ignore crucial differences in female occupational groups, types of activism, and levels of consciousness. An examination of distinctions between groups of working women, including those in the same industry, reveals previously unstudied facets of the relationship between work and family which are central to understanding the labor activity of both women and men. One of these facets is the extent to which women were temporary workers. This section will closely examine differences in the labor force participation of Troy collar women who were at different stages of the life cycle and from various household economies. Turning the conventional question on its head, the essay will explore how women's consciousness as workers reflects the extent to which their wage work was permanent. Examining the different forms of this permanency reveals that some individual women were permanent workers and some were part of social and ethnic groups which were a permanent and continuous segment of the labor force.

A look at collar laundresses' ages, marital status, and employment patterns reveals that the role of many working class women included that of provider.[7]

Census data and contemporary reports challenge the popular view that the majority of women wage-earners were young single girls who were not dependent on their income for survival, and cite evidence that a large percentage of collar women worked because they had to. Like other female occupational groups, not all collar women were young and single. In 1870, eighteen percent of collar laundresses were widows with small children who boarded or lived alone or with parents or other relatives. Of the remaining eighty-three percent who were single, not all were young; forty-five percent were twenty-five years of age and older.[8] According to Augusta Lewis, leader of New York City's female typographical union, and Susan B. Anthony, many collar laundresses had other relatives dependent on them for income (*New York Sun*, July 5, 1869). The laundresses' president, Kate Mullaney, supported her mother and two younger sisters (*New York World*, February 12, 1870).

Collar women's employment patterns also challenge popular assumptions.[9] Although women's work patterns were different than men's because their life cycle was different, the relationship between women's labor force participation and life cycle cannot be summed up with an ideal picture of young women working for only a few years before marriage. In keeping with working class families' assumption that family members would contribute to making a living, employment for women like Troy's laundresses was a familiar experience at every stage of life. Daughters who entered the labor force when they reached a suitable age had more than a few years of work ahead of them,[10] and those who did not marry remained in the labor force much longer.[11] Many women who left employment for marriage continued to earn money through home work or taking in boarders. The percentage of women who were widows or separated indicates that even young women who did not work before marriage might have to work later if their husbands died or left them.[12] Some collar women were employed for a good part of their lives, and others worked at one time or another, or during several stages of their lives either within or outside of their homes.[13]

Evidence suggests the existence of networks of women who worked in the collar laundries, and in later decades, in the collar industry as a whole. Collar work seems to have been a tradition in some families, partly because collar laundry work was especially attractive to women from Irish working class families. There were other opportunities for work in Troy but, as we shall see later, in the 1860s and 1870s collar laundry work was a good niche in the occupational structure for women of Irish descent. Just as sons often entered the same occupation as their fathers or older brothers, sometimes daughters followed their mothers or other female relatives into the same occupation, often working side by side in the same shop. Networks included more than family members. In Troy's closely-knit Irish working class community workers recruited friends, neighbors, and other relatives; women's networks must have included sisters-in-law, aunts, and female relatives. Contacts at work influenced community, ethnic, and family ties, and vice versa.[14] Family financial needs, the expectation among working class families that women contribute to making a living, and the fact that the collar industry provided stable employment for Irish working class women combined to make the social group from which collar women were drawn a permanent part of the labor force. Although not all individuals were permanent workers, collar women were part of a social group which supplied the labor force of the collar laundries in these decades.

There are good reasons to conclude that women in this segment of the labor force perceived of themselves as part of this group. The existence of networks suggests that individual women knew others with similar or different work histories. At any given time female relatives in the same household or neighborhood probably worked for wages in the collar laundries, and others worked there in the past or expected to be employed in the future. Moreover, the fact that collar laundresses' activism mobilized most of the workers in the industry and was sustained over long periods of time, rather than being tied to particular labor struggles, indicates that group awareness was continuous and not limited to sporadic periods of activism. A combination of close family ties and shared experience as workers and activists suggests that collar women were conscious of their shared interests as workers.

Speculation about women's perception of themselves as a group suggests that differences in household economy and stage of life cycle may explain some variations in women's labor militancy. Since Anthony's observation that "nearly all" the laundresses were supporting aged parents and younger siblings was based on a visit with the union's leadership,[15] her comments indicate that Kate Mullaney's family was not atypical (*New York World*, February 12, 1870). Other leaders were also the only wage-earners in their households. This suggests that women who were dependent on wages because of their household economy and stage of life cycle were more likely to be conscious of their shared interests and to translate their awareness into activism. The large proportion of collar women whose households included male wage-earners had other reasons to be committed to unionism which will be discussed later, but it is possible that they were less active in the union's daily operations. Women who were more dependent on wages to support themselves and others for an extended period of time probably formed an important part of the leadership.

This analysis suggests rethinking some conventional ideas about women workers and women's and men's labor activism and consciousness. Oversimplifying differences between women and men workers glosses over distinctions in the work patterns of women at different stages of life and from various family economies, and who work in localities with different industrial structures and populations. Just as obstacles to women's labor organizing do not constitute a framework for understanding women's activism, working women should not be assumed to be temporary workers with little or no identification with their work or awareness of themselves as having common interests as workers. Group consciousness does not stem only from work-related factors or from the type of labor force participation experienced by men. Partly because of ties to networks of family members and neighbors who shared similar identities, perceptions and experiences, individual women who may have been temporary workers were conscious of themselves as a group who shared common interests as workers (although their self-perception may have taken different forms). An examination of the interrelationship among family life, community and ethnic ties and, as we shall see later, workplace experience, contributes to an understanding of distinctions between the activism of workers in different industries, and to differences in consciousness and commitment to collective action of organized workers in the same industry.

A POSITION WORTH DEFENDING

Further examination of conditions contributing to women workers' ability to form sustained labor organizations also sheds light on other differences between female occupational groups and workers in the same industry, and on similarities between the experiences of some women and men wage-earners. Comparisons with less well-organized female workers, such as sewing women, shows that among Troy's working women collar laundresses were relatively privileged. In fact, collar laundresses, particularly ironers, shared many of the characteristics of male workers who organized successfully. Labor historians argue that in this period, as in other decades, the most well-organized workers were highly-skilled wage-earners on the highest levels of the working class. This was partly because workers in occupations which retained the characteristics of skilled crafts strongly identified with their trades and had a stake in defending their relatively high position on the social scale. Also, their labor was a comparatively scarce commodity which could be withheld in order to bargain with employers. Earning higher wages than most workers, they possessed the financial resources to weather hard times, including strikes (Montgomery 1967). While collar laundresses' situation differed from that of male workers, they shared with men an identification with their occupation and a relatively high status in the working class community, and they had good reasons to protect their rights as workers.

What was the position of Troy's collar laundresses in the community and the industry? Like many industrial workers, collar laundry women were largely of Irish descent. Immigration patterns in the United States partly explain the overwhelming proportion of Irish women employed in the laundries. Many Irish immigrants found their way to Troy because the Hudson River provided convenient transportation from New York City, and Troy's industries promised employment. But the position of Troy's Irish population differed from that of other urban centers where Irish immigrants were concentrated on the lowest levels of the working class. Walkowitz (1974) reveals that many of Troy's Irish immigrants achieved a relatively high status through employment in the skilled branches of the city's growing iron industry.[16] Census data indicate that while many collar laundresses came from families of unskilled workers, an even larger group came from skilled workers' families. The laundresses' status was consistent with both the low status of Irish workers in general and the relatively high status of many Irish families in Troy (Turbin 1979).

However, collar laundering was low on the occupational scale. Ellson and Pearson (1981) argue that occupations reserved for women are judged to be unskilled partly because manual dexterity and other abilities necessary for work such as sewing and ironing are considered natural female attributes.[17] Trained through long hours of work at home rather than informal apprenticeships, the learning process is invisible and thus unrecognized. But collar laundering had even less status than sewing because it had the added disadvantage of being "unladylike." While women from prosperous families may have done their own fine needlework, they rarely did their own laundry. People invariably compared laundry work to taking in washing, which was one of the most menial and poorly paid women's occupations. Thus, although laundry work was an industrial occupation, it was considered less genteel and respectable than dressmaking, millinery, or even routine hand stitching. Moreover, although laundering was probably not any more fatiguing and health-impairing than sewing and factory work, working conditions involved heavy physical labor which was distasteful to many women. Esther Keegan, the collar laundresses' vice president, reported that laundresses stood on their feet almost all of their eleven to fourteen hours of labor in shops as small as sixteen feet square. Temperatures reached the "nineties" in the winter, and in the summer it was so hot that the laundresses often had to "forgo their work for two to three weeks at a time from sheer inability to perform it." Ironers were required to continually lift hot heavy irons, and starchers' fingers became sore from constant immersion in starchy water. Keegan asserted that because of these conditions, laundresses frequently contracted consumption. "None but the strongest could stand it." Women from American backgrounds who had more options for employment probably preferred the more "ladylike" occupations of sewing and light industrial work (Turbin 1979).

While collar laundering was not attractive to women of American background who could get other work, it was a good occupation for Irish women who wished to escape employment in service occupations.[18] Working class women considered the work of cooks, chambermaids, and housekeepers degrading because it involved serving or cleaning up after others and did not provide the independence of a wage. Collar laundering did not have these characteristics and it also provided regular employment and relatively high earnings, in part because of the union. Combining the disadvantages of unladylike labor and the advantages of industrial work, collar laundering attracted on the one hand women from lower levels of the working class who sought to avoid domestic service, and on the other, those from higher levels who were willing to endure hard physical labor for high wages (Turbin 1979).

Of the laundering steps, collar ironing was the most prestigious and ironers were the best organized. Although ironing had lower status than other women's work, ironing in commercial laundries required a combination of manual dexterity and physical strength which could only be mastered with two to four weeks of intensive training. Proud of their ability to endure harsh working conditions and handle hot heavy irons for hours, collar ironers boasted that not every women was equal to the task.[19] Several incidents corroborate ironers' claims and indicate that the difficulty of finding good workers contributed to the ironers' ability to bargain successfully with employers.[20] During the ironers' major strike in spring 1868 laundry proprietors could not maintain full production levels during the strike while scab workers were being trained. As employers themselves admitted, it took "some time to teach the newcomers the business." Even with a few weeks of training, the inexperienced workers' abilities were not equal to the dexterity and speed of the striking ironers (Turbin 1979).

Partly because of this centrality in the production process, ironers could demand higher wages than starchers and washers, and indeed higher than those of most other women wage-earners. In 1872 the average earnings of working women amounted to $299.00 per year, or $6.96 per week, while the average working man earned $611.33 per year, or $13.44 per week. Collar ironers earned from $10.00 to $12.00 per week, about twice that of the average working woman and nearly as much as some working men. These relatively high earnings contributed to ironers' identification with their work and to establishing their status within their occupation and the community. High wages also provided resources which contributed to the strength of the union and to members' ability to weather strikes and hard times (Turbin 1978, 1979).

A strike over the introduction of machines suggests that ironers were willing to take drastic steps to preserve distinctions in wages and status based on expertise, but that these differences in earnings and prestige did not result in divisions which prevented collective action. In February 1886 the firm of Miller, Hall, and Hartwell installed ironing machines in their laundering departments and put ironers to work running the machines and folding finished collars and shirts. The firm's goal was both to raise production levels and to replace the piece work system with wages based on average output which would decrease the advantage of the more expert workers.[21] A spokeswoman for the 200 folders and machine operatives who walked off their jobs rejected the employers' claim that workers could earn as much as in the past for much less taxing work. She said that the strikers' goals were both to protect the ironers' expertise and the jobs of those who might be dismissed because of the machines' greatly increased output. Expressing pride in expert ironers' accomplishments mixed with resentment that less able hands might earn much more under the new system, she said "of two girls who have been running these machines the past week, one is a first class ironer who thoroughly knows her business and the other cannot work so fast or so neatly . . . Yet they both earned nearly the same wages on these machines" (*Troy Daily Telegram*, February 22, 23, 24, 1886). Stressing the importance of preserving jobs as well as expertise, this ironer was keenly aware of the implications of changes in the production process for ironers as a group as well as for individuals.

Collar laundresses had good reasons to protect their interests as workers, but ironers were in a better position to defend them. Ironers seemed to take a special pride in their work which resembled the attitudes of men in trades requiring skill and strenuous labor, and like well-organized male workers they possessed financial resources and could bargain relatively effectively with employers. Perhaps because of ties of family and ethnicity as well as bonds resulting from cooperation with other workers in small shops, ironers' greater resources and prestige did not lead to deep divisions among those who performed different tasks in the laundering process. Instead, like molders in the iron industry, ironers took the lead. Their leadership was probably a crucial ingredient in the labor activism of the entire industry.

FAMILY, ETHNICITY, COMMUNITY AND INDUSTRIAL STRUCTURE

Since collar laundresses were not craft workers whose labor was a scarce commodity, their strategies also depended on the support of Troy's well-organized, Irish dominated labor community. It was partly because of this tightly-knit labor movement that in Troy more relatively unskilled workers were organized than in some other industrial centers. Workers for whom there are barriers to organization (like women and less skilled workers in general) are more likely to organize in a community with a strong labor movement (Montgomery 1967). As leaders of this community, iron molders not only lent resources to less skilled neighbors, but they also articulated grievances and provided examples of success. Some groups who benefited from this support were day-laborers, sewing women, and women who ironed newly-manufactured collars for commercial laundries (Walkowitz 1974; Turbin 1978).

Women faced more barriers to organization than other less skilled workers. Despite male union officials' encouragement of women's unions, many men believed that women took men's jobs and reduced their earnings, and that the household, not the factory, was woman's "proper place." At best male unionists viewed women's unions as irrelevant because unmarried women were temporary workers and the goal of unions was to raise men's wages to a level sufficient to enable their wives to devote themselves to hearth and home.[22] However, in Troy some male wage-earners had more reasons to encourage women to organize than to be hostile or indifferent. Since most of Troy's industrially employed women were single or widowed, and the employment of daughters and widows without men to support them was congruent with working class families' expectations, the city's female industrial labor force was not a threat to traditional family structure.[23] Moreover, Troy's industrial structure fostered a firm alliance between important groups of women and men wage-earners, iron workers and collar women. Since the iron industry employed only men and collar factories employed predominantly women, male workers did not perceive women workers as a threat to their livelihood. In fact, well-organized women contributed to male unionists' goals of economic security and a strong labor movement.

Evidence indicates that from the 1860s to the 1880s collar laundresses (and sewers in the 1880s) provided an important contribution to iron molders' households. As we have seen, while many collar women were the only wage-earners in their families, a larger proportion lived in households which included male wage-earners. In many cases they were the daughters, sisters, and in-laws of iron molders.[24] Sharing the burden of their family's economic support with men, they may have had different attitudes toward the union and male unionists than women like Kate Mullaney whose families were entirely dependent on their earnings. But their family relationships gave them other reasons for having a stake in a strong and permanent union and provided one basis for cooperation between workers of different genders.

Family relationships do not always lead to cooperation. Daniel Walkowitz' and Barbara Abrash's film, *The Molders of Troy*, suggests that among Troy's Irish working class families commitment to unions was part of family lore and the household and community were places where union matters were discussed and sometimes resolved. But family tradition can work against labor organization just as it can reinforce it.[25] Family members who were loyal unionists did not always agree on strategies or attitudes toward union struggles. Strikes, lockouts, and other work-related emergencies called forth animosities as well as cooperation. In Troy, alliances between women and men were based on other factors fundamental to Troy's industrial and social structure.

The 1886 collar women's strike highlights the complex mix of factors which encouraged these alliances. Collar laundresses and sewers joined forces to form a local of the Knights of Labor in 1886, shortly before the ironers struck against machines in February (*Troy Daily Press*, February 11, 1886). In June about 200 starchers and ironers in the laundry department of George Ide's firm initiated another major strike by demanding an equalization of wages with other companies. The increase amounted to from one-half to one cent per piece, depending on the type of collar. When the women refused to return to work, employers responded by combining with other manufacturers to form an association and closed down all the shirt and collar factories in the city. The result was an industrywide lockout which involved thirty-three establishments and about 8,000 women, including home workers in Troy and vicinity. Although manufacturers and employees agreed on a compromise on wages in Ide's laundry within a few days, the lockout continued because employees insisted that the manufacturers' association recognize the Knights of Labor as the workers' representative. The employees won part of the increase they sought, but the demand that the Knights represent the collar women was rescinded (*Troy Daily Times*, *Troy Daily Press*, *Troy Daily Telegram*, May 15–June 23, 1886; *New York World*, May 15–June 22, 1886; *John Swinton's Paper*, May 15–June 29, 1886).

Family ties between iron molders and collar women seemed to have played a role in determining events. Locking out the entire industry over a demand for a small increase in one shop which was resolved fairly quickly makes sense only when the significance of the Knights' demands for recognition and some crucial events in the iron industry are considered. The collar women's five week strike coincided with a four month strike in the iron foundries. Both strikes ended within a few days of each other and both involved the Knights of Labor. Collar manufacturers, who sought to stem the influence of the Knights, were probably concerned that the newly-formed Joan of Arc Assembly would extend the Knights' influence into yet another segment of the labor force. But the fact that the molders' and collar women's strikes ended within days of each other suggests other relationships between the conflicts besides their association with the Knights. Labor leaders and other observers argued that the collar manufacturers were in league with the foundry owners; manufacturers locked out their employees because during the molders' strike families were dependent on the income of collar women who were molders' wives and daughters. Manufacturers hoped that throwing the women out of work would pressure iron molders to reach a settlement favorable to the foundry owners.[26]

The observers' claim that the factory owners' use of family ties to break the molders' strike supports the conclusion that family relationships in conjunction with Troy's industrial structure encouraged cooperation between workers of different genders. Since the city was dominated by two industries, one employing women and the other employing men, when men went out on strike they could rely on the earnings of female family members in the other industry and vice versa. Earnings of female family members were relatively certain since the collar industry employed thousands of Troy's women, both home and factory workers. Similarly, the iron industry employed a large proportion of Troy's male labor force (Walkowitz 1978). In both industries wages were relatively high and work steady, although there were slack periods. While this is not the only reason for Troy's high level of labor militancy, the relationship between industrial structure and family patterns is an important part of the explanation for Troy's strong labor community.

Ethnic and community ties also strengthened collar and iron workers' ability to hold out during strikes and hard times. Not all workers could depend on the earnings of relatives in the same household during strikes. Those who were the only wage-earners in their families probably depended on the resources of relatives in different households in the same or different neighborhoods, on friends and neighbors, and on benefits provided by the union's strike fund or on contributions (*New York World*, July 3, 1869). Living in the same neighborhoods and participating in Irish political and nationalist organizations, Troy's laundresses and iron molders were linked through community and ethnic ties as well as through family relationships.[27]

Examining shifts in the labor activism and alliances of collar sewers underscores the influence of family and ethnic ties on labor militancy. Collar sewers engaged in little labor activity before they organized with laundresses in the 1880s, and on one occasion when they did strike they refused help from the molders' union (*Troy Daily Times*, February 10, 1864). Two factors contributed to this change. First, by the 1880s collar laundries were incorporated into collar factories and sewers and laundresses were employed in the same establishments and faced the same employers.[28] Second, shifts in the ethnic composition of collar sewers resulted in closer ties to Troy's working class community. In 1865, nineteen percent of collar sewers were born in Ireland, in contrast to seventy-nine percent of collar laundresses. Five years later the percentage of Irish women employed as collar sewers doubled. In 1870, forty-four percent of the sewers were Irish, compared to eighty percent of the laundresses.[29] Thus by the 1880s collar sewers were not only part of the same industrial establishments as laundresses, but also a larger proportion of sewers were linked to laundresses and iron molders through family, community, and ethnic ties.

Other work supports the view that family relationships have a bearing on the characteristics of labor struggles. Mary Blewett's study of shoe workers in mid-nineteenth century Lynn, Massachusetts, argues that tensions between women workers' ties with male family members and ties with other women workers militated against firm alliances between women and men. Unlike Troy, Lynn and surrounding areas, were dominated by one major industry employing both women and men. In keeping with the strict sexual division of labor in which women worked as shoe binders at home or as stitchers in all female shops, women and men belonged to separate labor organizations. While women factory workers were part of a mobile labor force recruited from surrounding areas, home workers were largely wives or daughters of male shoe workers. Blewett's work on Haverhill suggests that factory operatives from other communities were not regarded as outsiders; coming from backgrounds and localities similar to that of the families with whom they boarded, strong ties developed between the young women and Haverhill's residents (Blewett 1979, 1983).

As in Troy, family relationships and women's contribution to the household economy were crucial ingredients in the web of alliances. In the 1860 regional shoe strike women factory workers (whom male workers had helped to organize) argued that improving women's wages was as important as improving men's wages. Also factory women sought to form an alliance with female home workers. Blewett argues that the male dominated strike committee refused to acknowledge the women factory workers' demands because they feared the decline of home work on which their families depended. Since the strike leadership ignored their demands, the female factory operatives' support was lost, although home workers continued to participate in the strike. The conflict ended in April with the issue of wages unresolved (Blewett 1983). Blewett's analysis and the example of Troy indicate that the influence of the relationship between family ties and industrial structure on labor organizing is a fruitful area of research for understanding labor militancy in nineteenth century cities.[30]

CONCLUSIONS

These findings have important implications for understanding working women in general. Avoiding stark contrasts between women and men and looking at conditions under which some women were able to organize successfully reveals subtle differences between male and female workers, and between women workers in the same industry and those in different occupations and communities. Moreover, while studies which focus on barriers to women's organization emphasize women's isolation from each other and lack of concern with common interests, the laundresses' experience suggests conditions under which some working class women may be conscious of their interests as a group. Consciousness takes different forms in different circumstances and may not always result in sustained organization, but it is important to see it as a possibility emerging from shared experience. Broadening the focus of labor history to include an examination of women who formed successful unions and perceived of themselves as a group having common interests contributes to a comprehensive understanding of working women and their organizations.

The preceding analysis also suggests a new perspective on the study of women, work, labor organizing and the family. It indicates that an area formerly thought of as especially suited to understanding women, the family, is also key for analyzing a subject thought to be the domain of men, labor activism, and indeed the entire labor movement in a community or region. This perspective is important because it reveals the limitations of looking at women's work force participation and labor activism mainly in terms of their family roles, and analyzing men's employment and union activity largely in terms of work-related factors. Reserving family life for understanding women and work experience for analyzing men leads to a narrow understanding of both sexes and neglects links between family, work, and industrial structure which contribute to an understanding of a community's complex social life.[31] An analysis of key facets of the interrelationship between family ties and work experience also suggests rethinking boundaries between academic fields. Like work and family life, areas of disciplines and interdisciplinary fields which study work and the family, women and men, are not distinct and separate, but are overlapping and systematically related.

NOTES

1. The discussion of Troy in the 1860s on pages 2 and 3 is based on material which originally appeared in Turbin (1979). Discussion of the 1880s is based on research completed since the publication of that essay.
2. Estimates are unreliable since home workers often do not appear in the manuscript census, but observers agreed that in the 1880s at least 3,000 women did home work in Troy and vicinity.
3. The discussion of the iron molders and Troy's labor movement is drawn from Walkowitz' important work on Troy (1972, 1974, 1978).
4. For example, Kennedy (1979) and Tentler (1979) stress factors which militate against women's sustained collective action. Studies of working class communities such as Dawley (1976) and Walkowitz (1978) discuss women's labor activism as well as barriers to organization, but they do not systematically examine specific conditions under which women organized successfully.
5. Kessler–Harris (1975, 1979) discusses ways in which male unionists' attitudes toward working women discouraged organization.
6. Louise Tilly (1981) is one of the few researchers who analyzes this question systematically.
7. This argument appeared in Turbin (1979). Also see Groneman (1977).
8. All percentages are drawn from New York State manuscript census schedules for 1865 and federal manuscript census schedules for 1870. This data is more fully discussed in Turbin (1978: 197–206).
9. The question of the extent to which women were temporary workers is complicated. Maintaining that women's work was a temporary stage before marriage was a means of reconciling contradictions between the ideology of domesticity and the reality of economic need which sent many women into the paid labor force. Related to this is the undercount of working women in the census. Women may have been reluctant to identify themselves as wage-earners and enumerators may have failed to asked questions about women's occupations. For a discussion of the undercount, particularly of home workers, see Bose (1983).
10. The youngest working women in the census are aged fourteen, but sources suggest that children left school sooner for wage work, after age twelve. See Walkowitz (1978: 115) and Kaestle and Vinovskis (1978) for a discussion of school leaving.
11. One unmarried woman who appeared in the 1860 census as a collar laundress when she was twenty-five was still working in the laundries in 1870 when she was thirty-six.
12. Widows did not always remain in the labor force. Some left work when their children were old enough to support them.
13. For further discussion see Turbin (1978: 198–200; 1979: 206).
14. Analysis of Troy's closely-knit Irish working class community is based on Walkowitz (1978). Hayner (1925: 635–6) suggests that women family members were often employed in the same company, with grandmothers, mothers, and daughters working in the same room in a shop. This pattern has been documented for other communities by Hareven (1977: 195), Wallace (1978: 59-61), and Dublin (1979).
15. Anthony's report was based on a visit to Troy in 1870. Delayed between trains, she took the opportunity to visit the union's failing cooperative laundry and meet with its managers, including Kate Mullaney and Esther Keegan. The union's leaders had been dismissed by employers after the 1869 strike. Harper (1969: 999–1000) notes that Anthony included references to this visit in speeches about the importance of the ballot for women's bargaining position with employers. She argued that if women were enfranchised the collar laundresses would have won their strike.
16. Walkowitz (1974) notes that men of Irish descent constituted the largest numbers of workers in each of the largest skilled branches of the iron foundries: molders, puddlers, and heaters and rollers.

17. Phillips and Taylor (1980) also discuss this point.
18. Walkowitz (1974) argues that skilled iron work also had more status for Irish workers than for those of American and British background.
19. Virginia Penny's (1863) compilation of employers' reports from the 1860s includes comments by proprietors of commercial laundries that good ironers were scarce and commanded high wages.
20. Another incident underscores this point. Having given in to demands for wage increases since 1864, in 1869 laundry proprietors tried to undermine the union by persuading nonunion ironers in the city's largest laundry to train new hands to replace workers in union shops. The owners would not have tried to weaken the union in this way if they could have simply fired the union ironers and replaced them with new hands. Kate Mullaney reported that the employers' tactics failed because the nonunion ironers, "seeing what the results would finally be, for their own protection, joined the union in a body." The owners' need for experienced labor enabled the ironers to strengthen the union even further (Turbin 1979: 210)
21. Manufacturers may have abolished the piece work system in order to increase their control over wages and the work process. Stone (1975) argues that piece work gave employees more control over wages, although it was also a source of divisions among workers.
22. For a discussion of the family wage, see Hartmann (1979: 16–17), Barrett and McIntosh (1980: 51–72), and May (1982: 400–408).
23. The small percentage of industrially employed married women was probably due to the collar industry's extensive home work system which enabled women to earn income at home. Home work in Troy is described by Greeley (1873: 614–615) and Weise (1877. 265).
24. Preliminary analysis of census data indicates that more collar laundresses were members of iron molders' families than working women in other industrial occupations. In 1865, fourteen percent of the laundresses' male relatives were molders. In contrast, molders constituted only eight percent of collar sewers' male relatives, and five percent of sewing women's male relatives. Although these figures are modest, they indicate that slightly more laundry women than other working women were related to molders (Turbin 1979)
25. Conflicts between family members during the laundresses' 1869 strike are described in the *Troy Daily Whig*, June 23, 1869. See Hartmann (1981: 367–8) for a useful analysis of conflicts and struggles which take place within families.
26. The argument that collar manufacturers were in league with iron foundry owners appears in: New York Bureau of Labor Statistics (1887: 44–77); *New York World*, May 19 and 20, 1886; *Troy Daily Times*, May 26, 1886; *John Swinton's Paper*, May 23 and June 23, 1886.
27. See Walkowitz (1974: 433–5, 1978) for a detailed and insightful analysis of Troy's ethnic, political, and community networks.
28. The organization of the collar industry from its inception to the 1870s is fully described in Greeley (1873: 614–615).
29. Discussion of these shifts is based on census data and on reports from the *Troy Daily Press*, *Troy Daily Times*, and *Troy Daily Telegram*, May 15 to June 23, 1886. Changes in the proportion of Irish collar sewers seems to be too great to be due to errors related to the small size of the population or limitations of census data. If in fact sewing was a more genteel although less remunerative occupation than ironing, it may indicate Irish upward mobility or changes in collar sewing which made the occupation less desirable to women of American background.
30. The role of family patterns in labor organizing has been analyzed by Foster (1974), Humphries (1977), and Benenson (1982).
31. This argument has also been made by Feldberg and Glenn (1979).

REFERENCES

Barrett, Michelle, and McIntosh, Mary. 1980. The Family Wage: Some Problems for Socialists and Feminists. *Capital and Class* 11: 51–72.

Benenson, Harold. 1982. Skill Degradation, Industrial Change, and the Family and Community Bases of U.S. Working Class Response. Paper presented at Social Science History Association, Bloomington, Indiana.

Blewett, Mary. 1979. The Union of Sex and Craft in the Haverhill Shoe Strike of 1895. *Labor History* 20: 352–375.

______. 1981. Shared but Different: The Experience of Women Workers in the Nineteenth Century Work Force of the New England Shoe Industry. In, *Essays From the Lowell Conference on Industrial History, 1980 and 1981*. pp. 77–85. Lowell.

______. 1983. Work, Gender, and the Artisan Tradition in New England Shoe-Making, 1790–1860. *Journal of Social History* 17: 221–248.

Bose, Christine. 1983. Determinants of U.S. Women's Work in 1900: A Household Resource Model. Paper presented at American Sociological Association, Detroit, Michigan.

Dawley, Alan. 1976. *Class and Community: The Industrial Revolution in Lynn*. Cambridge: Harvard University Press.

Dublin, Thomas. 1979. *Women at Work: The Transformation of Work and Community in Lowell, Massachusetts, 1826–1860*. New York: Columbia University Press.

______. 1981. Women and the Dimensions of Outwork in 19th Century New England. Paper presented at Berkshire Conference on Women's History, Poughkeepsie, New York.

Elson, Diane, and Ruth Pearson. 1981. 'Nimble Fingers Make Cheaper Workers': An Analysis of Women's Employment in Third World Export Manufacturing. *Feminist Review* 7: 93–95.

Feldberg, Roslyn, and Evelyn Nakano Glenn. 1979. Male and Female: Job Versus Gender Models in the Sociology of Work. *Social Problems* 26: 524–538.

Foster, John. 1974. *Class Struggle and the Industrial Revolution: Early Industrial Capitalism in Three English Towns*. New York: Saint Martin's Press.

Greeley, Horace, et al. 1873. *Great Industries of the United States*. Hartford: J.B. Burr and Hyde and Company.

Groneman, Carol. 1977. 'She Earns as a Child, She Pays as a Man': Women Workers in a Mid-Nineteenth Century New York Community. In, *Class, Sex, and the Woman Worker*, Milton Cantor and Bruce Laurie, eds. pp. 83–100. Westport, Conn.: Greenwood Press.

Hareven, Tamara. 1977. Family Time and Industrial Time: Family and Work in a Planned Corporation Town, 1900–1924. In, *Family and Kin in Urban Communities: 1700–1930*, Tamara Hareven, ed. New York: New Viewpoints.

Harper, Ida Usted. 1969. *The Life and Work of Susan B. Anthony*. New York: Arno Press. (First published in 1898.)

Hartmann, Heidi. 1979. The Unhappy Marriage of Marxism and Feminism: Towards a More Progressive Union. *Capital and Class* 8: 3–33.

______. 1981. The Family as the Locus of Gender, Class, and Political Struggle: The Example of Housework. *Signs: Journal of Women in Culture and Society* 6: 366–395.

Hayner, Rutherford. 1925. *Troy and Rensselaer County, New York*. New York: Lewis Historical Publishing Company, Inc.

Humphries, Jane. 1977. Class Struggle and the Persistence of the Working Class Family. *Cambridge Journal of Economics* I: 241–258.

Kaestle, Carl F. and Maris A. Vinovskis. 1978. From Fireside to Factory: School Entry and School Leaving in Nineteenth Century Massachusetts. In, *Transitions: The Family and the Life Course in Historical Perspective*, Tamara Hareven, ed. New York: Academic Press.

Kelly, Joan. 1979. The Doubled Vision of Feminist Theory: A Postscript to the 'Women and Power' Conference. *Feminist Studies* 5: 216–227.

Kennedy, Susan Estabrook. 1979. *If All We Did Was To Weep at Home: A History of White Working Class Women in America*. Bloomington, Indiana: Indiana University Press.

Kessler-Harris, Alice. 1975. Stratifying by Sex: Understanding the History of Working Women. In, *Labor Market Segmentation*, Richard C. Edwards, Michael Reich, David M. Gordon, eds. pp. 217–242. Lexington, Massachusetts: D.C. Heath and Company.

______. 1979. Where Are the Organized Women Workers? In, *A Heritage of Her Own: Toward a New Social History of American Women*, Nancy F. Cott and Elizabeth Pleck, eds. New York: Simon and Schuster.

______. 1982. *Out to Work: A History of Wage-Earning Women in the United States*. New York: Oxford University Press.

May, Martha. 1982. The Historical Problem of the Family Wage: The Ford Motor Company and the Five Dollar Day. *Feminist Studies* 8: 400–408.

Montgomery, David. 1967. *Beyond Equality: Labor and the Radical Republicans, 1862–1872*. New York: Vintage Books.

New York, Bureau of Labor Statistics. *Fourth Annual Report of the Year 1886* (Albany 1887).

New York, Secretary of State. *State Cenus Records of Rensselaer County, New York, 1855–1906, Troy, New York*. Microfilm of hand-written census records, County Court House, Troy, New York. Eleven Rolls. 35 mm.

Penny, Virginia. 1863. *The Employments of Women*. Boston: Walker, Wise, and Company.

Phillips, Ann, and Barbara Taylor. 1980. Sex and Skill: Notes Toward a Feminist Economics. *Feminist Review* 6: 79–88.

Stone, Katherine. 1975. The Origins of Job Structures in the Steel Industry. In, *Labor Market Segmentation*, Richard C. Edwards, Michael Reich, David M. Gordon, eds. pp. 27–84. Lexington, Massachusetts: D.C. Heath and Company.

Tentler, Leslie Woodcock. 1979. *Wage-Earning Women: Industrial Work and Family Life in the United States, 1900–1930*. New York: Oxford University Press.

Tilly, Louise A. 1981. Paths of Proletarianization: Organization of Production, Sexual Division of Labor and Women's Collective Action. *Signs: Journal of Women in Culture and Society* 7: 400–417.

Tilly, Louise, and Joan Scott. 1978. *Women, Work, and Family*. New York: Holt, Rinehart, Wiston.

Turbin, Carole. 1978. Women's Work and Women's Rights: A Comparative Study of the Woman's Trade Union Movement and the Woman's Rights Movement in the Mid-Nineteenth Century. Unpublished Ph.D. dissertation, New School for Social Research.

______. 1979. 'And We Are Nothing but Women': Irish Working Women in Troy. In, *Women of America: A History*, Carol R. Berkin and Mary Beth Norton, eds., Boston: Houghton Mifflin Company.

United States Bureau of the Census. *Ninth Census of the United States: 1870. Population of Rensselaer County, New York State*.

Walkowitz, Daniel J. 1972. Working Class Culture in the Guided Age: The Iron Workers of Troy, New York, and the Cotton Workers of Cohoes, New York, 1855–1884. Unpublished Ph.D. dissertation, University of Rochester.

______. 1974. Statistics and the Writing of Working Class Culture: A Statistical Portrait of the Iron Workers in Troy, New York, 1860–1880. *Labor History* 15: 416–460.

______. 1978. *Worker City, Company Town: Iron and Cotton Worker Protest in Troy and Cohoes: New York, 1855–1884*. Urbana: University of Illinois Press.

Wallace, Anthony. 1978. *Rockdale: The Growth of an American Village in the Early Industrial Revolution*. New York: Alfred A. Knopf.

Weise, Arthur James. 1877. History of the City of Troy and the Village of Lansingburgh. Troy, New York: William H. Young.

DANIEL J. WALKOWITZ

WORKING-CLASS WOMEN IN THE GILDED AGE: FACTORY, COMMUNITY AND FAMILY LIFE AMONG COHOES, NEW YORK, COTTON WORKERS

In much of the recent work characterized as the "New Urban History," sociologists and historians have focused on the relationship between social mobility and behavior within the nineteenth-century working class.[1] To a large extent this scholarship has tried to grapple with the question often posed by the New Left: "Whatever happened to the revolution?" Two alternative arguments have generally been put forth concerning working-class oppression and united or individual efforts towards social amelioration. In the first case, the oppressed working class organized and struggled—even violently—to gain some affluence and security through the labor movement. In the second case, workers individually achieved some mobility, and consequently little or no united effort was made to win a social revolution.[2] Something, however, of both these views may be correct: workers lived and worked under oppressive conditions, but workers achieved some significant measure of social mobility. Furthermore, considerable violence did occur in labor struggles, but no social revolution occurred.

These seeming paradoxes hinge on the contrast between working-class mobility as it was perceived by the members of the working class themselves and the attempt to make some "objec-

Professor Walkowitz is in the history department of Rutgers University.

This is an expanded version of a paper read at the annual meeting of the American Historical Association in Boston, December 30, 1970. Data for the paper were compiled from the United States manuscript census schedules for the city of Cohoes, Albany County, New York: Census Office, 8th Census of Population, 1860; Census Office, 8th Census of Manufactures 1860; Census Office, 10th Census of Population, 1880; and, 10th Census of Manufactures, 1880. Especially helpful also was Arthur Masten, *History of Cohoes, New York, From its Earliest Settlement to the Present Time* (Albany, 1877).

tive" assessment of the parameters of that mobility. This essay intends to examine the ways in which the cultural experience of the predominantly immigrant working class might have distorted their view of their social conditions and impaired their ability to focus on the origins of their oppression. Consequently, working-class violence, rather than being directed at the manufacturer, was directed at the ranks of the unemployed ready to claim their jobs. In this way, the working class did not engage in aggressive violence to win a social revolution so much as it fought defensive struggles to protect its modest gains.

Working-class behavior is not merely a response to objective social conditions but is fundamentally shaped by the *perception* of those conditions. Historians have correctly emphasized the poverty and fragility of working-class economic and social existence during the Gilded Age. For instance, a New York State Assembly Committee investigating laboring conditions declared that the testimony of 17 randomly selected employees of the Harmony cotton mills in Cohoes, New York, "very clearly establishes . . . [that] very few families are enabled to save money, while a majority of them barely manage to make both ends meet at the close of the year."[3] But these harsh social realities must be viewed in the context of the expectations—the social dream—and the alternatives open to the working-class community. While violence marked the struggle to control the conditions of industrial life, the equation between poverty and violent social behavior is not precise. The history of the Cohoes cotton worker community is a case in point.

Cohoes, New York, is a small city located eight miles north of Albany on the west bank of the Hudson River at the confluence of that river and the Mohawk River. The cotton mills of Cohoes provided job opportunities in light industry for female laborers, opportunities that helped to create an unusual social community: the mills attracted a high percentage of working women and almost one quarter of the cotton worker families was headed by a woman. Confronted by the values of Puritan America, subjected to the social paternalism of the Harmony Corporation and sensitive to the demands of their own ethnic traditions, these women were immersed in a patriarchal culture. What kind of security and status, then, could Cohoes offer these women and their families? And, equally important, how did security and status function? The history of Cohoes' cotton workers demonstrates that the factory and the community helped both to sustain the mill operatives and to secure some social mobility for them. However, the small degree of status and security they attained did not liberate them from economic and social worries; rather, these modest gains restricted their field of vision and alienated them from their own social reality. It is within this context that we must view labor violence that erupted in Cohoes during the early 1880s.

During the 1870s, in the midst of a national economic storm that produced many financial failures, bitter strikes and violence, the Harmony Mills had offered relative industrial calm—with the not inconsiderable financial security and stability that this represented, especially for the immigrant working-class family. The depression compelled the Harmony Mills to close only one month during that entire decade; and while wages fell, the workers never struck. However, the tone and temper of Cohoes industrial life changed suddenly in 1880. In that year, and in 1882, extended strikes were fought. The strikes and lockouts began usually over further wage reductions, but at their core was a conflict over union recognition and power. These struggles culminated in violent mob scenes where angry women cotton workers and their children confronted imported Swedish "scab" workers and their police bodyguards.

Why was the Cohoes labor movement dormant during the 1870s, and why did disorder and violence erupt after 1880? If as E.P. Thompson suggests,[4] class is a relationship between people, a shared consciousness, what then were the dominant needs and values that influenced working-class behavior? What institutions were most valuable to them? And what effect did the industrial experience have on the position and attitudes of women in nineteenth-century Cohoes? Did it permit them some measure of independence; did it give them some role in community life; did they suffer a loss of status by having to leave the home to work? Central to our concern is the relationship between the factory, the community and the cotton worker and her family.

Since the Industrial Revolution, woman as worker has been seen as a contradiction in terms, as some sort of sin against nature. This attitude underlay the widely held belief that for women to work would, as Richard Ely wrote in 1893, mean "the scattering of the members of the family and the breakdown of the home. . . ."[5] Carroll D. Wright, writing in the Tenth United States Census in 1880 identified the factory as the culprit: "The factory system necessitates the employment of women and children to an injurious extent, and consequently its tendency is to destroy family life and ties and domestic habits, and ultimately the home."[6] Wright's implications were clear: since the factory system removed mother from the home, it destroyed the family; therefore, remove women from the factory and the family would be saved.

Although they have disagreed on the causes, many historians have accepted the view that the working-class family was disorganized. Oscar Handlin has suggested, for example, that the urban industrial slum, "the disorganizing pressure of the environment," and not the factory, weakened the family.[7] In this way, the city, the factory and the immigrant experience, each have received the blame for the disorganization of the working-class family.

The history of the Cohoes, New York, cotton worker community, suggests the need to reconsider the impact of the factory and the city on the lives of the cotton worker and her family. Quite early in its history Cohoes had one distinct feature: by 1860 it had become a company town. Although both wool and cotton mills gave the city its title as the Spindle City, the Harmony Mills Company dominated the city, and by 1864 monopolized the town's cotton industry. But the Harmony Company controlled much more than Cohoes' cotton industry. In association with the wool manufacturers, company officials constituted an interlocking directorate that held virtually every major political and financial post in the city throughout this period.[8] And lastly, the company maintained considerable economic influence over the working-class community. The company built and rented the more than 800 brick tenement houses and five boarding houses that spread over Harmony Hill, the city's first ward where the cotton workers all lived. In addition, Harmony Mill paternalism oversaw the workers' lives from the child's attendance at the Sabbath School to the family's weekly food purchased from the Company Store.

Consequently, strike issues included not only wages and hours, but also such complaints as the credit system under which the cotton workers bought their food and the rent deducted from the family's pay.

The cotton mills, led by the Harmony Company, more than kept pace with the growth of the overwhelmingly working-class inhabitants of Cohoes, whose population numbered only 1,850 residents in 1840, 8,800 in 1860 and 19,416 in 1880. Consequently, while approximately one out of every four Cohosiers worked as a cotton hand in 1860, the ratio had risen to almost one in three in 1880. Most important, 60 percent of these cotton workers were women, and in 1860 more than half were immigrant Irish, while in 1880 four out of every five cotton workers were either first or second generation Irish or French-Canadian immigrants.

The experience of Cohoes suggests, however, that the factory and the working-class community play a more ambiguous part in the life of workers and their families than is traditionally thought. The cotton workers organized in response to this corporative omnipresence, and their activities touched all aspects of social life in the Harmony Hill community. The working class organized around the factory. Led by the skilled male spinners and female weavers, cotton workers organized unions which struck and won a wage advance in the Harmony Mills in 1858. During and immediately after the Civil War, the union activity waned, but the cotton workers did participate in the Short Hour Movement, the Workingman's Party and in the Workingman's Cooperative Store. Since working-class culture on Cohoes' Harmony Hill was also ethnic culture, mass strike rallies were addressed in both French and English to help unite the Irish and French Canadians around their common problems and needs. For certain issues involved social conditions which these people experienced together. So, to their laboring, political and ethnic activities must be added their role within the Harmony Hill community. For almost all cotton workers and their families lived on the Hill. There these workers had constructed a full and complex network of fraternal, religious and political clubs and institutions that offered them entertainment, security and some cultural nourishment. Usually several members of each family and occasionally whole families worked in the mills. These workers were not concerned only with narrow economic questions, but saw union activity as vital to the security of their family and community, security some had traveled as much as 3,000 miles to achieve. Thus, we have to view the working-class woman in the full context of her community. But before we can begin to understand behavior within the working-class community, we need to identify the workers and their families and see what changes take place in the Harmony Hill community between 1860 and 1880.

For Lucy Larcom[9] and her fellow workers in the 1830s, the cotton mill might have seemed like a boarding school for young ladies; but in Cohoes in 1857 the image of the factory and the factory girl had drastically changed. In reply to a series of letters from "A Factory Girl" in the local newpaper, a town teacher explains why she held these girls in contempt: "I *do* claim to be superior to the vulgar herd with which our factories are stocked, and I *do* consider them unfit to associate with me, or to move in the same society to which I belong. Such, too, is the sentiment of all 'Upper Tendom.' "[10] For the "elite" of Cohoes society who may well have spent their own girlhood in the mills, factory life had lost status. But it remains to be seen whether it had lost status for the large masses of Cohosiers who now worked in the mills.

The manuscript United States Census of Population for Cohoes in 1860 does not distinguish between cotton and wool workers,[11] but the average textile worker in the town was not a native American by birth .[12] Factory life had become predominantly an immigrant experience. More than one half the employees in 1860 were either Irish immigrants or their children, only one quarter were native Americans, while English and French-Canadian hands each constituted less than one tenth of the workers. The typical cotton worker had more than a single social and cultural identity: this worker was both Irish and female. Moreover, the Harmony Mills cotton hand was most likely an unskilled and unmarried woman between the ages of 15 and 25. Four out of every five Irish women between the ages of 15 and 19 worked in the mills in 1860 (Table 3).

Although fewer women and young men were employed among the other ethnic groups, they followed a common pattern: children entered the mills in their early teens and left increasingly in their twenties. Women then married and men found employment outside the mills. Only English males remained in the mills. Usually married and of middle-age they worked as skilled spinners, weavers, dressers and carders. The husbands of other cotton mill workers found other jobs. Americans established themselves in trades or business outside the factory, while the Irish and French-Canadians became unskilled day laborers on the Erie and Champlain canal network or on the factory maintenance staff.[13]

Thus, even before the Civil War, immigrant Irish families had found work for their children in the Harmony Mills. While the Irish clearly dominated the mills, they were joined by a sizable number of native American workers. Other ethnic groups also moved readily into the mills in numbers equal to their relative share of the city's population. Finally, the factory did not draw

TABLE 1
Factory (Textile) Workers (FW) and Ethnicity, 1860, and Cotton Workers (CW) and Ethnicity, 1880.

*1860	Male	Female	Total	Percent of Population	FW† (%)
All Textile Workers (Ten and Over)	778 41.4%	1103 58.6%	1881	28.3	100.0
Native American	197 40.2%	293 59.8%	490	22.8	26.0
Irish	377 37.9%	617 62.1%	994	31.6	52.8
English	101 57.7%	74 42.3%	175	30.0	9.3
Fr. Canadian	50 40.3%	74 59.7%	124	26.2	6.5
*1880					
All Cotton Workers (Ten and Over)	1280	1964	3244	21.3	100.0
Native American	136	148	284	9.1	8.8
Irish	514	958	1472	26.8	45.4
English	151	111	262	19.2	8.1
Fr. Canadian	435	674	1109	24.6	34.2

*Manuscript Census of Population data.
†Percentages of ethnic groups do not total 100% because small numbers of Scottish and German workers are omitted.

mothers away from their families. When they married and began raising families women did not work. Their children worked. The additional income especially from unmarried daughters could be put to good advantage. As Stephan Thernstrom discovered among the Newburyport Irish, income provided by the children enabled the family to gain some small measure of the security Ireland had not afforded–property. Similarly in the Cohoes working-class community of 1860, it was mainly a few families headed by Irish cotton workers who accumulated property: 11 percent of these Irishmen owned property in 1860, compared to only 5.9 percent of the Englishmen, 1.8 percent of the Americans and none of the French Canadians.

Cohoes differed from the early New England textile town. Not only did young immigrant Irishwomen dominate the Cohoes cotton mills in 1860, but also by this time weaving remained the only skilled trade in which women still readily found employ-

TABLE 2
Percentage and Relative Concentration* of Skilled and Unskilled Cotton Workers in Ethnic Groups, 1860 and 1880.

1860:	Unskilled		Skilled		Spinners (Males)	Dressers Carders (Males)
	Males	Females	Males	Females		
USA	25.3% 80	26.5% 84	2.4% 8	32.6% 103	16.6% 52	46.1% 145
IRE	48.4% 107	55.9% 114	36.6% 81	32.6% 67	25.0% 55	7.6% 17
ENG.	12.9% 130	6.7% 86	46.3% 468	32.6% 418	50.0% 505	30.7% 310
FR. CAN	6.4% 86	6.7% 97	0.0% 0	0.0% 0	0.0% 0	7.6% 103
N:	778	1103	41	46	12	13
1880:						
USA	10.6% 53	7.5% 37	11.1% 58	2.0% 10	0.0% 0	9.0% 44
IRE	40.2% 117	48.8% 139	44.4% 127	72.9% 200	60.0% 175	54.5% 159
ENG	11.8% 122	5.7% 70	11.1% 117	14.5% 177	33.3% 342	22.7% 233
FR. CAN	34.0% 121	34.3% 114	0.0% 0	4.1% 14	0.0% 0	4.5% 16
N:	1280	1964	9	48	30	22

*Proportion among gainful workers in all occupations = 100

ment: slightly more than half the Cohoes weavers in 1860 were women. The number of skilled workers distinguished by the census leaves much to be desired. But while the English filled skilled positions in the mills considerably in excess of their relatively small numbers in the town, Irishmen and women held skilled as well as unskilled positions (Table 2). This evidence shows the Irishmen did more than dig ditches and lay railroad track and Irishwomen worked in other than domestic services.[14] While the relative concentration of female English weavers was six times that of the Irish, in Civil War Cohoes, Irishwomen held as many skilled posts as weavers as did workers of American and English extraction. Native Americans still held about one quarter of the jobs, but by 1860 Cohoes' cotton mills had become largely Irish "institutions."

Between 1860 and 1880, Cohoes' Harmony Mills expanded greatly. New hands were needed to operate her spinning mules and looms. But how had the characteristics of the average cotton worker and her family changed during these decades? And again, in what ways did these changes reflect the absence of union activity and relative quiescence of the Cohoes' cotton worker then?

During the two decades in question, the most dramatic change in the mill labor force involved the native American and French-Canadian ethnic groups. Whereas one out of every four unskilled textile workers in Cohoes in 1860 had been of native American extraction, and less than one in ten had been of French

TABLE 3
Percentage of Cohoes Men and Women of an Age and Ethnic Group Employed as Cohoes Factory (Textile) Workers, 1860.

Ethnicity	**Age 10-14**	**15-19**	**20-29**	**30-39**	**40+**
American	5.4%	57.2%	34.8%	13.3%	6.9%
Irish	14.7%	81.9%	47.7%	13.7%	6.2%
Females					
English	11.5%	50.8%	31.8%	21.8%	9.2%
French Canadian	11.1%	77.0%	26.0%	12.1%	0.0%
American	6.4%	50.3%	24.9%	13.7%	7.4%
Irish	16.4%	67.6%	29.4%	18.1%	8.8%
Males					
English	3.6%	40.5%	52.1%	44.3%	23.6%
French Canadian	7.8%	58.0%	27.1%	25.0%	10.7%

Canadian origin, by 1880 the percentages were virtually reversed (Table 1). The Harmony Mills population had doubled, but the number of native American workers was almost one half its 1860 figure. The 124 French-Canadian textile workers counted in 1860, for instance, had increased by 1880 ninefold to 1,109 in the cotton mills alone; the number of native Americans dropped 42 percent during this period from 490 to 284. Almost half the workers were still Irish, but better than one in three unskilled cotton hands were of French-Canadian ancestry. Native American and English workers now comprised less than one in ten of each group. Even under the pressure represented by the influx of large numbers of "cheap" employable French-Canadian immigrant laborers, the Irish found additional employment in the mills. Similarly, the French Canadians found Harmony Hill to be a hospitable textile center. It is true that almost all teenage members of the family had to work for subsistence wages and everyone in the community depended heavily on company paternalism. The Harmony Mills, however, offered these people steady employment, solid brick-construction housing and a steady though meagre income. The French Canadian had found a home and, with friends, had established a community.

Although each ethnic group had distinct work patterns that reflected its separate cultural background, there were similarities among them. Two out of every three cotton workers in 1880 were female. The Irish and French Canadians maintained this ratio, while in contrast, the number of American-born men and women was almost even, and the number of English male workers continued as in 1860 to exceed the number of females in the mills. Native Americans had left the mills: 22.8 percent of the native population age ten and over labored in the textile mills in 1860, but by 1880 the percentage had dropped to 9.1 percent. Otherwise, among each of the three large immigrant ethnic groups—the Irish, French Canadians and English—the percentage of cotton workers remained about one out of every four or five "adults." Finally, as in 1860, the English contined to show a work pattern different from the other groups: the average English cotton hand was more likely to be a married male who was older than was his Irish, French-Canadian or native-American counterpart.

Thus, the typical unskilled cotton hand in 1880 was probably an Irish or French-Canadian woman. Not only was she a young unmarried woman, but the reverse was equally true: if one was a young Irish or French-Canadian girl growing up in Cohoes, the chance that she once worked, still worked or would shortly work in the Harmony Mills was most probable. It was also likely that she started work in the mills at an earlier age in 1880 than she would have in 1860, especially if she was of French-Canadian extraction (Table 4).

TABLE 4
Percentage of Female Factory (Textile) Workers, 1860, and Cotton Workers, 1880, in Selected Ethnic Groups who are under Twenty Years Old

	Age	U.S.A.	Ire.	Eng.	Fr. Can.
1860	0-14	2.7%	7.1%	10.5%	6.4%
	15-19	36.5	48.5	38.2	63.5
	Under 20	39.2	55.6	48.7	69.9
1880	0-14	16.7	15.6	13.5	27.3
	15-19	27.5	32.5	24.3	38.7
	Under 20	44.2	48.1	37.8	66.0

The percentage of workers under twenty remained at about 50 percent in both census years, but the percentage of children under 14 employed tripled between 1860 and 1880 from 7.4 percent of the entire work force in 1860 to 24.1 percent in 1880. And while the increase was more marked among boys than girls, both vastly increased; and children from all ethnic groups worked. The average age of the workers remained fairly constant, at approximately 20. However, the average age of the women *did* vary with ethnicity: for instance, two out of every three female French-Canadian cotton workers were *under* 20, while the same percentage of English were *over* 20. These differences suggest different attitudes toward the child's role in the family and the birth rate among the different ethnic groups. A higher number of English women did not work. The key here is that fewer English children worked. Married Englishwomen did not flock to the mills; rather, they appear to have remained at home and to have kept their daughters home or in school. This decision might have been motivated by a variety of concerns. The desire of the English to educate or protect their daughters, cultural animosities and the fear of loss of status through association with the mass of mostly Irish and

French-Canadian cotton workers may serve as explanations. For the Irish and newly arrived French-Canadian family, there was much more to be gained than lost by working in the mills. Children increasingly could and had to work the exhausting 72 hour work week under frequently dangerous conditions at absurdly low salaries; but their income enabled mother to stay home with the youngest children. For a young Irish woman or man the mills also offered the prospect of some occupational mobility. Achievement therefore related to the fortunes of the family. Many Irish appeared to have become skilled weavers and spinners as early as 1860. And by 1880 the Irish filled a majority of the skilled cotton mill positions. Irishwomen comprised 72.9 percent of the female weavers, and their sons and husbands fared equally well. Skilled Irishmen constituted 60 percent of the spinners and 54.5 percent of the dressers, carders and loom harness makers in 1880.

Consequently, while young girls of English and native-American origin may no longer have found factory work desirable, Irish and French-Canadian families wanted and easily obtained employment for their teenage daughters and sons and unmarried young women. So how may we evaluate the economic gains and social mobility experienced by the average cotton worker and her family between 1860 and 1880? High costs and low incomes made steady employment essential, and the Harmony Mills provided it.[15] The hours were long, the work among the whirling machines dangerous, but the Irish family procured work for as many children, relatives and neighbors as might turn up, and gained skilled positions. A few even translated money earned into some small property holdings. In this way, the history of Cohoes' working-class Irish and French Canadians suggests the need to reconsider Thernstrom's conclusion that the nineteenth-century working class did not exhibit the economic and social mobility celebrated in the American success myth.[16]

Thernstrom measured mobility in industrial and economic terms: occupational mobility and change in real estate and personal estate holdings. But these useful indices are too narrow. To grasp more fully the significance and character of social mobility in America, historians need to consider the goals and aspirations of the worker and her family on the one hand, and the form and function of status and power on the other. We can then assess the impact of technology, economic pressures and attitudes toward women. Might it not, for example, be the full realization of a social dream for the cotton worker family, freshly arrived in the new country with memories of famine still vivid, to find ample and steady employment in the mills, to maintain the security of the tenement home and to develop community fellowship? Cohoes' Irish found full employment in the Harmony Mills, and during the 20 years they increasingly dominated the skilled crafts. Life was not easy. But unlike many other factories during the depression, the Harmony Mills continued to provide regular monthly pay checks throughout the 1870s. The Company also maintained some unusually fine living conditions: well constructed apartments, paved streets, even some garbage collection and manicured lawns with room for a small garden. Compared to what one saw and heard of English manufacturing districts, and relative to the sorry conditions that impelled them to leave either Ireland or Quebec, it is easy to understand their desire to defend this small but for them not insignificant measure of security. Moreover, a woman had only to look at her Irish neighbors on the other side of town who worked at more menial service jobs–housekeepers and washerwomen–to recognize her preferred status. As the local newspaper noted, Cohoes' textile mills' employment of women made it "next to impossibility [sic] to get competent, reliable girls, who are willing to do housework at any price." The women had "the feeling that as operatives in the mills they take a higher place in the social scale than is accorded them when they do housework. The fact is, they don't like the idea of being servants, or being treated as such, and unless compelled by lack of the employment of their choice they avoid it with scorn."[17] So by 1880, as far as she was concerned, the cotton worker had achieved some measure of both status and security.

But what impact did the factory have on the cotton worker family? Did the company town tear the family apart? While there were considerable economic strains on the Cohoes cotton worker families, it is significant that working-class marriage patterns strikingly resembled the nonfactory family Richard Sennett described in the middle-class community of Union Park in Chicago during this same period. Except for the important presence of child labor among the working class, there appear to be surprisingly few structural differences between these working-class and middle-class families.

Whatever differences did exist between the marriage patterns of Union Park middle-class families and Cohoes cotton worker families seem to have arisen as much from the various ethnic cultural experiences as from disparities in economic position. For example, the percentage of married workers in the Harmony Mills follows the same pattern found in middle-class Union Park.[18] The average cotton worker couple married only when the husband had reached his early thirties, most likely when he felt somewhat more financially secure (Table 5). For the vast majority of the couples, no wide age difference separated the wife and husband (Table 6).

Table V
Percentage Married Within an Age Group, 1880, Among Cohoes Cotton Workers and Chicago's Union Park

Age	Workers	Middle Class Union Park Chicago*	Age
15-19	0.8%	3.5%	15-19
20-29	16.2%	20.4%	20-24
		43.0%	25-29
30-39	61.8%	60.3%	30-34
		60.3%	35-39
40-49	74.2%	70.7%	40-44
		72.0%	45-49
50-59	89.3%		

Percentage Married Within an Age Group by Sex and Ethnicity, 1880, Among Cohoes Cotton Workers

	Age	Ire.	Fr. Can.	Ethnicity Eng.	USA	Total
Females	20-29	8.0%	11.5%	13.0%	25.0%	10.3%
	30-39	44.2%	31.4%	83.3%	17.6%	41.0%
Males	20-29	24.0%	32.3%	39.3%	52.5%	29.1%
	30-39	80.7%	78.5%	91.6%	76.9%	90.6%

*Sennett, *Families Against the City*, 105.

In more than 80 percent of the marriages, the wife was less than ten years younger than the husband. And only Englishwomen married younger men with any frequency. Among 15.6 percent of all couples the wife was older than her husband, but among English couples the percentage was 25.3 percent. Women usually left the mills when they were married to assume the role of wife, mother and homemaker. But what of the relative size of the working-class and middle-class family? Once the family formed, conventional wisdom has it that the working class multiplied while the middle class exercised some reproductive restraint. Quoting Sennett on Union Park, "A host of sexual taboos and the prohibition of child labor in this middle-class community made abstinence not only possible but a compelling necessity."[19]

TABLE 6
Age Differences Between Husbands and Wifes of Cotton Worker Families, 1880.

	Marriages (N)	Wife Older (%)	Husbands 0-9 yr. older (%)	Wife less than 5 yr. older Husbands 0-9 yr. older (%)
Ir.	303	15.8	69.7	81.6
Fr. Can.	105	11.6	80.0	87.7
U.S.A.	50	12.0	72.0	80.0
Eng.	75	25.3	65.4	82.7
Other	18	16.7	66.6	77.7
	601	15.6	71.9	83.0

Cohoes, however, suggests again that the most important variable in terms of family size was ethnicity. The ratio of children under ten to the adult population in each ethnic group in 1860 (the "survival rate") demonstrates that family planning crossed class lines: the English and Irish couples averaged 30 percent and the French Canadians almost 50 percent more children than the couples of native-American extraction.[20] Finally, intermarriage figures between persons of different ethnic background demonstrate further the impact of ethnic culture. Almost 40 percent of the working-class English and native Americans who married wed outside of their own ethnic group. In contrast, French Canadians and Irish almost never married outside their ethnic community.[21] The reasons for this low rate of intermarriage would seem to be twofold: the Catholic injunction against marriage outside the religion, and the exclusiveness of both *Canadien* and Irish nationalist culture. In sum, working-class marriage patterns shared many of the same concerns for tradition, security and stability as the middle-class marriage. Each ethnic group, however, expressed these concerns in different forms of behavior.

Working-class households on Harmony Hill in 1880 again resembled those in Union Park. As in that middle-class community, working-class Cohosiers predominantly lived in nuclear families. By contemporary standards, however, cotton worker families experienced considerable disorganization. In a culture that celebrated a traditional two-parent family and the guiding role of the father, one-parent families, especially when headed by a woman, were considered incomplete and hence "disorganized." But it is crucial to examine the origins and dimensions of this

TABLE 7
Cotton Worker Household and Family Structure in Cohoes, 1880–Ward One, Harmony Hill.

Households	Ire.	Can.	USA	Eng.	Other	Total
Nuclear	323 72.7%	125 67.9%	35 60.3%	63 77.8%	18 81.8%	564 71.5%
Extended	42 9.5%	20 10.9%	6 10.3%	8 9.9%	2 9.1%	78 9.9%
Augmented	65 14.6%	38 20.7%	15 25.9%	10 12.3%	2 9.1%	130 16.5%
Mixed Adult Group* (MAG) & Single	14 3.2%	1 0.5%	2 3.5%	0 0.0%	0 0.0%	17 2.2%
	444	184	58	81	22	789
Families**						
Whole	302 68.0%	157 85.3%	47 81.0%	71 87.7%	17 77.3%	594 75.3%
"Broken"	128 28.8%	26 14.1%	9 15.5%	10 12.3%	5 22.7%	178 22.6%
Percentage of "broken" families headed by a female	89.8%	88.5%	88.9%	80.0%	80.0%	88.8%
Average No. Cotton Wkers/ family†	2.75	3.63	1.67	2.04	–	2.79

*The two boarding houses are not included.
**MAG & Singles not included.
†Based on first 250 families enumerated in Ward One.

"disorganization." Three quarters of the Irish and English male- or female-headed households were nuclear families (Table 7). These households, composed of first and second generation immigrants, were nuclear after the 3,000-mile migration. Households headed by native Americans or French Canadians had a percentage of families augmented by both relatives and boarders almost twice that of the other two groups. But it was the high percentage of one-parent families that distinguished the cotton worker family from other working-class and Chicago middle-class families.

One out of every four Cohoes cotton worker families on Harmony Hill was a "broken" family—a family headed by one parent. One-parent Irish families had raised the percentage considerably: 28.8 percent of the Irish families were "broken," compared to only about 14 percent of the families of other ethnic groups. Furthermore, almost all of these "broken" families were female-headed. Thus, almost one-quarter of the Harmony Hill families were headed by a "widow"—a woman whose husband had either left her or died. Family structure among the iron workers of Troy, New York, across the river, suggests that this extraordinary rate of family "disorganization" reflected conditions peculiar to the textile industry more than it did the general character of working-class life. Sennett found 10.9 percent of the Union Park families to be without one parent. Troy's iron workers, both skilled and unskilled, lived in "broken" homes to about the same extent.[22]

Differences did occur, however, *between* ethnic groups. In Troy and Cohoes the rate of one-parent Irish families outdistanced the other groups. Combining skilled and unskilled Troy iron workers, approximately 15 percent of the Irish, 6 percent of the English, and 10 percent of the native Americans lived in "broken" homes. Thus working-class and middle-class household and family structure strongly resembled one another: both were nuclear families with two parents. Differences were ethnic and industrial—in our case, especially among the Irish and the cotton industry. Why were so many of the cotton worker families one-parent in structure? Widowed women may have taken their families to Cohoes where their children could find employment in the Harmony Mills' light industry. Almost all the widows were over 40 years old with teenage children, and the cotton mills made it possible for mother to stay home with the youngest children while the older children earned the family's income.

Thus Cohoes' cotton worker families were more "disorganized" than Troy's iron worker families. But the high incidence of nuclear families suggests a problem with the term "disorganization." The term exposes the historical prejudice against the one-parent family and ignores the tensions that may have wracked many two-parent families. In addition, the cotton mill may have provided employment and a financial refuge for the widowed family. Thus Sennett's categories may be inadequate to understand the pressures on the nineteenth-century working-class family. In fact almost nine of every ten non-Irish cotton worker families were two-parent headed. Sennett is correct, however, when he insightfully suggests the importance of the stable family in a changing and complex industrial city. According to Sennett, "The family was enshrined out of a sense of its peril in the city."[23] For Sennett, fear that the stability and security of the family would not be maintained became a "guiding force" in the history of the nineteenth-century American city. The middle class clung to the family as the one stable institution in the midst of a rapidly changing world. Although the pressures on the family were immense, the family did not constitute the workers' single supportive institution. On the contrary, the factory and community also structured their social life. Thus, the working class, and the Irish in particular, made an effort to get their daughters and sons unskilled and skilled jobs in the mills and membership in the network of city fraternal and religious associations.

Why, however, was the Irish family so distinctly scarred? In her pioneering study of working-class Irish in mid-nineteenth-century London, Lynn Lees showed the continued dominance of the nuclear family in the Irish household, noted the similarity between the Irish and the English working-class family and concluded that the Irish had not suffered any unusual breakdown.[24] Lees, however, failed adequatedly to distinguish between families headed by two parents and those in which only one parent was present. In this regard, we were not told whether or not the Irish in London differed from the English. The evidence in both Troy and Cohoes suggests that the Irish family structure–though not household structure–differed from that of the other major ethnic groups present in these two cities. Statistics compiled by the United States Immigration Commission in 1910 corroborate this evidence: the Commission *Reports* listed 12.4 percent of the immigrant cotton workers born in Ireland as widowed, compared to percentages of 5.9 percent of the French Canadians and 7.1 percent for the English.[25] Significantly, these *Reports* suggested that this difference largely disappeared within one generation. For the second generation immigrant family–the first born in the United States–the percentage of Irish widows more nearly approximates the percentages for the other groups: the percentages for the American-born Irish, English and Canadian respectively are 5.9 percent, 4.8 and 3.8 percent. So, though some of the distinctions between the family structure of the Irish and other ethnic groups appear at face value to have diminished with a generation of acclimation, acculturation and without a 3,000-mile migration, the situation of the immigrant Irish family remains somewhat unique. The fragile Irish family reflected the problems that worried the immigrant in industrial America, i.e. considerable prejudice, high mortality and the intense pressures of industrial capitalism. But the higher number on one-parent Irish families may also have reflected distinct ethnic values. We may offer some preliminary suggestions for this. Peasant, semifeudal Irish cultural traditions celebrated Irish community life and kinship and then were patriarchal. Beyond this, though, the Irish families' willingness to allow young girls out of the home and into the factory during adolescence suggests that the Irish husband subscribed to a set of traditional family values distinctly different from those held by men of Protestant English and American origins.Lastly, the Irish peasants' culture had unregimented preindustrial work rhythms. Adjustment required by factory life, with its highly disciplined work patterns, made the Irish industrial experience disruptive and alienating.[26] Although more work needs to be done in this area, we see the importance of ethnic culture in shaping working-class experience.

What then can we say about the cotton workers and their families, their community and their adjustment to factory life during the Gilded Age? The history of Patrick Dillon and his family illustrates the life of one representative cotton worker family in Cohoes.[27] Patrick Dillon probably left Ireland with his wife Ellen and their six children during the potato famine. They arrived in New York around 1850, and by 1860 had added three more children to their family. At the outbreak of the Civil War the now 11-member family lived in a four- or five-room company tenement at 4 Willow Street in the heart of the Harmony Hill community. The family had managed to save approximately 300 dollars, but it had not been easy; four members of the family worked full time. Every morning the 45-year-old head of the household left home before six for work as a day laborer. The two eldest sons, Michael and William, age 20 and 18 respectively, answered the call of the Harmony Mills' bell, and walked down the street to the mill for a six-o'clock start, too. And Patrick, the 16-year-old son, joined his father as a day laborer. The father and son possibly worked on one of the canal or railroad labor gangs involved in area construction. They may well, however, have also worked for the Harmony Company—building new tenements or enlarging the newly acquired Ogden Mills. Mother, meanwhile, had her hands full at home. Matthew, age 14, and the 12-year-old twin girls did not yet work and only six-year-old James attended school. In addition, not only was Mrs. Dillon pregnant, but the baby, Bridget, who had only just celebrated her first birthday, and Margaret, age three, must have required considerable attention.

Meanwhile the men came home for lunch on their 40-minute noon break and then returned to the mills. At half past six the bell rang to close the mills for another day. For these 12 hours of work an adult common laborer received $0.75, while a skilled mule spinner received as much as $1.50. Women and especially children who labored in the mills received considerably less: an unskilled "back boy," for example, received $0.30 for his 12-hour day. When the monthly pay day arrived, the tenement house rent of between $5 and $7 was simply deducted from the salary.[28]

What happened to the Dillons during the next two decades? Did the family unit survive intact, did the family remain financially solvent and did they remain to establish themselves within the Cohoes' community? Patrick Dillon, Sr., had died late in the 1860s, but his widow continued to maintain the home on Willow Street. Family economics required that Mrs. Dillon open her small home to another family—John Kanal, his wife and two children—and to a boarder. Of her children, Patrick, Jr., died suddenly in 1870 at the age of 26 (shortly after his marriage) and James died September 15, 1874, at the age of 19—both from causes that are undisclosed. Michael and Matthew reappear periodically in the city directory as operatives in the Harmony Mills. Finally, while the older girls had most likely married, William, the second eldest son 20 years earlier, by 1880 had become head of the family, still located in their Willow Street tenement. The family once again sustained itself without boarders. William Dillon's first wife had died but he had remarried. His second wife, Elizabeth, was 15 years his junior, and was only nine years older than his son Patrick, now 15.[29] William now ran a "saloon" but his three youngest sisters, now 19, 20 and 22 years old, together with Patrick worked in the Harmony Mills, much as the family had for the past 20 years. Over the years the Dillon family had secured a place within the community for its remaining numbers but there had been many deaths in the family and most at relatively young ages.

Work in the mills had hardly changed. Wages for the now ten and a half to 11-hour day had dropped back from the high level maintained between 1867 and 1875 to their 1864 level: for a day's work a common laborer now received $1.12 ½, a skilled spinner $1.75, and a back boy $0.42. The Harmony Company continued throughout this period to play a central part in the life of the Dillon family: the Willow Street tenement remained a focus for the family, and the mills continuously employed the teenagers and adult Dillons and so helped to sustain the family. In fact, five of the seven members of the family in 1880 worked–four of them in the cotton mills. And, five years later the Dillons evidently felt secure enough to permit young Patrick, now 20 years old, to leave the mills and return to school. While living at home, Patrick Dillon–the grandson of his namesake who arrived in American almost 40 year earlier–had become a "student," with the considerable occupational and social mobility American society afforded the educated man. Though for many of his relatives, mobility had been only from the mills to the grave, young Patrick had achieved an avenue both he and the dominant American culture could celebrate.

Like other families in Cohoes, the lives of the Dillon family extended beyond the factory and was fuller and richer than this industrial portrait suggests. On Cohoes' Harmony Hill, the Irish and French-Canadian cotton workers like the Dillons had established by 1880 a diverse and full community replete with ethnic, religious, social and political club life. There were separate Irish and French Catholic churches; the Irish organized the Fenians and the Land League, and the French formed the St. Jean Baptiste Society; a French newspaper, *La Patrie Nouvelle*, was begun in the city in 1876; each ethnic group formed benevolent societies; and while Cohoes Irishmen usually voted Democratic, it was not uncommon for French Republican groups to form before the fall elections.

Carl Wittke has emphasized the competition between the Irish and the French Canadians. This competition supposedly stemmed from the French-Canadian support of the Republican Party and their reluctance to organize.[30] There were, however, certain fundamental similarities in their experience as well. Whether the workers were Irish like the Dillons, or French Canadian, both were Catholic, both came to America in search of economic advancement. Both worked side by side in the mills and were neighbors on the Hill. And together both struggled against the manufacturers to preserve their jobs and to control their work conditions. Work for the women and children in the Mills was indeed taxing. But through the depression, families like the Dillons gained some security and status. There were openings in skilled positions and some families had even become property holders. The factory did not provide "pin money," especially in the case of the large number of widowed families. The factory offered women jobs and made it possible to hold the female-headed family together and to maintain a nuclear family. In this way, rather than destroying the family, for the cotton workers, the Harmony Mill helped to sustain it.

In addition, urban Harmony Hill did not necessarily alienate the family. While living conditions left something to be desired, the close relationships and organization of the community also helped sustain the cotton worker family. When the workers went out on strike, the whole city was affected. Community pressure helped to maintain the strike: some businessmen offered discounts and contributions to striking workers; one woman, for instance, complained to the local press that the family above her had been persecuting her family for working, and that the day before she had been hit on the head by a bottle thrown by one of them; various tenants who wanted to work complained of "bulldozing"–intimidation from striking neighbors. But community pressures weakened the strikers, too; many striking weavers would return to Cohoes to work because they and their girls were homesick. As Miss O'Brien wrote from Forestdale, R.I., "This [Forestdale] is a very pretty place, but not like home [Cohoes]."[31]

So, why did violence erupt in Cohoes in the early 1880s? This seemingly optimistic portrait was deceptive. The family, community life and occupational mobility in the factory were enclaves against a threatening and insecure urban industrial life. Cohoes cotton workers lived in poverty. That they could endure three wage reductions during the 1873-1877 depression demonstrates how their depressed lives had lowered their expectations. At least the Harmony Company had not closed. In this way, they felt they had gained some success and had established a home. But they continued to live on the edge of fear–low pay, technological changes in the industry and an always ample supply of surplus labor threatened to destroy the small part of the social dream they had been able to realize. In addition, the increasing competition of industrial capitalism demanded increased production, lower costs and greater efficiency. To secure and maintain their profits the Harmony Mill manufacturers felt it necessary to reduce wages and control all aspects of mill life. Unions stood in their way. When the cotton workers' wages were reduced for the fourth time in seven years, they saw their minimal success, status and security threatened. Central to the struggle was control. At issue were not simply salaries, but the survival of the entire community. When, after six months of strikes, the manufacturers brought in disciplined, Protestant, Swedish immigrant families to replace the strikers, the women and children cotton workers responded directly and vigorously. They gathered at the mill entrances to "greet" the Swedes with stones. Police were brought in to protect the "scabs," and violence ensued. Although the strike was crushed, the working-class community then united and two months later elected the strike leader to the State Assembly.

In conclusion, the behavior of the Cohoes cotton worker community suggests the need to understand the place of ethnic traditions in the context of working-class achievements and perception. Furthermore, we need to reassess the impact of the community and factory on the working-class family. Many working-class cotton mill families *were* broken. Child labor was necessary. Industrial capitalism divested the worker of control over work conditions and threatened the family's quest for social and economic security. Both the factory and the urban experience intensified the problems of adjustment for preindustrial peoples, subjecting them to new and alienating work and to the strange heterogeneity of the city. But it must be remembered that by 1880 both the factory and the community had come to sustain the cotton worker family, and especially the female-headed household, in important ways. Together the mills and community provided another avenue to social fulfillment and achievement for the Irish and French Canadians of Harmony Hill. Thus, ironically, the argument that urged women to be taken out of the factory did much to rob many families of their one vital source of income. For in the textile mills at least, the women who worked not only needed the money desperately, but were usually unmarried adolescents, not mothers. Lastly, the Cohoes cotton worker community illustrates the *embourgeoisement* of the working class; the working class had begun to acquire certain middle-class attitudes about the values of status, security, property and the privatized nuclear family. Thus the final irony of cotton worker mobility: on the road to success, the pressures of industrial capitalism had reduced the cotton worker and her family to perceptual cripples, alienated from and by their own conditions. Cohoes' working class did engage in violence, but the violence was defensive–an attempt to protect their modest social position. There is perhaps no greater testimony to how difficult these people's lives had been, how fragile their economic existence remained and how fearfully they faced the future, than the energetic manner in which the women of Cohoes' Harmony Hill cotton worker community defended and celebrated the modicum of status and security they had achieved. Enmeshed in this difficult, fragile and fearful existence, the working-class dream had become a nightmare.

FOOTNOTES

1. See Richard Sennett and Stephan Thernstrom, eds., *Nineteenth-Century Cities: Essays in the New Urban History* (New Haven: 1969).

2. There are, of course, variations on each theme. The first view is widespread in the literature of the labor movement. (One popular refinement of this view emphasizes the

considerable oppression of the working class and argues that this suffocated its radicalization.) The second view is expressed by Stephan Thernstrom in the conclusion to his article in a New Left anthology. Stephan Thernstrom, "Urbanization, Migration, and Social Mobility in Late Nineteenth-Century America" in *Towards a New Past: Dissenting Essays in American History*, Barton J. Bernstein, ed. (New York: 1968), 158-75.

3. New York State Bureau of Statistics of Labor, *2nd Annual Report, 1884* Legislative Assembly Document 26 (1882), "Establishing the Fact of the Existence of Child Labor in the State," (Albany: 1885), 112.

4. Edward P. Thompson, *The Making of the English Working Class* (New York: 1963), 9-10.

5. Richard Ely, "Introduction," in Helen S. Campbell, *Women Wage-Earners* (Boston: 1893), n.p.

6. Carroll D. Wright, quoted in Campbell, 90.

7. Oscar Handlin, *The Uprooted* (New York: 1951), 167.

8. The biography of William E. Thorn, the agent and treasurer of the Harmony Company from 1867 to 1910, well exemplifies the social, financial and political institutions that Cohoes textile manufacturers controlled. Thorn was both the son-in-law of Commodore Cornelius Vanderbilt and the nephew of Thomas Garner, the owner of the Harmony Mills. After coming to Cohoes in 1867, Thorn served on the Board of Directors of the Cohoes Company (the water power company), was secretary and treasurer of the Cohoes Gas Light Company (both controlled by the Garner interests), was director and first president of the Manufacturers' Bank of Cohoes and was instrumental in organizing the Cohoes Mechanics' Savings Bank. Finally Thorn was elected mayor of Cohoes in 1878 and 1880 and served as a Republican Presidential elector in 1892. See James H. Manning, *New York State Men* (Albany: 1920).

9. Lucy Larcom, *A New England Girlhood* (New edition, New York: 1961). See Edith Abbott, *Women in Industry: A Study in American Economic History* (New York, 1918), 114-16. Abbott writes of the Lowell, Massachusetts, mills that "all operatives were required to live in the company boarding houses . . . organized to resemble . . . big boarding schools." And, "Lowell had a high reputation for good order, morality, piety, and all that was dear to the old-fashioned New Englander's heart."

10. "A Factory Girl" to the editor, *Cohoes Cataract*, April 18, 1857.

11. One encounters various problems working with census data. In Cohoes all mill hands are simply enumerated in the 1860 Census of Population as "Works in Factory." The Census of Manufactures, however, suggests that the cotton and wool worker situation did not vary much. The statistics from the Census of Population for textile workers closely approximates the Census of Manufactures data for the Harmony and other cotton mills in the city. Therefore, one must interpolate from the former to the latter. In 1880 cotton workers and sections of town are distinguished.

12. Unless otherwise indicated the father's place of birth is used to define ethnicity. Thus a native American is someone whose father was born in the United States.

13. The percentage of Irish and French-Canadian men in their thirties and forties who worked as laborers doubled and tripled respectively the percentage of those in their twenties. The actual number also rose markedly. For example, 49 Irishmen or 17.2

percent of those Irishmen in their twenties were laborers, but among those in their forties the number rose to 95 or 54.3 percent.

14. See Oscar Handlin, *Boston's Immigrants, 1790-1865: A Study in Acculturation* (Cambridge, Mass.: 1941), 61-75; Thomas N. Brown, *Irish-American Nationalism: 1870-1890* (Phila.: 1966), 18-19; William V. Shannon, *The American Irish* (New York: 1963), 28, 95; Carl Wittke, *The Irish in America* (Baton Rouge, La.: 1956).

15. In 1880, between four and five people worked in the average Irish and French Canadian household respectively; in contrast, only two or three people worked in the average English and American cotton worker household.

16. Stephan Thernstrom, *Poverty and Progress: Social Mobility in a Nineteenth Century City* (Cambridge, Mass.: 1964), 146.

17. *Cohoes Daily News*, May 11, 1881.

18. See Richard Sennett, *Families Against the City: Middle-Class Homes of Industrial Chicago, 1872-1890* (Cambridge, Mass.: 1970), 105.

19. Sennett, *Families Against the City*, 118.

20. Comparative birth rates for Cohoes in 1860 can be approximated by comparing the ratio between the adult population of each ethnic group and the number of children in that group below a given age. (I have chosen age ten, but the figure can be adjusted easily.) Multiplied by one thousand, the birth rate (actually a "survival rate") per thousand population in 1860 reads:

Native Americans	209
English	263
Irish	277
French Canadians	308

21. Only six of 298 French Canadians in Cohoes Harmony Hill (2.0 percent) married someone from another ethnic group. Forty-two of 596 Irish men or women (7.0 percent) intermarried.

22. Thirteen and eight-tenths percent and 12.2 percent of Troy's skilled and unskilled iron workers respectively lived in one-parent households. See Daniel J. Walkowitz, "Statistics and the Writing of Working-class Culture: The iron workers of Troy, New York, 1860-1880," forthcoming, 1972, in a book edited by Herbert G. Gutman.

23. Sennett, *Families Against the City*, 116-19.

24. Lynn Lees, "Patterns of Lower-class Life: Irish Slum Communities in Nineteenth-Century London," in *Nineteenth-Century Cities*, 359-85.

25. U.S. Immigration Commission,*Reports of the Immigration Commission to Congress*, 1910, 10, part 3, *Immigrants in Industries*, 154-55.

26. Thompson, 436-44.

27. This biographical sketch is based upon the original federal manuscript census schedules. Most important also was the *Troy Directory, also Cohoes. . .*, 1867-1885; Masten, *History of Cohoes*; and, Census Office, 10th Census, 1880, *Reports*, 20, "Statistics of Wages. . . ," 361-63.

28. Caroline F. Ware, *The Early New England Cotton Manufacture*, 244, presents a picture of the wage structure in New England cotton towns that is sensitive to the dependence of the employee on meagre wages, the ways in which salary was tied to their total social condition through rent and store pay and the reduced wages of women and children.

29. This 15-year age difference between William Dillon and his second wife reflected the usual pattern. When widowers remarried there is almost always a larger age gap with the second wife than with the first. This suggests something of the poor odds against a widow's remarrying. For an extended discussion of this problem, see William J. Goode, *World Revolution and Family Pattern* (New York: 1963), 318-19.

30. Carl Wittke, *We Who Built America* (New York: 1940), 315-28.

31. *Cohoes Daily News*, August 15, 1882.

Homesteading in Northeastern Colorado, 1873–1920: Sex Roles and Women's Experience

KATHERINE HARRIS

In this article, Katherine Harris describes the sharing and respect for women expressed among homesteading families in northern Colorado. This mutuality seems to contradict the distinct sex roles inherent in the Cult of True Womanhood, which most historians have seen as restricting women's opportunities in the West. Harris suggests that the western emphasis on the role of helpmate gave women more opportunities than they had had before because they had a greater share of responsibility and decision-making in the family. Above all, she shows the economic importance of women's activities in the homesteading period.

Historians debate what preceded the Cult of True Womanhood. Some believe that white women in colonial America had a greater range of options than their nineteenth-century descendants, that women had higher status in the colonial period because their labor was essential. Other historians, however, question the notion of women's opportunity during the colonial period, saying that earlier agricultural families were extremely patriarchal. These scholars, like Harris, see the Cult of True Womanhood as liberating compared to earlier patriarchal family roles. Whichever view one prefers, Harris's work indicates that a restrictive ideology did not determine the lives of homesteading women in Colorado in the late nineteenth century, and reminds us again to look beyond prescriptive literature to the actual circumstances of people's lives.

Much of the recent historiography describing women on the agricultural frontier has produced a bleak picture of their condition. According to these interpretations, women were coerced and exploited participants in a venture undertaken primarily for the benefit of men.[1] My study of homesteaders in Washington and Logan counties in northeastern Colorado does not support this conclusion.[2] In the years between 1873 and 1920, thousands of individuals and families worked to establish claims under the homestead laws. Women were significantly represented among the land entrants, and their success rate was approximately the same as men's.[3] Among the female population, however, only spinsters and widows were eligible to enter claims, so that other parameters of the homesteading experience must also be explored to gain a broader understanding of its

Grandma Pryor, Pryor Homestead, near Kit Carson, Colorado. Courtesy Colorado Historical Society.

effect on women. One of these, the impact of pioneering on gender-linked work and behavior patterns, is the subject of this paper.[4]

For the white, native-born Americans making up the bulk of those migrating to northeastern Colorado, culturally prescribed rules for behavior derived from nineteenth-century eastern, urban, middle- and upper middle-class models of propriety. A historian of American women, Barbara Welter, has labeled this ideal the Cult of True Womanhood and noted its emphasis on the role of women in maintaining harmonious relations between the sexes. Yet the cult was prescriptive for men, as well. Both sexes ideally confined their activities to separate spheres. Women were to occupy themselves with the moral and practical issues relating to the nurturance of children and the management of the home. They were also to cultivate personal qualities of purity, piety, domesticity, and submissiveness to better meet the needs of husbands, fathers, and children. Men, on the other hand, were to restrict their actions largely to the world of wage work and public affairs. They were expected to be aggressive and competitive, yet not too concerned with moral issues, for men were generally thought to possess spiritual natures intrinsically inferior to women's.[5]

There is some question when, where, and how completely the Cult of True Womanhood was assimilated by native, white agrarians. A study of mid-nineteenth-century midwestern migrants on the Overland Trail found no evidence of the cult's penetration into their lives. Instead, these families were organized along pre-industrial, patriarchal lines with women dominated by men in nearly all aspects of their lives.[6] Nonetheless, the evidence is strong that during the latter half of the nineteenth century, midwestern farm families became well acquainted with the cult's ideals. Popular magazines, books, and newspapers with a wide circulation through much of rural America carried countless articles and advice columns stressing women's domestic responsibilities as mothers of children and helpmates to husbands.[7] It was this role of helpmate that made the urban Cult of True Womanhood compatible with the farm economy. As their husbands' helpers, women could work outside their proper sphere and still maintain the integrity of the ideal.

There is little doubt that northeastern Colorado's homesteaders were familiar with the behavioral prescriptions broadcast by the popular press. Most of the immigrants' families of origin were midwestern agrarians. Those with urban roots were even more likely to have assimilated these ideals. Eastern social customs and styles were evident in the way many settlers lived. And eastern-based churches, clubs, and lodges distinguished town life at an early date.[8]

While it appears certain that homesteaders were familiar with eastern notions of propriety, how completely they acted on them before migrating west is open to question. It it, however, possible to discover how women, men, and children related to each other after they arrived in Colorado. The weight of the evidence indicates, first, a large measure of mutuality, or sharing, between the sexes, and implies a relaxation of culturally determined barriers dividing men and women. And, second, it reveals a pattern of childrearing that imposed many responsibilities on children, regardless of gender, yet allowed them a great deal of freedom as well. Both in the community and in the family, the homesteading experience enhanced female status and autonomy.

Among notheastern Colorado's homesteaders, role-sharing between the sexes was more likely to occur in relations with neighbors than within the family. But the performance of some community obligations remained strongly gender-linked. Women, for example, nearly always had the task of dispensing hospitality by feeding and bedding down visitors to the homestead. And childbirth, an event involving both family and community, was usually an exclusively female occasion, when women friends and relatives provided both emotional support and their skills as midwives to the expectant mother. Women also tended their communities' ill and injured, frequently sharing the task of helping a stricken family.[9]

Yet ministering to the infirm was by no means a wholly feminine role. Martin Skiles, according to his daughter, "would sit up with sick people" and "was also called to doctor sick horses and cows." Other men, too, served as nurses for their sick and dying neighbors. And during the crisis caused by the influenza epidemic of 1918, perhaps as many men as women tended the stricken.[10]

Just as men sometimes assumed the role of nurse and care-giver usually reserved for women, women might undertake "male" duties when death followed illness or injury. Sarah McDonald "quite often conducted funeral services of neighbors" in the vicinity of Fleming where for some time there was no minister.[11] And according to an early-twentieth-century resident of Logan County, one woman "made coffins . . . , buried people, and did everything that could be done, other than preaching the sermon."[12]

The shared responsibilities of men and women were also evident in the process of establishing schools and churches. The first community building to be erected in any neighborhood was nearly always a school. The time between settlement and the construction of a schoolhouse varied widely, depending on the perceived needs of homesteaders in a given locale and their ability to finance the undertaking. In a Washington County community settled largely by Danish bachelors, no school was built for at least ten years after their arrival in the mid-1880's. Even where families with school-age children were more concentrated, tax money might be insufficient to support a teacher.[13] If money were available, it was often barely adequate, so that school terms were typically short, often only three months. Pupils sometimes attended sessions in two districts at different times of the year. Where there were no schools, children might be tutored by their parents, with either the mother or the father assuming this responsibility.[14]

The construction of churches lagged behind that of schools; the presence of families again was a determining factor. (Those same Danish bachelors had no church services, either.) An important practical consideration, of course, was the availability of the schoolhouse, or even settlers' homes, to serve secondarily as places of worship.[15] Also, the fact that homesteaders represented many different denominations delayed, although it did not necessarily prevent, the members of the community from working together to build a church. Many congregations had a notably ecumenical makeup, including not only a variety of Protestants but sometimes Catholics as well. For this reason, churches were crucial to the process of community building by uniting people from diverse religious backgrounds.[16]

Organizing Sunday schools, as religious meetings were known when no preacher was presiding, was primarily the work of women. But men also showed their eagerness to attend by the fact that families often traveled many miles, sometimes on foot, to meetings. In the absence of a minister, services consisted of classes taught by both women and men.[17] With or without a minister Sunday was a high point. No matter how lonely, dull, or difficult the rest of the week might be, homesteaders could look forward to the Lord's Day as a time for resting from some kinds of work, for sharing religious feelings, and for visiting with other families. Indeed, the social aspects of religion can hardly be overemphasized. Families routinely shared Sunday meals with each other, and on those occasions when a revival was under way, they might spend as long as a month together.[18]

Community-wide family attendance characterized the secular as well as the religious gatherings of homesteaders. Dances, picnics, box suppers, spelling bees, baseball games, card parties, "literaries," and other events involved the whole family. The mixed attendance at literaries was, in fact, contrary to the practice of the closest parallels to these events in towns: "ladies'" Fortnightly Club meetings. Among homesteaders, literary nights were occasions for individuals of all ages and both sexes to take turns performing before their neighbors. Debating at these functions was apparently a male preserve, but it was not without hazard to masculine prestige. One man remembered his feelings of astonishment when, as a boy, he discovered that "grown men could be afraid to get up and speak before a group of their friends."[19]

A leveling effect was not the only consequence of shared social experience. Another was the relatively weak development of female networking. Women did, of course, seek out each other's company. After the turn of the century some women organized more or less formal groups, such as the Merrie Minglers Sewing Club and the Sunshine Club, to provide more opportunities for female sociability. But frequently when these groups met, the husbands came along and visited with each other or played cards, checkers, or horseshoes.[20]

The extensive mingling of the sexes, as well as the degree to which gender roles were muted in all areas of community life, can largely be attributed to the simple fact of geography. Homesteads were more or less isolated from one another. But distances were usually not extreme, and homesteaders were able to meet relatively frequently.[21] Still, for reasons of safety, convenience, and the desire to communicate with someone outside the family, settlers' gatherings generally included everyone.

Beginning in 1893, woman suffrage may have had a subtle effect, making many women less eager to segregate themselves in female groups, and stimulating a greater mutuality between the sexes. In both Logan and Washington counties the measure passed by nearly two-to-one, a considerably greater margin of victory than it received state-wide. The strength of the favorable vote by men implies that women and men had already shared some decision-making powers. Moreover, there is evidence that women themselves worked in behalf of their enfranchisement, suggesting a self-image in disparity with legal constraints.[22]

The muting of gender-role distinctions, evident in homesteaders' community activities, also affected the division of labor between males and females in families. Necessity frequently required men and women to assume each other's tasks, leading to the development of unfamiliar skills, especially among women. Children grew up with fewer constraints on their behavior and work patterns than their parents had known. A few even acquired a conscious recognition of equality within the family circle.

Among the routine chores, hauling water, gathering cow chips for fuel, and milking were relatively free from gender connotations. In a given family either the husband or wife might perform these tasks, although the responsibility often shifted to the children as they grew older.[23] Churning cream to make butter, on the other hand, was a job reserved for women, and children under their supervision. Butter production, along with eggs from the chickens women raised, were important elements of the domestic economy, for money received from their sale was sometimes the only cash income a family had. Women sold their butter locally, or shipped it to Denver, and even to the East, earning from ten to thirty cents a pound for as much as fifty to one hundred pounds produced every week. For comparison, at a time when butter brought twelve cents per pound (in the late 1880s and early 1890s), eggs sold for five cents a dozen and corn for seven cents a bushel.[24]

Women's other work within homesteading families encompassed those tasks traditionally assigned to their sex. They "kept house"—cooked, canned (meat, fruit, and vegetables), sewed, washed, and ironed. They tended very young children and usually kept a garden. Toward the end of the nineteenth century, mechanization had begun to produce changes in the nature of some jobs. One of the most important acquisitions for domestic work on a homestead was a sewing machine. As one matron commented, "only women who have struggled along sewing by hand can realize what a sewing machine meant to me."[25] A second device, the hand-operated washing machine, ameliorated what was perhaps the most arduous task of all, doing the family laundry. Its basic mechanism was simply a paddle with a handle for manually agitating the wash. The principal labor-saving feature of the machine was that children could readily be assigned the task of operating it, thus relieving their mothers from the backbreaking job of scrubbing clothes on a washboard.[26]

Men had no day in their weekly routine to compare with women's washday. Their labor was more seasonal, with intense periods of activity during planting and harvest. Through the rest of the year, their work probably had less variation than women's, centering largely on the care of stock and occasional construction and repair jobs.[27] An important though understated side to men's work was their role in parenting. In many families, children of both sexes started doing fieldwork and cross-country errands by age nine or ten. Their chores included helping with the planting, hoeing, and harvesting; herding cattle; hauling feed, fuel, and water; trading at local stores; and taking crops to market.[28] In performing these tasks, children were often supervised by their fathers. This nurturance implies a paternal influence on daughters who may have internalized male role models to some extent. This may have been enhanced by the competition between brothers and sisters performing the same "masculine" jobs.[29]

In some families girls, as well as boys, continued to perform additional farm duties as they grew older. Most assumed jobs out of necessity: perhaps they had no brothers old enough to do the work. Thus the Middlecoff sisters cut and shocked corn with their father; and the Nelson girls drove the family's cattle the twenty-five miles to the Sterling winter feedlot. Eva Morris assumed the farming when her father was absent. In her case, however, an unusually clear statement illuminates her attitude toward men's work. As one family member related, "farming and working with animals was her main love—housework was for girls, not for Eva." [30]

In many, if not most, homesteading families work was in such demand that the gender of the laborer was relatively unimportant. Pioneering, nonetheless, had a different impact on daughters than on wives and mothers. While most daughters were expected to learn "household duties," [31] they appear to have had greater scope for their behavior than married women, probably because girls' sexual identities were often incidental to their contributions to the family. Wives and mothers, on the other hand, had fewer opportunities to alter gender-role patterns because their sexual identities defined their work in the family. Whether acting out of necessity or preference, they generally performed nontraditional tasks in the context of helping husbands and children.

Disregarding those cases where women and girls apparently preferred nontraditional over "female" domestic pursuits, we may ask to what extent the helpmate role may have been a device for exploiting women's labor.[32] Although there is no unequivocal answer, the subject may be approached obliquely by looking at instances where men did jobs ordinarily assigned to women.

Women's work did not have the same prestige as men's. The boys in one family, for example, helped their sisters sew carpet rags only as a punishment. Moreover, the record shows many more girls and women transcending gender-defined work roles than boys and men. Males probably did less nontraditional work than females, but another factor was men's reluctance to mention the "female" tasks they performed. Thus, Clark Woodis never recorded in his diary the fact that he washed dishes and cleaned the house, although entries for the same dates by his wife, Ruth, indicated that he did these chores.[33]

Clark's motivation for performing domestic tasks was the same governing many, if not most, women who labored in the fields: necessity. Ruth suffered from a heart condition, and she was often unable to work. Men also helped their wives when the need to do so could not be described as dire. To be sure, Orrin Hall carried water to fill the washtub and irrigate the garden for his wife, Ruth, who, by her own description, was not a strong woman. Yet he also ironed her clothes (including the artificial bosom of starched ruffles worn under Ruth's "full chested shirt waist") during the period she taught school—a job that provided their household with much needed cash income.[34] The evidence certainly is not conclusive, but the fact that some men filled the helpmate role argues against wholesale exploitation of wives' labor.

Part of the vital work associated with homesteading was the earning of cash income. Everyone except the smallest children might contribute to the family cash economy, but each member did so in ways that ordinarily varied in relation to age and gender.

While the primary source of married women's cash income was from marketing the surplus butter and eggs, some women also marketed their garden vegetables or other domestic products such as bread, sausages, and cheese. Most cash-producing jobs matrons performed were carried on in the home environment, or at least did not take them away from the homestead for extended periods. Commonly, women took in boarders (usually teachers, but also railroad workers), charging them at the rate of ten dollars per month for food, accommodations, and such additional amenities as washing, ironing, and mending. They also washed, ironed, and sewed for local bachelors, worked as dressmakers for their neighbors, and served as postmistresses.[35]

Daughters sometimes took over the domestic chores to give their mothers the time to earn money. But daughters also earned wages. Some found employment in the hotels of nearby towns; a few even owned and operated restaurants. Others worked as domestics in private homes. Salaries for housework were low—about two dollars a week in the 1890s. Teaching, on the other hand, paid three or more times as much and was therefore, considerably more desirable. Many wage-earning daughters, of course, lived with their families. Certainly, their role in helping to support their families was important, although the portion of income they kept for their own use is unclear. Another class of daughters—those who entered homesteads to expand family holdings—probably had more control over their wages. Lois Ervin, recalling her experience as a homesteading daughter, said the money she received from teaching was her own. Amy Dickinson Worthley, on the other hand, said her earnings and those of her siblings were pooled to pay for their education. She added, however, that she thought this practice was unusual.[36]

Young unmarried men, like young women, probably kept some or all of the money they earned. Many young males taught school because the salaries were relatively high: twenty-five to forty dollars a month around the turn of the century.[37]

The amount varied according to the affluence of the school district, the date, and probably the number of students. But there is no evidence that the sex of the teacher affected the pay. Nevertheless, men made up only a small percentage of teachers,[38] in part because males had many more kinds of work available to them than did females.

Male settlers held a nearly endless variety of jobs, even discounting those who owned businesses and homesteaded as a sideline. They not only worked weekdays in town, but they also traveled, sometimes hundreds of miles, to secure employment for months at a time.[39] These absences had a significant impact on women and children, increasing their workloads and their importance.

The contribution of women and children to the family economy of the homestead was acknowledged in the degree to which they could direct the allocation of resources. Children received material assets in accordance with whatever parents could spare. Indeed, one way parents recognized their children's increasing autonomy was to allow them to keep a larger proportion of their earnings as they grew older. Another was through the gift of livestock. One father gave each of his sons and daughters a heifer calf; the issue of that animal was also the child's property. In time, the growing herd provided income for clothing, tuition, and school supplies. Another family provided each of twelve children with a filly. When these daughters and sons left home as young adults, they took with them their own herd of horses, in addition to a milk cow given as a kind of "going-away" present.[40]

Within marriage, decisions for allocating resources appear to have been shared. This finding contradicts studies indicating women's second-class status in farm families, a conclusion based on investment of capital in additional land and farm machinery rather than in domestic labor-saving devices or improvements to the home.[41] In the native-born white families of northeastern Colorado, there were many examples of husbands spending time and money for the well-being of wives. But women also played an active role in determining how sizeable sums of money were to be spent. When Ollie and Willis Barden moved to their homestead in 1903, they lived in a "half dug out." Three years later they moved into a three-room frame house. Meanwhile, Willis used a walking plow that someone had given him for breaking sod. Orrin and Ruth Hall had a bumper wheat crop in 1917. They invested their profit in a four-bedroom frame house with indoor plumbing. Ruth eagerly anticipated "all this luxury after eight years in the little sod house." But Orrin was in no hurry to move, thinking their new quarters should "cure for a while." Ruth strongly disagreed, and she got her way: "the wildlife could have the soddy. I was getting out. So we moved into our new house in April 1918." Amy Dickinson Worthley's mother inherited money which she used to buy a farm next to the Dickinsons' place in Nebraska. When the family moved to Logan County, the sale of her land helped buy the new farm. But Mrs. Dickinson was distressed at losing title to her own real estate, so her husband made her a co-owner of the Colorado property.[42]

Wives' power to command resources and direct expenditures was evident in many other circumstances. When Mary and Samuel Wright decided to buy new furniture, one of their purchases was a sewing machine; Mary Hayes bought a sewing machine and lace curtains with money she earned from taking in boarders; Jessie Hassig Challis had title to her own cattle, and her own brand.

At least some wives retained control of property they had acquired before marriage. Lois Ervin had proved up a claim in her own right. Using the $1,600 from the sale of her homestead, she bought a second quarter section. In 1925 this land sold for $4,000 and ten years later Lois invested the money from this venture in her son's trucking business.[43] Typically, she used her resources to promote her family. Nonetheless, within the constraints of habit and custom governing female behavior, the decision to do so was hers.

The foregoing examples strongly suggest women's considerable status within the family. Men and women generally had different roles to play, but the mutuality between the sexes enforced by the needs of homesteading expanded women's power to negotiate and win. Inevitably, the strength of women's position affected the power dynamics of the whole family; this conclusion is supported by an uncompromising statement from a man whose mother and father homesteaded in 1908. He wrote, "our parents taught us [children that] . . . each member of a family is equal."[44] This does not mean, of course, that equality actually existed in homesteading families. But the fact that it occurred even as an ideal is significant.

The high status that at least some women homesteaders experienced was sometimes overshadowed by painful feelings associated with changing roles and disrupted relationships caused by the move to Colorado. Usually, those who felt most disoriented were middle-aged or older; a few were used to an urban environment. Yet the loneliness some women felt was inconsistent with an objective evaluation of their lives. Women were generally in daily contact with family members. They saw neighbors once a week or oftener, and homesteaders of both sexes made regular trips to town.[45] Women's close personal friendships with other women formed much of the meaningful fabric of their former lives. These rich emotional relationships, with their associations of place and time, had no easy substitutes. New relationships of similar intensity were necessarily slow to develop and in the meantime, some women experienced an intense sense of isolation. Yet for other women this same emotional vacuum seems to have encouraged a closer rapport with men.

Unreserved enthusiasm for homesteading was almost always associated with youth. Jessie Nolan, who was fifteen when her family came to Colorado, reported that she and the other children were "jubilant" about the move. Ollie Barden, a bride in 1902 when she and her husband settled near Haxtun, wrote, "we lived and were happy, had good neighbors and we were One Big Family." Young single women often viewed homesteading as a personal, romantic adventure. An excerpt from Mary Anderson's autograph album illustrates this point. In 1886, Mary and a friend, Bee Randolph, homesteaded adjoining quarter sections and shared a shack built over the property line. Mary's wedding the following year caused some melancholy for Bee, who composed the following:

> Dear Mame—Here we are in our little preemption home for the last time together, at least for some year [sic] to come. But I hope sometime we may visit it again. We cannot be happier than we have been here, although we may have wealth and other great pleasures. Can you not almost remember every day from the first, what has happened? Our laughing, singing, playing, working, our company, etc.[46]

For these young women, one of the essential attractions of homesteading was the independence that proving up a claim offered. Self-determination was not an option generally available to their sex. Yet homesteading held out that possibility, sanctioned by laws whose original intent was to encourage settlement by families and, thereby, social and political stability on the agricultural frontier. Moreover, the legal right of single women to patent government land had an unforeseen result. The elevated status and autonomy of this very visible group in the local female population served as an inspiration to all women and especially to girls, who were most receptive to novel ways of acting. To be sure, the labor shortage and the relative isolation of the family unit, which forced its members to greater reliance on each other, also played a part in promoting mutuality between the sexes. But the possibility of acquiring land raised the expectations of all females in the homesteading community. "Why can't I have some [government land], too?" was a question that surely more than one spinster asked herself.[47] And while wives could not enter claims, they probably acquired some psychological benefit from the unprecedented opportunities for land ownership available to their daughters and to others of their sex. It is true that for some women, the climate of enhanced freedom of action and elevated economic status was not worth the disruption of well-defined sex roles and the physical hardships pioneering imposed. But for those of a more resilient disposition, homesteading in northeastern Colorado had much to offer.

As I noted earlier, my findings of high status and opportunity for women on a portion of Colorado's agricultural frontier conflict with the conclusions reached by many recent studies of westering women. The explanation for this disagreement does not lie solely in the evaluation of the data. Several factors relating to time, place, the nature of women's economic role, and the focus of research on a particular phase of the pioneering process may account for differences in interpretation.

The variable of time is clearly responsible to a large degree for women's high status among northeastern Colorado homesteaders. Other studies have considered events predating the first settlement of Logan and Washington counties by as much as four or five decades. Agrarians of these earlier generations were unlikely to have yet emerged from the rigid patriarchy characteristic of pre–industrial and colonial families. Indeed, John Faragher specifically identified his subjects as living under this kind of family organization.[48] The homesteaders of northeastern Colorado, on the other hand, had assimilated the Cult of True Womanhood and its elevation of women within their proper sphere.

It is probable, too, that distinct family types not only evolved over time, but became geographically segregated, as well. One historian has classified within pre–industrial patriarchy three family patterns based on the relative power exercised by the eldest male. In the most rigidly hierarchical families, which he called "evangelical," the father's power was limited only by his obedience to God. This type of family was threatened by even the modest power sharing that occurred within "genteel" and "moderate" families; therefore, evangelicals tended to remove themselves from contact with other groups.[49] In the nineteenth century, family variations probably became even more complex with the development of companionate marriages arising out of the Cult of True Womanhood. Further, although the shift over time has generally been away from hierarchical and toward more companionate family styles, both styles have continued to coexist. The historian studying white, native-born women on the agricultural frontier must, therefore avoid generalizing. What may be true for one population may not accurately describe another, because family organization with its consequences for women probably varied significantly over the American West.[50]

Finally, the oppression of women described by some historians may be related to frontiers where women were, for some reason, constrained from entering claims. In addition, studies that look only at the migration[51] necessarily exclude women's entrepreneurial activities during settlement and focus instead on a part of the pioneering process likely to have inflicted the greatest physical and psychological pain. As a frontier business enterprise, homesteading was probably unique because of the relatively large numbers of women who directly participated by acquiring land patents, and because of the rising expectation their success generated among others of their sex.

Further study of women on homesteads and in other agricultural settings is needed to explore variations in women's status on the farmers' frontier. Nevertheless, in the light of recent publications, the data from northeastern Colorado suggest that the experience of pioneer agrarian women was more diverse and complex than might previously have been suspected.

Notes

1. John Mack Faragher, *Women and Men on the Overland Trail* (New Haven, Conn.: Yale University Press, 1979); Julie Roy Jeffrey, *Frontier Women: The Trans-Mississippi West, 1840–1880* (New York: Hill and Wang, 1979); Joan Jensen, *With These Hands: Women Working on the Land* (New York: Feminist Press and McGraw-Hill Book Co., 1981); Lillian Schlissel, *Women's Diaries of the Westward Journey* (New York: Schocken Books, 1982); Christine Stansell, "Women on the Great Plains, 1865–1890," *Women's Studies* 4 (1976): 87–98. Exceptions are Glenda Riley, *Frontierswomen: The Iowa Experience* (Ames: Iowa State University Press, 1981); and Sandra L. Myres, *Westering Women and the Frontier Experience, 1800–1915* (Albuquerque: University of New Mexico Press, 1982)

2. This paper is based on a larger study of homesteading women. See Katharine Llewellyn Hill Harris, "Women and Families on Northeastern Colorado Homesteads, 1873–1920" (Ph.D. diss., University of Colorado, 1983). The research was directed by Lee Chambers-Schiller and Ralph Mann, who were the first and second readers, respectively.

3 As many as 18 percent of the land entries in the period after 1900 were made by women, and 55 percent of these entrants patented land. Figures for homestead land entries in Logan and Washington counties were compiled from the land office tract book records available on microfilm from the Bureau of Land Management.

4. Although oral histories provided important evidence, written reminiscences comprised the bulk of the source materials for this study. See especially the family histories collected in the following volumes: Washington County Museum Association, *The Pioneer Book of Washington County, Colorado* (Denver: Big Mountain Press, 1959), hereafter cited as *PBWC;* Washington County Museum Association, *The Pioneer Book II of Washington County, Colorado* (Fort Morgan, Colo.: Print Shop; Aurora, Colo.: Rocky Mountain Press, n.d.), hereafter cited as *PBWC II;* Dorothea Safford and Helen Taylor, eds., *No Fuss and Feathers—Crook: A History of the Crook Community* (Fort Collins, Colo.: Crook Historial Society, Economy Printing, 1977), hereafter cited as CHS, *No Fuss and Feathers;* Fleming

Historical Society, *Memories of Our Pioneers* (Iowa Falls, Iowa: General Publishing and Binding, 1971), hereafter cited as FHS, *Memories*. The homesteading women of Washington and Logan counties did not leave a rich legacy of letters and diaries. This lack is particularly regrettable because of the tendency of the memory to suppress whatever was stressful and to recall, sometimes in embellished form, the pleasanter aspects of an experience. I have tried to keep this phenomenon in mind when weighing statements made years after the events they describe.

5. Barbara Welter, "The Cult of True Womanhood, 1820–1860," *American Quarterly* 18 (Summer, 1966): 151–74.

6. Faragher, *Women and Men on the Overland Trail*, p. 244 n.5, pp. 119, 138–40.

7. Norton Juster, *So Sweet to Labor: Rural Women in America, 1865–1895* (New York: Viking Press, 1979). Mary P. Ryan placed the beginnings of widespread dissemination of the cult after 1830, the year low-cost printing technology was invented. See her *Womanhood in America from Colonial Times to the Present* (New York: New Viewpoints, 1975), p. 143, cited in Faragher, *Women and Men on the Overland Trail*, p. 244 n.5.

8. *PBWC*, pp. 70, 223, 276, 278, 324, 367, 369–70, 379; CHS, *No Fuss and Feathers*, pp. 49–50; *PBWC II*, p. 207.

9. *PBWC*, pp. 31, 324; *PBWC II*, p. 426; CHS, *No Fuss and Feathers*, p. 49.

10. *PBWC*, pp. 222, 73, 163; *PBWC II*, pp. 126–27, 181, 381, 396, 427, 585.

11. FHS, *Memories*, pp. 50–51.

12. Opal Covington, tape-recorded interview with Margaret Cooley, Akron, Colo., 15 May 1975; *PBWC*, pp. 163, 190, 222.

13 *PBWC*, p. 56; FHS, *Memories*, p. 238.

14. *PBWC II*, pp. 49–50, 139–40; *PBWC*, p. 220; FHS, *Memories*, pp. 76, 242.

15. *PBWC*, p. 379.

16. Ibid., pp. 352, 175, 195–96.

17. Ibid., pp. 27–28, 45, 141, 379, FHS, *Memories*, p. 180; *PBWC II*, p. 355.

18. *PBWC II*, pp. 230–31; *PBWC*, p. 137

19. Glen R. Durrell, "Homesteading in Colorado," *Colorado Magazine*, Spring, 1974, p. 105. Durrell's reminiscences date from 1908 to 1916 in neighboring Lincoln County (*PBWC II*, pp. 349–50).

20. *PBWC*, pp. 198, 356, 380; PBWC II, pp. 275–76, 451, 515.

21. *PBWC II*, pp. 44, 396, 523.

22. Across Colorado, 55 percent of the voters approved woman suffrage. State of Colorado, *Abstract of Votes Cast for State Officers at the General Elections of the Years 1892–1900 Inclusive* (Denver: Smith Brooks Printing Co., 1901), p. 7.

23. *PBWC*, pp. 322, 117, 345, 362; *PBWC II*, pp. 354, 410, 426, 601; FHS, *Memories*, p. 206. Collecting chips was usually a job for women and children on the Overland Trail. Myres, *Westering Women*, p. 105.

24, Eggs, butter, and cream were often simply traded for groceries and other items. *PBWC II*, pp. 252, 515, 601; *PBWC*, pp. 43, 64, 167–70; FHS, *Memories*, p. 159. The importance of butter and egg production as a source of cash income has been noted for other parts of the agricultural frontier. See, for example, Glendy Riley, *Frontierswomen: The Iowa Experience* (Ames: Iowa University Press, 1981), pp. 86–87.

25. *PBWC*, pp. 353, 131; *PBWC*, pp. 325, 529; FHS, *Memories*, p. 31.

26. *PBWC II*, pp. 111, 353, 553; *PBWC*, pp. 131, 382.

27. Diaries of Ruth and Clark Woodis, *The Story of a Colorado Homestead, 1913–1928* (n.p., 1976). Ruth and Clark Woodis homesteaded near Deertrail, west of Logan and Washington counties. Ruth's chores appear to have been much more varied than Clark's.

28. *PBWC*, pp. 31, 42–43, 117, 322; FHS, *Memories*, pp. 104, 216.

29. This hypothesis is supported by Teresa Jordan's oral history of modern ranch women. See her *Cowgirls: Women of the American West* (New York: Anchor Press, Doubleday and Co., 1982), pp. 24–25, 39–41, 50–51, 66–67.

30. Eva Morris was born in 1898. FHS, *Memories*, pp. 195–96, 204, 246; *PBWC*, pp. 149, 173, 259, 342; *PBWC II*, pp. 66, 197.

31. *PBWC II*, p. 460; FHS, *Memories*, p. 216.

32. In support of the idea that men exploited women's labor on the agricultural frontier, see especially Stansell, "Women on the Great Plains," p. 93; and Faragher, *Women and Men on the Overland Trail*, pp. 59–65, 115, 183–87.

33. Diaries of Ruth and Clark Woodis, 5 May 1918 and 5 March 1919.

34. Ruth Schooley Hall, *Soddie Bride* (Fort Collins, Colo.: Robinson Press, 1973), pp. 34, 70, 80.

35. *PBWC*, pp. 138, 147–48, 160, 163, 170, 192, 350; *PBWC II*, pp. 20, 125–26, 231, 354–55, 426, 695; FHS, *Memories*, p. 167.

36. Lois Ervin, tape-recorded interview with Katherine Harris, Sterling, Colo., 7 June 1980; Amy Dickinson Worthley, tape-recorded interview with Katherine Harris, near Sterling, Colo., 7 June 1980; Helen Alishouse, tape-recorded interview with Margaret Cooley, Akron, Colo., 12 Nov. 1975; *PBWC*, pp. 87, 173, 248, 264.

37. For comparison, ranch hands at the turn of the century earned about fifteen dollars a month (*PBWC*, pp. 29, 88, 265); *PBWC II*, p. 183.

38. *PBWC*, p. 60.

39. Ibid., pp. 160, 162, 177, 192, 258, 284–85, 321, 359–60; FHS, *Memories*, pp. 41, 126–27, 161, 175, 194–95, 201, 207; *PBWC II*, pp. 18, 101, 125–26, 348–49, 396, 449, 588; Nell Brown Propst, *Those Strenuous Dames of the Colorado Prairie* (Boulder, Colo.: Pruett Publishing Co., 1982), pp. 77–78.

40. *PBWC*, pp. 150, 380

41. Stansell, "Women on the Great Plains," p. 91; Mary W. M. Hargreaves, "Women in the Agricultural Settlement of the Northern Plains," *Agricultural History* 50 (January, 1976): 187.

42. Mrs. Dickinson was native of Denmark, but her husband was American-born. Worthley, interview; Hall, *Soddie Bride*, pp. 122–23; FHS, *Memories*, pp. 30, 216; *PBWC*, p. 176.

43. Ervin, interview; *PBWC*, pp. 157, 163, 353.

44. FHS, *Memories*, pp. 206–207, 209. The family consisted of a father, mother ("who could keep up with a lot of men when it came to . . . [doing any] . . . homestead job"), two sons, and a daughter.

45. Ibid., pp. 131, 214; Hall, *Soddie Bride*, p. 95; Clara Watson, "Homesteading on the Plains," *Colorado Magazine*, April, 1961, pp. 142–43; *PBWC II*, pp. 175, 201, 585, 596. For a similar observation concerning women of the Iowa frontier, see Dorothy Schwieder, "Labor and Economic Roles of Iowa Farm Wives, 1840–80," in Trudy Huskamp Peterson, ed., *Farmers, Bureaucrats, and Middlemen: Historical Perspectives on American Agriculture* (Washington, D.C.: Howard University Press, 1980), p. 165.

46. *PBWC*, pp. 159–60; *PBWC II*, pp. 398–99; FHS, *Memories*, p. 31.

47. *PBWC II*, p. 673.

48. Faragher, *Women and Men on the Overland Trail*, p. 244 n.5.

49. Philip J. Greven, *The Protestant Temperament: Patterns of Childrearing, Religious Experience, and the Self in Early America* (New York: Alfred A. Knopf, 1977), pp. 12–18, 25–28, 124–40. Recently Joan Jensen pointed out geographically distinct differences in the agrarian experience, in an unpublished paper given at the Sex/Gender Division of Labor: Feminist Perspectives Conference, 13–15 May, 1983, University of Minnesota, St. Paul campus. See her "The Sexual Division of Labor on American Farms: 1750–1850."

50. One of the diarists in Schlissel's *Women's Diaries*, p. 78, hinted at the difference in family organization when she unfavorably compared Missourian with Yankee husbands. Further suggestive evidence is the early granting of the vote to Colorado women, which may have been related, in part, to a high concentration of companionate families in the state.

51. Schlissel, *Women's Diaries*; Faragher, *Women and Men on the Overland Trail*.

The Chicana in American History: The Mexican Women of El Paso, 1880–1920—A Case Study

Mario T. García

The author is a member of the history and Chicano studies departments in the University of California, Santa Barbara.

ALTHOUGH MEXICAN WOMEN have made significant contributions to the growth of a Chicano working class in the United States, their history has received little attention. Interpretive and historiographical pieces have been written, but no in-depth scholarship on the subject has emerged.[1] One factor that may explain this shortcoming is the absence of female Mexican

---

The author wishes to thank Ramón Eduardo Ruiz, W. Elliot Brownlee, Mary Brownlee, and Ileana Rodríguez for their helpful comments on this paper.

[1]General and interpretive works based on secondary sources include Martha P. Cotera, *Diosa y Hembra: The History and Heritage of Chicanas in the U.S.* (Austin, 1976); María Linda Apodaca, "The Chicana Woman: An Historical Materialist Perspective," *Latin American Perspectives*, IV (Winter and Spring 1977), 70–89; and Flor Saiz, *La Chicana* (N.p., 1973). For contemporary history based on recent census data, see Laura E. Arroyo, "Industrial and Occupational Distribution of Chicana Workers," *Aztlán*, IV (1973), 343–382; and Rosaura Sánchez, "The Chicana Labor Force," in Rosaura Sánchez and Rosa Martínez Cruz, *Essays on La Mujer* (Los Angeles, 1977), 3–15. On historiography, see Judith Sweeney, "Chicana History: A Review of the Literature," in Sánchez and Martínez Cruz, *La Mujer*, 99–123; and Rosalinda M. González, "A Review of the Literature on Mexican American Women Workers in the U.S. Southwest, 1900–75" (Unpublished paper available in the Chicano Studies Library, University of California, Berkeley). Also, consult the following bibliographies which have sections on history: Roberto Cabello-Argandoña, Juan Gómez-Quinoñes, and Patricia Herrera Durán, eds., *The Chicana: A Comprehensive Study* (Los Angeles, 1975); and Cristina Portillo, Graciela Rios, and Martha Rodríguez, eds., *Bibliography of Writings on La Mujer* (Berkeley, 1976). For interpretive articles on contemporary

American historians. Moreover, Chicano history, like most history, while showing slow but healthy development recently, only now has begun to focus on the role of Mexican American women.[2] A "Chicana" writer finds it "disheartening" to discover scant mention of women in the latest publications on Chicano history.[3] Yet "her history" is an integral part of the Mexican saga in the Southwest. As one scholar has observed, Chicano history without the Chicana would be "false" and "truncated."[4] This study attempts to help correct the omission of women in Chicano history and suggests some of the major research areas that might be explored, using the case study of Mexican women in El Paso, Texas, between 1880 and 1920.[5]

Women of Mexican descent appear early in the story of the Southwest. On the whole, most were wives and mothers, and their story has yet to be told. Wives accompanied their husbands on the long and perilous trek to the United States during the late nineteenth and early twentieth centuries. The family, of course, represented the most important institution transferred across the border by Mexican immigrants. The Dillingham Commission report of 1911 on the state of foreign immigration to the United States, authorized by the United States Senate, noted that a high percentage of Mexican laborers in western

---

Chicanas, the following sample can be consulted: Noemi Lorenzana, "La Chicana: Transcending the Old and Carrying Out a New Life and Self-Image," *De Colores*, II (1975), 6–14; Jennie V. Chávez, "An Opinion: Women of the Mexican-American Movement," *Mademoiselle*, LXXXII (April 1972), 150–152; and Adal Riddel, "Chicanas and El Movimiento," *Aztlán*, (1974), 155–165. For a more recent and general treatment, see Alfredo Mirandé and Evangelina Enríquez, *La Chicana: The Mexican-American Woman* (Chicago, 1979).

[2] For a discussion of recent publications in Chicano history, see Juan Gómez Quinoñes and Luis Arroyo, "On the State of Chicano History: Observations on Its Development, Interpretation, and Theory, 1970–1974," *Western Historical Quarterly* 1976), 155–185.

[3] Noemi Lorenzana, "Hijas de Aztlán," *De Colores*, I (Summer 1974), 43.

[4] Sweeney, "Chicana History," 99–100.

[5] Besides being the most important point of entry for Mexican immigrants, El Paso also served as a major urban employer of Mexican workers. Mexican men, for example, readily found jobs at the smelter, the railroad yards, in construction, clerical work, and in a variety of other low-skilled occupations. A special El Paso census conducted in 1916 recorded that out of a total population of 61,482, Mexicans represented 32,724 or 54.8 percent of the city's inhabitants. Except for San Antonio, El Paso by 1920 contained the largest urban concentration of Mexicans in the U.S., and the border city was the only southwestern metropolis possessing more Mexicans than Anglo Americans. For more on El Paso and its Mexican population, see Mario T. García, "Obreros: The Mexican Workers of El Paso, 1900–1920" (Ph.D. dissertation, University of California, San Diego, 1975); and Oscar J. Martínez, *Border Boom Town: Ciudad Juárez since 1848* (Austin, 1978).

industries had brought their wives from nearby Mexico. According to the commission, some 58.2 percent of Mexican railroad workers in the survey reported that their wives were with them in the United States. This figure was much higher than that for other immigrant railroad workers in the West who had arrived from more distant lands, such as southern Europe and Asia, and the commission suggested, although without evidence, that "the conditions under which section hands live are less uninviting to the Mexican women than to the women of any other race."[6] One railroad line, the Santa Fe, by 1910 was encouraging the migration of Mexican families in order to stabilize working conditions. As a Santa Fe engineer put it, hiring married men resulted in better and more productive workers.[7] Investigators for the Dillingham Commission also discovered a similar condition in urban-related work. Sixty percent of Mexicans employed as construction workers by street railways, for example, admitted they had their wives with them.[8]

In Mexico at the turn of the century, the urban working class and rural family appear to have constituted a strong social and economic institution. Ernesto Galarza, in his autobiographical *Barrio Boy*, recalls that his family in rural Nayarit included not only his mother (who divorced Galarza's father prior to his birth), but also his aunt, three uncles, and two cousins. In the Galarza household, the men went to labor in the fields during the day while the women and children remained and performed the housework and cooking.[9]

Leaving Mexico and entering the United States, the Mexican family seems to have remained strong and retained its native character rather than being weakened by the immigration process. The majority of Mexican immigrant families, as revealed in a sample taken from a 1900 El Paso census, were either nuclear or extended (see Table 1). Over half of the immigrant household units were nuclear families living by themselves or in an augmented relationship with nonrelated household resi-

[6] "Immigrants in Industries, Part 25: Japanese and Other Immigrant Races in the Pacific Coast and Rocky Mountain States," 61 Cong., 2 sess., *S. Doc. 633* (1911), Vol. III, Part I, pp. 11–12 (cited hereafter as *Dillingham Commission*).

[7] Judith Fincher Laird, "Argentine, Kansas: The Evolution of a Mexican-American Community: 1905–1940" (Ph.D. dissertation, University of Kansas, 1975), 121.

[8] *Dillingham Commission*, Part 25, Vol. III, Parts I and II, pp. 39 and 86.

[9] Ernesto Galarza, *Barrio Boy* (Notre Dame, 1971), 3–71.

TABLE 1
HOUSEHOLD COMPOSITION, EL PASO, 1900
(PERCENTAGES ROUNDED OFF)

	Mexican National	Mexican American	Non-Spanish Surname
Nuclear family households			
Husband, wife and children	38% (58)	45% (11)	29% (65)
Husband, wife, no children	7% (10)	4% (1)	10% (23)
Broken families			
Husband and children	3% (4)	0 (0)	3% (7)
Wife and children	19% (30)	0 (0)	9% (21)
Single-person households	7% (12)	4% (1)	20% (42)
Extended-family households[a]	13% (20)	16% (4)	5% (13)
Augmented-family households[b]	11% (17)	30% (7)	19% (40)
Extended-augmented family households[c]	0 (1)	0 (0)	2% (6)
Total Number (393)	(152)	(24)	(217)

[a] Nuclear family living with one or more relatives.
[b] Nuclear family living with nonfamily members, such as lodgers, in the same household.
[c] Nuclear family living with both relatives and nonfamily members
SOURCE: U.S. *Manuscript Census, 1900.*

dents, such as boarders. In addition, 13 percent were extended families. More Mexican immigrant families lived in nuclear households than did non-Spanish surname families. Perhaps reflecting greater personal mobility, a larger percentage of non-Spanish surnamed individuals resided in single-person households than did Mexican immigrants. On the other hand, more broken homes could be found among the Mexican immigrant population, especially those involving a mother and her children; however, it is possible that in some cases husbands were not recorded due to jobs outside the city. Still considerably more Mexican Americans than Mexican immigrants lived in nuclear families. Many Mexican Americans also apparently took in boarders.[10] Since the 1910 and 1920 manuscript cenuses are not

[10]U.S. manuscript census, 1900, El Paso County, Vols. 35 and 36. There are 3,123 family units included in the 1900 census for the city of El Paso. To acquire a representative sample, every eighth unit was recorded commencing with the second unit of the First Ward (the census encompassed El Paso's four wards). The total number of units in the sample amounted to 393. For sample methodology, see Peter R. Knights, *The Plain People of Boston, 1830–1860: A Study of City Growth* (New York, 1971), 3–10. I wish to thank Carl V. Harris of the Department of History, University of California, Santa Barbara, for his assistance in determining the sample. In a study of the Mexican

yet available to scholars, no comparisons can be made, but it is possible that over this twenty-year period a pattern of chain migration set in and extended-family households grew among Mexican immigrants as other relatives arrived, especially those from the northern Mexican states.

Although some Mexican women in El Paso and throughout the urban Southwest contributed to household incomes by taking in wash or lodgers, no disintegration took place in the traditional pattern of men being the chief wage-earners and women doing household work. The sample taken from the El Paso census of 1900 shows that no mothers and few daughters, most of the latter being too young, in an immigrant family headed by the father worked outside the home.[11] As wife and mother the Mexican housewife was primarily responsible for caring for the Mexican male worker and her family. Under a division of labor which relegated nearly all of them to housework, Mexican women, like most women, had to maintain the male work force as well as reproduce it. Within the family, Mexican males not only found relief from their job alienation, but nourishment for another day's hard work. Consequently, the family, and the women's role in it, performed a significant economic task.[12]

Too poor to afford their own domestics, Mexican women in the border city performed their housework under depressed living conditions. "Chihuahuita," the largest Mexican settlement in El Paso and adjacent to the Rio Grande River border, contained the city's worst and most congested housing. While no legal restrictions prohibited Mexicans from living in the better homes found in American neighborhoods, lack of occuptional

---

community in Los Angeles between 1850 and 1890, Richard Griswold del Castillo also found that most Mexican immigrants lived in nuclear families. Griswold del Castillo, "La Familia Chicana: Social Change in the Chicano Family of Los Angeles, 1850–1890," *Journal of Ethnic Studies*, III (Spring 1975), 41–58.

[11] *Manuscript Census, 1900*. In a sample of 152 immigrant households, of those with a working father not one unit contained a mother working outside the home and only seven units had working daughters.

[12] For interpretive works on the role of women as housewives and mothers, see Shiela Rowbotham, *Woman's Consciousness, Man's World* (Middlesex, England, 1973); Rowbotham, *Hidden from History: Rediscovering Women in History from the 17th Century to the Present* (New York, 1976); Alva Buxenbaum, "The Status of Women Workers," *Political Affairs*, LII (Nov. 1973), pp. 31–42; and Wally Secombe, "The Housewife and Her Labour under Capitalism," *New Left Review*, LXXXII (Jan.–Feb. 1974), 3–24.

mobility, in addition to race and cultural prejudice, kept Mexicans segregated in *barrios* (slums). Mexicans adjusted to these conditions, however, because of acquaintance with poverty, plus the mistaken belief they would soon return to Mexico with ample savings.

Unfortunately, the adjustment of Mexicans left them open to exploitation and neglect by landlords and city officials. Due to their small wages, Mexican workers had to live in *jacales*—adobe homes—with dirt floors. Reporter Lewis Gilbert of Missouri noted in a visit to El Paso in 1900 that the huts, home to the Mexicans, had from one to three rooms. In sharp contrast to their adobe houses, the Missourian observed, Americans built their structures of bricks. For heating and cooking, the Mexicans gathered firewood from timber that flowed down the Rio Grande. Some resorted to stealing coal from nearby railroad cars. Tragically, the burning of these fuels often led to fires which destroyed the jacales. Furthermore, little sanitation existed in the Mexican barrios. Since they did not own property, except for their huts, Mexicans found it difficult to acquire municipal services paid by local property taxes. American property owners in Chihuahuita, who rented land to Mexicans, delayed improvements by claiming they could not afford increased taxes. Unlike the American sections, for example, the Mexican districts contained few sidewalks or paved streets. In 1897 the Spanish language newspaper, *El Monitor*, complained about poor street conditions in the Mexican area where rubble and latrines could be found. Already crowded, the addition of new immigrants and refugees, especially during the Mexican Revolution of 1910, only increased the high population density of Chihuahuita. Jacales at times housed two or three families. Although tenements had replaced some of the huts by 1916, the new buildings quickly became congested and unsanitary due to the Mexican's poverty, continued immigration, and neglect by landlords.[13]

Under these conditions, Mexican housewives did the hard manual labor which allowed immigrant families to live on husband's and sometimes childrens' limited earnings. Mexican

[13] *El Paso Times*, Jan 9, 1900, p. 6; *El Monitor*, Oct. 31, 1893, p. 3. Also, see chapter 5, "Chihuahuita: The Making of a Barrio," in García, "Obreros," 212–260.

women had to haul water for washing and cooking from the river or public water pipes. To feed their families, they had to spend time marketing, often in Cuidad Juárez across the border, as well as long, hot hours cooking meals and coping with the burden of desert sand both inside and outside their homes. Besides the problem of raising children, unsanitary living conditions forced Mexican mothers to deal with disease and illness in their families. Diphtheria, tuberculosis, typhus, and influenza were never too far away. Some diseases could be directly traced to inferior city services. Charity official, Mrs. E. Kohlberg, complained in 1909 that much of the increase in tuberculosis among the Mexican population could be blamed on the sanitation department which swept the streets of Chihuahuita without first sprinkling them with water, "thus scattering dust in every direction and releasing millions of germs." As a result, Mexican mothers had to devote much energy caring for sick children, many of whom died. The *El Paso Times* commented later in 1909 that out of thirty-six deaths during the previous week, twenty involved children less than three years of age. Almost all were Mexicans. "Death seems to be a frequent and common visitor in the homes of the Mexican element," the newspaper remarked. Lack of sewers, water, paved sidewalks, and streets plus overcrowded homes made housework one of the most arduous jobs in the Mexican settlement.[14]

The Mexican housewife, although oppressed under a sexual division of labor, helped sustain the family's male workers and indirectly El Paso's economy which grew and prospered from the labor of Mexicans. Without the woman's housework, Mexican men could not have adjusted so easily to an American urban environment. "If we are to understand the lives of the working class," one scholar stresses, "we must look at the lives of the women as well as those of the men, in the household as well as in the workplaces."[15]

---

[14] Garcia, "Obreros," 238–244; *Times*, Nov. 24, 1909, pp. 1–2, and May 13, 1910, p. 4.

[15] Susan J. Kleinberg, "Technology and Women's Work: The Lives of Working Class Women in Pittsburg, 1870–1900," *Labor History*, XVII (1976), 58. Interpreting the modern role of housewives as a result of industrial capitalism, Ann Oakly writes that "the work of women has received very little serious sociological or historical attention. Their unpaid work in the home has scarcely been studied at all." Ann Oakly, *Women's Work: The Housewife, Past and Present* (New York, 1976), 3–78.

Besides their roles as housewives, Mexican women guarded Mexican cultural traditions within the family. Not only did the family represent the most fundamental institution brought by Mexican immigrants, but it proved to be the most resistant barrier to American assimilation.[16] Due to a lack of economic options, much Mexican popular culture in El Paso and throughout the Southwest centered on family activities. It is difficult with the scarcity of documentation on Mexican families to present an accurate picture of family life in El Paso, but anthropologist Manuel Gamio noted certain customs being practiced during the 1920s by Mexican immigrant families in El Paso as well as other Mexican settlements throughout the United States. Gamio observed that while Mexican immigrants accepted American material goods, they also retained earlier customs. These included folklore, songs and ballads, birthday celebrations, saints' days, baptisms, weddings, and funerals in the traditional style. Because of poverty, a lack of physicians in the barrios, and adherence to traditional customs, Mexicans continued to use medicinal herbs. Immigrant women interviewed by Gamio acknowledged that for the most part they cooked "Mexican style."[17] Mexican folk customs both inside and outside the family also included a variety of oral traditions. These involved *cuentos* (Mexican tales), children's stories, legends, ghost and goblin stories, such as "La Llorona" (The Weeper) and *dichos*—sayings and proverbs. Perhaps the most popular form of oral literature were the songs and ballads called *corridos* which were based on the Spanish romance and which the Mexicans sang in Spanish with their families and fellow-

[16]Ernesto Galarza, "Mexicans in the Southwest: A Culture in Process," in Edward H. Spicer and Raymond H. Thompson, eds., *Plural Society in the Southwest* (New York, 1972), 276–277.

[17]Manuel Gamio, *Mexican Immigration to the United States* (New York, 1971; originally published Chicago, 1930), 76–83, and Gamio, *The Life Story of the Mexican Immigrant* (New York, 1971; originally published Chicago, 1931), 82–83, 161–166. The existence of such folk traditions emphasizes what Emilio Willems discovered in his study of the German Rhineland town of Negle: the persistence of earlier preindustrial cultural practices within a modernized society or what sociologist Herbert J. Gans refers to as an "urban village." See Emilio Willems, "Peasantry and City: Cultural Persistence and Change in Historical Perspective—A European Case," *American Anthropologist*, LXXII (1970), 528–543; and Herbert J. Gans, *The Urban Villages* (New York, 1962). Also, see Herbert G. Gutman, *Work, Culture and Society in Industrializing America* (New York, 1976), 3–78.

workers. Singing in the family involved songs sung by mothers to their children or while doing housework. According to one folklorist, singing formed part of the evening's entertainment along with prose narratives, riddles, and games. All family members participated in these evening performances and the singing ranged from *corridos* to children's songs.[18] In addition, Mexican women instilled in their children faith in Mexican Catholic beliefs and practices. Although Mexican culture in El Paso and along the border changed over the years as Americanization modified various customs and values, Mexican housewives must nevertheless be credited with helping to keep alive native culture, thus making it easier for Mexican immigrants to adjust and work in the United States.[19]

While housework formed the most important work activity for Mexican women, some in El Paso also found jobs outside the home. El Paso, for example, had one of the earliest concentrations of Mexican female wage workers in the United States. Mexican women, as other women, worked either to augment the earnings of male family members or due to the loss of the male breadwinner. As one scholar correctly observes, "work was not a choice but a necessity."[20] A sample of 393 El Paso households taken from the 1900 manuscript census reveals that almost a fifth (17.11 percent) of Mexican households contained a working woman. American women also had to enter the labor

[18] Américo Paredes, *A Texas-Mexican Cancionero: Folksongs of the Lower Border* (Urbana, 1976), xvii, xix–xxii; and Gamio, *Life Story*, 218.

[19] While Mexican women aided in the retention of cultural traditions within the family, it should also be pointed out that such traditions maintained the woman in a subordinate position within the family. For sociological, anthropological, and psychological views on the Mexican family in the United States, see Maxine Baca Zinn, "Chicanas: Power and Control in the Domestic Sphere," *De Colores*, II, no. 4 (1975), 19–31; Zinn, "Political Familism: Toward Sex Role Equality in Chicano Families," *Aztlán*, VI (1976), 13–26; Miguel Montiel, "The Social Science Myth of the Mexican American Family," *El Grito*, III (1970), 56–63; Miguel Montiel, "The Chicano Family: A Review of Research," *Social Work*, XVIII (March 1973), 22–31; Robert Staples, "The Mexican-American Family: Its Modification over Time and Space," *Phylon*, XXXVII (1971), 179–192; Nathan Murillo, "The Mexican American Family," in Carrol A. Hernández, *et al.*, eds., *Chicanos: Social and Psychological Perspectives* (St. Louis, 1976), 15–25; Peter Uhlenberg, "Marital Instability among Mexican Americans: Following the Patterns of Blacks?" *Social Problems*, XX (Summer 1972), 49–56; Betty Garcia-Bahne, "La Chicana and the Chicano Family," in Sánchez and Martínez Cruz, *La Mujer*, 30–47; and Leo Grebler, *et al.*, eds., *The Mexican-American People* (New York, 1970), 350–377.

[20] Apodaca, "The Chicana Woman," 71.

force and the census sample indicates that 11.21 percent of American households had a female worker. Mexican women who worked, according to the census, were either unmarried daughters, mothers with no husbands, or single women. Of the 31 Spanish surnamed households in the sample with a working female, 17 had daughters or other young relatives with jobs while the remaining 14 contained working mothers with no husbands or single women. On the other hand, married Mexican women, both foreign and native born, within a nuclear or extended family, did not work. The sample revealed no instance of a woman with an employed husband having a job.[21] Age and fertility help explain this condition. In the 1900 sample, 41.08 percent of married Mexican immigrant women were between fifteen and thirty years of age, a period when women generally give birth. Moreover, 38.44 percent of married Mexican immigrant women were between thirty and forty, a period when most women had children at home. Indeed, 77.44 percent of all married Mexican immigrant women in El Paso had children twelve years of age or under or children listed as attending school; of these 39.93 percent had children five years of age and under.[22]

If age and fertility worked against Mexican women finding jobs outside the home, so too did Mexican cultural traditions. Mexican men resented women, especially wives, working or wanting to work for wages. Most males believed their work a man's duty and that woman's consisted of raising children and keeping house.[23] As one working class newspaper in Mexico during the age of Porfirio Díaz emphasized: "To be a wife is to be a woman preferably selected amongst many other women, for her honesty, for her religiousness, for her amiability, . . . for

---

[21] *Manuscript Census, 1900.*

[22] *Ibid.* Virginia Yans-McLaughlin in her study of Italian immigrant families in Buffalo also discovered a preponderance of married immigrant women of child-bearing age who did not work outside the home. See Yans-McLaughlin, *Family and Community: Italian Immigrants in Buffalo, 1880–1930* (Ithaca, 1977), 180–217. Most married women of child-bearing age in the United States in the early twentieth century did not work. Valerie Kincade Oppenheimer, *The Female Labor Force in the United States* (Berkeley, 1970), 1–63.

[23] For attitudes of Mexican men toward wage-working women, see Paul S. Taylor, "Mexican Labor in Los Angeles Industry" (unpublished manuscript, Paul S. Taylor Collection, Bancroft Library, University of California, Berkeley), part 2; and Gamio, *Life Story*, 46.

her industriousness, [and] for her docility. . . ."[24] Despite such attitudes, the Mexican family in the United States did not remain static. Over the years more Mexican women, especially daughters, became wage-workers to augment the family income. Also, as the economy expanded, especially during the "Roaring Twenties," El Paso and southwestern industries and services began to recruit more Mexican women workers. Mexican men may have more easily accepted their daughters working outside the home than their wives, but the cultural challenge and adjustment that resulted from wage-working women within the traditional male-dominated Mexican family represents a little understood and important topic for future research.[25]

The increase in Mexican female wage-workers in El Paso by 1920 can be seen in census figures for that year. The census reported that 3,474 foreign-born females, almost all Mexicans, ten years of age and older were engaged in a gainful occupation. Foreign-born female wage-workers represented half of all females ten years and over who held jobs in El Paso. Most female workers in El Paso (3,112 females or 45 percent of all employed women) did "women's work." The two largest occupations were servants (1,718) and laundresses (710)—jobs familiar to women in Mexico—where the majority of Mexican working women could be found. Due to deficiencies in skills and schooling, as well as prejudice against them, few Mexican women, unlike their American counterparts, were in such skilled professional occupations as teaching, nursing, or office work.[26] Table 2

---

[24] As quoted in Margaret Towner, "Monopoly Capitalism and Women's Work during the Porfiriato," *Latin American Perspectives*, IV (Winter–Spring 1977), 93. Like Mexican men, most males in the United States did not look with favor on women, especially married ones with children, working outside the home. Oppenheimer, *Female Labor Force*, 40–42.

[25] McLaughlin points out in her study of Italian immigrant families in Buffalo that acculturation, including women working outside the home, did not necessarily lead to a breakdown of traditional male authority in the family. See McLaughlin, "Patterns of Work and Family Organization: Buffalo's Italians," in Michael Gordon, ed., *The American Family in Social Historical Perspective* (New York, 1973), 140. A recent study suggests that increased numbers of married Mexican women are now working. See Rosemary Santana Cooney, "Changing Labor Force Participation of Mexican American Wives: A Comparison with Anglos and Blacks," *Social Science Quarterly*, LVI (1975), 252–261.

[26] U.S. Bureau of the Census, *Fourteenth Census of the United States, 1920: Population* (Washington, D.C., 1923), IV, 263; U.S. manuscript census, 1900; and Carlos B. Gill, "Mascota: A Mexican World Left Behind" (Ph.D. dissertation, University of California, Los Angeles, 1975), 127.

TABLE 2
NUMBER AND PERCENTAGE OF SPANISH-SURNAMED DOMESTICS AND LAUNDRESSES, 1889, 1910, AND 1920

Year	Number	Percent of Total Workers (Mexican and American)
	DOMESTICS	
1889	61	49.73
1910	447	65.37
1920	1528	76.18
	LAUNDRESSES	
1889	40	34.90
1910	220	64.48
1920	516	92.17

SOURCE: El Paso city directories for 1889, 1910, and 1920. The 1890 city directory was not used because no copies for that year could be found. The discrepancy between the 1920 census figures and those of the city directory is probably the result of a more limited survey by the compilers of the city directory.

shows the number and percentage of Spanish-surnamed women listed as domestics and laundresses in the city directories of 1889, 1910, and 1920.

Victor S. Clark, a Bureau of Labor inspector, noted in 1908 that Mexican "immigrant women have so little conception of domestic arrangements in the United States that the task of training them would be too heavy for American housewives."[27] Yet domestic work proved to be the most readily available source of jobs for Mexican women. Clark correctly recognized that women from preindustrial cultures might have difficulty adjusting to the new electrical devices of middle-class American homes, although he failed to understand that the employment of Mexican maids saved southwestern housewives from having to buy the new appliances. Mexican domestics did their work by hand. Elizabeth Rae Tyson, who grew up in El Paso, remembered the extensive use of Mexican maids by American families. "Owing to the large Mexican majority," she recalled,

> . . . almost every Anglo-American family had at least one, sometimes two or three servants: a maid and laundress, and perhaps a nursemaid

[27] Victor S. Clark, "Mexican Labor in the United States," *U.S. Bureau of Labor Bulletin No. 78* (Washington, D.C., 1908), reprinted in Carlos E. Cortés, *et al.*, eds., *Mexican Labor in the United States* (New York, 1974), 496.

> or yardmen. The maid came in after breakfast and cleaned up the breakfast dishes, and very likely last night's supper di-hes as well; did the routine cleaning, washing and ironing, and after the family dinner in the middle of the day, washed dishes again, and then went home to perform similar service in her own home.[28]

Mexican women, besides working as servants, found other employment opportunities. Many worked as washerwomen, either in American homes or in their own as well as in the various laundries of El Paso. In laundries, they learned such other skills as the use of sewing machines and received from $4 to $6 a week. In 1917 the El Paso Laundry, the largest in the city, employed 134 Spanish-surnamed workers out of a total of 166 employees, and Mexican women, mostly doing collar and flatwork, composed what appears to have been over half of the Mexican employees. That same year the Elite Laundry had 76 Spanish-surnamed female workers out of a total of 128 employees. Another of the larger laundries, the Acme, employed 75 Spanish-surnamed females out of 121 employees in 1917. The same pattern prevailed in the smaller laundries. For example, the Post Laundry had 33 Spanish-surnamed women in their work force of 49. While many of these laundresses lived in El Paso, some came from Cuidad Juárez. The daughter-in-law of Frank Fletcher, who owned the Acme Laundry, remembers that when she arrived in 1926, a laundry truck picked up the Mexican women at the border, took them to work, and returned

---

[28]As quoted in Mary Wilson Barton, "Methodism at Work among the Spanish-Speaking People of El Paso, Texas" (M.A. thesis, University of Texas, El Paso, 1950), 15. Some Mexican women also worked as maids in office buildings. See Pay Roll, Mills Building, Sept. 1, 1911, in H. Stevens Collection, No. 761, University of Texas, El Paso, library. The continued employment of Mexican domestics after 1920 in El Paso suggests that the use of new household technology by middle-class Americans did not lead to a total displacement of Mexicans as domestics. It appears that Mexican women, many of them commuter workers from Ciudad Juárez, learned the use of the new technology and at the same time continued to receive low wages. The 1970 census for El Paso lists 1,394 women as private household workers out of a total Spanish-language or Spanish-surname working population of 54,789 (U.S. Bureau of the Census, *Census of Population, 1970—Character of the Population*, Part 45: *Texas* [Washington, D.C., 1973], Sect. 1, p. 714). The persistence of Mexican women as domestics in El Paso and along the border goes counter to the national trend of the new household technology replacing domestics. See Ruth Schwartz Cowan, "The 'Industrial Revolution' in the Home: Household Technology and Social Change in the 20th Century," *Technology and Culture*, XVII (1976), 1–23.

them in the evening to the international bridge. The use of nonresident Mexican women limited already low wages.[29]

In addition to service jobs, some Mexican women labored as production workers, especially in El Paso's early garment factories. In 1902 Bergman's factory, which turned out shirts and overalls, reported that it had three American women and a large number of Mexican females. Yet, according to a newspaper account, Bergman concluded that he could get more and better work out of his Americans and consequently paid them $10 to $14 a week while the Mexicans received no more than $9 a week. Several years later, in 1919, the El Paso Overall Company advertised in a Spanish-language newspaper that it needed Mexican women for sewing and for general work. Mexican women likewise worked in the Kohlberg cigar factory. Although the exact nature of their work cannot be determined, 22 Mexican women out of 113 employees labored in the plant in 1917. Some women also found jobs as clerks and sales personnel in the downtown stores. An *El Paso Times* ad in 1905 read: "Wanted - 5 experienced American and Spanish salesladies." The Mexican newspaper, *El Día*, in 1919 praised Panchita Salas for her "work and charm" at the El Globo Department Store run by the Schwartz family. That same year, the White House Department Store, one of El Paso's largest, publicized in *La Patria* that it needed young women clerks in all its departments. Still other Mexicans worked as cooks or dishwashers in restaurants. In more unfortunate cases, Mexican women sold food on the streets of Chihuahuita.[30]

Finally, as in other societies, some women inhabited the saloons and gambling halls of the red-light district. The *Lone Star*, an early El Paso newspaper, in 1885 expressed shock over a twelve-year-old Mexican girl's activities. "It is rumored," the newspaper sermonized, "that she is a prostitute and most any hour of the day she can be seen in the streets with different men." When the city government enforced an ordinance in

[29] *La Patria*, Sept. 12, 1919, p. 4; *Labor Advocate*, Oct. 31, 1919, p. 4; *El Paso Herald*, June 23–24, 1917, p. 7; July 28–29, 1917, p. 16; May 26–27, 1917, p. 15; Dec. 15–16, 1917, p. 4; and telephone interview with Mrs. Frank Fletcher, Jr., El Paso, Aug. 15, 1975.

[30] *Times*, Sept. 26, 1902, p. 8; *La Patria*, Oct. 30, 1919, p. 4; *Herald*, June 9–11, 1917, p. 15; *Times*, Dec. 19, 1905, p. 7; *El Día*, Feb. 18, 1919, p. 3; *La Patria*, Oct. 30, 1919, p. 4; *Times*, Dec. 8, 1903, p. 7; and *Herald*, Aug. 1, 1916, p. 14.

1903 to move the district further from the center of El Paso, the *Times* reported that many of the prostitutes "propose to go across the river, among the number being the Mexicans, which include the dance hall girls." Two years later when Lou Vidal attempted to open his dance hall, police raided the establishment and arrested his employees, which included dance hall girls María González, Josefa González, Lola Beltran, and Senida García.[31]

Not only did employers hire Mexican women for jobs characterized as "women's work," but they paid them the lowest wages in the city. Although it appears that poor wages for Mexican women can be partly explained by their work inexperience and initial low productivity, employers nevertheless used such arguments to maintain wage differentials between Mexicans and Americans and to insure profits for themselves. As a result, persistent low wages for all Mexicans, men and women, whether for economic or racial reasons, or both, served to support job and educational discrimination against Mexicans in El Paso, which kept them in a state of restricted economic mobility and near poverty.[32]

Specific attention to the wages of Mexican women in El Paso occurred as the result of hearings held in the border city in November 1919 by the Texas Industrial Welfare Commission. During three days of testimony by employers as well as female employees, the commission discovered that Mexican workers in the laundries and factories of the city received less pay than American women in other industries. The Mexicans also obtained less than the salaries of laundry and factory workers in other Texas cities who performed similar work but did not face Mexican competition. According to the commission, these differences made it more difficult to set a minimum wage throughout the state. The reason for the problem, the commission stated, could be found in the Mexican's lower standard of living,

---

[31] *Lone Star*, Aug. 22, 1885, p. 3; *Times*, Feb. 4, 1903, p. 2; Feb. 3, 1905, p. 3. For information on El Paso's redlight district, see C. L. Sonnichsen, *Pass of the North* (El Paso, 1968), 277–304. In 1910, the city government abolished the red-light district.

[32] On occupational and educational differences between Mexicans and Americans in El Paso, see Mario T. García, "Racial Dualism in the El Paso Labor Market, 1880–1920," *Aztlán*, VI (1975), 197–218. For a recent theoretical treatment of race and class, see Mario Barrera, *Race and Class in the Southwest: A Theory of Racial Inequality* (Notre Dame, Ind., 1979).

"and that is a condition which, it seems, cannot be remedied." The members of the commission concluded, although without evidence, that "the Mexican workers find it possible to 'live comfortably' on a wage that Anglo workers would regard as 'starvation wages.' "[33]

Despite the commission's conclusions, Mexican women who appeared before it refuted those who claimed that Mexicans did not need higher wages because they had a lower standard of living. One group of laundry workers who had gone on strike for higher wages testified that the laundries had paid them $4 to $5 a week. Manuela Hernández, who had worked for several years at the Acme Laundry, told the commission in Spanish that she received $11 a week. While her wages made her the highest paid Mexican woman in the plant, American women averaged $4 to $6 more, although it is not clear if the Americans performed the same work. "I find it difficult to live on my wages," Hernández commented, "which I turn in to the family budget." She estimated that it would take $16 a week for her family to live "comfortably." María Valles testified that she worked at the Elite Laundry and received $4.50 a week. She lived with her family and supported a nine-year-old daughter. "I have to support her and myself," she stated, "but I have to make great sacrifices, some days going without food, for lack of means." She believed she could live well on $15 a week. Mexican women employed in the El Paso Overall Company also testified before the commission about their need for higher wages. The *El Paso Herald* described one of these workers, Daniela Morena, as "a woman along in years," who stated that she made $7 to $8 a week and supported her mother and two children. She believed that she required at least $15 a week, "but if alone might get along with $8 or $9 a week, as she 'dressed very humbly.' " Other garment workers gave similar testimonies. The Mexican women's arguments, unfortunately, had little impact. Low wages for Mexicans, both men and women, continued to characterize the El Paso economy.[34]

---

[33] *Times*, Nov. 20, 1919, p. 5.

[34] *Ibid*., and *Herald*, Nov. 20, 1919, p. 10. For a more thorough discussion of the Texas Industrial Welfare Commission's hearing in El Paso, see García, "Racial Dualism," 201–206.

In addition to their roles as housewives and wage workers, a third major activity of Mexican women in the United States was their participation in labor unions and labor strife. Though relatively few women were active in unions or labor protests, Mexican women nonetheless were involved in some of the largest and most important labor strikes in the Southwest.[35] In El Paso, the laundry strike of 1919 is illustrative of the numerous class conflicts of the post-World War I years in the United States.[36] Unlike domestics who worked alone, the Mexican laundresses labored in close physical proximity in the same plant. Consequently, a sense of community developed in the laundries that helped promote the organization of workers who demanded higher wages and union recognition. In October 1919 some of the Mexican women, together with state and local American Federation of Labor organizers, established the Laundry Workers' Union. The union then began to organize workers, almost all Mexican women, in the Acme Laundry of El Paso. When this plant refused to accept the union and fired two of the organizers, Isabel and Manuela Hernández, the rest of the almost two hundred workers went on strike demanding that the employers rehire their co-workers. "We asked for the reinstatement of the two girls . . . ," Acme employee Francisca Sáenz told a meeting of the Mexican strikers. "Isabel Hernandez," she explained, "is a marker, sorter and inspector getting $11 a week with four years experience and Manuela is getting the same wages as marker and sorter and started in six years ago." F. B. Fletcher, the president and manager of Acme, denied any knowledge of a union and claimed he had dismissed the two workers for other reasons. According to Fletcher, one of the women had been fired because "she had made talk about the laundry that was not to his liking. . . ." As for the other,

[35]The two most significant strikes involving Mexican women are the San Antonio Pecan strike in 1938 and the more recent Farah strike in El Paso in the early 1970s. Seedon C. Menefee and Orin C. Cassmore, *The Pecan Shellers of San Antonio: The Problem of Underpaid and Unemployed Mexican Labor* (Washington, D.C., 1940); Harold A. Shapiro, "The Workers of San Antonio, Texas, 1900–1940" (Ph.D. dissertation, University of Texas, Austin, 1952); and The San Francisco Bay Area Farah Strike Support Committee, *Chicano Strike at Farah* (San Francisco, 1974).

[36]On the numerous incidents of class strife in the United States in 1919, such as the steel strike and the Seattle general strike, see Jeremy Brecher, *Strike* (Greenwich, Conn., 1972), 133–180.

Fletcher alleged that she had been working at another laundry while insisting she had been sick and claiming pay from the Acme.[37]

When three other laundries attempted to do the work of Acme, the Mexican women at those plants joined the strike. Owners of two more laundries at first agreed to recognize the union, but then changed their minds. The women at these places also struck. In a few days somewhere between 300 and 575 workers, including some men, had gone on strike against all of El Paso's laundries. At a meeting of the Central Labor Union where representatives of the A. F. of L. addressed the laundry workers, the Mexican women unanimously agreed to stand by the union. "Truly this was a sight that would do the heart of any one good to see these girls and women," the *Labor Advocate*, the A. F. of L. organ in El Paso, reported. "[S]ome of them hardly in their teens and some of them bent with age, standing up and solemnly promising that no matter what may come or what may happen, they would stand together for the mutual good of their fellow workers."[38]

Besides the workers' own solidarity, the A. F. of L.'s support proved important in maintaining the strike. The Central Labor Union not only endorsed the action, but various locals raised funds for the women strikers. The *Herald* reported shortly after the work stoppage that the machinists of both the El Paso & Southwestern Railroad and the Galveston, Houston & San Antonio Railroad had gathered $400 for the laundry union in addition to $100 donated by the carpenter's local. Other unions which contributed included those representing plumbers, iron-workers, bricklayers, electrical workers, sheetmetal workers, freight handlers, musicians, plasterers, painters, and taxi drivers. The Central Labor Union also organized a committee headed by William J. Moran, the *Advocate*'s editor, to negotiate a settlement with the laundries. The A. F. of L.'s willingness to organize and assist the Mexicans, however, did not represent a departure from Samuel Gompers' policy of excluding alien

[37] *Advocate*, Oct. 24, 1919, p. 1 and Oct. 31, 1919, p. 1; *Herald*, Oct. 27, 1919, p. 4; and *Times*, Oct. 28, 1919, p. 3.

[38] *Advocate*, Oct. 24, 1919, p. 1 and Oct. 31, 1919, p. 1; *Herald*, Oct. 30, 1919, p. 4; *Times*, Oct. 31, 1919, p. 8; and *La Patria*, Oct. 31, 1919, p. 8.

workers. "The strike of the Laundry Workers in our area is somewhat unique," the *Advocate* editorialized, "for often we have taken it for granted that these workers were practically all Mexicans, hence we gave but little concern, but this is not the case. True it is, that they are nearly all of Mexican origin but they are by no means all of Mexican citizenship. The large majority are residents of El Paso and citizens of the nation, but nevertheless, let us look at the facts that are fundamentally the cause of this strike." Besides the nonrecognition of the union by the laundries and the dismissal of the women organizers, the strike concerned the low wages paid to the workers. These ranged from $4 to $6 a week. In comparison, laundry workers in Fort Worth, Dallas, Galveston, Houston, and San Antonio averaged $14 a week. "[T]here is no question," the *Advocate* stated, "but that the treatment of the laundry workers of El Paso has been disgraceful and disgrace rests upon the laundry owners."[39]

The laundry workers obtained further assistance from various Mexican social organizations in El Paso, composed of both Mexican Americans and Mexican nationals. *La Patria*, the city's major Spanish-language newspaper, expressed its support of the Mexican women and called upon other Mexican groups to do likewise. Although it did not usually favor strikes, believing them to be counterproductive as well as the work of radicals and agitators, *La Patria* believed the laundry workers' struggle was a just one: "[I]f our congenial women compatriots deserve praise," *La Patria* emphasized, "so too does the Central Labor Union and other American unions who have provided unselfish assistance as well as moral support." A delegation of twelve women and four men from the laundry union also received the endorsement of the influential mutual society, the Círculo de Amigos, which had been organized by Mexican American city employees. In a letter to all Mexican societies, Círculo officials expressed their support of the strikers "who are giving an example of character, strength and racial solidarity." Believing it important not to abandon the women in their hour of need, the Círculo called on

[39] *Herald*, Oct. 30, 1919, p. 4; *Advocate*, Oct. 27, 1919, p. 4; *Times*, Oct. 28, 1919, p. 1; *Herald*, Oct. 27, 1919, p. 4; *Times*, Oct. 28, 1919, p. 1; *Advocate*, Oct. 24, 1919, p. 1 and Oct. 31, 1919, p. 1.

all other Mexican organizations and the Mexican community to attend an informational meeting on how best to "help our sisters." To raise funds for the workers, the Círculo sponsored a dance.[40]

Hearing of the laundry strike, some Mexican workers outside El Paso voiced their support. José L. Payen of Local No. 84 of the International Union of Mine, Mill, and Smelter Workers of Metcalf, Arizona, stressed at an El Paso strike rally the need for unionization and justice for workers. Payen, however, put forth a class ideology which went beyond the more limited union consciousness of the Mexican women and the Central Labor Union:

> Comrades in arms, we, who through our labor turn our sweat into gold, should be united, especially in these times when it appears the world is going to encounter a terrible catastrophe. We should be united to demonstrate to the capitalists that our religion is our Union and our weapon is the strike and our sights a brilliant future created through the honorable medium of our labor, and if anyone dares to destroy our sacred ideals, then they will pay the price, and we will be satisfied that we have done our sacred duty.[41]

Despite organized labor's support and that of the Mexican societies, the laundry workers faced considerable opposition. El Paso newspapers, with the exception of the *Labor Advocate* and *La Patria*, carried reports favorable to the laundry owners. A *Herald* reporter, after a visit to the Acme Laundry, noted that the entire plant appeared to be clean and well-ventilated. Besides sanitary toilets and cooking facilities, the *Herald* writer informed his readers that he had found "a Victrola in the upstairs main room where Mr. Fletcher says the girls have dances each noon." Interviewed by the *Herald*, Fletcher denied that the average wage given laundry workers amounted to $5.50 a week. Acme, according to Fletcher, paid an average of $9 a week for a nine-hour day and a fifty-four-hour week. Fletcher, however, neglected to tell the reporter what he would testify before the Texas Welfare Commission less than a month later: that the $9 average resulted from paying Mexican workers an

[40] *La Patria*, Nov. 1, 1919, pp. 3–4; Nov. 3, 1919, p. 2; and Nov. 11, 1919, p. 3.
[41] *Ibid.*, Nov. 11, 1919, p. 2.

average of $6 per week and American workers $16.55 a week. Although the *Herald* believed that workers, especially foreigners, needed to be awarded "fair pay for a fair day's work," it also agreed with New Mexico Governor O. A. Larrazolo, who warned that "reckless agitators [from] within were foes more dangerous to the United States than any foes without."[42] The *Herald* did not specifically link the Mexican women with radicalism, but the newspaper's concern with class agitation could not help but influence public opinion against the Mexicans.

To emphasize growing class conflict not only in the United States but also along the U.S.-Mexican border, both the *Herald* and the *Times* carried reports during the strike that literature printed by the Industrial Workers of the World had been seized by El Paso border officials. Some of the literature, claimed the newspapers, had been printed in Spanish and had been distributed to Mexican workers in the United States. The newspapers observed that the "Wobblie" pamphlets advocated nationalization of all industries and land in Mexico, free love, and the overthrow of existing governments. While no evidence exists of I.W.W. influence in the laundry strike nor among El Paso workers, the *Herald* nevertheless warned citizens:

> That the I.W.W. has advance guard going about the country blazing the trail for the main body and the city of El Paso has already been so blazed is the interpretation placed by some to the presence on the wall of a men's rest room in El Paso of the following lines of mystery:
>
> W
> J T N G E T N G No. 2
> I WW
> TEX[43]

While hurt by unfavorable newspaper publicity, the laundry workers' main problem concerned the owners' ability to hire strikebreakers as well as retain some of their employees. F. Ravel, proprietor of the Excelsior Laundry, refused to sign a union contract because his operation had not been seriously hampered by the strike. "Some of my Mexicans quit," he told a

[42] *Herald*, Oct. 31, 1919, p. 3; Nov. 20, 1919, p. 10; and Oct. 30, 1919, p. 6.
[43] *Ibid.*, Nov. 17, 1919, p. 1; and *Times*, Nov. 18, 1919, p. 13.

reporter, "and I put Americans in their places. In a few weeks every workman in my shop will be American." Ravel contended that American labor proved to be more productive and efficient than Mexican. Besides hiring unemployed Americans, the laundries also found it easy to hire numerous Mexican workers both in El Paso and Cuidad Juárez. The *Advocate* pointed out that even though 486 women and men had gone on strike, hundreds of other Mexicans were asking for work in the laundries. How many of these were citizens and how many were not is impossible to determine. Frustrated, the strikers verbally attacked their replacements by calling them "scabs" and labor leaders demanded that the city government stop the laundries from employing other workers. The city attorney, however, ruled that no municipal ordinance prohibited employers from hiring whom they pleased.[44] Unfortunately for organized labor and the Mexican women, the A.F. of L.'s own refusal to organize or support Mexican alien workers only added to the availability of Mexican strikebreakers.

To compound their problems, the laundry workers failed to maintain the laundry drivers' support, despite an initial endorsement by the Laundry Drivers' Union. "As the first blow in a fight against Bolshevism," the *Herald* noted, "the American Legion endorsed Friday the action of the ten drivers for the Acme Laundry who withdrew from their union and stood by their employers." Unlike the laundry workers, all of the truck drivers were Anglo-Americans. The Mexican women received an additional setback when an ad appeared in the *Herald* signed by thirty-four workers, including twenty-seven Mexicans, who had remained on the job at the El Paso Laundry. Addressed "To the Public," the notice stated that the undersigned "old employees" of the laundry "have at all times been treated in a most considerate manner, and our welfare has never been neglected; . . . we are not in sympathy with the laundry workers' unfair strike and positively will not support it."[45]

El Paso's laundry strike continued until the end of 1919, but it had been lost almost from the start. The existence of a large

[44] *Advocate*, Dec. 19, 1919, p. 1; *La Patria*, Nov. 1, 1919, pp. 1 and 4; and *Herald*, Oct. 31, 1919, p. 5.

[45] *Times*, Oct. 31, 1919, p. 8; *Herald*, Oct. 31, 1919, p. 3; and Nov. 4, 1919, p. 8.

pool of surplus Mexican labor both in El Paso and across the border proved to be the decisive factor. Although no doubt irritated by the strike, and by the fear of class disturbances in the city, laundry owners simply hired other workers, both Mexican and American. Hampered by El Paso's large number of Mexican aliens, plus its refusal to organize or support them, the A.F. of L. assisted as best as possible the laundry workers, but could not overcome organized labor's liabilities along the border. As for the Mexican women who went on strike, it appears most never regained their jobs. Their struggle, however, represents one of the earliest displays of union consciousness and ethnic solidarity among Mexican female workers in the United States. The fact that many of the women apparently were Mexican Americans rather than Mexican nationals must also be seen as a major factor in the laundry workers' ability to organize. More permanent, knowledgeable, and secure in their rights as American citizens, unionization of Mexican American workers symbolized a process of acculturation to an industrial and urban culture.[46] Hence, the laundry strike of 1919 stands as an example of Mexican women workers in the United States actively resisting class exploitation and in the process forging their own history.

This case study of Mexican women in El Paso between 1880 and 1920 has attempted to demonstrate some of the major research themes on women that might be pursued in Chicano history. The general topics of Mexican women as housewives, as wage workers, and as participants in unionization and labor strife constitute the most important activities that have affected Mexican women in the United States. An investigation of them by historians of the Chicano experience will contribute not only to an understanding of the history of Mexican American women, but to the history of all Mexicans north of the border. The history of Chicanos, especially Chicano workers, is only half complete without an appreciation of the contributions Mexican women have made. As one Mexican American woman has concluded: "History is filled with the activities of the Chicana."[47]

---

[46] For a treatment of industrialization's impact on early women factory workers, see E. P. Thompson, *The Making of the English Working Class* (New York, 1963), 413–417.

[47] Apodaca, "The Chicana Woman," 88.

William Harris

WORK AND THE FAMILY IN BLACK ATLANTA, 1880[1]

Discussion of the long-lasting effects of the slave experience on the subsequent history of black Americans has centered on two areas: work and the family. By confining slaves to unskilled, rural tasks requiring no formal education or training, slavery, it is said, left blacks unprepared for any productive role in the growing cities of the nation.[2] Even more crippling, according to a view until recently widely accepted, was the destruction of family life among slaves. According to this view, slavery "emasculated" the black male, depriving him of his rightful role as family breadwinner, and displaced ultimate family authority onto the white master. The slave woman was, moreover, subject to sexual as well as economic exploitation by the master. The threat, too often carried out, of arbitrary separation by sale hung over the heads of the parents. For these reasons, continues the indictment, slavery created an unstable family life with the mother as the dominant figure and the father at best an uncertain presence. This unstable, "matriarchal" or "matrifocal" family under slavery persisted after emancipation and provides at least a partial explanation for "weak" family structure in today's black ghettos.[3]

This whole view has come under increasing attack from several directions in recent years. Studies of slave life by John Blassingame and Eugene Genovese have pointed out that slave families were considerably more stable than earlier scholars had assumed, and that family ties of affection were indeed a great resource in enabling blacks to resist on their own terms the fearful dehumanizing effects of the "peculiar institution." Some of the demographic work on slavery by Robert Fogel and Stanley Engerman has lent support to the new interpretation.[4] Since sources for the study of slavery offer little direct quantitative evidence about family and household structure among slaves, other scholars have turned to the census returns of 1870 and 1880 for information about recently emancipated slaves. Such studies show that most black families had two parents present, and have thus contributed to the undermining of the traditional view of slavery's effects.[5]

A significant gap in this new knowledge of black family life is the lack of a comparative dimension.[6] For example, did black communities have a much higher proportion of fatherless families, or a lower proportion of nuclear families, than did white? Did families and economic opportunities of former slaves differ significantly from those for the Irish immigrants of the 1850s – another poor, rural, largely uneducated group thrust suddenly, and in massive numbers, into a new urban environment? This paper attempts to help fill that gap with an investigation of the occupational distribution and family structure among both blacks and whites in post-Civil War Atlanta. The sources for the paper are samples, generally ranging in size from four hundred to five hundred for each race, of adult men and of households, taken from the manuscripts of the censuses of 1870 and 1880.[7]

I chose Atlanta because it is in many respects an ideal place to look for evidence about the adjustment of newly freed slaves to urban life. The city grew rapidly in the postwar years, and before 1880 it was already considered untypical of southern cities in its social instability and in the dominance of values and pressures we commonly associate with life in modern cities.[8] Atlanta had few slaves and almost no free blacks before the war, so its adult black population in 1870 and 1880 was made up almost entirely of recent migrants, the overwhelming majority of them former slaves, and nearly all of them new to the city.[9] Comparison of this black community to Atlanta's whites, and, where appropriate, to other nineteenth-century communities, both black and white, can add an important perspective to our knowledge of black life both before and after the Civil War.

I

Table I summarizes some data from samples of adult males in Atlanta, drawn from the census manuscripts for 1870 and 1880. It shows that economic prospects for blacks were far worse than for whites, yet it also shows that these prospects were by no means uniformly bleak. Already in 1870 nearly a quarter of all black men were skilled workers. By 1880 there was a slight improvement in the black occupational structure, with fewer unskilled or service workers, and more in each of the other categories.[10]

Table 1. Occupations of Males Aged 20 and Over in Atlanta[a]

	Black, Number	1870 %	Black, Number	1880 %	White, Number	1880 %
Unskilled labor/ service	263	62.6	238	53.1	21	5.3
Semiskilled	47	11.2	56	12.5	40	10.1
Skilled	99	23.6	125	27.9	99	25.0
All Manual	409	97.4	419	93.5	160	40.4
All Nonmanual	9	2.1	20	4.5	221	55.8
Other/none	2	0.4	9	2.0	15	3.8
Total	420	99.9	448	100.0	396	100.0

[a]Percentages may not add to 100 due to rounding

SOURCE: Manuscript schedules of the Ninth Census (1870) and the Tenth Census (1880) for the city of Atlanta.

A comparison here of Atlanta's blacks with the Irish of Boston in 1850 is illuminating. These Irish immigrants were also recently removed from a poor rural environment; most had been landless farm tenants until the Great Famine in Ireland in the 1840s. In the 1850s they were the focus of intense nativist and anti-Catholic sentiment which captured considerable political influence in northern cities, including Boston.[11] As Table 2 indicates, Atlanta's blacks were not worse off insofar as the occupational distribution is concerned.[12] The former slaves were in fact more likely to have skilled jobs, and only a little less likely to be in nonmanual occupations. Nor do we find that blacks in Atlanta were in a more difficult economic position than blacks in New Orleans, with its unique pre-Civil War free black community, or in a northern city like Detroit. In New

Orleans in 1880, for example, slightly more than half of all black men were common laborers or servants, and about one-fourth were, as in Atlanta, skilled workers.[13] David Katzman has reported that more than two-thirds of Detroit's black men were unskilled laborers or servants in 1880.[14] Robert Fogel and Stanley Engerman have estimated that about 12 percent of adult male slaves in 1850 were skilled workers, while another 7 percent each were semiskilled or nonmanual workers.[15] This suggests that blacks in slavery were, in an economic sense, perhaps as well prepared for nineteenth-century urban life as, for example, those newly arrived Irish immigrants of the 1850s.

Table 2. Occupations of Males Aged 17 or Over[a]

	Blacks in Atlanta, 1880[b]		Irish in Boston, 1850[c]
	Number	%	%
Unskilled/service	266	54.6	59.5
Semiskilled	64	13.1	14.8
Skilled	126	25.9	16.6
All Manual	456	93.6	90.9
All Nonmanual	20	4.1	7.6
Other/None	11	2.3	1.6
Total	487	100.0	100.1

[a]Percentages may not add to 100 due to rounding

[b]SOURCE: Manuscript schedules of the Tenth Census (1880) for the city of Atlanta.

[c]SOURCE: List of occupations of Irish immigrants in Oscar Handlin, *Boston's Immigrants* (New York: Atheneum, 1970), pp. 250-251.

The way these occupational groups functioned in the black (or white, or Irish) community is inherently more difficult to assess, and cannot be determined precisely from a quantitative or structural picture. Yet it seems clear that black artisans and craftsmen formed a resource of great social and cultural, as well as economic, potential. Eugene Genovese has emphasized that artisans were "the proudest and most independent" among the slaves, with a greater knowledge of the world, and formed a natural political and cultural leadership which was highly respected by the slave community. Their role was potentially analogous to that of artisans in America, England, and France in the advanced political and social movements of the eighteenth and nineteenth centuries.[16] The potential was never entirely fulfilled, as this class came under increasing pressure both from industrialization and from the racist attacks of their white competitors, who drove them out of many skilled occupations by 1900.[17]

The weight of the evidence, in any case, indicates that slavery in itself was not the cause of the lack of social mobility among nineteenth-century urban blacks – a phenomenon ably described by Stephan Thernstrom.[18] Even the Irish immigrants, Thernstrom has pointed out, advanced much faster up the occupational ladder. We are more likely to find the cause in the specific environments of the postwar black and Irish communities. The whole political arena, for example, was closed to blacks after Reconstruction, while the Irish found in politics both a source of immediate economic advantages and an important direct route of upward mobility.[19]

II

If a background of slavery was in itself not the crucial element in the economic chances of blacks following emancipation, did it perhaps exert a more decisive influence on black family life? Table 3A shows the proportion of one- and two-parent households among Atlanta's blacks and whites in 1880. As in occupations, a significant (though much smaller) difference emerges.[20] Black households were more likely to be headed by women. Black children, not surprisingly, were less likely to be living with both parents than were white children (see Table 3B). This difference is greater than might be expected from the difference in family and household heads, because while white female-headed families had fewer children than white male-headed families, the reverse was true among blacks: female-headed families had slightly more children on the average.[21]

Table 3. A. Percentages of One- and Two-Parent Households[a] in Atlanta, 1880[b]

	Black	White
Two-parent households	70	79
One-parent households	30	21
male head	(2)	(2)
female head	(28)	(19)

B. Percentages of Children Age 15 and Under, by Type of Family,[a] in Atlanta, 1880[b]

	Black	White
Two-parent family	64	85
One-parent family	33	14
father	(3)	(1)
mother	(30)	(13)
Neither parent present	3	1

[a]For definition, see footnote 7.

[b]SOURCE: Samples including 437 black households and 402 white households from the schedules of the Tenth Census (1880) for Atlanta.

This disparity between white and black households cannot be explained in any simple way by differing mortality rates between the two races. The ratio of families headed by widows to families headed by males among blacks is indeed higher than among whites, but the main reason for the disparity is that black families are more likely to be headed by women who are divorced, separated, or unmarried, as shown in Table 4.[22]

Table 4. Ratio of Household[a] and Family[a] Heads Who Are Widows, and of Other Female Heads, to Male Household and Family Heads, in Atlanta, 1880[b]

	Blacks		Whites	
	Households	Families	Households	Families
(1) Number of male heads	306	326	322	358
(2) Number of widow heads	87	101	67	79
(3) Number of other female heads	37	52	4	6
(4) Ratio of (2) to (1)	.28	.31	.21	.22
(5) Ratio of (3) to (1)	.12	.16	.01	.02

[a]For definitions, see footnote 7.

[b]SOURCE: Samples including 437 black households and 402 white households taken from the manuscript schedules of the Tenth Census (1880) for the city of Atlanta. Households consisting entirely of related adults have been excluded.

It is far from certain, however, that "slavery" explains this higher frequency of fatherless households among blacks. An important factor may have been different sex ratios in the white and black populations. The city directory for Atlanta in 1874 reported ratios of 109 males per 100 females among whites and only 78 males per 100 females among blacks.[23] It is difficult to judge the accuracy of the figures, but a low ratio among blacks would tend to increase desertions and the frequency of fatherless households. Another possible cause for a higher proportion of fatherless households among blacks is economic and class distinctions between blacks and whites. A majority of white family heads, for example, were in nonmanual occupations in Atlanta in 1880, while the overwhelming majority of black male family heads were in manual jobs, and about half were unskilled or service workers.[24] If we could compare all households or families by social class, as well as by race, we might well find similar proportions headed by females, regardless of race. Unfortunately, our sources provide no reasonable basis for a class breakdown of female-headed households. Occupations of women are not a useful guide here, since many women did not work, and those who did were limited to a few types of jobs; in any case the most relevant information would be the occupation of the dead or missing husbands, or of the fathers, of the female heads.

We can get some evidence for class influence on family structure by comparing white and black households headed by men of similar households. Table 5 shows several comparisons of households headed by male skilled workers, the only occupational classification in which both races are broadly represented in my samples. No significant differences emerge, whether in overall family structure, number of children per family, or frequency of school attendance.[25]

Table 5. Households[a] Headed by Male Skilled Workers in Atlanta, 1880[b]

A. Percentages of all Households Whose Structure Was:

	Nuclear[c]	Extended[c]	Augmented[c]	(Number)
Whites	77.6	18.1	4.3	(94)
Blacks	75.9	13.2	10.8	(83)

B. Number of Households in Which the Primary Family[a] Included:

	No children	1-2 children	3-4 children	5 or more children
Whites	29	36	17	12
Blacks	17	35	18	13

C. School Attendance by Children, 8-15 Years Old, in Primary Family:

	Total Number	Number Who Attended School Previous Year
Whites	79	52 (65.8%)
Blacks	69	45 (65.2%)

[a]For definition, see footnote 7.

[b]SOURCE: Samples including 437 black households and 402 white households taken from the manuscript schedules of the Tenth Census (1880) for the city of Atlanta.

[c]Nuclear households include parents and children or childless married couples; extended households include other persons related to the household head; augmented households include other persons unrelated to the household head (boarders). Households consisting only of adults, except married couples, are excluded here.

This information about Atlanta family structure points toward three related conclusions. In the first place, most black families in 1880 were not in any obvious or structural way "matriarchal" or "matrifocal"; they were rather like other families of the same place, social class, and time. Second, the influence of slavery may have resulted in a somewhat higher incidence of fatherless families and households among blacks, but the evidence for this is not conclusive. Third, and as an important qualification to the second point, the relative differences between blacks and whites in proportion of fatherless households was far less one-hundred years ago than it is today, when that proportion is nearly three times greater among blacks than among whites.[26]

These conclusions are strongly reinforced by information available so far about family structure in other nineteenth-century cities. In seven southern cities in 1880, reported in four separate studies (including this one), the proportion of female-headed families or households among blacks ranged from 23 percent to 30 percent.[27] In four northern cities the same year, from 14 percent to 16 percent of black families or households were headed by women.[28] This indicates that families in antebellum free black communities were more likely to include both parents than communities where former slaves predominated, but other evidence makes such a causal connection questionable. Southern rural areas in 1880 show proportions of female-headed families about equal to proportions in northern cities at that time.[29] Studies of Philadelphia in 1838 and of Boston in 1880 show no greater frequency of fatherless households among those born in slavery than among those born to free parents in the north.[30] There can be no doubt, however, that the two-parent household predominated among blacks throughout the country in the years following the Civil War.

We have less information about white family structure in the nineteenth century, but what is available lends support to the idea that in relative terms white families were more like black families than they are today. John Blassingame found that in New Orleans, 19 percent of white families were headed by women in 1880, while 23 percent of black families were headed by women.[31] In Buffalo in 1855, 13 percent of Irish households were headed by women, while another 5 percent were headed by men with the mother dead or absent, so altogether 18 percent of all households had only one parent.[32] In Paterson, New Jersey, in 1880, 19 percent of Irish and 21 percent of native-white households and subfamilies were without husbands or fathers present.[33]

As in the case of occupational distribution, it is necessary to go beyond quantitative measures, and try to assess the quality of family life – a task whose dimensions are only suggested here. There can be no question that cultural factors are at least as important as economic ones in this area. For example, Italian and Jewish families in early twentieth-century cities were far more likely to have both parents present than the black or Irish (or native-white) families of the mid-nineteenth century, despite a preponderance of unskilled or semiskilled occupations among these later immigrants. It may be that attitudes brought from the peasant village or European ghetto were decisive in these cases.[34] We must ask as well how different types of families functioned in different communities. Sociologist Jacquelyne Johnson, summarizing recent scholarship, has noted that black mothers without husbands may be more effective than white mothers in the same situation. If this was true in the past, black children raised in such families would not have suffered harm comparable to white children.[35]

Whatever our ultimate conclusions about the social history of America's blacks, it is clear that the information about blacks in Atlanta does not support the notion that slavery had crippled them so much that they lagged far behind such groups as the poorest of the nineteenth-century European immigrants. Recently emancipated slaves seem to have been no worse off, economically and socially, than the recent Irish immigrants had been twenty-five years before. It was not where they started, but what happened along the way that left blacks behind on the road to economic security and social stability. Believing that, by many economic and social measures, black Americans today have a place in society analogous to that of some former immigrant groups, one writer has asserted that "the Negro today is like the immigrant yesterday."[36] This may be true, but it is perhaps more important that the Negro yesterday was like the immigrant yesterday. The relevant historical question is why the todays of black Americans are so much like the yesterdays.

FOOTNOTES

1. The author wishes to thank Blaine Brownell, David Donald, Jack Censer, Hugh Graham, and Willie Lee Rose, who read earlier versions of this paper and made many useful comments and suggestions.

2. See, for example, Clement Eaton's remarks that slave labor in general was too "careless, ignorant, and inefficient" to be suitable for the use of machinery or labor-saving tools, in *The Growth of Southern Civilization, 1790-1860* (New York, 1961), pp. 65, 66-67. Eaton also notes the development of skills among slave workers in "individual" cases; see *ibid.*, pp. 84-85.

3. Perhaps the best-known discussions of the supposed effects of slavery on contemporary black life are found in Gunnar Myrdal, *An American Dilemma: The Negro Problem and Modern Democracy* (New York, 1962), pp. 930-31, and Daniel P. Moynihan, *The Negro Family: The Case for National Action*, which is reprinted in Lee Rainwater and William Yancey, *The Moynihan Report and the Politics of Controversy* (Cambridge, Mass., 1967), pp. 39-124. References to slavery are on pp. 15-17 of the original Moynihan report, and on pp. 61-63 in Rainwater and Yancey. Both of these depend heavily on the classic work of E. Franklin Frazier, *The Negro Family in the United States* (Chicago, 1939). The most important historical work of recent times which emphasizes this traditional view is Kenneth Stampp, *The Peculiar Institution: Slavery in the Ante-Bellum South* (New York, 1964), which discusses the family in chs. 6 and 8. Another influential work which accepted the traditional view is Stanley Elkins, *Slavery: A Problem in American Institutional and Intellectual Life* (Chicago, 1968).

4. John Blassingame, *The Slave Community: Plantation Life in the Ante-Bellum South* (New York, 1972); Eugene Genovese, *Roll, Jordan, Roll: The World the Slaves Made* (New York, 1974), pp. 450-524 *passim;* Robert Fogel and Stanley Engerman, *Time on the Cross: The Economics of American Negro Slavery* (Boston, 1974), pp. 126-144.

5. See especially Herbert Gutman, "Le phénomène invisible – la composition de la famille et du foyer noirs après la Guerre de Sécession," *Annales: Économies, Sociétés, Civilisations* 27 (1972): 1197-1218; see also below, pp. 10-11.

6. An important exception is John Blassingame, *Black New Orleans, 1860-1880* (Chicago, 1973), especially ch. 4.

7. The data for Atlanta's population were based on systematic samples taken from the manuscript schedules of the Ninth Census (1870) and the Tenth Census (1880) for the city of Atlanta. I have tried to follow the definitions for household and family used in the 1970 census, which may be found in the introduction to the section on population in the *Statistical Abstract of the United States,* published each year. A "household" comprises all persons who occupy a house, apartment, or other group of rooms, or a room that constitutes "separate living quarters." I excluded the small number of households consisting of one person, or of unrelated adults. Also excluded are "group living quarters" such as barracks, hotels, houses of prostitution, and the like. A "family" is a group of two or more persons related by blood, marriage, or adoption and residing together in a household. Primary families include the household head and persons related to the head. Secondary families include families living as lodgers, whose members are unrelated to the household head. A "subfamily" is a married couple, with or without children, or a single parent with unmarried children, living in a household and related to, but not including, the household head. In my sample, if two or more families were listed as being boarders, and were otherwise unrelated to the household head, each such family was classified as a separate household. In this essay, "families" means all primary, secondary, and subfamilies.

When proportions of some characteristic (for example, the proportion of nuclear households) of a *population* are estimated from a *sample* of size 400 taken from that population, we should think of the estimated proportion as being within about 4 or 5 percent, plus or minus, of the true, or actual, proportion. More specifically, if the proportion of nuclear households in a population is 50 percent, then 19 out of 20 random samples of 400 households would show between 45 percent and 55 percent of nuclear households. (Extreme proportions will be estimated more accurately; if 10 percent of households are nuclear, then 19 of 20 such samples would show between 7 percent and 13 percent to be nuclear.) In statistical terminology, at the 95 percent confidence level, the confidence interval for samples of size 400 is ±4.9 percent if the true proportion is 50 percent.

8. Grigsby Wotton, *New City of the South: Atlanta, 1843-1873* (Ph.D. diss., The Johns Hopkins University, 1973), pp. iii, 6, 10-11, 209-210.

9. *Ibid.*, pp. 57-61. Atlanta's population included 1914 slaves and only 25 free blacks in 1860. There were about 16,000 blacks in Atlanta in 1880. The proportion of blacks in the population went from 20 percent to about 45 percent in this same period.

10. By a chi-square test the differences between the figures for blacks in 1870 and 1880 is significant beyond the .05 level; so the probability is less than 1/20 that the improved occupational position reflects chance variation between the samples, rather than actual differences in the black populations in 1870 and 1880.

11. Oscar Handlin, *Boston's Immigrants: A Study in Acculturation* (New York, 1969), pp. 201-206.

12. The data in Table 2 on Irish workers were derived from the list of occupations of Irish men in Boston in Handlin, *Boston's Immigrants,* pp. 250-251. I classified these lists in a

manner consistent with my classification of Atlanta's male workers. The tailors among Boston's Irish were classified as semiskilled, consistent with Handlin's description of that occupation (pp. 74-77). The four tailors in my Atlanta sample – two white and two black – were classified as skilled workers. Also, 2227 servants were subtracted from Handlin's totals, since this many female servants were included in his list (p. 61).

The figures for Atlanta's blacks in Table 2 are slightly different from the figures in Table 1, because Table 2 includes workers aged 16-19, to make the data consistent with that reported by Handlin.

13. These figures were calculated from the list of occupations of black males in 1880 in Blassingame, *Black New Orleans*, pp. 226-228, with classification made consistent with my classification of occupations for Atlanta's male workers.

14. David Katzman, *Before the Ghetto: Black Detroit in the Nineteenth Century* (Urbana, Illinois, 1973), p. 218. Katzman classified occupations somewhat differently from the method used in this essay for Atlanta, in a way which would lead to a slightly higher percentage of workers in the lowest category; a reclassification would not affect the conclusions here.

15. Fogel and Engerman, *Time on the Cross*, pp. 38-40. Skilled workers were far more common among free blacks in the antebellum urban South; see Gutman, "Le phénomène invisible," p. 1206.

16. Genovese, *Roll, Jordan, Roll*, pp. 392-394.

17. Gutman, "Le phénomène invisible," pp. 1215-1217.

18. Stephan Thernstrom, *The Other Bostonians: Poverty and Progress in the American Metropolis, 1880-1970* (Cambridge, Mass., 1973), ch. 8 and pp. 250-255.

19. See, for example, William Shannon, *The American Irish* (New York, 1963), pp. 62-63.

20. The difference is significant beyond the .001 level by a chi-square test. Among *families*, 27 percent among a sample of 639 black families from the 1870 census were headed by females, while the corresponding figure in 1880 is 32 percent. Such an increase is significant at about the .05 level for samples of this size, meaning there is a high probability (.95) that an actual difference exists between the proportions of female-headed families in these two years. While *statistically* significant in this sense, it is hard to see what other significance the increase might have, considering the large migration both into and out of the city in these years. Family relationships must be inferred from names and living arrangements for 1870, since the census for that year, unlike the 1880 census, did not specifically ask about these.

21. The figures are: white male-headed households: 1.93 children; white female-headed households: 1.13 children; black male-headed households: 1.73 children; black female-headed households: 2.13 children. These figures are for children of the household head, aged 15 or under.

I also compared black and white households in terms of the proportions of nuclear, extended, and augmented structures, both overall and separately for male- and female-headed households. No significant differences were found. In each case about two-thirds of all households were nuclear in structure, about one-sixth to one-fifth extended, one-tenth to one-eighth augmented, and about 2 percent consisted of related, but unmarried, adults. (These terms are defined in Table 5.)

22. Thus, the information in Table 4 shows that Atlanta differed from New Orleans, where the larger proportion of female-headed households among blacks in 1880 can be attributed to the higher proportion of widows, and not to the greater frequency of desertion or separation. See Blassingame, *Black New Orleans*, pp. 103-104. The disparity between the

races in Atlanta in this respect may be exaggerated if white women household heads were more likely to tell census takers they were widowed, when in fact they had been deserted, or had had illegitimate children. A study of birth certificates might provide more accurate information in this regard. I believe the disparity between blacks and whites is too large to be explained entirely on these grounds, however.

23. The 1880 census does not break down sex ratios by race, but the figures in the directory would give results close to those reported for the total population for breakdowns for sex and race (separately) for Atlanta in the census. These are given in U.S. Census Office, *Report on the Social Statistics of Cities* (Washington, 1887), Part 2, p. 157. The figures from *Beasley's Atlanta City Directory* are reported in Wotton, *New City of the South*, p. 215, fn. 28. A recent study of black families in seven Ohio Valley cities from 1850 to 1880 found no relationship between sex ratio and frequency of female-headed households (Paul Lammermeier, "The Urban Black Family of the 19th Century: A Study of Black Family Structure in the Ohio Valley, 1850-1880," *Journal of Marriage and the Family* 35 [1973]: 446-447). Sociologist Jacquelyne Jackson, however, believes that sex-ratio disparities are a significant cause of female-headed households and family instability in modern cities (Jacquelyne J. Jackson, "Family Organization and Ideology," in Kent Miller and Ralph Dreger, eds., *Comparative Studies of Blacks and Whites in the United States* [New York, 1973], pp. 411-412). If further research indicates that sex-ratio imbalances were significant in causing more female-headed households, this would reintroduce the factor of higher mortality among black males as an indirect cause of that phenomenon. It is, however, almost impossible, even today, to find out just why census returns report a "shortage" of young black men; see comments on this in Moynihan, *American Negro Family*, p. 43.

24. The figures for occupations of household heads were calculated separately from the figures for adult males in Tables 1 and 2, and are based on entirely separate samples. However, the overall picture is quite similar in both cases, so the figures for household heads will not be reproduced here. Among female household heads, about one-third of whites were reported as having an occupation other than "keeps house"; about four-fifths among blacks were so reported.

25. By a chi-square test, the differences between whites and blacks shown in Table 5 are not significant at the .10 level for any of the three comparisons.

26. In 1971 28.9 percent of black families had female heads, while 9.4 percent of white families had female heads. Families and not households is the relevant category here, since the household category in 1971 includes a much higher proportion of single adults and all-adult households than was true in the nineteenth century. In 1971 only 2.6 percent of all families did not live in their own household (U.S. Bureau of the Census, *Statistical Abstract of the United States, 1972* [Washington, 1972], pp. 38-39).

27. The cities, besides Atlanta, are New Orleans, reported in Blassingame, *Black New Orleans*, pp. 240-241; Savannah, reported in John Blassingame, "Before the Ghetto: The Making of the Black Community in Savannah, Georgia, 1865-1880," *Journal of Social History* 6 (1973): 475; and Richmond, Mobile, Natchez, and Beaufort, S.C., reported in Gutman, "Le phénomène invisible," p. 1207. The conclusions here are supported also by Peter Kolchin's comparative study of a sample of Alabama census districts in 1870. Kolchin's conclusions – that black and white households were basically similar – is based on a considerably more indirect method than the one in this paper, and is not strictly comparable to it. See Peter Kolchin, *First Freedom: The Response of Alabama's Blacks to Emancipation and Reconstruction* (Ph.D. diss., The Johns Hopkins University, 1970), pp. 125-130.

28. The cities are Buffalo (for 1875) and Troy, N.Y., reported in Gutman, "Le phénomène invisible," p. 1207; Boston, reported in Elizabeth Pleck, "The Two-Parent Household: Black Family Structures in Late Nineteenth Century Boston," *Journal of Social History* 6 (1972):

17; and Pittsburgh, reported in Lammermeier, "The Urban Black Family," p. 443. Lammermeier also reports 21 percent and 23 percent, respectively, of black families in the border cities of Cincinnati and Louisville were female-headed in 1880.

29. Gutman, "Le phénomène invisible," 1207.

30. Theodore Hershberg, "Free Blacks in Ante-Bellum Philadelphia: A Study of Ex-Slaves, Freeborn, and Socioeconomic Decline," *Journal of Social History* 5 (1971-72): 194; Pleck, "The Two-Parent Household," pp. 18-19.

31. Blassingame, *Black New Orleans*, pp. 240-241. It is possible that the frequency of fatherless households in 1880 reflects the deaths of soldiers in the Civil War, especially among southern whites, but likely that the effects were quite small by that time. It would be impossible to give any precise estimate of such effects without a knowledge of such things as the remarriage rate among widows, the proportion of soldiers who were married, and so forth, but perhaps a rough guess is in order. An estimated 260,000 Confederate soldiers died as a result of service during the war. If we assume the 6 million whites in the Confederacy were divided in roughly 1.2 million households, and that one-half of the casualties were heads of households, then about one-tenth of Confederate households were left without husbands or fathers in 1865. If we assume further that one-half of the widows remarried by 1880, and that in one-half the remaining households all the children had left the household, we can get a very approximate estimate that 2 or 3 percent of southern white households in 1880 were fatherless because of the Civil War. None of the households would include children under 15. If we take into account that normal mortality would in any case have left many of these households fatherless by 1880, and that the process of emancipation, and combat casualties among black soldiers, had disrupting effects on black families, it seems unwise to attribute much significance to Civil War combat in so far as differences in family structure between whites and blacks are concerned.

32. Laurence Glasco, *Ethnicity and Social Structure: Irish, Germans, and Native Born of Buffalo, New York, 1850-1860* (Ph.D. diss., State University of New York at Buffalo, 1973), p. 147. Paul Lammermeier reported that 26 percent of families in one "predominantly Irish" ward in Cincinnati were headed by females in 1860 (Lammermeier, "The Urban Black Family," p. 444).

33. Herbert Gutman, "Work, Culture, and Society in Industrializing America, 1815-1919," *American Historical Review* 78 (1973): 562.

34. *Ibid.*, p. 588, and Virginia McLaughlin, "Patterns of Work and Family Organization Among Buffalo's Italians," *Journal of Interdisciplinary History* 2 (1971): 304.

35. Jackson, "Family Organization and Ideology." Evidence for deficiencies of such families comes largely from the higher frequency of delinquency, unwed pregnancies, and low levels of schooling among children in such families (there is a summary of evidence in Moynihan, *The Negro Family*, ch. 4). For the most part we cannot measure these aspects of family life in 1880, but we can observe the relationship between family structure and schooling. The table below shows that both black and white children in two-parent households were more likely to have attended school the previous year than children in fatherless households:

Percentage of Children, 8-15 Years old, Who Attended School the Previous Year in Atlanta, 1880:

	White	Black
Male-headed Households	78	68
Female-headed Households	52	50

The lack of economic opportunities for women would have been a powerful source of pressure on fatherless households. In 1870, only 28 black females in the entire population of Atlanta reported owning property worth as much as $100, while 322 black males reported property worth that much in the census of that year. Perhaps the genealogical reconstruction of ordinary black families over long periods of time will ultimately prove as feasible as it has been for colonial American families, though the sources for such an effort have not yet been exploited, if they exist.

36. Irving Kristol, "The Negro Today Is Like the Immigrant Yesterday," *New York Times Magazine*, September 11, 1966, pp. 50-51 ff.

FAMILY TIME AND INDUSTRIAL TIME

Family and Work in a Planned Corporation Town, 1900-1924

TAMARA K. HAREVEN
Clark University

The role of the family in the adaptation of workers to industrial life, a central concern for sociologists for some time, has only recently begun to interest historians. Neil Smelser has shown that during the early years of the industrial revolution in Britain, working families carried their own habits into the factory setting and often continued to function as units.

Author's Note: *This paper is part of a book in progress on "The Laborers of Manchester, New Hampshire, 1880-1940: The Role of Family and Ethnicity in Adjustment to Urban, Industrial Life." The project was supported by Grant No. RO 8963-73-500 from the National Endowment for the Humanities, and by a research grant from the Merrimack Valley Textile Museum, with matching funds from Amoskeag Industries, the Cogswell Benevolent Trust, and the Norwin and Elizabeth Bean Foundation. The oral history interviews were supported by the New Hampshire Council for the Humanities and the United Textile Workers. I am indebted to Dr. Thomas Leavitt, Director of the Merrimack Valley Textile Museum, whose initial support helped launch this project. Research was carried out at the Manchester Historic Association and the Baker Library, Graduate School of Business Administration, Harvard University. I am indebted to Randolph Langenbach for his important discoveries in the history of the Amoskeag Corporation in his own study of the architectural and urban planning history of the Amoskeag Mills. Herbert Gutman, David Montgomery, Maris Vinovskis, John Modell, Howard Chudacoff, Daniel Walkowitz, and David Grimsted provided valuable criticisms.*

William Goode went further to argue that the family was an independent agent in the process of industrialization. Rather than being a passive recipient of social and economic change, the family acted as a catalyst in activating changes in the larger society.[1]

This revisionist sociological view of the role of the family in the process of industrialization has been reinforced by the work of some labor historians. Following the route of cultural anthropologists, they have demonstrated that workers, while adapting to the industrial system, also succeeded in modifying it in terms of their previous cultural traditions and work habits. The continuous influx of immigrants from the same or similar backgrounds tended to reinforce the impact of preindustrial immigrant traditions on the new system.[2]

Several recent historical studies have emphasized the active role of the family in the migration process and its function as a source of continuity and stability under the pressures of adjustment to new conditions. Some of these studies now argue that not only did the family not break down, it in fact retained active control over the careers of its members. As the transmitter of premigration culture, the family kept ethnic traditions alive, and its cultural heritage guided the family in its adaptation to new conditions.[3]

Such revisions of the stereotypes of family passivity and breakdown in the industrial process have engendered new extremes. The filiopietism which has been emerging over the past years tends to exaggerate the strength of the immigrant or working-class family and its autonomy as an institution. This neo-romantic interpretation of the role of the family could easily result in another stereotype, as removed from historical reality as earlier ones.

Now that the ghosts of social breakdown are being exorcised from historical scholarship, we must ask: to what degree, under varying circumstances, was the family in control of its own decisions, and to what degree was its behavior guided by external pressures and incentives? To answer these questions it is necessary to study more closely the family's role in the industrial environment, an approach which must be *contextual* as well as *dynamic*. Contrary to the prevalent approach which studies the family in isolation in the household, it is necessary to see the family as it actually existed in constant interaction with other social processes and institutions.[4]

For laborers such an approach links family organization and traditions to the experience of industrial work. It takes into account the interrelationships between the family and technological change, the work process, demands for work discipline, job mobility, ethnicity, and economic behavior, within the framework of industrial capitalism. Such a model by necessity views the "family" as a process which unfolds over its entire cycle rather than as a constant at one point in time. It takes into account the fact that family structures, functions, relationships, and needs differed at each stage of the family cycle and that these internal changes were related to larger societal processes.[5]

If the term "industrial time" designates the new time schedules and work discipline imposed by the industrial system, "family time" refers to the internal and external timing of family behavior at different stages of individual and family development, particularly to the timing of major demographic events. An understanding of how the two different times affected each other, the areas in which they conflicted or reinforced each other, provides a model for the study of the family's role in the larger society. While families responded to external pressures and adjusted their timing accordingly, they also often timed their own behavior in accordance with their internal "clock." It is the historian's task to determine to what degree, under what changing circumstances, the family's behavior was timed in response to external conditions, and to what degree it moved in accordance with the family's internal and traditional timepiece.[6]

This essay will explore the family's interaction with the industrial system on two levels: it will first examine the workers' adjustment to industrial life. Secondly, it will examine the internal timing of family behavior along the family cycle in response to the external pressures and demands of the world of work.

This exploration focuses on the experienced French-Canadian immigrant laborers of the Amoskeag Manufacturing Company in Manchester, New Hampshire, at the peak of the corporation's industrial development during the first two decades of the twentieth century. At the turn of the century Manchester had 70,000 inhabitants and was the seat of the world's largest textile mill–The Amoskeag Corporation–which employed an average of 14,000 workers each year in the period preceding World War I.[7]

Originally developed by the Amoskeag Corporation as a planned New England textile community, Manchester, unlike its sister communities of Lawrence and Lowell, continued to be dominated by the corporation that originally founded it in the 1830s.[8] Similar to the textile manufacturing towns on which it was patterned, the Amoskeag Corporation recruited its early labor force from rural New Englanders. From the 1850s on, immigrants from England, Scotland, and Ireland began to replace native American workers. In the 1870s, following the textile industry's discovery of the French Canadians as the most "industrious" and "docile" labor force, the corporation embarked on the systematic recruitment of laborers from Quebec. By 1900, French Canadians constituted about 40% of the labor force in the mill, and about one-half of the city's population. While their migration continued through the first two decades of the twentieth century, the corporation was also absorbing small numbers of Germans and Swedes, followed by increasing numbers of Polish and Greek immigrants in the second decade of the twentieth century.[9]

As a planned industrial town, Manchester did not experience the classic problems of social disorganization generally attributed to urban living. The carefully designed and maintained corporation space, encompassing the mill yard and housing for a large segment of the work force, enclosed the workers in a total environment. From the late nineteenth century on, Manchester developed cohesive ethnic neighborhoods which were organized along kinship and ethnic lines, and which surrounded the corporation housing, radiating east, south, and west of the mill yard.[10] The problems that Manchester's laborers were facing, therefore, did not derive from urban anomie, but rather from the pressures of industrial work and discipline. These conditions allow the historian to examine the role of the family in the process of industrialization without the interference of factors generally connected with the pressures of life in a large city.

The surviving historical record utilized for this study is unusually rich, allowing an exploration of conditions and developments from the perspectives of the workers as well as the corporation. The unique collection of cumulative, individual employee files which were recorded for the period 1910-1936 provides detailed data for the reconstruction of the workers' careers. Particularly important are the entries in each employee file listing the reasons for his or her leaving the job, as well as the reasons given by overseers for the dismissal of workers. The linkage of this data with marriage and insurance records, as well as with oral histories, permitted a reconstruction of the workers' life and work histories with a wealth of information unavailable in census records.[11]

FAMILY INTERACTION WITH THE CORPORATION

In their day-by-day relationships, the corporation and the family were two interacting institutions. Although the two were not equals, they were exercising checks and balances on each other. In a paternalistic system such as that of the Amoskeag Mills, the corporation not only perceived itself as a family, but also was aware of the family's powerful role in the workers' lives and consciously attempted to utilize that force as an instrument to control the workers. It therefore relied on the family to recruit the workers and to socialize them into industrial work.[12]

The Amoskeag Corporation and its immigrant workers demonstrated a remarkable fit in their respective ideologies of work and of social hierarchy and authority. Nineteenth-century paternalistic ideology, still alive in twentieth-century Manchester, viewed industrial management as a family affair. In the tradition of industrial paternalism the corporation perceived itself as a large family, and the workers within it as its children. "More than 15,000 persons work in these mills. . . . It is true that the large company to which they sell their labor treats them as its own children," read a typical corporation advertisement in French-Canadian newspapers. The corporation's own management and organization were structured along family and kinship lines. Even in the early part of the twentieth century, when workers were hired as individuals, the corporation continued to employ entire families where possible. Family hiring was more advantageous to the corporation since the effort invested in recruitment and transportation could be maximized through the number of textile workers provided by one family. This also held true for housing arrangements where the corporations preferred to utilize the space by placing families with several working members in the corporation tenements.[13]

In the beginning of the twentieth century, the corporation embarked on a series of new employee welfare programs. With the exception of the superannuation of a limited number of older workers, these programs were aimed primarily at the workers' families, rather than at individuals. They included a homeownership plan for workers who had stayed in the corporation's employ five years or longer, a playground and dental care program for children, and a visiting nurse and home instruction program for mothers. Management hoped to socialize the children through these programs, to Americanize the workers, and to develop a permanent, stable, and loyal industrial labor force.[14] The new welfare program introduced in 1910 was combined with an efficiency program, which under the influence of Taylorism, tried to centralize and rationalize hiring policies, and to increase the speed of production.[15]

Corporate paternalism struck a responsive chord in newly arrived immigrant workers. The work ethic and customs of a preindustrial culture were woven around the traditional view of the family as a work unit. The workers transferred this tradition into the industrial system and realigned their family work relationships in accordance with the needs and expectations of industrial work. This is not to argue that the tasks and division of labor which the French-Canadian farm family had traditionally carried out in rural Quebec were automatically transferred to the American industrial system. Child labor in the factory, the work of mothers outside the home, and the regimentation of life to an industrial schedule were all novel experiences.

The basic tradition of family work and of the economic role of each member, however, was carried over from the agricultural background. The important continuity was in the perception and experience of the family as a work unit, even when the locations of the job and the work process were different. Daughters and wives who had earlier contributed to the family's economic efforts on the farm transferred these work roles to industrial labor. Even though the tasks they were performing differed from those in their premigration setting, the basic traditional assumptions that guided family work roles were not disrupted.[16] The one area of conflict concerned the issue of women's work. French-Canadian customs, reinforced by the Catholic Church, regarded women's work outside the home as a threat to the family. This did not stop two-thirds of all married French-Canadian women in the town from working in the factory. In their own minds, they reconciled the conflict by arguing that their work was temporary. Many, however, claimed such temporary conditions till the end of their lives. Married women continued to work over their entire careers with intermittent interruptions for childbirth.[17]

The relationship between the workers and the corporation was one of mutual interaction. The degree of their cooperation or withdrawal depended on a variety of factors for each: on the corporation's side, the relationship was governed by the availability of the labor force and by the fluctuation of the textile market. In periods of labor shortage prior to World War I, when the corporation had to compete with other industries over the labor supply in the city, it was forced to tolerate the autonomous behavior of the workers and their resistance to modernization. On the other hand, during its continuous decline in the post-World-War-I period, and until its shutdown in 1936, the corporation's gradual curtailment of its labor force allowed the workers less freedom to manipulate the system.[18]

The workers were by no means equals to the corporation in this balance of power, but they were able to exercise a certain degree of autonomy under limited conditions. The workers' response depended on the changing work conditions and demands of the corporation, and on individual and family considerations. The availability of alternative employment opportunities in the city, economic needs, traditional work habits, and family values all influenced their behavior. Demographic patterns had a crucial impact on the workers' careers, especially those of women. The degree of their dependence on industrial work or independence from it, especially mobility in and out of the mill, was determined by individual and family needs which changed over the stages of the family's development. Particularly significant in this scheme was the shifting margin of poverty and subsistence at different stages of the family cycle. Unmarried individuals in their late twenties had a different attitude toward work than fathers of families of five, for example, or widows in their fifties.[19]

This model suggests, therefore, that both the worker's family and the corporation were flexible institutions. Their relationships and patterns of interaction fluctuated and changed over time, in response to internal conditions as well as under the impact of larger historical processes. The family was most effective in making an impact on work patterns in two areas: (1) it facilitated the adjustment of its members by acting as a labor recruiter, a housing agent, and as a source of support in critical life situations, and (2) it exercised its own controls, even if limited ones, against the corporation by encouraging labor turnover, by influencing the job placement of its members, and by affecting job control in the daily routine of work.

THE ROLE OF FAMILY AND KIN IN INDUSTRIAL ADJUSTMENT

Acting as a conveyor belt, facilitating the workers' movements and cushioning the shock of adjustment, the family and the kin group served as the labor recruiters, the organizers of migration routes, and housing agents. Within the factory, the family group directed the work choices of its members, influenced their placement in different departments, and prepared them for industrial work. Kinship ties were especially instrumental in facilitating the workers' experimentation with alternative careers.[20]

French Canadians were streaming to Manchester in response to systematic recruitment propaganda issued out of Manchester through their own ethnic organizations and through communications from relatives. Their kin met them on arrival, placed them on their first job, and located them as temporary boarders until they found a corporation flat or rented an apartment in the growing French-Canadian section of the city's West Side.[21]

Chain migration through the kin group was not limited to Manchester. Kinship networks were pervasive throughout the entire industrial region in New England. The presence of clusters of kin in a variety of New England industrial towns offered laborers of the Amoskeag Mills the opportunity to migrate through a series of mill towns with the hope of improving their conditions. Their migration was not terminal. It followed a circuitous route through other textile mills in Maine, southern Massachusetts, and Rhode Island, where relatives were working.[22] Workers moved back and forth, from Manchester to Quebec and back to Manchester. Leaving the mills often for two or three summer months, they visited relatives in the Quebec countryside or took on temporary jobs, only to return again to the textile mills in Manchester.

Family ties thus formed a network of employment opportunities as well as temporary and permanent stations for migration. A reconstitution of the migration patterns on the basis of the employee records of the Amoskeag Company suggests that prior to 1922 about one-fourth of the employees studied immigrated to the other New England mill towns in search of better jobs. In most of these instances, the presence of relatives in other towns facilitated their temporary sojourns. Migration did not destroy the family and kin group. It transposed a formerly localized family pattern over an entire industrial region in New England.[23]

Flexibility in corporation employment policy, which emanated primarily from the need for cheap labor, enabled the family to exercise some controls over the recruitment and placement of its members. The continuous informality in corporation hiring policies, and especially the overseers' autonomy in their departments, facilitated personal connections between overseers and the workers' relatives. The character of a department was basically determined by its overseer, and a workroom frequently containing 100 or more workers was still identified by the overseer's name. Workers continued to obtain jobs directly from the overseer, even after the introduction of a formal employment office.[24] When there was a vacancy in a workroom, the overseers generally filled it by asking one of the workers to bring in someone he knew. Most workers ignored the employment office and turned directly to the overseers for jobs and the placement of relatives. Since the workers were continuously coming and going, this informal placement network was quite extensive.

The family group thus infiltrated the mill and made its direct impact on the composition of the workrooms. Kin and ethnic clusters developed in most departments. Members of one family often clustered in a variety of jobs working near each other in the same room, and childhood friends, cousins, and neighbors often worked side by side for years. About one-fourth of all French-Canadian workers studied in this group met their spouses in the mill and continued to work there after marriage.[25]

Such arrangements enabled the workers to exercise some controls over the work pace. Especially following World War I, as the corporation accelerated its pressures for speed-ups, workers assisted relatives and friends in meeting quotas, even if it meant a loss in pay on their own piece-rate work. The presence of relatives reinforced the workers' collective strength in resisting corporation pressure, especially when the demand for speed-up became overwhelming. The pervasiveness of family groups also enabled the workers to try out different jobs in various departments by passing for one of their relatives, to take turns going to work, and to substitute for each other by switching their employee passes, or by having several members utilize the same pass.

From the late 1920s on, the corporation was becoming nervous about the ethnic and kin alignment in the workrooms: "Refrain from requesting the employment of relatives of persons in charge of units in the same units," read the instruction of management to overseers. An inspector reporting his conversation with various overseers to the management concluded: "For instance, I did not believe it was really good for any unit of the mill to be wholly comprised of relatives and friends of the operatives also of the same race." In that particular workroom, 90% of the labor force was made up of the same ethnic group.[26]

The strength and resilience which workers derived from their families was reinforced by ethnic ties. Ethnicity provided the major organizational scheme for the workers' adjustment to the pressures of the factory work and life in the city. The ethnic group offered the commonality of a cultural heritage, language, residential cohesion, entertainment and rituals, religious ties, and mutual benefit associations. Most of the work and residential patterns were organized around the laborers' family and ethnic ties. Tight-knit clusters of ethnic residential areas appeared in Manchester from the 1880s on.[27] Ethnic enclaves developed in the corporation housing as well. Although corporation flats had to be secured through individual family applications, residents managed to cluster along ethnic lines in corporation housing in the same manner in which they succeeded in aligning themselves in the workroom. Officially, applications for residence in corporation housing had to be submitted long in advance, and workers had to wait their turn.

In reality, friends and relatives notified prospective tenants of vacancies and managed to secure those flats ahead of their turn through the help of acquaintances in the office. Sons of former workers recall the invisible, but clearly reinforced, boundaries between ethnic youth gangs in the corporation tenements.[28]

FAMILY TIME: THE STAGES OF THE FAMILY CYCLE

Internal family considerations and demographic conditions, but primarily economic need, influenced the patterns of the workers' persistence and migration. In the pre-World-War-I period, families decided who of their members would go to work, what son or daughter should start first, at what point the wife should stop, when she should return to work, and who should explore alternative employment outside the mill.

This process of family decision-making emerges both in the analysis of the employment files, where workers frequently cited family reasons for leaving their jobs, as well as in the oral history interviews. Aside from involuntary reasons such as illness, accidents, retirement, and death, laborers left because: "husband did not want wife to work," "wife did not approve of husband's work in the night shift," "parents want son to go back to school," "girl takes care of young children at home." As long as the employment system was flexible, family members could decide whose labor was needed to maintain the family's income, who should work in the mill, who should stay home, and what department or workroom he or she should be sent to.[29]

What factors governed the family's decision on the timing of entrance into the labor force, taking on new family obligations, or migration into new areas? What were the internal and external factors which directed the family's interaction with the world of work?

The timing of behavior followed the family life cycle and was governed by the external pressures of the industrial system. The decision as to when people were leaving home, marrying, giving birth to their first child, spacing the births of their subsequent children, or sending their children to work or to school were timed by the internal clock of family traditions as well as by the external pressures of the factory system and by economic needs. Historians are only now beginning to unravel what specific processes were involved in this timing, and how they varied among different socioeconomic and cultural groups under different circumstances.[30]

For the French-Canadian immigrants, industrial work meant family employment. It is not surprising, therefore, that they were recognized as textile workers par excellence. French Canadians had the highest birth rate of all industrial workers in the United States. Their large numbers of children made them particularly suitable for family employment. In New England their average family size was 7.2, while the Irish, a group also well known for high fertility, had an average of 5 members per family. French Canadians also boasted the highest average number of family members working in the textile industry (3.9). Large family size which had served well the work needs of farmers continued to be an asset in industrial work in the late nineteenth century.

Changing conditions in the textile industry from the early part of the nineteenth century, however, dictated a modification of demographic behavior after the end of the nineteenth century.[31] The first major impact or the industrial system on demographic behavior was in the postponement of marriage, particularly for women. By the second decade of the twentieth century, women who had migrated to Manchester in their teens and second-generation immigrant women began to delay their marriage until their late twenties or early thirties. This was a direct response to the conditions of industrial work. Because much of the family's income depended on the work of more than one member, marriage did not offer an escape from work outside the home.[32]

Postponement of marriage was also dictated to women by their own parents. Since single women workers carried a significant share of the burden of their families' support from the moment they were able to work, parents counted on their daughters' wages as an essential addition to the family income. As unmarried daughters sixteen and older began to work full-time, their parents and younger siblings were gradually withdrawing from work. Several investigations of New England textile towns, including Manchester, which were carried out by the U.S. Bureau of Labor Statistics revealed that while sons committed only 83% of their income to their parents' budgets, daughters delivered 95% of their pay. Parents tried to influence daughters to delay their marriage in order to continue to rely on them as a source of income.[33]

Aside from economic need, women also worked because they enjoyed their occupations. Numerous testimonies in the oral history interviews provide this insight which has escaped historians who rely on quantitative data only. "I loved my work," said one retired weaver (now 94 years old). Work in the mills provided an experience of partnership and sociability which was organized along sex lines, but which nevertheless carried a family ambiance into the workrooms. "We were all like a family," remarked another retired worker.[34]

For most young immigrant women workers, marriage did not provide an escape from industrial work; it actually added the new burden of housekeeping and childrearing to factory labor. Caught between the traditional definition of sex roles in their own culture and the economic needs of their family, women found themselves working in the mill as well as tending to their domestic tasks. Most female textile workers continued to work after marriage until giving birth, and returned to the mill as soon as they weaned their infants. They worked until the birth of their next child and then stopped temporarily, only to return again.[35] The woman's mother next door, or an aging aunt or other female relative provided day care. Where no relatives were available, women either left their children with a neighbor or deposited them each day at the orphanage which, in addition to its regular inmates, by necessity took in children of working mothers.

About one-half of the married men working in the Amoskeag Mills also had their wives working with them, in order to supplement the family income. This experience was not unique to Manchester. It was characteristic of employment patterns in the textile and shoe industries in general, which in 1930, for example, had the highest ratio of females to males ten years and above, reporting gainful employment.[36]

Once they had children, however, women's careers became more checkered and less stable. Married women with children made up the major proportion of the Amoskeag Mills' reserve labor force. While the group of regularly employed workers consisted of a higher percentage of young women under age 35, the reserve labor force included a higher percentage of women between the ages of 35 and 55. There was no comparable age discrepancy between males in the regular and the reserve force. Among workers older than 55, there was no major difference in the percentage of men and women in the reserve labor force.[37]

The pattern of the work cycle of married women was thus articulated to the family cycle: during their childbearing and childrearing years, women did not work to their full capacity. For family reasons as well as corporation needs, they found themselves in the reserve labor force, rather than as regular workers. During the period of optimal family earnings, when their children were grown, but still living at home and working, the women worked only occasionally. The marriage or departure of the last child drove the mothers back to the mill. This explains why one finds a much higher proportion of married women aged 55 and up on the regular labor force, rather than on the reserve. The most intensive periods in the employment of married women came before age 35 and after age 55. In the intervening periods, their intermittent work patterns depended on the availability of temporary jobs in the mill. Prior to 1922, there was almost always a job to be found in one department or another. After the strike, as a consequence of gradual and continuous curtailment, married women were most vulnerable to permanent job loss if they left work to raise children.

One of the important functions of delayed marriage, especially in the second generation of immigrants, was a curtailment in the number of children born. In some respects, this decline in fertility was a manifestation of a gradual secularization and relaxation of traditional norms. It also represented, however, changing conditions in the employment market. With the passing of the New Hampshire Child Labor Law in 1905, the employment of children under sixteen became increasingly risky. In this case, the corporation decided to comply with the new law, since it had nothing to lose at a time when changes in production and experimentation with efficiency made the work of young children obsolete. The decline in the child labor market turned large numbers of children into economic burdens on the family. It was advantageous, therefore, to limit the number of children, especially since childbirth impaired the mother's effectiveness as a breadwinner; it imposed on her patterns of intermittent employment and therefore undermined her chances of occupational advancement.[38]

Even though they were not actually entering factory work before age sixteen, children were socialized to the work experience in the mill at an early age. Industrial labor became part of their lives even before they actually worked. The experience of their parents, and the proximity of their homes to the mills, prevented any real separation between the world of childhood and the world of work. Children carrying lunch pails to the mills at the noon hour were a familiar part of the Manchester scene, where school children earned their first money by bringing lunches from the boarding houses to the mills. Most youths attending high school worked regularly in the mills during the summer. The expectations that children would have to work as soon as the law permitted were strongly impressed on them from an early age by their parents. The family economy, as well as the family's work ethic, was built around the assumption that children would contribute to the family's economic effort from the earliest opportunity.

By the time they entered the mill, young people had become familiar with the entire work process. Parents and older brothers and sisters provided a variety of models of occupational behavior. Oral history interviews have revealed consistently that most young boys and girls commencing work in the mills learned initial tasks from relatives rather than from strangers. An informal family apprenticeship system was thus infused into the formal structure of the world's largest textile mill.

When they came to take their first job, the children were already familiar with the names of overseers and second hands, knew the gossip about various transactions in the workrooms, and were familiar with a number of shortcuts and tricks. They also knew from an early age that the Amoskeag Corporation was the single largest employer in the city and that they could not afford to be blackballed by the Amoskeag Company, because they would not be able to find work anywhere else in northern New England.

Work roles along sex lines were also inculcated at an early age. Girls knew that until their marriage, their work would be regulated by parents and that most of their income would be ploughed back into the family's resources. They were also prepared for the fact that if the family could afford to send any of its children to school after age fourteen, the boys would go first. Within the limited occupational structure of the mill town, they were prepared for the fact that the highest rank of skill a woman could aspire to would be that of a weaver, while men could hope to become loom fixers, expert dye mixers, master mechanics, and eventually even overseer, the most coveted position.

This advance knowledge of the limits of opportunity cast the daughter into the role of back-up person for the son's career. It meant that her work would serve to facilitate her brother's occupational mobility. Girls were directed to the mill and were expected to work steadily, in order to plug the holes in the family's income, so that their brothers could afford the flexibility of experimentation in search of better occupations. As long as the daughter maintained a consistent income, the sons could afford the freedom to transfer from one department to another in the mill, or could take the risk of experimenting with outside jobs. It is not surprising, therefore, that unmarried women under thirty (who might generally be expected to have a higher turnover on the job) showed a higher persistence rate except for situations where they moved because they followed husbands or parents to another mill town or to another job.[39]

Commencement of work did not mean independence from parental and family controls. Young men and women working in the mill continued to live in their parents' or relatives' households until marriage. Those without parents boarded with relatives, usually with married brothers and sisters or with aunts and uncles under similar arrangements. They were paying, in effect, for their room and board and were using the remainder of their pay for supplies and personal savings. While in large commercial cities young men and women tended to leave their homes and to board with strangers, industrial workers in Manchester continued to live at home or with relatives until they married. They rarely boarded with strangers. Only those men and women in their twenties and thirties who had no relatives in the city turned to corporation or commercial boarding houses.[40]

Family regulation of the individual careers of its members significantly cut down initiative for migration and experimentation with other occupations. The employment of several members in the same enterprise made the entire family vulnerable to fluctuations of the labor market and the shifting of occupational opportunities. During periods of layoff and curtailment of production, an entire family group found itself without work. This particular vulnerability was dramatized during the strike of 1922, when whole families were unemployed and on the verge of starvation during the nine-month shutdown of the mills. The strike clearly revealed that workers who had spouses or other relatives employed in the shoe industry were more inclined to strike than those whose entire source of support depended on the textile industry. Disagreement over the strike tore families apart. Brothers and sisters stopped talking to each other after their initial disagreement over whether they should strike. The almost total dependency of entire families on the textile industry deprived them of the opportunity of assisting each other during that critical situation.[41]

CONCLUSION

Family or surrogate family organization thus provided the central organizing scheme in the workers' living and work experience. These arrangements had their own built-in flexibilities which were governed by the family's decisions, or by external pressures, as conditions might dictate. On what basis the family made its decisions and what considerations and motives were involved in the decision are questions still open for exploration.

Immigrant families in factory towns timed their behavior by the internal clocks which were wound by their traditional customs, as well as by the factory bells. Under what circumstances did they respond to their traditional rhythms of time, and under what circumstances did they conform to industrial time? This is one of the key issues of social, cultural, and economic history. The data in this study suggest that at certain stages of their cycle families were more independent than at other stages, and that the differences in their behavior at different points in time were governed by internal family conditions as well as by the pressures and requirements of the industrial system. While these tentative conclusions await careful testing and further detailed research, it is clear now that the family was a flexible institution, and that given the historical circumstances or the opportunity structure, it was a dependent agent at certain times and an independent agent at other times.

While sociologists have been arguing that the isolated nuclear family was the form most fit for the industrial environment, this study suggests that the most adaptable family type was the extended family. With elaborate kin networks in Manchester as well as in Quebec, and with extensions in several other industrial New England towns, such families were best able to offer their members flexibility in the immigration process and in adaptation to new industrial conditions. Their major strength was in their ability to manage their resources and to direct their members into the labor force in accordance with their own needs.[42]

Despite the sophisticated structures of industrial capitalism, families continued to function as production units, even though the workplace shifted from the home to the industrial plant. Within the limited flexibility of a corporation-controlled factory town, the family could continue to make its own labor force decisions and to maintain controls over the careers of its members, as long as the market was open. Migration to an urban setting and industrial work did not drastically challenge paternal authority and traditional sex roles.

The family's interaction with the system was based on cooperation and mutual exploitation of needs and opportunities. The family succumbed to the pressures of industrial work during periods of labor surplus, but maintained its own controls during periods of labor shortage. It offered its members important resources to fall back on during times of crisis or critical life situations. While it prepared its children for industrial work, it also cushioned them from the potential shock and disruptions which they encountered under new industrial conditions. In its effort to protect its members from such exposures, the family developed its own defense system and brought its cultural traditions to bear on its environment and the industrial system.

The immigrant laborers of Manchester, New Hampshire offer the historian the rare opportunity to explore intensively a group of industrial villagers living in a twentieth-century city still dominated by nineteenth-century paternalism. Several unique facets of their experience might lead us to question the feasibility of generalizing on the experience of the family and industrial work: patterns of family employment were different in the textile industry, which is female-intensive, than in steel communities, where women's occupations were segregated from male occupations.[43] Secondly, the continuation of paternalism in a community this size is not typical of American industrial towns in general. Finally, the particular immigrant group studied here in detail—the French Canadians—had the flexibility of "commuting" to and from the homeland, which other immigrants did not enjoy.

Despite the unique conditions of Manchester, it is possible to generalize from its experience about most early twentieth-century textile communities in the northeastern United States. It is not surprising that the patterns found in Manchester have strong parallels in mid-nineteenth-century Lancashire, England, and in late-nineteenth-century Stockport, England and Amiens, France—all of which were centers for the textile industry.[44] What is more surprising is that the kin and family patterns described in this study bear resemblance to patterns found in London's Bethnal Green and Boston's West End in the 1950s.[45]

This study does not provide a universal interpretation of the interaction of the family with the world of work. Instead, it invites historians to pursue these questions in a variety of communities under different historical conditions in order to derive deeper insights into the relationship between the family and the process of industrialization.

NOTES

1. Neil Smelser, *Social Change and the Industrial Revolution* (Chicago, 1959). William Goode, *World Revolution and Family Patterns* (New York, 1963). See also Sidney Greenfield, "Industrialization and the Family in Sociological Theory," American Journal of Sociology, 67 (1961), 312-322.

2. For crucial revisions of traditional working-class historiography, see E. P. Thompson, *The Making of the English Working Class* (New York, 1963); Herbert Gutman, "Work, Culture and Society in Industrializing America, 1819-1918," American Historical Review, 78 (1973), 531-588; David Montgomery, "Immigrant Workers and Scientific Management," in *Proceedings of the Conference on Immigrants in Industry, Eleutherian Mills, 1973* (forthcoming). On recent working-class historiography, see Paul Faler, "Working-Class Historiography," Radical America, 3 (1969) and Robert H. Zieger, "Workers and Scholars: Recent Trends in American Labor Historiography," Labor History, 13 (1972).

3. The most well-documented work in support of this thesis is Michael Anderson, *Family Structure in Nineteenth-Century Lancashire* (Cambridge, 1973). Specifically on American immigrant families, see Virginia Y. McLaughlin, "Patterns of Work and Family Organization: Buffalo's Italians," Journal of Interdisciplinary History, 2 (1970).

4. For the emphasis on family and household structure as the major unit of analysis, see Richard Sennett, *Families Against the City* (Cambridge, Mass., 1970). Sennett errs in defining "extended family" only within the household, thus ignoring the significant presence of kin outside the household.

5. See Tamara K. Hareven, "The Family as Process: The Historical Study of the Family Cycle," Journal of Social History, 7 (1974). For conceptualization and definition of the family cycle, see Paul C. Glick, "The Family Cycle," American Sociological Review, 12 (1947), 164-174; Reuben Hill, *Family Development in Three Generations* (Cambridge, Mass., 1970).

6. On the concept of "industrial time," see Pitirim A. Sorokin and Robert K. Merton, "Social Time: A Methodological and Functional Analysis," American Journal of Sociology, 42 (1937).

7. On the Amoskeag Mills, see Waldo Brown, *A History of the Amoskeag Company* (Manchester, N.H., 1915), a company history. Daniel Creamer and Charles W. Coulter, *Labor and the Shutdown of the Amoskeag Textile Mills*, Works Project Administration, National Research Project, Report No. L-5 (Philadelphia, 1939).

8. On classic planned New England textile towns, see Caroline F. Ware, *The Early New England Cotton Manufacture* (New York, 1942); John Armstrong, *Factory Under the Elms* (Cambridge, Mass., 1968); Vera Shlakman, *Economic History of a Factory Town: Chicopee, Massachusetts* (New York, 1935). On the significance of the architectural design of the Amoskeag Mills and the relationship between corporate paternalism and control of the city, see Randolph Langenbach, "An Epic in Urban Design," Harvard Bulletin (April 15, 1968), and "Architecture and Paternalism: A Study in Social Space," unpublished manuscript. For the corporation's Welfare Program see Tamara K. Hareven, "Continuities and Discontinuities in Corporate Paternalism," unpublished manuscript.

9. In 1911, French Canadians constituted 37.6% of the labor force; native-born Americans (many of whom were of Irish and Scotch descent) constituted 18.6%; the Irish, 14.7%; the Poles, 10.8%; and the Greeks, 8%. By 1923, French Canadians constituted 46%. On the textile workers of Manchester in the context of other textile communities, see *Report on the Condition of Women and Child Wage-Earners in the United States*, vol. I, Cotton Textile Industry (Washington, D.C., 1910), Senate Doc. No. 65, 61st Congress, 2nd session. Manchester was one of the communities investigated in this report. See also Ralph Vicero, "The Immigration of French-Canadians to New England, 1840-1900," Ph.D. dissertation, University of Wisconsin, 1966.

10. A reconstruction and mapping of the neighborhoods from the Manchester City Census of 1881, from the Federal Manuscript Censuses of 1860 to 1880, and from the most recently opened census of 1900, is now in progress.

11. This project utilized the following data: a 5% random sample of the individual employee files kept by the corporation from 1912 to 1936. The sample consists of 2,000 individual files. Individual workers' careers were reconstructed from these files over each worker's entire work period. They were subsequently traced

through city directories, and wherever relevant and possible, workers' careers were reconstructed for the period prior and subsequent to their employment by the corporation, as well as during intermittent periods. The individual records were then linked with marriage records and were augmented by corporation records, newspapers, and a collection of oral history interviews of former employees. The records of French-Canadian workers were also linked with insurance records.

12. Recruitment before 1930 was carried out primarily through returning relatives to Quebec villages. From 1900 on, after the organization of the Association Canado-Americaine in Manchester, the corporation utilized the newspaper published by this organization for propaganda and recruitment of workers. The paper published major articles on the Amoskeag Mills, the copy for which was supplied by the Amoskeag Corporation. See *Le Canado-Americain* (1913-1915).

13. *Le Canado-Americain*, November 10, 1913. On corporation housing, see Langenbach, "Architecture and Paternalism: A Study in the Planning of Social Space."

14. The corporation published regular descriptions of the program in *The Amoskeag Bulletin*, 1-4 (1912-1918). The corporation's welfare and efficiency system is discussed in greater detail in Hareven, "Continuities and Discontinuities in Corporate Paternalism." On the strike, see *History of the Amoskeag Strike During the Year 1922* (Manchester, New Hampshire, 1924).

15. On the French-Canadian background, see Phillippe Garigue, *La Vie Familiale des Canadiens Francais* (Montreal, 1967).

16. Compare with Smelser, *Social Change and the Industrial Revolution*, and Anderson, *Family Structure in Nineteenth-Century Lancashire*. See also Louise Tilly and Joan Scott, "Women's Work and the Family in Nineteenth-Century Europe," Comparative Studies in History and Society, (forthcoming).

17. This is based on oral history interviews as well as on an analysis of the women's employment patterns.

18. On the fluctuation of the textile market and its impact on the Amoskeag Company's hiring policies, see Creamer and Coulter, *Labor and the Shutdown*.

19. On the internal economic conditions of the family and their impact on labor market behavior, see U.S. Congress, *Report on Conditions of Woman and Child Wage Earners* I; Modell, "Family, Economy and Insecurity," paper delivered at the annual meeting of the Orgainzation of American Historians, April 1974, and "Economic Dimensions of Family History," The Family in Historical Perspective Newsletter, No. 6 (1974). Tamara Hareven and John Modell are embarking on a study of family budgets in the early part of the twentieth century. The margin of poverty has been defined by early social investigators of the urban poor. See B. Seebohm Rowntree, *Poverty: A Study of Town Life* (London, 1922), and Robert Hunter, *Poverty* (New York, 1904).

20. On the role of kinship in migration, see Charles Tilly and C. Harold Brown, "On Uprooting, Kinship, and the Auspices of Migration," Journal of International Comparative Sociology, 7 (1967). On French Canadian Kinship see Phillippe Garigue, "French Canadian Kinship and Urban Life," American Anthropologist, 58 (1956).

21. This is a recurring pattern described in the oral history interviews.

22. Labor turnover and patterns of migration are discussed in detail in Tamara K. Hareven, "The Laborers of Manchester, New Hampshire, 1910-1922: Patterns of Adjustment to Industrial Life," Labor History, (forthcoming). See also, *Report on the Conditions of Woman and Child Wage Earners* I, 127.

23. It is now possible for the first time to reconstruct such patterns of migration, because the employee records actually state where individuals went on leaving the corporation. See also U.S. Department of Labor, Women's Bureau, *Lost time and Labor Turnover in Cotton Mills: A Study of Cause and Extent*, Publication No. 52 (Washington, D.C., 1926), Part I, 109-113.

24. The overseer was the man in charge of production, management, and discipline in an entire department, which consisted of several workrooms.

25. The trace of the original 2,000 employee files gathered for the study turned up an additional 500 of their relatives who were also working in the mill. This does not represent all the possible kin combinations. It contains only the immediate ones that could be traced through vital records. If one allowed for second cousins and a variety of relatives that are not mentioned in the interviews, the number of kin could be considerably higher.

26. Evidence for kin clustering in the workrooms is derived from the reconstruction of kin groups by place of work. See also "Memo to Mr. Hagan," October, 1934, Amoskeag Files, Baker Library, Harvard University.

27. Based on oral history interviews and on a preliminary survey of the residential clustering in the corporation's tenements and boarding houses by Tamara Hareven and Randolph Langenbach. For comparison, see two significant studies of the social space of the urban working class, Pierre Chombard de Lauwe, *La Vie Quotidienne des Familles Ouvrières* (Paris, 1956) and André Michel, "La Famille Urbaine et la parenté en France," in Reuben Hill and René Konig, *Families in East and West: Socialization Process and Kinship Ties* (Paris, 1970). On ethnicity and residential cohesion see Herbert Gans, *The Urban Villagers* (New York, 1962). For a comparative experience in a textile community, see Donald B. Cole, *Immigrant City* (Cambridge, Mass., 1957).

28. Based on oral history interviews. See also Gerald D. Suttles, *The Social Order of the Slum: Ethnicity and Territory in the Inner City* (Chicago, 1968).

29. The reasons for leaving have been computed for the individual employee files.

30. Hareven, "The Family as Process," and Anderson, *Lancashire*. For an analysis of women's family cycles, see Peter Uhlenberg, "A Study of Cohort Life Cycles: Cohorts of Native Born Massachusetts Women, 1830-1920," Population Studies, 23 (1968).

31. *Report on the Condition of Woman and Child Wage Earners*, I.

32. U.S. Department of Labor, Women's Bureau, *The Share of Wage-Earning Women in Family Support*, Bulletin, No. 30 (Washington, D.C., 1923), 137-140.

33. Ibid.

34. Oral history interviews.

35. These patterns emerge from the reconstruction of the work careers of 1,000 women from the employee files, and from oral history interviews.

36. See *The Share of Wage-Earning Women*.

37. Creamer and Coulter, *Labor and the Shutdown*.

38. Wilson H. Grabill, Clyde V. Kiser, and Pascal W. Whelpton, *The Fertility of American Women* (New York, 1958), 404-406; J. Hill, "Fecundity of Immigrant Women," U.S. Congress, Immigration Commission, *Reports of First and Second Generations of Immigrants in the United States–Fecundity of Immigrant Women* (Washington, D.C., 1911), Senate Doc. No. 282, 61st Congress, 2nd Session.

39. This is based on the reconstruction of the work histories and the computation of the number of times hired and dismissed for each worker. See also, *Lost Time*, 29-32, 67-72, 84-87.

40. See John Modell and Tamara K. Hareven, "Urbanization and the Malleable Household: An Examination of Boarding and Lodging in American Families." Journal of Marriage and the Family, 35 (1973), pp. 467-479.

41. Most of the interviewees still refer to the strike as the most traumatic experience of their lives. Some of them are still not on speaking terms with former friends and relatives.

42. See Talcott Parsons and R. F. Bales, *Family, Socialization and Interaction Process* (New York, 1955), Bernard Farber, *Guardians of Virtue* (New York, 1972), Sennett, *Families Against the City*.

43. For comparisons, see Susan Kleinberg, "Women's Work Patterns and the Occupational Structure of Cities," paper presented at the Brockport Conference, October 1974, and Elizabeth Butler, *Women and the Trades* (Pittsburgh, 1907-1908).

44. Compare with Anderson, *Lancashire*, and with Louise Tilly and Joan Scott, "Daughters, Wives, Mothers, Workers: Peasants and Working Class Women in the Transition to an Industrial Economy in France," paper presented at Second Berkshire Conference on the History of Women, October 1974, Cambridge, Mass. The study is based on data gathered and analyzed by Howard Chudacoff and Burr Litchfield.

45. See Michael Young and Peter Wilmott, *Family and Kinship in East London* (London, 1957, revised 1962) and Gans, *Urban Villagers*.

IMPERFECT UNIONS
CLASS AND GENDER IN CRIPPLE CREEK, 1894-1904

Elizabeth Jameson

Western mining towns were class-conscious and masculine, and Cripple Creek, Colorado, was no exception. From 1894 to 1904 the Cripple Creek district, with its twelve towns, was a stronghold of radical labor. Centered around nine locals of the militant Western Federation of Miners (WFM), thirty-six unions organized everyone from waitresses and laundry workers to bartenders and newsboys.[1] Through successful organization workers achieved a large measure of control over job conditions and over the social, political, and economic life of the towns. This effective degree of labor control meant that a secure homelife was at least partially attainable by working-class families, and helped insure that middle-class concepts of appropriate sex roles were not challenged in Cripple Creek. Although the industrial structure of gold mining supported both passionate class allegiances and genteel definitions of manhood and womanhood, it made class concerns of primary importance.

The emphasis on class concerns resulted from dramatic changes in western metal mining. In less than twenty years small-scale placer mining (panning ore from streams or gravel beds) was replaced by lode or "quartz" mining (deep shaft operations which removed rock from which the ore had not been separated, and which was later milled and refined). The profitable development of mining required railroads, advanced technology, large refining facilities, a specialized work force, and considerable capital.

Corporate mining, therefore, drastically altered the relationship of miners to their labor and transformed social relationships in mining communities. Older understandings of work and ownership heightened their awareness of loss. In the old mining districts ownership of a claim required work and occupation in good faith, nothing more—or less.[2] A miner kept virtually all that he produced.

Elizabeth Jameson is one of the founders of the University of Michigan Papers in Women's Studies, the Women Studies Program at the University of Colorado, and FRONTIERS. She will teach women's history and social history at the University of Virginia next year. She has a B.A. from Antioch, an M.A. from the University of Michigan, Program in American Culture, and currently is completing her Ph.D. at Michigan. An expanded version of this article will appear in Class, Sex, and the Working Woman, forthcoming from Greenwood Press.

The product of his labor was precious metal. More than any other commodity, gold was tangible wealth. Under the wage system, that wealth was not kept by the men who mined it, but was given in profits to absentee owners who neither worked nor lived in mining towns.

Mining was dangerous work, and miners' wives, unlike the owners or resident managers, shared the hazards which endangered workers' health and wages. Women were well aware that without the unions corporate power could jeopardize family security. Labor organization in Cripple Creek was bounded by two critical miners' strikes. The first, in 1894, like most of the period, was defensive, called to oppose mine owners' attempts to cut wages and lengthen the work day. It was the only mining strike of the time in which state power was used to protect civil peace rather than mine owners' property. Populist Governor Davis Waite was the exception in a long line of state executives who sent the militia to help break unions. Waite helped negotiate the agreement which guaranteed a $3 minimum daily wage, an eight-hour day, and the right to union membership for district miners. That agreement lasted until "the" Cripple Creek strike of 1903-04, when employers, state, and military power crushed the miners' unions.[3] The Western Federation was the keystone for Cripple Creek workers: it protected other district labor from 1894 to 1904. But the support of other workers could not prevent its defeat, and the defeat of the miners' locals marked the end of all organized labor in the district.

The Western Federation of Miners (1893-1916), later the International Union of Mine, Mill, and Smelter Workers (1916-1967), has long been considered one of the nation's most radical unions for its endorsements of socialism and because it developed a coherent class ideology to counter corporate control of mining. The WFM did not favor regulation of the trusts or a return to individual enterprise, but supported instead an end to private ownership of basic industry and of the wage and profit system. The union advocated workers' control of production and the establishment of a socialist cooperative commonwealth. Its slogan from the beginning was "Labor Produces All Wealth--Wealth Belongs to the Producer Thereof."

Such principles animated the Cripple Creek labor community from 1894 to 1904. The mutual aid and class understanding shared by the men and women of Cripple Creek were fairly typical of analyses and associations throughout the mining west. While feminism was not of central concern, a variety of radical and reform sentiments flourished in the district: everything from populism and the single tax to self-help through cooperatives. Socialism, both utopian and scientific, had many adherents. Workers dissatisfied with the emerging corporate order believed that they could build a new society "within the shell of the old." The nature of that society was debated as they moved from free silver to socialism and proposed a variety of reforms, often in combination with a class analysis which denied the effectiveness of piecemeal measures.[4]

Given this high degree of class awareness, Cripple Creek provides a particularly significant insight into the overlapping claims of class and gender in America. Women shared the class understandings and social support of the labor community, but organized labor rarely addressed the private world of the family or the specific situations of women in mining towns. The failure to integrate comprehensions of class and of sex roles not only weakened class action, but also left women subordinate, privatized, and often alienated.

Both labor organization and family roles were based in the work structure of gold mining, the only major industry in the district. The towns were largely working class and the work force was largely male. By 1900 some 8,000 men--roughly a fourth of the district's total population--were engaged in mining labor, and other wage work consisted of support services either for the mines or for the miners and their families.[5] The population was similarly male-dominated. Although females outnumbered males under age twenty-one, the adult population was predominantly male. The sex ratio was closest in the town of Cripple Creek, the commercial center, where more jobs for women existed. There were proportionately more men in Victor, "The City of Mines," and in smaller towns like Anaconda, Altman, and Goldfield, which were residential centers for miners and their families.[6]

Virtually all adult women were economically dependent upon male breadwinners. With a male-dominated work force and an excess of men of marriageable age, paid work for women was limited. Their jobs were largely "domestic" in nature: women were cooks, waitresses, seamstresses, retail clerks, dance hall workers, and prostitutes. Many were small proprietors of boarding and rooming houses, restaurants, and groceries. Schoolteachers were the largest group of women professionals. Still, an unusual number of professional women practiced in the district: at least four physicians, one osteopath, one dentist, and twenty-five nurses in 1902. Married women, however, rarely worked outside the home. They might take in laundry, cook, clean, or manage boarding houses, but could not teach or engage in public business. "Women just didn't get jobs, women belonged in the home."[7]

There were three groups of women in Cripple Creek who could reasonably be considered working class: women wage workers; prostitutes and dance hall women; and the women of male workers' families, who were by far the largest group. Most women were considered working class because their husbands, fathers, or brothers worked for wages. Their security depended on the men's incomes, health, and generosity, and on the regularity of work in the mines. Even women wage laborers who "earned" their class position were still subordinate to male unionists. Although it was possible for a single woman or a widow to support herself, all district workers relied on the economic control of the miners' locals. Their leverage was powerful, since merchants depended on the patronage of miners and their families.

The roles and expectations of working-class women were based on two interlocked ideologies: the understandings of class which were formed as mining came under the control of corporate capital in the late nineteenth century, and the concepts of womanhood and manhood produced by the earlier shift from household manufacture to factory production which began around 1820. The class experience was paramount. Relationships between women and men did not appear to jeopardize workers' communities and control. Capitalist employers were a much more obvious and tangible threat.

Working-class women also saw this threat; they shared the class philosophies of male workers and espoused them with eloquence. In 1902 a Cripple Creek stenographer informed Colorado's Bureau of Labor Statistics that there was no essential difference between chattel and wage slavery. "Chattel slaves labor for their masters, are poor, dependent upon the whims of owners for food, clothing, and shelter and are kept in mental darkness. Free laborers (God save the world) toil for their employers, are poor, dependent upon the caprice of monopolists for wages with which to procure food, clothing, shelter. . . . One system of exploitation is simple and direct in its execution, the other is complex and roundabout."[8] Similarly, a Cripple Creek housemaid declared that the point had been reached "where there is a clear, well-defined class interest which separates the laboring class from their employers. . . . The working class must become class conscious and enter politics through the Socialist movement." She wanted to end the wage system and establish an industrial government

> not to manipulate politics and parcel out patronage, but to take charge of and direct and control production and distribution. The actual workers in each industry will control that industry, waste will be eliminated, earnings will be vastly increased, and the hours of labor will be shortened to less than half what they are at present. Almost all the work now is performed by people who are working for wages. They would surely work better if they were getting all that they earned, instead of a very small part of it. . . . [R]eform measures may help a little, but not until we get the co-operative commonwealth will the question be settled so that it will stay settled.[9]

However powerful these responses to capitalism, neither directly addressed the experience of most women. But Mabel Barbee, the daughter of a Cripple Creek prospector, recognized the harshness of her mother's life: "the bare, ugly camp, so alien to her nature; the wide gap between her dream of a home and the drab reality of the house on Golden Avenue; her never-ending loneliness."[10]

There is a vast distance in feeling and outlook between the cramped loneliness of the prospector's wife and the class outlook and faith in political action of the two working women. That distance reflects an important contradiction for working-class women, who were expected to accept a class analysis of industrial conditions and definitions of "natural" sexual attributes which transcended class lines.

If the world of work was divided into laborers and employers, the world of women was divided into good women and bad. Men were defined by their relationship to production, women by their relationship to men and morality. Like class awareness, concepts of sex roles were rooted in economic change. As production moved from households to factories, married women were no longer so important as manufacturers of commodities, and a new definition of sexual sphere developed which reflected women's loss of central economic roles and restricted them to a special social function. What Barbara Welter has called "The Cult of True Womanhood" developed in this context between 1820 and 1860: the ideal woman was pious, pure, submissive, and domestic. Women were to preserve the national morality through influence within the family household.[11] They were expected to provide a stabilizing moral center, while men were trained to be aggressive, acquisitive, and competitive.

Both roles were defined as "natural," common to all women or men regardless of class. All men were expected to work to provide for themselves and their families. All women were to be private, decorative, and supportive of men engaged in purposive economic activity. All homes were intended to be comfortable and comforting retreats from the competition of the marketplace.

Neither True Manhood nor True Womanhood was a fully human role. Both roles required the repression of human capacities, and neither was completely attainable. Concepts of manhood and womanhood had been formulated in an age of laissez-faire individualism, which judged deviation from accepted sexual spheres as an indication of individual failure. Yet these roles could be achieved only by those few who succeeded in a competitive world: urban entrepreneurs, manufacturers, professionals, and their wives. Cripple Creek workers considered the achievement of genteel sex roles to be an important measure of collective success, but they realized that union organization was necessary to gain genteel homes, and the sexual ideologies of an earlier manufacturing age took on more complex and social meanings for workers in the age of corporate mining.

Union control over wages and working conditions helped maintain the wide distance between home and work, a separation which could not have been so clear had low wages forced married women's entry into the work force. Concepts of sexual sphere remained essentially unchallenged in Cripple Creek because the unions were strong enough to guarantee wages sufficient for a man to support a family. Both manhood and womanhood were redefined in class terms: true men were unionists and true women were loyal union wives.

Although men and women challenged industrial capitalism, neither questioned traditional relationships with the other. Men judged themselves by their abilities to support families. Women were presumed to be morally superior and economically dependent, and their place in the home was not questioned. They were told that class allegiance derived from responsibility to husband and household, and that their own potency lay in being class-conscious housewives and mothers. The strongest demonstration of class loyalty was to "find a man who's a union man." In a WFM song, "Scab, Scab, Scab," a suitor was rejected for his opposition to unionism.

> And when I popped the question she said, "You make me sad,
> Do you know I can marry a union man? Do you think I'd
> look at a scab?
> My father is a W.F.M., my brother is the same,
> My mother joined the Auxiliary--I guess I'll not take
> your name."[12]

After marriage, the worlds of husbands and wives were often separate. Women were home-centered; men's lives revolved around work and work associations. Those work relationships could be very close. Many men considered themselves "partners," a term implying cooperation in work, close friendship, and frequently shared living arrangements.[13] After work, men often spent their time downtown at the bars, gambling rooms, or at union and lodge meetings.[14]

The district union newspaper, the Cripple Creek Daily Press, reflected the masculine dominance of the mining camp. The frequent prize fights were front-page news and union and lodge smokers received full coverage. Lydia Pinkham never advertised in its columns, but a wide variety of "male complaint" remedies were touted, indicating preoccupation with sexuality and inadequacy.

"Real men" were not only concerned with strength and sexuality; they also worked hard and supported their families. The high wages gained by unions made that support possible, and manhood was less tied to rugged individualism than to militant unionism. Workers believed that a "man who is not alive to his interests enough to join a union of his craft is unworthy to be the husband of a good woman or the father of innocent children."[15] Scabs were derided for their "lack of manhood"; to be an active unionist was to be a "man--not a makeshift."[16] Manhood was understood both in terms of traditional "masculine" qualities and in relation to class membership. Womanhood was similarly defined in traditional terms, but for women class membership was indirect. Women's class status derived from their men's relationship to the means of production, and their class involvement was dependent on male organization.

Western labor assumed, with some accuracy, that it treated women in an enlightened manner. Many demands of the middle-class women's movement had been achieved. There was equal pay for equal work, if not equal work. Women had the vote in Colorado and were considerably more active in district politics than in the unions. They held public office and participated regularly in party politics.[17] It was not unusual for women to vote in the old mining districts, and they were granted the vote in school elections when Colorado achieved statehood in 1876. In 1893, during a Populist insurgency, women achieved the full franchise, since, as Governor Waite declared, with the limited franchise "the heavens have not fallen and the efficiency of the public schools has been greatly improved."[18]

District labor prided itself on these achievements, defined them as valuable working-class tools, and considered them sufficient to women's needs. As with the suffrage movement nationally, womanly virtue became a justification for granting women electoral equality. But it was assumed that with the franchise women's concerns had been met, and that only class issues remained. Women's public and social influence was given class meaning. Both the ballots and the purchasing power of working-class women were seen as weapons to be used in behalf of organized labor.

Prevailing national concepts of sex roles, home, and family were incorporated into labor's critique of industrial capitalism.

Workers opposed capitalism partly because it forced women to work and destroyed the home; one measure of the unions' strength was their ability to protect women and children from wage labor. The Press insisted that a man should receive wages "sufficient to keep his wife and children out of competition with himself, and give them the same opportunities for improvement and intellectual and moral training and comfortable living as are enjoyed by those who do not labor. No other condition of society is just."[19] Tying respectable family life to unions, Cripple Creek gold miners contrasted the homes they had won through organization with those in areas with no unions.

> A comparison of the interior of the home of the average industrious miner of the Cripple Creek district and a comparison of its contents with that of a coal miner in the eastern states . . . would be a revelation to that class of people who look upon a man who delves in the earth and who gets black and dirty when on shift as an inferior sort of animal, ignorant and brutal, drinking up his wages and beating his wife and living in dirt and squalor. Instead of those conditions the opposite are the rule. Their homes are neatly furnished, carpets on the floors, kitchen furnished with all the conveniences a good housewife is so proud to own. . . . The father, when off shift, is neatly dressed, and with his papers and books becomes intelligent and well posted. The mother, though often hard worked, finds time to put on a neat, clean dress in the evening. The children attend school, and are comfortably clothed and well fed. . . .[20]

Union control made Cripple Creek a considerably more pleasant place than most mining camps. It was a stark contrast to coal towns, where workers lived in company houses, traded at company stores, sent their children to company schools, and were paid in company scrip. Cripple Creek was a single-industry area devoted solely to gold mining, but not a company town. Workers owned or rented their own homes, were paid in cash, traded with private merchants, and elected school officials and most other office-holders. For women, such benefits meant greater material and social security, emotional support, and a clearer analysis of the ugly reality than most of their class.

The unions did much to relieve the dislocations of industrialization for working-class people. Enormous human loss accompanied corporate mining. Violence, in the form of sickness, injury, and death, was a daily fact of mining life.[21] Industrial hazards affected not only miners, but their families as well. Women were all too aware of the human costs of mining, costs for which mining corporations took scant responsibility. "Now, I happen to know that the Hull City Placer mine is in a most dangerous condition. . . . [M]y husband worked there; he is an old time miner and a good one, too. When he explained the dangerous position he was daily placed in I insisted on him drawing his time, which he did. . . ."[22] Not all women were so lucky or so adamant, and deaths and accidents occurred each day, from falling rock, improper timbering, dynamite explosions and missed shots, or faulty machinery.

One of the first tasks of union locals was to provide relief for sickness and death. Major expenditures went to care for widows and children, for sick benefits, and for funerals and shipping bodies elsewhere for burial. In 1903 the WFM locals cared for the victims of at least 193 accidents and conducted the funerals of thirty-five members. The Altman local alone paid $2,235 in sick benefits in 1898-99. Further security was provided by the life insurance offered through the unions.[23]

Emotional support was as important as material assistance. When Henry King, a prominent member of the Victor Miners' Union, died in a mining accident, it was his wife's "express desire that a union man make whatever remarks are deemed necessary or appropriate." The service was held in the union hall, the eulogy delivered by a district labor leader. When Mrs. King went to Denver to bury her husband, she was accompanied by members of lodges to which she belonged, a woman friend from the Ladies' Auxiliary, and a representative of the Daily Press.[24] This level of support was typical. The Press contains sadly frequent notices for unionists to attend funerals and numerous announcements of fundraisings for the families of departed members. Nothing could totally ameliorate these losses or economic uncertainty; but the unions did a great deal to relieve suffering, to provide friendship and support, and to give class meaning to life—and death—in the district.

Such support meant at least as much to workers' wives as to the men. The women were more alone at home than were the men in their workplace. Union functions and friends provided some relief from loneliness and isolation. Women suffered indirectly when the men's incomes were insecure and when unions could not effectively counter the power of mine owners. The pain which derived from economic and emotional ties to working-class men could be alleviated in part by class ideologies which provided social explanations for the plight of working-class families. Sharing the community and vision of organized labor, women's auxiliaries expressed their own blend of love and militance. The Victor Women's Auxiliary reflected these sentiments when a woman died whose husband had been imprisoned during the 1903-04 strike.

> Women's Auxiliary No. 2 of Victor has parted with a beloved sister. For labor's cause she has suffered. The crown of thorns pressed against her brow, the "cross" laid on organized labor in this district rested heavily on her shoulders, and the patience with which she endured her burden, the loyalty she displayed to our cause, has endeared her to organized labor throughout the Cripple Creek district, and her death has cast a deeper gloom, a deeper sorrow over our hearts than words can express. To her bereaved husband this auxiliary extends its sympathy and sorrow.[25]

Mutual assistance was given larger meaning by recognition of shared loss, anger, and oppression, all of which lent coherence to working-class experience and gave it social, rather than individual, meaning. Human caring and militant class interpretation were both central to Cripple Creek's working-class community. But neither caring nor social relief could achieve ultimate class aims.

Reforms and mutual aid might help insure class survival locally until workers were sufficiently well organized nationally to achieve the cooperative commonwealth. But a socialist state could not be achieved through local union organization alone, and if larger goals were to be achieved, crucial concerns had to be the extension of working-class education and organization. Both were successfully pursued in Cripple Creek, and both involved women.

With the possible exception of Butte, Montana, also a WFM stronghold, the Cripple Creek district was probably the most organized area in the country. By 1902 a clear majority--some estimates run as high as 70 percent of the district's workers--belonged to a union.[26] The educational and social events they sponsored enhanced daily life for laboring people, provided enjoyment, and advanced political and economic education. The unions operated free public libraries in Victor and Cripple Creek, and for four years published the Cripple Creek Daily Press, established to counter the capitalist press and to provide a forum for union news and class education. The largest daily in Teller County, its masthead read "The Only Daily Newspaper Owned By Organized Workingmen."[27]

Education was necessary to working-class organization, but it was often merged with sociability. The union halls were centers for social and political activities which included unionists' families in class politics and education.[28] Social life helped provide for labor's survival: locals and auxiliaries sponsored events to raise money for strike support and to meet legal costs. While labor controlled the district, these functions aided workers in other localities. During the 1903-04 strike, the Women's Auxiliary raised relief funds by presenting a play and holding a Leap Year Ball, tickets to which were "furnished free of charge to sisters whose husbands were out on strike."[29]

The unions' effectiveness depended on workers' leverage in the local exchange economy. In an area where almost all consumers were laborers, consumer boycotts went far to enforce union demands. By successfully advertising and boycotting establishments which refused to meet the demands of the smaller unions, organized labor forced merchants to grant six o'clock closing to retail clerks, prevented laundries from shipping clothes out of the district to nonunion shops, made boarding houses and restaurants hire union help, eliminated nonunion products from saloons, groceries, and other retail houses--in short, enforced demands for union recognition, wages, and hours for all district workers.[30]

These tactics depended upon the women. Since purchasing power was a vital union weapon, women were courted for their control of household budgets and told that they belonged to unions through their husbands. "My husband is a member of a labor union. Am I not his better half? The good husband brings his union wages to his wife. That is as it should be. But if the wife spends the union wages for nonunion goods, she is undoing the work of the labor unions."31 The District Trades Assembly decided to form a Women's Auxiliary to organize feminine support for union label drives. "The results of researches made by the home industry committee have convinced the assembly that so long as the wives and home keepers of union men remained in a measure indifferent to the sources from which the necessities of life were supplied, just so long would their efforts in behalf of the blue label be but partially successful."32

Boycotts worked only for trades which produced items for home consumption; they were ineffective for workers in heavy industry, especially for gold miners. Miners relied on successful strikes, informal organizing drives, and on social pressure both at work and in the towns. These tactics were sufficient until 1904. For ten years women benefited from union control, and confronted contradictions between class and sex roles from within an established labor community. With their security and home life dependent on male organization, women placed class loyalty above their own needs.

Women whose primary loyalty was to their class were isolated from exclusively women's organizations. The local Women's Clubs were largely the province of the wives of merchants and professionals. More preoccupied with women's rights and civic projects than with class, they sometimes came into conflict with organized labor. For example, when the Victor Women's Club planned to petition Andrew Carnegie for funds for a town library, the unions objected. Labor preferred to build its own reading rooms and regarded "Carnegie's money as 'blood money,' coined from the sweat and blood of our fellow workmen, and therefore consider[ed] such a proposition an insult to organized labor and refus[ed] to patronize any library or reading room established in whole or in part with Carnegie's money."33 The conflict between the Women's Club and the Trades Assembly was understood totally as a class issue.

Class seemed more crucial than gender because conditions in hard rock mining exerted the greatest influence on the lives of all the people in the district, because class awareness came from a much more immediate experience than concepts of womanhood, and because workers by no means accepted the inevitability of their class position. Cripple Creek workers had either been present during the creation of a wage-labor class in mining or knew people who had lived through that transformation. They had not so directly experienced the redefinition of manhood and womanhood. Sex roles therefore appeared natural, unchanging, and biologically determined, while class relationships had an obviously historical, changing—and changeable—character.

Although an analysis which satisfactorily fused class and gender would not have guaranteed labor's triumph in its battles with mine owners, the failure to achieve that analysis created crucial rifts in working-class programs. Believing that a middle-class feminist movement was sufficient and that its aims had been locally achieved,

Cripple Creek workers projected class goals that were confused by allegiances to genteel sex roles. Labor's analysis of industrial capitalism was not complete: it did not address the relationship of the household to the total economy or include the social and economic value of housework. Visions of an equal and humane socialist society did not include projections of equality between men and women or challenge economic dependence within the family. It was assumed that if workers did achieve the cooperative commonwealth, that socialism would guarantee a secure family unit, with a working husband and a wife who would not be forced to work outside the home, but who could devote herself to being a wife and mother. Unresolved tensions in the workplace increased tension and hierarchy at home, both of which were heightened by women's dependence on the alienated labor of men. The uneasy coexistence of strong loyalties to class and to middle-class family roles created rifts among women and within the working class. Possibilities for achieving either class or feminist goals were diminished.

Women workers received an inconsistent blend of support as workers and chivalrous patronage as women. It was assumed that women held jobs only if absence of a male breadwinner or an inadequate income forced them. The common fear prevailed that women took men's jobs and depressed wages. For every woman who worked, a man would "be out of a job through the ingenuity of capitalism to economize on the profit reaping system."[34] District unions organized female labor to avoid that threat, but male workers shared the belief that women worked temporarily, and only to support themselves, not families.

Equality in the workplace would have been problematic had it ever been confronted. It never really was. There were no women miners; Most women were married and at home, and others hoped to be. Unionists believed their treatment of women progressive, and for the time it was. The Typographical Union was proud that it was "the first organization of men to recognize the rights of women to equal work."[35] Not all district workers agreed, however, and many considered women incompetent to work outside the home. R. E. Croskey, a socialist, secretary of the District Trades Assembly, and national President of the Hotel and Restaurant Employees Union, believed that no woman could "cook in a restaurant or hotel" because when "you put a woman at a range with three half springs to keep broiling with a long fork and a bowl of consomme coming up at the other end, she gets flustered."[36] Deviation from accepted work spheres was sexually as well as economically threatening. Deeper masculine fears surfaced when the Denver Women's Club requested that a woman police officer be hired. The <u>Press</u> was opposed, claiming that hiring a woman for the job would "result in the effeminacy of the human race." Worse yet, wives would "confer with the young lady next door who is working the night shift on the force, and those aged and sacred excuses for coming home at 2 in the morning will not hold as much water as a sieve."[37]

Several hundred Cripple Creek women belonged to unions, especially to the Retail Clerks, Laundry Workers, Cooks and Waiters, Hotel and Restaurant Employees, and the Typographical locals. Clerks and typographers, who most often had equal work and wages, benefited particularly from union membership. But women's and men's work were generally distinct, and women unionists often received lower wages than men. The 1900 census of manufacturers, which probably underrepresents women wage workers, lists fifty women working in the district for an average $368.09 annually and 735 men whose average annual wage was $838.68 in nonmining manufacturing.[38] The wage scale enforced by the Cripple Creek Laundry Workers was generally lower than the $3 minimum daily wage for miners, and the lowest wages were for "female" jobs. The scale for a sixty-hour week ranged from a minimum of $15 for drivers to $8.50 for towel supply girls and $7.50 for mangle girls. Laundry wages were slightly better in Victor, where the weekly scale ranged from $9 for mangle girls to "[m]en working inside, not less than $18" for fifty-four hours.[39]

Women's wages in Cripple Creek were somewhat higher than national scales, but their work was often irregular. Ten waitresses hired temporarily to serve a convention overflow crowd staged a walkout in 1902 because they received the standard $14 a week and board instead of the $3 a day and board usually paid temporary help. When the grievance committee of the Hotel and Restaurant Employees could not resolve the issue, the union struck. One woman explained the strikers' position. "[W]e wait a week or a month for two days' employment, and get four dollars for it. Extra work is during a rush. It is hard and wearying work because there are so many people to wait upon, and a waitress earns every cent she gets. My brother earns four dollars a day at the mines, and comes home fresh and ready for a frolic, but I am so tired and weary that I must go to bed if I would be in any shape to work the next day."[40]

Even in "women's" occupations, women were seldom a majority of the work force, and all the unions were male strongholds. The "thirty-eight beautiful women all members" of the Cooks and Waiters, who graced a Labor Day float, belonged to a local which had a total membership of some two hundred.[41] Few women achieved union leadership. Several served as secretaries of the Clerks' locals, but more were found on arrangements committees for socials and in other more "feminine" roles. Nellie Kedzie, one of the few prominent women unionists, represented the Cripple Creek Federal Labor Union at the State Federation of Labor convention in 1900. She "spoke well for early closing," and "seemed at home, too." But her influence in the masculine convention atmosphere was such a novelty to male unionists that one facetious reporter could only associate Kedzie's forcefulness with the fact that she had survived when "she had once been run over by a street car in Denver."[42]

If district labor was conflicted about working women, at least the women's class and moral status was unambiguous: they were workers and they were good women. Class and morality interacted with greater complication for workingmen's wives and for "bad" women. Prostitutes performed wage labor, but a prostitute's class status depended on her race and on the class of her clientele.[43]

Unionists' reverence for "good women" stood in stark contrast to the "row" and to living and working conditions there. In 1901-02 the Press covered at least fifteen suicide attempts among prostitutes and dance hall women, most of them attributed by the male reporters to desertion by pimps or lovers. The "soiled doves," could not be approved, but could be seen as victims of exploitation, forced into their vocations by a capitalist economy. "Under our present social and industrial system the breeding and propagation of the female prostitute class is as inevitable and unavoidable as the appearance of the maggot in the putrid carcass that lays in the July sun."[44]

Dance halls compromised men and women, but it was hard to condemn the women who worked there, especially since, despite professed veneration of True Women, many male workers obviously tolerated a fair amount of feminine "falseness." Labor reserved its greatest venom for employers. "[T]he inmates of such places . . . deserve pity rather than censure. They are victims of conditions which should not exist in any country. But for the men who live from the product of these women's shame, we have no words adequate to express our contempt."[45]

Despite the partially developed economic analysis of prostitution, allegiance to genteel morality was sufficiently strong that organizing dance hall workers, much less prostitutes, was never seriously considered. But true to the union spirit of the community, dance hall women called a strike in 1902 to oppose a 10 percent reduction in their share of liquor sales and established a Dance Hall Girls' Protective Association. The strike succeeded, but the union was apparently short-lived and the women never applied for membership in the Trades Assembly.[46]

For union men, it was enormously important to protect "good women" from the taint of the tenderloin. It was impossible to eliminate gambling and prostitution, but numerous campaigns were waged to regulate them. Although men could move between the "half world" and the home world, a woman could rarely regain her virtue, and it was a source of male pride that union wages saved "families from the soup house and the brothel."[47] But the definition of union wives as "good women" failed to distinguish them from middle- and upper-class women, including the few women mine owners. The boardinghouse keepers and restaurant owners whom organized labor boycotted for anti-union hiring practices were True Women, too.

Women accepted the notion that they should provide a refuge from the workplace. If a working man provided a comfortable home, he expected wifely support. One woman wrote that a working man should be able to come home to a "rosy wife" who could "sing at the wash tub" and find "nothing under the sun that makes her as merry as housecleaning." She should save money and be agreeable since "the working man has all the vicissitudes he wants when he goes to his work." But she recognized that women's supportive roles derived from economic dependence and suggested that a happy marriage required that a woman take "to the altar a sum of money to give her some share of independence for life."[48] That role was difficult; housework absorbed most waking hours, and life was often tense and uncertain. Women were rarely economically independent, and the reliance of the whole family on a male breadwinner did much to reinforce an ideology of natural sexual spheres.

Women were assumed to be preoccupied with home, morality, children, and femininity. One page of the Sunday Press was devoted to news of the various unions and to columns on labor philosophy. The page also contained fashion items. Next to a story about a waitresses' strike or an article "For the Abolishment of the Wage System" appeared fashion photos of "A Moire Blouse Jacket," "The 'Zenana' Coat," and "Smart Paris Costumes." Working-class women were encouraged to be pretty and popular, to strive for male approval. They were advised to "look always young and charming, be as happy as you can. Dress as well as your means will allow, dress becomingly and dress modestly; give every attention to your underclothing."[49] While men were lauded for their civic and work activities, the Press ran popularity contests for women: for the most popular teacher, the most popular married lady, the most popular clerk in the district.[50]

Labor demanded respect for feminine gentility. Even union politics could not absolve the man who swore in the presence of a lady.

> Residents of Victor Avenue in the vicinity of Sixth Street are incensed over the speech of one Jim Olvie in that locality yesterday noon. . . . Yesterday Mrs. Ed. Vinton, wife of a letter carrier, remarked that the president [McKinley] was growing better. Olvie is alleged to have expressed his regret with much profanity and some obscenity in the presence of ladies and particularly to Mrs. Walenberg. The latter is the wife of P. Walenberg, a member of the executive board of the miners' union, and is a lady of respectability and refinement. Olvie, she states, referred to the president as a s- of a b- and hoped he would die.[51]

Chivalrous amenities were appreciated--even demanded--by women as well as men.[52] Not all women were happy, though, and everyone knew ways out. Fifty-six divorces were reported in the Press from July, 1899, through December, 1901. Many couples lived apart and wives left the district for months at a time. Separations were generally explained in acceptably genteel terms: vacations were for the benefit of the wife's health, and couples lived in different cities for the health of the family or for the children's education.[53] The exercise of these options hints that some workers' homes were not fully satisfying. It also may help to explain why traditional family roles received so much public allegiance, and why women were so strongly encouraged to support class goals without challenging their own roles.

The supposition that women were either good or bad, and the further assumption that working-class women were "good" and therefore preoccupied with home, family, and civic morality, shaped understanding of women's social power and had an important effect on labor politics. The WFM decided to organize Women's Auxiliaries in 1902 partly because it was moving to a policy of political action and it was "estimated that by organizing the women just about 200,000 votes will be added to the political strength of the organization."[54] Cripple Creek unionists had recognized women's political importance earlier, and announced that "the question of trusts, imperialism, free silver, and other political issues are of no consequence or importance whatever compared to the emancipation of women."[55] There was, however, more opportunism than conviction in this assertion, since it was intended to encourage women to oppose an anti-union politician who had also opposed suffrage. While attention to women's issues was often simply recognition of their political power, district labor was progressive to encourage women's participation in politics for any reason.

Suffrage brought women some recognition, but it was often given in genteel terms. It was assumed that women were less partisan than men and that special appeals were necessary to win their votes. Those appeals were based on neither feminist nor class goals, but on the supposed moral and home concerns of working-class women. Women were asked to support Democrats in 1900 because Republicans squandered education funds, and because women were "more intimate with the home and school life of the children than the husband."[56] Appeals to womanly virtue created political hostility toward prostitutes, probably the largest group of women wage earners in the district. This attitude diminished possibilities for the political success of organized labor, as exemplified in an important local election in 1899.

In 1899 the unions formed the Co-operative Party, and joined with the Populists to run a labor slate for county offices. Assuming that union strength guaranteed male support and that the women's vote must be won, organized labor made the only real campaign issue the suppression of gambling and prostitution. The "good civic housekeeping" argument of the national suffrage movement was adopted, and women were asked to prove their right to vote by opposing local vice. "The ladies have an opportunity to show that the right of suffrage has not been thrown away upon them--the opportunity to throw their influence for purity in politics."[57] Voters were reminded that "every gambler, every keeper of a bawdy house, every man in the Cripple Creek district who makes a living by violating the law, is working and fighting for either the democratic or republican candidates for county offices."[58] But purity was no vote grabber. The Co-operatives came in an abysmal third to the Democrats and the Republican-Silver Republican coalition, and for the next few years organized labor supported the Democrats.[59]

Neither nonunion power nor the class analysis developed by organized labor sufficiently explain the tactics adopted in the 1899 election campaign. A highly organized and class-conscious labor community projected political goals and tactics, not from class understandings, but from genteel concepts of home, family, and sex. Perhaps working-class women were not primarily concerned with prostitution; perhaps working-class men considered it necessary to their public and self-image to oppose prostitution, but did not really desire its elimination; perhaps everyone knew that no political party could end prostitution in any event. An unconflicted class analysis might have led to demands for legalized prostitution, but adherence to genteel morality meant that raising such an issue was both inconceivable and politically unwise. Nor were working-class women encouraged to formulate their own political demands, which might, for instance, have involved issues like the extension of sewer lines to working-class neighborhoods. It was clear, however, that class concerns were more likely to insure political success than were issues of social morality. When labor candidates concentrated on such measures as support of a state eight-hour law and raising mine owners' taxes, they won in Cripple Creek. Nor was the 1899 defeat a simple matter of old party allegiances. In 1903 organized labor elected the secretary of the District Trades Assembly to the office of county tax assessor on an independent ticket.[60]

Part of the difficulty was that few goals remained in Cripple Creek which were susceptible to local political solutions. Like an eight-hour day and a living wage, a secure home and women suffrage were important gains. But those achievements could protect neither labor nor women when union control was threatened in 1903. Socialism could not be won locally, and workers were prevented from extending union benefits even to the nearby smelter workers of Colorado City, who refined Cripple Creek ores, and for whom, in 1903, Cripple Creek miners risked all that they had achieved.

Local concerns were not at issue in the 1903 strike.[61] True to the WFM's commitment to industrial unionism, the strike was called to support the smelter workers, who toiled longer hours for less pay than the miners, and who were blacklisted when they attempted to form their own locals. The WFM struck Cripple Creek mines that shipped ore to smelters which had fired union laborers, hoping that this economic pressure would force the smelters to re-employ unionists.

Both miners and mine owners were fully class conscious, and both sides thought that they dealt from strength. The unions were well-organized, had ample treasuries, and controlled most public offices. But the Mine Owners' Association had important allies, including the Governor, Republican James Peabody. A Canon City banker, Peabody had helped organize his local Citizens' Alliance, an association of anti-union business people and professionals. Cripple Creek merchants organized a district Citizens' Alliance and cut off credit to strikers. The WFM quickly established four cooperative stores to distribute strike relief.

The strike was initially uneventful, but in September, 1903, local business petitioned Peabody for troops. With scant investigation, without talking to labor, and over the objections of local officials who denied any danger to civil order, Peabody sent in the militia. Military salaries were guaranteed by a mine owners' loan to the state. Led by Adjutant General Sherman Bell, who was superintendent of large Cripple Creek mining interests and who promised to "do up this damned anarchistic federation," the soldiers did little to preserve peace. They arrested unionists wholesale and held them without charge. Claiming as legal justification that there was _limited_ martial law in the district, the military defied _habeas corpus_ orders. Soldiers invaded the Teller County Court House, surrounded it with Gatling guns, and trained a cannon on it. Peabody declared full martial law in early December, after someone pulled spikes from train tracks and after an explosion in the Vindicator mine killed two men. Strikers were held for both acts, though the mine was under military guard and although there was strong evidence that an employers' detective had staged the train wreck and had warned the engineer to prevent its occurrence.

Employers instituted a work permit system in March, 1904, and denied employment to union men. The end came for the miners on June 6, when a train depot was blown up, killing fourteen scabs. Labor insisted that the explosion was a mine owners' plot to justify destruction of the unions. However, the charge was not investigated as local officials were deposed by mine owners and the Citizens' Alliance, who took over the legal apparatus of the county. (They gave the Sheriff a choice of resigning or being hanged.) The mob then destroyed union halls and stores, rounded up prominent unionists, and deported them to Kansas and New Mexico. The deportees who tried to return were beaten, re-deported, and threatened with death should they try again. The employers' slogan was "They Can't Come Back."

With the strike broken, all unions were suppressed. Union miners were blacklisted and merchants refused to employ any union help. All retail clerks were forced to surrender their union cards and all locals were required to withdraw from the District Trades Assembly. Washerwomen who had sympathized with the strikers were prohibited from working in the district, though some apparently eked out a precarious living.[62] Unions were never again permitted in the Cripple Creek district, and the class aid and communalism they had supported could continue only at considerable risk of discovery by the mine owners or the militia.

During and after the strike, women performed valuable service to the unions and to one another. Notions of feminine weakness and gentility were used as class weapons in publicizing the excessive force used against labor. When the Women's Auxiliary was invaded by soldiers, women and children beaten by mine owners' gunmen, and women separated from their husbands, the employers and the state were attacked for violating womanhood and destroying the home.[63] Women, however, could sometimes do things which men could not, and they were also praised for their strength and bravery during the strike. They crossed military lines without being imprisoned or shot; they and their children taunted scabs and soldiers, and otherwise harrassed them. The militia tried to stop the women, but did not jail them.

> Mrs. James Prenty and Mrs. Blixer, both prominent in the women's auxiliary . . . were in custody, though not under arrest, for about an hour today. They were charged with having indulged in insolent criticism and denunciation of the military. They were allowed to sit on the stairs leading to the bullpen for a while and were then taken before Provost Marshal McClelland, who gave them a lecture on the necessity of using caution in their public speech.[64]

After the deportations, organization and relief work fell to the women. They raised bail bonds, provided food for the incarcerated miners, and distributed strike relief. Margaret Hooten and Estella Nichols, both Auxiliary members, were arrested and told to stop the relief effort; after that the work went on in secret.[65]

Even before the brutal aftermath, the strike produced its heroine. Financial difficulties forced the Press to fold, and the only other pro-labor paper in the district, the Victor Record, agreed to publish WFM statements. In an attempt to silence the Record, the militia jailed its work force. Emma Langdon, a union linotypist, crawled in a back window, worked all night, and brought out the paper with the headline, "Somewhat Disfigured But Still In The Ring." For her action she became the first woman elected an honorary member of the WFM and was hailed as a "Colorado Heroine."[66]

Women joined the battle as allies and were among the casualties. They shared an analysis which explained their experience in class terms, and they still had the material and social support of the WFM and other unions.[67] But class support could not stop the destruction of unionism or its human toll.

Women watched helplessly as their husbands were deported and endured separation and poverty when the men were not allowed to return. Harriet Minister, the wife of a deported union man, told a newspaper reporter: "They sent my man away, and he will not come back, if he takes my advice, until things are quite different from what they are now. I make my living taking in washing. It is better than begging. One who has six mouths to feed has to work pretty hard."[68]

For some it was even worse. Emil Johnson, a deported member of the Altman miners' union, turned on the gas in his Denver rooming house and killed himself. The Denver papers reported that Johnson was driven to suicide by concern for his family. "Johnson's wife and children, at Altman, had been refused provisions because of an order issued by General Bell. When Johnson heard of this he was driven almost to the verge of madness to think his innocent family should be made to suffer so much on account of his insisting on his rights. He brooded over this, at times laboring under the hallucination that his family was starving. . . . The suicide was the result."[69]

Fred Minister and Emil Johnson were both WFM members. But in the polarized strike situation there was no neutral ground, and some nonunionists suffered as well. The small middle class was forced to take sides, and union sympathizers were punished along with the striking miners. W. H. Morgan, an assayer who supported the strikers, was among the first to be deported from the district. Frightened that he would be arrested and taken back to the military bullpen, and despondent about his family's welfare in his absence, Morgan also committed suicide. Several letters from his wife were found on his body.

> Willie was beaten badly by one of the soldiers last night because he would not tell where you were hiding. . . . Two or three of the neighboring women have been to see their husbands but have not been allowed to see them. Mrs. W. says her man was not even allowed to change his underwear, and he called to her that most of the men were bothered with vermin. . . .

> I saw General Bell tonight to let me get some groceries and he said he hoped Denver would soon be put under martial law so he could search for you. He said he would fix it so no union man could vote at the next election. He talked awful to me. . . . Please stay in hiding and do not let this horrible man and his soldiers get hold of you, for they will never let you get away. I hope to God this terrible thing will soon be settled in some way, so you can return to your home again. I do not see why innocent men should be made to suffer. You say you are discouraged. Brace up and write soon to GAY[70]

The Morgans, the Johnsons, and the Ministers were not alone in their anguish. However conflicted the lives of working-class women, those conflicts were less painful than their suffering as the unions were destroyed.

When class action became imperative, women left their homes and violated prescribed roles. The "good women" of Cripple Creek were good resisters. Emma Langdon, who believed that "women's natural sphere should be in the home and not in public life," nonetheless acted as a worker in the strike. "[T]hey are brothers. . . . We are both subjected to the same conditions. He is on strike today. I may be tomorrow. We both stand for the same cause--unionism."[71]

Langdon later wrote a history of the strike. Like many union women, she performed that work in addition to her household duties. "I have compiled the work, set the type, read the proofs, and made the pictures from which many of the illustrations are made, folded the pages and while getting out the work have taken care of my work as usual, doing my own sewing, baking, washing, and ironing and other work that falls to the lot of women. . . . I have worked at my trade sufficient to pay the greater part of the expenses of halftones and press work. I attended the trials of my union brothers and fulfilled my duties as secretary to orders and membership on committees."[72] Combining the roles of woman, worker, and class activist, Langdon became an organizer for the WFM and for the Socialist Party.

For Emma Langdon, as for the now anonymous stenographer, housekeeper, and miners' wives, class identity was real and important. Unions made a significant difference for many Cripple Creek women: they provided social and material aid, a community of class understanding, a place to go to escape household isolation. As significant as these benefits were, they were insufficient to the needs of women or of organized labor.

Industrial change not only produced class militance, but also separated production from the home and made wage work the province of men. To protect their homes and their women, unionists diluted their social programs and political action. It is not surprising that women and households did not become an integral part of class understanding; that analysis has begun to be formulated only recently as the economic role of the household has become more narrowly restricted to consumption, and as married women have moved in greater numbers into the paid work force. So long as family and productive roles were kept separate, men could be seen primarily as workers and women primarily as homemakers. It is only as the spheres have become less separate that their relationship has begun to receive serious analysis.

Nor is it surprising that the working-class women of Cripple Creek desired a stable home life and did not clamor for the drudgery of the work world. They gave primary allegiance to their class rather than to their sex because class organization, indirectly at least, achieved a great deal for them. But it could not overcome the loneliness of the isolated household, nor protect that household when corporate power crushed the unions.

Cripple Creek workers who developed collective means to confront the power of corporate capitalism accepted definitions of sexual sphere which undermined class action. True Womanhood belonged with laissez-faire capitalism if it belonged at all. By idealizing women's economic dependence on their husbands and men's economic responsibility for their families, True Womanhood and True Manhood made it more difficult for men to escape alienated work. If women were dependent on male wages, men were equally dependent on unpleasant jobs; they could not easily risk unemployment by individually challenging working conditions. The individualism implicit in concepts of manhood not only impeded collective action, but also meant that men could feel only solitary failure if they did not successfully provide for their families. Cripple Creek workers combated individualism by providing social explanations and solutions for the economic position of working-class men. But successful unionism paradoxically insured that the sex roles of an individualist age were not challenged.

The contradiction between class and gender existed partly because the class battle was not won; the home still served to absorb some of the tensions of the workplace. But idealization of the home endangered the class cause and left women with only escapist alternatives. If they did not accept their status as miners' wives, women could only leave town, commit suicide,or sue for divorce.

That women did not challenge their genteel roles is understandable. A comfortable home was not a real possibility for many working-class women, and without the local unions, women's lives would have been more difficult and uncertain. Nor is it easy to project a situation in which women might have demanded to enter the paid work force and risk their lives underground along with the men. Economic dependence was the root of sexual inequality within the working class, and it is difficult to imagine an alternative in a nineteenth-century mining town. But it is significant that the ability to provide for one's family was such an important measure of male success that the sexual ideologies which surrounded that measure were idealized rather than questioned.

If labor's understanding of industrial capitalism had been extended to encompass division of labor within the family and to embrace an historical rather than a "natural" understanding of sex roles, then women might have participated more fully in the formulation of class goals and policies. Had women been encouraged to formulate demands around their own needs, an anlysis which related class and gender inequalities might have begun to be formulated.[73]

But these things did not happen, and one reason that feminist demands were not met in Cripple Creek is that women did not raise them. The most significant feminist achievement in the district, suffrage, was inadequate when employers could depose elected officials. The absence of feminism in Cripple Creek was only partly the failure of the national women's movement, which in the 1890's paid inadequate attention to the needs of working-class women. The most important cause was the importation of unequal work relationships from the mines to the family households.

Although corporate capitalism made class needs more immediate and crucial than feminist goals, the two were inseparable. Unequal attention to either class or feminism created contradictions in both. Restricting its goals narrowly to suffrage, the national feminist movement sacrificed immigrant, black, and working-class women, and achieved only a partial victory. Accepting sexual spheres as "natural" and unchanging, Cripple Creek workers advocated conflicting programs and made the mistakes evident in the 1899 election campaign. Class cut across sex lines and sex cut across class lines; feminist and class goals had to be pursued together or each would succeed only partially.

A class understanding that was not strained by sexual inequality would not have guaranteed the end of household isolation in Cripple Creek. Like wage labor, the household had an economic base which could only be changed through collective action. But a perfect union of class and gender would have meant that labor confronted capitalist power untorn by internal contradictions. As it was, working women remained subordinate within the unions, prostitutes were attacked politically, and married women could enter the union hall only after the dinner dishes were done and the children tucked in. Like Emma Langdon's list of tasks, class and gender were combined in Cripple Creek, but never successfully merged.

Working-class women and men might have had more satisfactory relationships with one another had they challenged their traditional roles and fought class battles as equals. Adherence to the genteel household meant that they were separate even in defeat. The women remained at home with the children while the men were deported. It would have been small comfort, but an equal and unified working class would have been deported together. That small comfort would have meant a great deal to Harriet and Fred Minister, to Emil and Katie Johnson, to Gay and Will Morgan.

NOTES

Research for this article was sponsored by the American Association of University Women, through the Sara McAnulty Nevins-Myra Bigelow Wilson and Martha Hoag Clifford Endowed Fellowships. Some of the ideas developed in conversations with Marilyn Young, Ann Markusen, and Robert Conrow. I am grateful to Milton Cantor for thoughtful editing and to Carol Pearson and Robert Sklar for their helpful comments. Above all, I want to thank John Graham, whose critical and supportive help more than demonstrated the value of shared work.

[1] Eighth Biennial Report of the Bureau of Labor Statistics of the State of Colorado, 1901-1902 (Denver: The Smith-Brooks Printing Co., 1902), pp. 66-82. Separate locals also existed for barbers; bricklayers and masons; musicians; printers; painters and paper hangers; retail clerks; sheet metal, tin, iron, and cornice workers; tailors; typographers; newspaper writers; stage employees; electrical trainmen; miners; stationary engineers; and mill workers. Two Federal Labor Unions and two Junior Federal Labor Unions included all other workers.

[2] Charles Howard Shinn, Mining Camps: A Study in American Frontier Government (1884; rpt. New York: Harper and Row, 1965), pp. 280-83.

[3] For accounts of the 1894 strike, see Jenson, Heritage of Conflict, pp. 38-53; Benjamin M. Rastall, The Labor History of the Cripple Creek District (Madison: University of Wisconsin, 1908); and Emma Langdon, The Cripple Creek Strike (1903-4-5; rpt. New York: Arno Press, 1969), pp. 34-44.

[4] For samples of unionists' political opinions see Seventh Biennial Report of the Bureau of Labor Statistics of the State of Colorado, 1899-1900 (Denver: The Smith-Brooks Printing Co., 1900), pp. 102-19; and Official Proceedings of the Tenth Annual Convention, Western Federation of Miners (Denver: Colorado Chronicle, 1902), pp. 106-07.

[5] Report of the State Bureau of Mines, Colorado, for the Years 1903-4 (Denver: The Smith-Brooks Publishing Co., 1905), pp. 20-21, gives these figures for district miners: 1896, 3,575; 1897, 5,386; 1898, 5,764; 1899, 7,925; 1900, 7,920; 1901, 6,484; 1902, 5,940; 1903, 5,200; 1904, 5,667. Cripple Creek "boosters" claimed a population of 50,000 at the turn of the century, but the 1900 census for Teller County enumerated only 29,002. Robert Guilford Taylor, Cripple Creek (Bloomington: Indiana University, 1966), p. 205, contains probably the most accurate population estimates for the area. Taylor places the 1900 population at 32,000.

[6] In 1900 there were 12,144 men to 9,968 women over twenty-one in the district, and earlier the sex ratio was even more unbalanced. Twelfth Census of the United States, Population, Part II, Vol. II. (Washington: United States Census Office, 1901), pp. 177, 212-13.

[7] Interview with Mrs. Clara Stiverson, age 81, a resident of the district from 1899-1925, conducted July 29, 1975, in Golden, Colorado.

Figures for women's occupations were obtained from the Cripple Creek-Victor Mining District Directory (Cripple Creek: The Directory Publishing Co., 1895), and Cripple Creek District Directory, 1902-3 (no city: The Gazetteer Publishing Co., 1902). The 1895 Directory lists 353 women, of whom 117 (33 percent) have no listed occupation; the 1902 Directory lists 1,521, 703 (46 percent) with no occupation. From those who listed occupations, the following figures were computed. Dressmaker or seamstress: 11 percent (1895, 1902); rooming, boarding house, or restaurant proprietor: 29 percent (1895), 21 percent (1902); other proprietor: 6 percent (1895), 3 percent (1902); clerk: 8 percent (1895), 12 percent (1902); stenographer: 3 percent (1895, 1902); cook: 3 percent (1895, 1902); laundress or laundry worker: 12 percent (1895), 9 percent (1902); waitress: 8 percent (1895), 7 percent (1902); housekeeper, maid, or domestic: 7 percent (1902); schoolteacher: 6 percent (1902); telephone or telegraph operator: 4 percent (1902); other: 15 percent (1895), 12 percent (1902). The 1902 figures do not add to 100 percent due to rounding. The actual numbers are certainly underestimates; there are both boarding-house keepers and professionals who advertise in the local press, but are not listed in the 1902 Directory. Prostitutes, of course, are not listed. However, comparisons with newspapers and other sources suggest that the proportions approximate women's occupational participation, and that they accurately reflect jobs available for women.

8 1901-02 Bureau of Labor Statistics Report, p. 47.

9 Ibid., pp. 55-56.

10 Mable Barbee Lee, Cripple Creek Days (Garden City, N.Y.: Doubleday, 1958), p. 169.

11 Barbara Welter, "The Cult of True Womanhood: 1820-1860," American Quarterly (Summer, 1966), pp. 151-74.

12 Miners' Magazine (Jan. 1904), p. 15.

13 This term is widespread in local newspapers, and appears with some frequency as a household relationship in the 1900 Manuscript Census for Teller County.

14 In 1895 the district held fifty-three saloons; by 1902 there were 106. District Directory, 1895, pp. 448-50 and District Directory, 1902-3, pp. 607-10.

15 "Labor Notes," Cripple Creek Daily Press, June 22, 1902, p. 2.

[16]"Business Interests Demands Strong Unions," Press, Aug. 14, 1901, p. 4. See also "Cripple Creek News Notes," Colorado Springs Gazette, Sept. 15, 1901, p. 2.

[17]Lists of delegates to party conventions from the city to the congressional levels, 1900-03, indicate that roughly one-fifth of all delegates were women. The figures range from no women at one Republican gathering to one-third at some Democratic conventions. Women were most often elected city clerks or treasurers; almost always the county school superintendent was female. Delegate lists were printed in the Cripple Creek Daily Press.

[18]Quote in Charles Hartzell, History of Colorado During the Turbulent Reign of "Davis the First" (Denver: C. J. Kelly, 1894), p. 14. See also Billie Barnes Jensen, "The Woman Suffrage Movement in Colorado," M.A. Thesis, University of Colorado, 1959. The Cripple Creek district ratified woman suffrage in 1893 by a vote of 548 to 254; Altman, then the labor stronghold, favored suffrage 92 to 27. "Official Vote of El Paso County," Colorado Springs Weekly Gazette, Nov. 16, 1893, p. 5.

[19]"Labor Notes," Daily Press, Oct. 5, 1902, p. 2.

[20]"Business Prosperity Depends on Labor," Press, April 23, 1901, p. 4.

[21]The Report of the State Bureau of Mines, Colorado, 1903-04 (Denver: The Smith-Brooks Printing Co., 1905), p. 25, gives the following state figures for hard rock mining accidents: 1896: 103 fatal, 107 nonfatal; 1897: 110 fatal, 169 nonfatal; 1898: 108 fatal, 184 nonfatal; 1899: 103 fatal, 481 nonfatal; 1900: 107 fatal, 526 nonfatal; 1901: 121 fatal, 633 nonfatal; 1902: 82 fatal, 561 nonfatal; 1903: 67 fatal, 494 nonfatal; 1904: 101 fatal, 539 nonfatal. Reports of accidents in the Cripple Creek Daily Press indicate that a significant number were not reported. Although these were seemingly minor, a bruised hand from falling rock meant the loss of several days' work.

[22]Daily Press, Nov. 9, 1902, p. 4.

[23]Official Proceedings of the Eleventh Annual Convention Western Federation of Miners (Denver: Western Newspaper Union, 1903), pp. 86-88. "Good Work," Daily Press, Dec. 13, 1899, p. 1.

[24]"Our Fallen Chief," Press, March 10, 1903, p. 1 and "Solemn Ceremony at Henry King Funeral," Press, March 11, 1903, p. 1.

[25]Miners' Magazine, Sept. 17, 1903, p. 7.

[26]1901-02 Bureau of Labor Statistics Report, p. 88. James T. Smith, Deputy Labor Commissioner, supplied the 70 percent estimate; WFM membership figures suggest this may be an inflated figure. In 1903, when the district's population was some 30,000, the District Trades and Labor Assembly reported 5,300 members. Since this was after the 1903-04 strike had begun, and many union miners had left the district, a 50 to 65 percent estimate is probably reasonable. See "The Situation in Colorado," Miners' Magazine, Dec. 24, 1903, p. 8.

[27]The Press, which published during 1899-1903, was purchased by thirty-four of the district's then thirty-five unions. Besides national, state, and local news, the Press covered union activities and reported gossip and daily social life for all the towns. It furnishes a wealth of material for understanding Cripple Creek working-class culture, and reflects in its news coverage, advertising, and editorials the juxtaposition of conflicting understandings of class and gender. While I have footnoted several examples for my conclusions in this article, there are literally hundreds of items in the Press which document important beliefs and associations. A nearly complete run of the Press is available at the Western Historical Collections, University of Colorado, Boulder, and a microfilm copy is available at the Wisconsin State Historical Society, Madison.

[28]See for example "Engineers' Union--Musicale and Entertainment," Press, Oct. 27, 1901, p. 2; "Greatest Labor Day Celebration That Was Ever Held in Cripple Creek," Press, Sept. 3, 1901, p. 1; "Cooks and Waiters Entertain," Press, Feb. 2, 1903, p. 1; and "Open Meeting at Victor," Miners' Magazine, April 4, 1904, pp. 11-12.

[29]"Dramatic Performance by Ladies of Victor Ladies Auxiliary No. 2," Miners' Magazine, April 14, 1904, p. 11 ; and "The Woman's Auxiliary," Miners' Magazine, April 14, 1904, pp. 12-13.

[30]See for example the following articles: "Waiters Win Out," Dec. 12, 1899, p. 1; "Dry Goods Stores Close at 6," Dec. 30, 1899, p. 1; "Must Do Work at Home," May 13, 1902, p. 1; "Trades Assembly Demands Union Made Cigars," Nov. 11, 1902, p. 14. A typical unfair notice read: "The following eating and boarding houses have been declared unfair by Cooks' and Waiters' Union No. 24, and the Trades Assembly of Cripple Creek. . . . It is charged that the ladies do not treat their employees right," Aug. 12, 1900, p. 1. All articles from the Daily Press.

[31]"How Women Can Help," Daily Press, Dec. 21, 1902, p. 4.

[32]"Address to the Toilers," Press, March 16, 1902, p. 2. See also "Labor Notes," Press, June 8, 1902, p. 2; "Labor Notes," Press, March 29, 1903, p. 11; and "Women's Work in Label Agitation," Press, June 29, 1902, p. 2.

[33]"Union Men Do Not Wish Library From Andrew Carnegie," Press, April 8, 1902, p. 1.

[34]"Labor Notes," Press, Dec. 21, 1902, p. 3.

[35]Ibid., April 20, 1902, p. 2.

[36]"Hotel and Restaurant Employees in Session," Press, May 31, 1901, pp. 1, 5.

[37]"Women for Policemen," Press, Dec. 25, 1901, p. 4.

[38]Twelfth Census of the United States, Manufactures, Part II, Vol. VIII (Washington: United States Census Office, 1902), 67.

[39]"Oppose Barela Amendment," Press, Aug. 5, 1902, p. 1; "Shipping Laundries Declared to be Unfair," Press, Aug. 19, 1902, p. 1.

[40]"Waitresses Walked Out of National," Press, Aug. 5, 1902, p. 1.

[41]"Greatest Labor Day Celebration That Was Ever Held in Cripple Creek," Press, Sept. 3, 1901, p. 1.

[42]"Convention Notes," Press, June 17, 1900, p. 4.

[43]Leland Feitz, Myers Avenue A Quick History of Cripple Creek's Red-Light District (Denver: The Golden Bell Press, 1967), p. 18.

[44]"Regulate It," Press, Aug. 24, 1899, p. 1.

[45]"Abate the Nuisance," Press, Feb. 4, 1903, p. 4.

[46]"A Strike in Dance Hall," Press, April 23, 1902, p. 8; "Labor Notes," Press, April 27, 1902, p. 2.

[47]Miners' Magazine, Feb. 4, 1904, p. 5.

[48]Augusta Prescott, "The Kind of a Woman a Workingman Should Marry," Press, Feb. 15, 1903, p. 12.

[49]"Women and the Home," Press, Jan. 30, 1901, p. 1.

[50]See for example: "Miss Jennie Wolf Winner Daily Press Voting Contest," Press, Nov. 9, 1901, p. 1.

[51]Press, Sept. 12, 1901, p. 5.

[52]See Anna Kirk, "Anna Kirk's Experience on a Car," Press, Nov. 10, 1901, p. 11.

[53]See "News of the District," Press, passim. Examples are: "Mrs. Warren Wise of Denver is here on a visit to her husband. He is a pumpman on the Legal Tender." ("Goldfield," Press, April 25, 1901, p. 5.) "Mrs. Jerry Kelly, wife of the local secretary of the Miners' Union, has returned with her children from Canon City, where she went to seek improved health." ("Victor Brevities," Press, March 24, 1901, p. 8.)

[54]"Miners Will Have Women's Auxiliary," Press, June 3, 1902, p. 1.

[55]"Bonynge and Women Suffrage," Press, Oct. 13, 1900, p. 4.

[56]"What Will Women Do?" Press, March 21, 1900, p. 4.

[57]"To the Ladies," Press, Oct. 8, 1899, p. 4.

[58]Press, Oct. 21, 1899, p. 2.

[59]"The Official Count," Press, Nov. 6, 1899, p. 1.

[60]See for instance: "Candidates for the Legislature," Press, Nov. 2, 1902, pp. 1, 5; Langdon, The Cripple Creek Strike, pp. 160-61.

[61]For further information on the 1903-04 strike, see the only full-length treatment of the strike, Benjamin M. Rastall, The Labor History of the Cripple Creek District (Madison: University of Wisconsin Press, 1908). Accounts also may be found in Melvyn Dubofsky, We Shall Be All (New York: Quadrangle, 1969), pp. 49-55 and Vernon Jenson, Heritage of Conflict, pp. 118-59. Leslie Doyle Spell and Hazel M. Spell, Forgotten Men of Cripple Creek (Denver: Big Mountain Press, 1959), pp. 128-44, contains an eyewitness account of the Citizens' Alliance attack on the Victor Union Hall. See also Langdon, The Cripple Creek Strike, for a contemporary history.

[62]"The Situation in Colorado," Miners' Magazine, June 16, 1904, p. 10; June 23, 1904, p. 11; June 30, 1904, p. 10.

[63]See for example: "The Situation in Colorado," Miners' Magazine, January 28, 1904, pp. 8-12; July 7, 1904, pp. 8-11; July 14, 1904, pp. 8-11; Langdon, The Cripple Creek Strike, pp. 224-25.

[64]"The Situation in Colorado," Miners' Magazine, June 16, 1904, p. 9.

[65]Ibid., June 23, 1904, pp. 11-12.

[66]Ida Crouch-Hazlett, "A Colorado Heroine," Miners' Magazine, March 30, 1904, pp. 11-12.

[67]See for example: "The Colorado Labor Convention," Miners' Magazine, Jan. 21, 1904, pp. 3-5; Mrs. M. R. Stephenson, "A Woman Surveys the Field," ibid., May 26, 1904, p. 11, and Mrs. Annie Ballard, "Some Pertinent Questions," ibid., July 7, 1904, p. 11. Relief reports, Official Proceedings of the Twelfth Annual Convention, Western Federation of Miners (Denver: Western Newspaper Union, 1904), pp. 89-107 and Official Proceedings of the Thirteenth Annual Convention (Denver: The Reed Publishing Co., 1905), pp. 160-86.

[68]"The Situation in Colorado," Miners' Magazine, Nov. 3, 1904, p. 7.

[69]Langdon, The Cripple Creek Strike, pp. 357-58.

[70]"The Situation in Colorado," Miners' Magazine, July 14, 1904, p. 9. Morgan worked primarily as an assayer, but was also president and general manager of the Grouse Mountain Gold Mining Company, which was probably one of the many small mining companies that leased their properties or had small-scale operations in the district. He was a strong union sympathizer, and probably depended on assaying for his livelihood. In one of her letters, Gay Morgan said that she would try to send her husband some money. "We have only $31 left. You took $10 when you left and we have used the rest."

[71]Langdon, The Cripple Creek Strike, pp. 410, 244.

[72]Ibid., p. 249.

[73]For an example of a situation in which this did occur, see the film Salt of the Earth, which is based on a strike of the International

Union of Mine, Mill, and Smelter Workers in Bayard, New Mexico. There the women began by asking that the union include in its demands running water and nonwood stores for the company housing furnished Chicano miners. Ultimately, the women took over picket duty when a court injunction prevented the union from picketing, and they demanded an equal voice in union decisions.

VIRGINIA YANS-MCLAUGHLIN

A FLEXIBLE TRADITION: SOUTH ITALIAN IMMIGRANTS CONFRONT A NEW WORK EXPERIENCE

What happens when peasants immigrate to modernizing societies? What impact does immigration have upon internal family dynamics and upon the family's relationship to the rest of society? How, in particular, do traditional families relate to these new work experiences they find in modernizing societies? These are bold, expansive questions. The subjects who will help us to answer them–south Italians who immigrated to Buffalo and upstate New York at the turn of the twentieth century–are more humble, but they play a significant role nevertheless.

A variety of approaches and methodologies are available to historians seeking to examine family change. Conventional sociology, for example, long viewed the family as an end product of socio-economic forces and as an institution which functions to maintain the existing social order. Thus, by definition, clear dichotomies would exist between folk and modern families. Applied to immigration history, this meant that families who crossed the ocean experienced enormous stress and frequent disorganization as they made their transition from peasant village to industrial nation. At the very least, this transition remolded the traditional family into a mobile, detached, nuclear form whose roles, relationships and values "fit" the demands of a more "rational" industrial economy.[1] One of the clearest expressions of this position, the one we are concerned with here, suggests that "almost as a matter of definition we associate the factory system" and other industrial work patterns "with the decline of the family and social anonmity."[2]

Because this approach seemed so inadequate an explanation of evidence I found concerning Italian-American families, I turned to cultural anthropologists interested in cultural and historical change. Instead of defining the family as an institution functioning to maintain social equilibrium, some see it as a flexible organization using alternatives within the social order, as well as traditional forms and ways of relating, to suit its needs in a given context. Some anthropologists emphasize that tradition–familial or otherwise–plays a significant part in social change, that it satisfies some basic human need, even

Professor Yans-McLaughlin is in the history department of the City College of New York.

in modernizing societies. Social change, they argue, does not necessarily imply a systematic fit of institutions, but adaptations of one institution to another. The relationship between modernity and tradition is, then, not dichotomous but dialectical.[3] Using this approach, I was able to understand not only how the family was transformed by modern society, but how the traditional family transformed itself.

We can also learn something from anthropologists about the modernizing societies which play host to these families. These societies do not have the ruthless and homogenous invincibility they are often assumed to possess as they move toward economic rationality. A range of alternatives exists here too; all kinds of adaptations, reorganizations and adjustments are possible.[4]

To understand familial change among Buffalo Italians or any other group, past traditions, historical context and particular situations–which, to be sure, exclude some possibilities and include others–require examination. This is not a simple linear view which argues that past experiences determine future behavior, that because south Italian families behaved in one way in Italy, we can understand why they behaved in similar ways in America. Nor is it a static functional explanation that sees culture and social structure as mere "reflexes" or "mirror images" of one another.[5] We are examining a dynamic process, a give and take, between new conditions and old social forms.

This theoretical perspective facilitates historical understanding of immigrant Italian family behavior, especially the work experiences of these families. Persisting traditional modes and their relatively smooth transition from folk to modern society cannot be well understood without it. This became clearer when I examined evidence for Buffalo Italians who endured all the economic and social deprivations usually associated with lower-class family instability. Most of the men, for example, were low-paid, unskilled seasonal workers, unemployed six or seven months out of twelve. They experienced little vertical or horizontal occupational mobility. These Italians found themselves residentially and socially segregated. They were denied political power. The last large immigrant group to enter the city, they became the unfortunate target of nativist stereotypes and discriminatory practices. Black Americans, who did not begin significant Buffalo settlement until relatively late, did not assume this burden from them until the 1920s and 1930s.

Despite these pressures, all the usual indices indicate remarkable family cohesion. Italians had low desertion rates, low illegitimacy rates, few broken families and they requested welfare aid infrequently. Other evidence points to the persistence of traditional values, especially among the first generation.[6]

Struggling to fill their economic needs, these families entered a new work world in order to meet them. Buffalo's peculiar occupational structure and job discrimination limited their options, but they perceived alternatives for themselves. They chose work styles and occupational modes which permitted minimal strain upon accustomed family arrangements. By constructing and interpreting their own social reality in terms of past experiences, they managed to adapt themselves to a new social context with relative ease.

If past experiences help explain Italian family behavior, we must journey backwards in time to nineteenth-century southern Italy. Our goal is to examine family work experiences there to achieve more empathetic understanding of how these immigrants perceived their new situation.

In southern Italy, clear connections existed between an individual's economic role and his or her family role. But strong cultural traditions frequently intervened, so any statement positing equivalence between the two would be hazardous. Consider the father first. He presided over his family and maintained its livelihood by his labors. Because he rarely owned or rented land enough to support his family, he generally hired himself out as a day laborer. Seasonal unemployment or underemployment—usual facts of peasant life—and the daily and sometimes weekly absences from home required by his work search did not seriously undermine his authority. Cultural traditions supported it strongly.[7]

But he had a competitor. The Italian family has been described as "father-dominated, but mother-centered." Some argue that matriarchal traditions without any immediate economic basis help explain the mother's relatively powerful position, but her economic importance to the family played some part.[8] Wifely functions were extremely important in this peasant economy; it would be unwise to undervalue them by projecting backwards in time present day market values which define "work" in terms of wages received for services performed outside the home. The fact of the matter is, however, that Italian peasants themselves attributed greater prestige and importance to male contributions to the family economy. A wife's clearly defined family and household responsibilities included obedience to her husband, family loyalty, thrift and, most important, childbearing. She oversaw family resources, prepared and purchased food, mended and made clothing and ordered children in household tasks. Peasants looked disdainfully at wives who left the home to work, and few did so unless poverty required it. Sicilians held very strictly to this rule. But an expected part of a wife's year-round labors could include joining the family in crop harvesting. Seasonal migrations also drew entire peasant families away from their villages, but girls and women rarely worked in non-agricultural occupations because few factory towns existed in the *Mezzogiorno*.[9] Women who left home to labor generally worked as members of a family unit earning a portion of the family wage. They did not regard themselves (nor were they regarded) as independent wage earners. Women did not derive their status within the family from their position as wage earners, nor did the wages they earn challenge the husband's position as chief breadwinner. His frequent absences from home suggest that even her household powers—always subject to his will—accrued to her by default. A Sicilian study reports, for example, that the father's "authority in his house is final, and there is no official redress to his commands."[10]

Although the peasants loved their children and treated them well, they too had responsibilities. As Covello observes, "the economic basis of married life was reflected in the evaluation of children primarily as an economic asset."[11]

Their economic value as work hands shortened the period of childhood. Despite government efforts to curb child labor, in 1911 almost one-half of all children aged ten to fifteen were gainfully employed. Peasants completely ignored child labor legislation applying to agricultural work.[12]

Returning to the American scene, we can see how these family relationships fared in a new context. Buffalo Italians, most of them Sicilians, who journeyed to northwestern New York's food processing factories and the fields surrounding them are the basis for our discussion. Although some assume that the factory's impersonality, industrial discipline and work routines prevented possibilities for continuity, these Italians had a very different experience.

Early in this century rapidly growing fruit and vegetable processing companies throughout the nation recruited employees from country areas and immigrant quarters in nearby cities. These perishable products required many hands working long hours during the busy June to October season. Although precise figures are not available, contemporary reports establish that Buffalo Italians commonly journeyed all over New York State to join other *paesani* engaged in this labor.[13]

Substantial Italian colonies existed in all large cities near the canneries, but upstate manufacturers still reached far west to Buffalo for their labor forces. Buffalo's peculiar economic structure partly explains their choice. Other nearby cities such as Rochester, Syracuse, Utica and Troy had enough homework and light industries to absorb female and child workers, but Buffalo had different labor demands. Heavy industry and transportation, its most rapidly expanding sectors, presented greatest demands for male labor. Although industrial work opportunities for unskilled women and children existed and other ethnic groups took them, Italians generally did not. Husbands and fathers feared the liberalizing influence contact with American workers might have.[14]

While south Italians seemed to have a special preference for this type of work, manufacturers found it difficult to employ American-born workers, who preferred regular employment of fathers to seasonal employment of the whole family. And each year, more and more Polish women, who had once labored in the canneries, expressed their preference for year-round domestic work in Buffalo's private homes. Because Italian family mores concerning women working in another man's home discouraged it, this option presented no realistic alternative for unskilled women. Cannery work, on the other hand, presented the possibility of extending community controls upon the family into the factory, and this explains why it seemed more respectable to Italians than other occupations did. The canneries provided a unique work opportunity where laboring and living spaces existed in close proximity. In the living quarters, ever present parents and kin kept a watchful eye on all community members. That children remained directly under parental control was only one asset. Adults could work assured that their young ones were safer than they would have been left home alone or playing in the streets.[15]

So come summer, south Italian women and children became migrant laborers and left their Buffalo homes—sometimes without fathers and husbands, who sought summer construction jobs in the city or wherever else they could find them. At first glance such an arrangement seems surprising. South Italian mores required a husband to guard his wife and daughters jealously.

But was going to the cannery really such a break with tradition? Seasonal migrations had not been an unusual recourse for peasant families who followed harvests throughout the *Mezzogiorno*. And temporary family dissolution was no strange experience either. Immediate need had justified its risks before, when many job-seeking fathers journeyed throughout the Italian south or across the sea, not to escape family responsibilities, but to fulfill them. Once in America, the same kind of thinking motivated risks and adjustments. And though many fathers remained in Buffalo, some could find employment with their families, as factory mechanics or harvesters.[16]

Removal of the family to the country had another aspect reminiscent of the Italian situation: the profitable use of children could continue without fear of reprisal for violation of factory codes or child labor laws. Legislation limiting the number of hours women could work was also difficult to enforce. The canners, for their part, tended to ignore statutes limiting weekly work hours for women and for children under sixteen on the grounds that their trade's special conditions exempted them. And although processing shed labor was industrial in character, not until 1913 did unsuccessfully enforced factory legislation codes attempt to control these establishments. In the meantime canners worked their employees for a thirteen and one-half hour day or more. Because the season lasted from mid-June to mid-October, parents also violated and avoided compulsory school attendance laws. In the country, school authorities could be easily circumvented.[17] The work situation, then, made it possible for the immigrant family to maximize its profits over a very short period.

Cannery wages varied according to speed and skill because employers paid by the piece for both shed and field work. In a typical cannery, no one earned less than $1.00 a day; most foreign-born men and women earned from $1.25 to $1.75. Family income sometimes exceeded what a male head of household alone could earn in the city in railroad or industrial work,[18] and child labor laws prevented younger children from incrementing family income in the city. Wage supplements lowered family living costs for the season. In many cases, canners provided housing, fruits and vegetables *gratis* or at a nominal fee. Italians laboring in New York canneries could get along on as little as $.50 to $1.00 a week. "Very thrifty" families, the Immigration Commission reported, saved "considerable sums" of money every summer, enough to get through a winter of probable unemployment of fathers. For some who could not find work, it presented the only opportunity to earn a living.[19] Foremost among the economic assets of working in the canneries, however, was the fact that Italians could earn a family wage. An Italian social worker described the immigrants' practical conception of family economics in a manner recalling the south Italian situation: "dal numero delle braccia di una famiglia dipende la prosperita della medesima . . . " or "a family's wealth depends upon the number of hands it has."[20] In short, because these immigrant families both perceived and seized this opportunity to earn a supplementary cash income, they found a way to minimize the tensions which their low urban living standard could have produced.

A work situation which minimized family strains because it permitted mother and child to labor together constituted reason enough for Italians to become migrant laborers. Even in cases where mother and children went alone to the canneries, they stayed away from home for only short periods, and apparently immigrants did not perceive their absence as a serious challenge to the family's well being. One gets the impression that they may have viewed it as a chance for wife and children to return to a familiar agricultural environment.[21] Recall also that in Italy the mother supervised household tasks and production independently of her husband. Several observers noted that south Italians especially tended to organize cannery work along family lines. The labor–weeding, harvesting and preparation for preserving–was light enough for women and children to engage in and, a government investigation reported, "since the women and children can work efficiently, the laborers, particularly the south Italians make the family the working unit. This means that the whole family engages in farm labor or berry picking and the earnings all go into the family fund."[22]

The canners' mode of recruiting south Italians reflected their recognition that priority must be given to their family needs. The companies usually brought migrant workers from the city in family groups. An Albion company, which employed about three hundred Buffalo Italians, instructed its *padrone* to "secure families whenever possible." "It is found," the Immigration Commission stated, "that when the family is employed as a whole on the farm all are more contented and more apt to remain for the season than when part remain in the city and part go to the country."[23]

Those who defended recruitment of families for migrant labor and use of child employees claimed that the foreign parents would not come to the rural areas without their children. Some canners stated that they actually did not wish the children to work there, but the parents insisted.[24] Eager adults worked their children in the fields, even when employing farmers, who feared the young ones might damage crops, opposed it.[25]

The general division of work among family members at the canneries shows further adaptations of south Italian practices. Close integration of economic and family roles as well as sex role differentiation continued. Fathers either remained in the city or worked apart from women and children, so disciplinary activity and work direction stayed in the mother's hands. If a woman had evening work, the father sometimes cared for the family's young, but an elder daughter or some older woman more typically assumed these responsibilities. The entire family together might work the bean, pea and corn fields in weeding and harvesting processes, just as it had in Italy. In grape-growing areas, all tended vines and picked the fruit.[26] Until child labor legislation was enforced in the canneries, children who once assisted in domestic chores in Italy now helped their mothers prepare crops for canning or snipped and husked vegetables while the women packaged and labeled them.[27]

Comparison of Italian and native-born working-class conceptions of the child's role and the use each made of their children points to some useful distinctions. While ninety percent of American-born children, many of them local residents, came to the canneries as independent workers, all foreign youngsters worked and traveled with their parents. This suggests the foreign parents' unwillingness to relinquish economic and familial control over their offspring.[28] A "working investigator" disguised as a laborer noted that where "American" help was used in snipping or husking, work rarely commenced before seven in the morning. Where foreigners–that is, Italians–labored, work began at four or four-thirty A.M. during the rush season. Where Americans were employed, children seldom did other work during the day, but Italian parents often roused their children at dawn to snip beans until daylight, when they went to the fields to pick beans. At night they went to the sheds and worked again. The investigator claimed that "Cases in which American mothers force their children to work are, however, the exception and not the rule . . . . " Even when American children did work, she claimed, they eagerly awaited going to the "sheds where there are many other children and where they can earn a little spending money."[29]

Parental motivations in forcing the children to work are clear. A social worker at Albion's Olney Canning Company observed that strong economic motives drove the Buffalo Italians working there. The Italian people, she said, considered their "children as so much money value." The social workers had great difficulties manipulating intractable parents who failed to accept that the children belonged in cannery schools, not in factory sheds. Throughout the entire summer, the social worker claimed, she and her colleagues frequently failed to keep children under ten–the legal working age for labor of this kind–out of the sheds and off the harvest fields. "You understand," she reported, "the disposition of the mothers . . . was to make money out of the children."[30] An Italian government agent who visited the canneries at about the same time concurred. "The canners," she said, "like the cheap labor of the Italians and their children, and the parents for their part go with pleasure because it gives them a way to earn off their children." Italian adults, she noted, were the hardest drivers. Lamenting the "precocious old age" of Italian youth, she observed that little ones "old enough to hold a bean are made to work by their parents." While softer American parents permitted their young ones to leave work, the *Mezzogiorno's* children struggled on.[31]

Shed labor organization, to the extent that parents determined it, indicated juvenile subservience to adults among all groups. Whether they wanted to or not–and these children, like most, had a special proclivity for not wanting to–young ones followed parental orders. Adults, especially the Italians, definitely maintained the upper hand in delegating work tasks.[32] An Italian-born social worker who visited canneries where Buffalo Italians labored elaborated further. The mothers were "hard on the children," she commented:

> Although they love their children, they do not love them in the right way sometimes. They think they must bring in something and that is

> the Italian idea. They like to have children because they help to lift the burden.
>
> Q. The more children the more work?
>
> A. Yes.

Noting that children in Italy were expected to work, she continued that she saw nothing wrong in this because it prevented them from becoming lazy.[33] Like the migrant laborers she commented upon, this woman also interpreted the situation in terms of her own cultural attitudes.

The style of parental discipline of Italians and Americans varied, the former being particularly relentless, the latter more indulgent. The Italian investigator who asked children in a cornhusking shed why they continued to work so long received the reply, "We'd get licked."[34] Testimony given the Factory Investigating Commission relating to the situation at a cannery where many Buffalo Italians worked speaks for itself:

> The parents were constantly urging the children to work. One little boy, aged 11, was throwing some bean snippings at another little fellow and had stopped work a second. His father hit him brutally across the face and set him again to work. Everywhere parents were forcing children to work .... If they did not work they would shake them and sometimes hit them depending on the parent. This is not true of all parents, but the majority of the Italian parents were forcing their children to work. Most of the American parents were not forcing them to work. Take for instance, the woman, Mrs. McGaffie, the woman I have mentioned here. She had a little girl aged 10 in the factory. She did not use such stringent methods of forcing the children to work as the Italians did, but she kept the child constantly at work for 6 or 7 hours a day. But she was not so brutal about it as the Italians were, and she did let the child go home to meals, and stopped when she pleaded and pleaded with her mother that she was tired.[35]

A Factory Commission inspector's report concerning a cannery where many Buffalo Italians worked tells of a twelve-year-old Italian child, little Jack, whose family woke him at three in the morning. He snipped beans from 4:30 A.M. to 10:00 P.M. with only a few minutes off for supper. After this long day's work, his only comment to the investigator was "My fingers is broke." That day he went to sleep at midnight and woke up at three in the morning. He was, he said, "awful tired," but his mother made him work. Finding his hands swollen, he tried to leave work several times. His mother also constantly scolded his ten-year-old sister, who could "hardly keep her eyes open," to continue her work. Jack earned $1.40 that day. He could keep none of his wages. But, he said, labor like this was nothing compared to the pea season when his mother and sister returned home at one and two in the morning and "They was so sick they fell down and vomited."[36]

The Factory Investigating Commission neatly summarized differences between Italian and American attitudes toward work and child rearing. For foreigners the shed was "distinctly a place for work." But for the American child the shed was more like a "playground where they play at work till they get tired and then quit."[37] The disposition of the funds earned by Italians and Americans also tells us something about their differing cultural attitudes toward the child's family role. American children, the Commission's report noted, worked to earn spending money, to buy a bike, a toy or shoes. But Italian and Polish parents required their children to submit their wages to the family budget.[38] Indeed, since parents, not children, received the wage, it is highly unlikely that the latter ever saw their earnings. An Italian government reporter's comments put it well: "In general the child is considered as a tool and appendix of the mother, and it is she who is paid, not them."[39] As in Italy, the child did not achieve even this symbolic recognition as a wage earner.

Because of this transference of family discipline into the factory, canners had few problems obtaining the highest possible output from children. As one factory investigator put it, the "severe manner of the mothers rules the house and family in largely the same manner as she controls the family in the shed or field."[40] Goaded by sheer economic necessity and in some cases the need to earn enough income for the whole year during the summer, such parents were far more effective taskmasters than the factory owners could have been. Indeed, the chief factory inspector testified that so far as the canners were concerned, children remained free to come and go: the parents, he claimed, especially the foreigners, forced the children to work. Similarly, Italian parents, not the manufacturers, sent their children running away when the canning inspector, representative of the public interest in their young ones, arrived.[41] The canners felt no compulsion to keep records of the children's working hours for, as one scholar of child labor put it, "They knew that the parents would keep their offspring at work, just as tenement parents did, in order to increase the family 'piece work pay'." Or, aptly put by the Commission, "The canners supply the materials to work on, the parents do the driving."[42]

At least one canner permitted a school on his premises for children under working age, but Italian mothers resisted allowing their children to attend. In fact, the women began what was described as "practically a riot . . . [though] not as bad as that," when a plant superintendent, attempting to comply with labor codes by keeping children under ten out of the sheds, was beseiged by angry Italian women, one of whom bit his finger "right through."[43] The Commission did not fully clarify the circumstances of this disturbance, but all witnesses agreed that many mothers, wishing their children to work rather than attend school, participated–not just the single female assailant. And clearly this "riot" resulted from the factory supervisor's interference into what the parents considered their exclusive domain.

Most observers did not attribute the harshness of this situation to parental hard-heartedness, but to low family wages. The Factory Investigating Commission noted, for example:

> Nor are the parents alone to blame. Their parental love is often dulled by the hard grind of necessity. Manifestly a canner who pays low wages

> to parents cannot argue convincingly that the children should not be permitted to snip beans to increase the meager earnings of the family. If children should not be permitted to work, the cannery owner would still be under the necessity of obtaining the labor of their parents and unquestionably would soon have to pay the parents approximately what is now the total family income.[44]

Apparently, American working-class parents could better afford to be "much more careful in caring for their children" than less fortunate foreigners who had little choice but to conceive of their children as economic assets and use them accordingly.[45]

Italian parents avoided, ignored or protested against state intervention in family affairs just as they had in the Old World. Although the goals of parents and canning manufacturers differed, the effective results were the same. Usually, the two formed a cooperative partnership to avoid child labor and truancy regulations. It is easy to understand the employers' motivations. Manufacturers generally perceived that so long as they made no attempt to undermine Italian family organization—take, for example, their recruitment policies—they could expect to receive optimum output from every family member. Moreover, the use of child labor usually worked to their advantage, so why—except for an occasional public demonstration of good will, such as allowing the North American Civic League to establish immigrant schools on their premises—attempt to challenge it? Immigrant parents had economic needs as well, but they also rejected American legal endorsement of community interest in the disposition and care of their children. Legal definitions of the child as a separate personality with rights more important than his family obligations made no sense to them, simply because such individualistic notions conflicted with more familistic south Italian ones. The former peasants saw the child as a member of the family group in which no outside influence had a right to interfere. What one scholar of child labor wrote of nineteenth-century American parents, who also brought a traditional culture with them to the factory, applies equally to Italians of this later period. "The average New Yorker," he wrote, "was as opposed to interference in the family as he was to state meddling in the market place."[46]

Because Polish, Italian and an earlier generation of American-born parents exhibited similar attitudes to child labor, one could argue that similarities in class and economic position, not cultural tradition, explain their behavior. And indeed our evidence suggests the beginnings of a lower-class subculture cutting across ethnic lines. But I do not see the cultural and class explanations as mutually exclusive. The choice of explanations, it seems to me, depends upon what one wishes to explain. In this instance I am less concerned with proving that most peasant cultures adapted uniformly to industrial society than I am with the adaptation of one traditional culture to that society. Others will have to assume the larger task. In the meantime I would hazard the guess that original distinctions among traditional cultures moving into American society played some role in differentiating each group's response.

Additional evidence points to the persistence of traditional Italian cultural attitudes despite the new work situation. Extremely poor housing conditions, which certainly encouraged the deterioration of sexual controls and "moral degeneration," failed to undermine Italian morale.[47] Housing arrangements generally allowed little or no separation of the sexes. Facilities varied according to the cannery. Tenements, barracks and separate houses were each used in different places. Not uncommonly, entire families, regardless of their size, resided in one room. Worse, several families might be housed together, separated only by a canvas. Adults of both sexes slept, dressed and washed in the same area. Often, young adolescent children, male and female, used the same sleeping quarters. Boarders frequently intruded into a family's already limited privacy. In one colony, unmarried men and women of an undetermined nationality lived in the same barracks with only a broken partition separating them.[48] In spite of these circumstances, community pressures prevailed in the Italian quarters, where the people kept "good humor."[49] Other ethnic groups living under similar conditions apparently did not exercise the same degree of control. For example, Buffalo's Health Commissioner, himself of Polish origin, traced a number of illegitimate births in the Polish community to these circumstances. Despite his knowledge of Italian living conditions both in Little Italy and at the canneries, he made no mention of Italian illegitimacy.[50]

The work situation itself also challenged traditional moral concepts. The manager of a Geneva, New York, cannery which employed Buffalo and Syracuse south Italians noted that despite the close association of the sexes both in the dormitories and at work, moral conditions remained "excellent."[51] But there is no doubt that factory organization tested Italian female morality. A social worker, disguised as a laborer, wrote in her diary of "fresh" bosses and timekeepers at the canneries, each of whom had power over the women. "The situation," she said, "is much like that of a department store where the floor walker has a lot of girls under him, receiving low wages and all more or less at his mercy." Male cannery superintendents apparently did not consider it beneath their dignity to offer the young women an opportunity to earn extra money, and the fact that much cannery work took place at night made the situation more threatening for the women.[52] Another social worker had actually been drawn by the women into their protective community. They warned that the time-keeper was "fresh" and that she had best avoid him. Protection extended outside the immediate Italian community and the basic family group when an Italian girl warned her that "one must be careful not to get fresh with the Italian boys, because they are dangerous."[53] Sexual identification apparently triumphed over ethnic loyalty.

An additional circumstance reinforcing community feeling among the Italians, despite the shifting nature of the migrant population, was that the work force contained other sometimes hostile and competitive groups—country people living near the canneries, Poles and Syrians. As one commentator has put it, "confined in a single rural factory [they] were unlikely to form much of a bond with another."[54] Considerable conflict existed between the Syrians and Poles, who gladly accepted low salaries, and the Italian women, who wished to strike for higher pay. As for the Americans, they would side with the American employer rather than join the "Eye-talians" in a strike.[55] Those strikes which occurred were attributed to the Italians; they provide testimony to their sense of solidarity, especially where bread and butter issues were concerned.[56] The closely-knit Italian women frequently joined together, hoarding work under their skirts and chairs in an effort to save piece work for themselves. In this manner they earned the resentment of less united, but equally discontented women.[57] The same sense of solidarity prevailed between an Italian foreman and female workers when the foreman gave the "Buffalo tables" more than their share of the work.[58]

Italian immigrants sought other occupational arrangements in American cities which permitted easy adaptation of traditional practices. For example, they found homework, another semi-traditional occupation, attractive. Like the canneries it provided a transitional step for recently arrived peasant groups attempting to cushion the full leap into industrial society. A New York State Factory Investigating Commission report on three hundred New York City families emphasized the peculiar preference Italians seemed to have for this work style:

> The large proportion of Italians engaged in homework is significant of the fact that their home traditions lend themselves with peculiar readiness to the homework system. The Germans accept homework as a trade and adapt themselves to specific phases of it at which they may become expert. They do not do finishing, but do fine custom tailoring, making vests complete or fine hand-made button holes .... The Irish and Americans adopt homework only as a last resort. They do it only when they are poverty stricken and driven to it by necessity. The Italians come usually from rural districts and know little about factory work and organized industry. The men become laborers and fall into seasonal trades where the wages are small and irregular and must be supplemented. As a rule they have strong home associations, they expect their girls to marry young, and they do not like them to go out into factories. Accustomed in Italy to depend upon the labor of their children in the fields, they expect them in this country to yield a financial return at the earliest possible moment and are, therefore, ready to have them adopt homework, a system that lends itself to the exploitation of women and children.[59]

In both homework and cannery industries the family continued as the basic productive unit and the organization of work, if not its substance, closely resembled Italian practices. The mother's role as arbiter of household tasks and disciplinarian of children was reinforced by her economic position as work manager, be it artificial flower-making, sewing or canning. She maintained her inferior position to her husband because she had not become the chief breadwinner. As in Italy, these families viewed income earned by wives and children who ventured to migrant labor camps or worked at home as a supplement to the father's wages, not a replacement. In neither case did the Italian male relinquish his support obligation, nor did he forfeit his control and authority. And women and children who worked at the canneries or at home did not drift as separate individuals into the labor market. They were recruited, lived and worked as family members under the close scrutiny of other Italian-Americans, many of whom were associates, *paesani* and kin. Social controls, including those regarding traditional sexual attitudes, operated as effectively in the canning factory as they did in the neighborhood. The visible and public nature of work and living conditions, continually emphasized throughout the Factory Commission's investigations, also partially explains why these controls functioned so effectively. Finally, like the household, the migrant labor camp permitted close integration of living and working quarters and therefore did not separate the family's productive and child-rearing capacities. A close association of economic and family functions similar to what existed in Italy prevailed in both situations. Italians found such arrangements agreeable because they brought income in but minimized sex role conflict.

Other studies suggest that these kinds of adaptations were not peculiar. They also show that employers seeking high output at cheap prices had a flexibility of their own. New Jersey silk-weaving firms, for example, frequently hired whole Italian families, probably because these employers, like cannery owners, recognized the family's potential as a well disciplined work unit. Smelser's study of the English Industrial Revolution observes similar phenomena in the recently mechanized weaving industry, and studies of modern Japan emphasize how its economic institutions operate under traditional political and personal concepts. Finally, a study of south Italian factory laborers in Pittsburgh shows the same transference of kin control occurring in an urban situation. In this instance, Italians did permit women and children to enter industrial occupations outside the home because proximity to the ethnic neighborhood and the presence of other Italians in the work force provided props for expected behavior.[60]

One could argue that both the canneries and homework industries were semi-traditional occupations, and that immigrant adjustment to them does not challenge customary notions concerning the relationship between the family and industrialization. But such an argument does not explain the immigrants' behavior in more typical urban settings and it obscures some important distinctions about them and the industrial society they helped to create. We tend to simplify what the creation of such a society means. Geertz reminds us that "economic development can take place within a context of general social and economic conservatism in which essentially traditional values and social structures are so adapted as to be capable of integration with more efficient economic practices."[61]

Sometimes with their employers' cooperation and sometimes without it, Italian immigrants transformed canning factories into communities where Old World social attitudes and behavior could continue and where kinship ties operated to maintain them. The way in which these families fit themselves into their new context confirms that despite requirements for efficiency and rationality, modern economic institutions were quite capable of incorporating such traditional needs.

There was a lot of room in industrial America for immigrants wishing to avoid a head-on collision with a new way of life. But immigrant preference for fringe occupations shows how tradition influenced both their perception and their use of work options. Without taking their perceptions into account, we cannot understand them *or* their history.

FOOTNOTES

1. Oscar Handlin, *The Uprooted* (New York: Grosset and Dunlap, 1951) is the most famous example of an immigration historian adopting the folk society to modern society dichotomy. The most noted exponent of the more sophisticated functional view is Talcott Parsons. His work on the family is discussed in Morris Zelditch, "Cross-cultural Analyses of Family Structure" in Harold F. Christensen, ed., *Handbook of Marriage and the Family* (Chicago: Rand McNally and Co., 1964), 492 ff.

2. Neil Smelser, *Social Change in the Industrial Revolution* (Chicago: University of Chicago Press, 1959), 193.

3. I am indebted to Lloyd I. Rudolph and Susanne Hoeber Rudolph, *The Modernity of Tradition* (Chicago: University of Chicago Press, 1967) for this approach. See especially their Introduction. Although these authors are concerned with Indian politics, they adopt the flexible approach used by many anthropologists.

4. Clifford Geertz, *Peddlers and Princes: Social and Economic Modernization in Two Indonesian Towns* (Chicago: University of Chicago Press, 1963), 145 takes this position.
5. Clifford Geertz, "Ritual and Social Change," *American Anthropologist*, Vol. LIX, No. 1 (Feb., 1957), 32-54 is a critique of such a position.

6. Virginia Yans McLaughlin, "Like the Fingers of the Hand: The Family and Community Life of First-Generation Italian-Americans in Buffalo, New York, 1890-1930," (unpublished Ph.D. dissertation, State University of New York at Buffalo, 1970) contains evidence supporting these statements.

7. Leonard W. Moss and Walter H. Thomson, "The South Italian Family: Literature and Observation," *Human Organization*, Vol. XVIII (Spring, 1959), 40 and 38 argue that the male's high status could not have derived entirely from his economic role because he retained it even if unemployed. They argue, therefore, that the dominant cultural tradition tended to support the male. See also Constance Cronin, *The Sting of Change: Sicilians in Sicily and Australia* (Chicago: University of Chicago Press, 1970), 104.

8. Moss and Thomson, "The South Italian Family," 38 and Leonard Covello, "The Social Background of the Italo-American School Child: A Study in Southern Italian Family Mores and Their Effect on the School Situation in Italy and America," (unpublished Ph.D. dissertation, New York University, 1944), 377. I am indebted to Louise A. Tilly in her comments on an earlier version of this paper (Anglo-American Conference on Comparative Labor History, April, 1973) for the distinction made here between "market" and "peasant" economic values.

9. As Tilly, Ibid., wisely points out, because conditions varied considerably throughout Italy, generalizations concerning women's work roles are hazardous. But figures from the 1901 census do support my generalization that southern women rarely labored outside

the home in non-agricultural occupations. The figures for women 9 years of age and over engaged in work outside the home (including domestic servants) are: Abruzzi and Molise–11 percent; Basilicata–11 percent; Calabria–30 percent; Campania–19 percent; Sicily–15 percent. Figures are computed from Italy, *Annuario Statistico, 1905-1907* (Rome: Istituo Centrale di Statistithe 1907), 111 ff. And as Tilly, Op. Cit. correctly pointed out, these are gross figures making no allowance for urban and rural distinctions. I suspect that the figures for women working outside the home would be lower if peasants alone were considered. I would also like to suggest that even if this small percentage of women did work outside the home, we cannot assume that their behavior was socially acceptable.

Seasonal migrations are discussed in Robert E. Dickinson, *The Population Problem of Southern Italy* (Syracuse: Syracuse University Press, 1955), 67-74; Italy, *Atti della giunta per la Inchiesta Agraria e sulli Condizione della Classe Agricola*, Vol. XIII, Tome II, Fas. IV (Rome: Forzani, Typografi del Senato, 1885), 20 ff.; Robert Foerster, *The Italian Immigration of Our Times* (Cambridge: Harvard University Press, 1919), 532-33 discusses family migrations; see also Sydney Sonnino, *La Sicilia nel 1876*, Libro Secondo, *I Contadini* (Florence: Tipografia di G. Barbera, 1877), 84, 98, 117. Louise Odencrantz, *Italian Women in Industry: A Study of Conditions in New York City* (New York: Russell Sage Foundation, 1919), 27 ff. and U.S. Senate, *Reports of the Immigration Commission*, Vol. IV, 61st Congress, 3rd Sess., *Emigration Conditions in Europe* (Washington, D.C.: Government Printing Office, 1910), p. 160 comment on the lack of industry in the Italian south.

10. Moss and Thomson, "The South Italian Family," 38; Cronin, *The Sting of Change*, 104.

11. Covello, "The Italo-American School Child," 357, 359.

12. Ibid., 365.

13. Amy Bernardy, "L'emigrazione delle donne," *Bollettino dell'Emigrazione*, No. 1 (1909), 69, 85-7; U.S. Senate, *Reports of the Immigration Commission*, Vol. XXII, 61st Congress, 2nd Session, *Immigrants in Industry*, part 24, *Recent Immigrants in Agriculture*, Vol. II, 500; New York State, *Second Report of the Factory Investigating Commission* (hereafter cited as *FIC*), Vol. II (Albany: J.B. Lyon Co., 1913), 792.

14. For a discussion of these points see Virginia Yans-McLaughlin, "Patterns of Work and Family Organization: Buffalo's Italians," *The Journal of Interdisciplinary History*, Vol. II (Autumn, 1971), 299-314.

15. U.S. Senate, *Recent Immigrants in Agriculture*, Vol. II, p. 491 indicates the decreasing popularity of canning work among Poles and American-born workers. Ibid., p. 497 indicates that even Italian men looking for work considered canning work more respectable for themselves than railroad work. The importance immigrants assigned to control of their young is indicated in Consumer's League of New York, *Behind the Scenes at the Canneries* (New York: Consumer's League of New York, 1930), 48; and in *FIC*, Vol. II, 1297.

16. Maria Maddalena De'Rossi, Segretariato femmenile per la tutela delle donne e dei fanciulli emigranti, Relazione, "Le donne ed i fanciulli italiani a Buffalo e ad Albion" (Rome: Tip. Forense, 1913), 18.

17. The labor law was amended a number of times regarding the number of hours women and children could legally work in factories. The New York State Factory Investigating Commission was particularly interested in including the canneries under the factory acts and eventually succeeded in doing so. See Jeremy Felt, *Hostages of Fortune: Child Labor Reform in New York State* (Syracuse: Syracuse University Press, 1965), 25,

170; Bernardy, L'emigrazione delle donne," 66; *FIC*, Vol. I, 125; editorial by Virtus, "La schiavitu delle donne e dei fanciulli," Buffalo, *La Fiaccola*, July 28, 1910, 1.

18. U.S. Senate, *Recent Immigrants in Agriculture*, Vol. II, 508, 494.

19. U.S. Senate, *Recent Immigrants in Agriculture*, Vol. II, 494, 496, 150; see also Virtus, "La schiavitu," *La Fiaccola*, July 28, 1910, 1 and Buffalo, *Il Corriere Italiano*, Dec. 2, 1905, 1.

20. De' Rossi, "Le donne ed i fanciulli," 18.

21. Bernardy, "L'emigrazione delle donne," 88.

22. U.S. Senate, *Recent Immigrants in Agriculture*, Vol. II, 491.

23. Ibid., 507, 492. The agent who went into the Italian quarter claimed he always received more applications than he needed. Important abuses normally associated with the padrone system, however, especially that recruits pay the padrone for securing employment, do not seem to have been serious. By 1911, for example, many farmers did their own contracting, wages had become better established, and workers could find positions on their own without using agents as go-betweens. See Ibid., 493.

24. *FIC*, Vol. I, 141; see also testimony of the plant supervisor where Buffalo Italians were employed, Ibid., Vol. III, 423.

25. Luciano J. Iorizzo, "Italian Immigrants and the Impact of the Padrone System" (unpublished Ph.D. dissertation, Syracuse University, 1966), 190.

26. "Looking Over the Canneries," Buffalo *Express*, Aug. 16, 1912, 7; Consumer's League of New York, *Behind the Scenes at the Canneries*, 47; *FIC*, Vol. II, 954; U.S. Senate, *Recent Immigrants in Agriculture*, Vol. II, 509.

27. George Mangold, *Migratory Child Workers* (New York: National Child Labor Committee, Pub. No. 354; 1929), 4; U.S. Senate, *Recent Immigrants in Agriculture*, Vol. II, p. 509; *FIC*, Vol. II, 775.

28. *FIC*, Vol. II, 802.

29. *FIC*, Vol. I, 135-38.

30. Testimony of Jennie Bowen, Dec. 10, 1912, *FIC*, Vol. IV, 1933.

31. Bernardy, "L'emigrazione delle donne," 67, 62-4.

32. Testimony of Mary Chamberlain, social worker disguised as laborer, *FIC*, Vol. III, 1013.

33. Testimony of Madeline De' Rossi, social worker, North American Civic League for Immigrants, Dec. 10, 1912, in *FIC*, Vol. IV, 1945.

34. Bernardy, "L'emigrazione delle donne," 67.

35. Testimony of Mary Chamberlain, taken from the diary she kept when working as a disguised laborer at the cannery, *FIC*, Vol. II, 1007.

36. *FIC* Vol. II, 785.

37. Ibid., 781, 786.

38. Ibid., 786, 789.

39. Bernardy, "L'emigrazione delle donne," 67.

40. *FIC*, Vol. II, 1296.

41. Ibid., 949, 775.

42. Felt, *Child Labor Reform*, 174; *FIC*, Vol. I, 166.

43. De'Rossi, "Le donne ed i fanciulli," 19-21; testimony of Jennie Bowen, Dec. 10, 1912, *FIC*, Vol. IV, 1916-23; testimony of Robert Mulree, Superintendent of Olney Canning Co., Aug. 15, 1912, *FIC*, Vol. II, 423-24; see also testimony of Miss De'Rossi, Dec. 10, 1912, Ibid., Vol. IV, 1943.

44. *FIC*, Vol. I, 166.

45. Ibid., Vol. II, 781.

46. Felt, *Child Labor Reform*, 9.

47. Bernardy, "L'emigrazione delle donne," 88.

48. *FIC*, Vol. II, 884-87; Virtus, "La schiavitu," 1.

49. Bernardy, "L'emigrazione delle donne," 88.

50. *FIC*, Vol. II, 887.

51. U.S. Senate, *Recent Immigrants in Agriculture*, Vol. II, 502.

52. Testimony of Mary Chamberlain, Nov. 26, 1912, *FIC*, Vol. III, 10014.

53. Ibid., 1016.

54. Felt, *Child Labor Reform*, 170.

55. Consumer's League of New York, *Behind the Scenes at the Canneries*, 44; *FIC*, Vol. I, 167.

56. *FIC*, Vol. II, 872.

57. Testimony of Mary Chamberlain, *FIC*, Vol. II, 1016.

58. Consumer's League of New York, *Behind the Scenes at the Canneries*, 45.

59. *FIC*, Vol. II, Appendix IV, "Manufacturing in the Tenements," 684-85.

60. Foerster, *The Italian Immigration of Our Times*, 346, discusses the New Jersey situation; Smelser, *Social Change in the Industrial Revolution*, 182 ff.; Geertz, *Peddlers and Princes*, p. 144 mentions a Japanese study by James G. Abbegglen, *The Japanese Factory: Aspects of Its Social Organization* (Glencoe, Ill.: Free Press, 1958); George H. Huganir, "The Hosiery Looper in the Twentieth Century: A Study in Family Occupational Processes and Adaptation to Factory and Community Change, 1900-1950" (unpublished Ph.D. dissertation, University of Pennsylvania, 1958) *passim* discusses Pittsburgh Italians.

61. Geertz, *Peddlers and Princes*, 144.

NEW IMMIGRANT WOMEN AT WORK: ITALIANS AND JEWS IN NEW YORK CITY, 1880-1905

by Thomas Kessner and Betty Boyd Caroli

The concurrent surges in both feminist history and the new urban history have produced divergent streams with few scholars in one area incorporating methodology, materials or findings from the other. Women's histories have generally directed their attention to middle-class reformers and professionals while scholars of the urban past focus on "anonymous Americans" to illuminate the lives of laborers and other overlooked individuals. Pointedly, however, attempts to study the nation's history from the "bottom up" have concerned themselves mostly with men.

New York offers a particularly compelling setting for investigating women's work. The largest and richest of all American cities, it led in the industrial transformation that propelled the country's economy to prosperity and consequently offered women new employment opportunities. Early in the nation's history, Alexander Hamilton and other advocates of an urban-industrial America observed the manufacturing economies utilize their female populations more effectively by drawing them out of the house and into the factory. By the end of the nineteenth century, Hamilton's vision of large numbers of employed women had become a reaility in many urban areas.

In 1880 New York City reported 11,339 industries employing almost 72,000 women. Tobacco and textiles, among the most swiftly growing businesses, accounted for almost half of the female work force. Across the East River, neighboring Brooklyn was expanding at an even faster pace than Manhattan. Its manufacturing concerns numbered over 5,200 and employed more than 7,000 women. Brooklyn's female work force was diversified over a broader range of occupations in such industries as the cord, twine, boot, hat and textile factories which skirted the residential sections.[1]

A heterogeneous labor force, including Italians and Russian Jews, assisted New York and Brooklyn in their economic progress. From the early days of the republic, New York's busy port had witnessed the arrival of workers from various parts of the globe and many of these immigrant men and women settled in the prospering city to stake out new lives. By 1880 more than half of Manhattan's workers claimed foreign birthplaces and 45 percent of Brooklyn's laborers were not native-born. In the last two decades of the nineteenth century southern and eastern Europeans formed an increasingly larger part of this influx so that by 1900 Greater New York included over 145,000 Italians and 178,000 Russians.[2]

Several questions arise concerning the economic roles of Italian and Jewish immigrant women in the American metropolis. How did women from these two groups react to an urban environment and its economic imperatives? Did

---

THOMAS KESSNER and BETTY BOYD CAROLI teach History at Kingsborough Community College, in New York City.

The Journal of Ethnic Studies 5:4

they leave the home for the factory? If they did, what occupations did they enter? How did their female offspring fare in the city economy, bearing the twin burdens of being foreign and female in an economy not fully comfortable with either? Did ethnicity, which recent studies indicate was an economic determinant of significant effect, play a role in the choice of women's work?

Published data, available in the Federal Census for 1880, provide a general picture of working women from several ethnic groups in New York, Brooklyn and 48 other cities. This material indicates variations along ethnic lines in choice of occupations. Irish-born and native-American women show the largest percentages in domestic service while German _frauen_ apparently preferred factory positions.[3] Unfortunately these data do not distinguish Jewish and Italian women into separate categories but absorb them under "all other female workers."

In order to describe the economic roles of Italian and Jewish women in New York City, the manuscript schedules of the 1880 federal census were utilized to provide a sample of immigrant families with information on ethnic, occupational and other characteristics.[4] No federal census of New York's population is available with such information in later periods. However, the State of New York periodically conducted its own census and the hand-recorded schedules of the 1905 survey provided a second sample. Comparisons of occupational distributions can thus be made between New York's Italian and Jewish women over the period, 1880-1905.

Of the 450 Italian households examined for 1880, only 30 reported wives working outside the home. This small number supports few conclusions beyond the point of their scarcity, but a glance at the occupations reported shows most of the women at the very bottom of the status ladder (See Table 1). Nearly half worked as unskilled ragpickers and common laborers with most of the rest involved in the production of textiles, food and leather goods. Only three Italian wives, of all the households sampled, claimed white-collar employment.

Twenty-five years later the 1029 Italian families that constituted the 1905 sample showed a total of 59 wives employed outside the home. With about 6 percent claiming employment in both samples, one might conclude that the generation between 1880 and 1905 brought little change in the economic lives of Italian women, were it not that these workers exhibit a discernibly altered occupational distribution. By 1905 few wives toiled at the fringes of the urban economy in ragpicking and common labor. They were found instead in skilled and semiskilled jobs in tailoring shops and textile factories. In spite of this progress out of the unskilled categories, one might conclude from the small number of employed married women that they left family support to their husbands.

This conclusion would be wrong. Despite the fact that the census data seem to support such a position, one that differs sharply from impressionistic and contemporaneous reports, these findings are weakened by the fact that the census did not gather occupation information on "homework," thereby ignoring the single most important source of employment for married Italian women. As a recently settled _signora_ told an investigator of industrial conditions, "Italians are different from American women. They don't like to work in

TABLE 1

OCCUPATIONAL DISTRIBUTION FOR ITALIAN WIVES AND HUSBANDS, NEW YORK CITY, 1880–1905

	1880		1905	
Occupational Group*	Husbands	Wives	Husbands	Wives
Upper white collar[a]	2.0%	3.3%	2.3%	0.0%
Lower white collar[b]	24.9%	6.7%	17.8%	10.2%
Skilled blue-collar[c]	13.1%	20.0%	21.8%	39.0%
Semiskilled blue-collar[d]	6.9%	23.3%	16.3%	30.5%
Unskilled blue-collar[e]	53.1%	46.7%	41.9%	20.3%
Number	450	30	1015	59
Total Households Sampled	456		1029	

*A discussion of the classification system used in this study can be found in Stephan Thernstrom, The Other Bostonians, 289-302. Important material on such classification is contained in Alba M. Edwards, "A Social Economic Grouping of the Gainful Workers of the United States," Journal of the American Statistical Association, XXVII (1933), 377-87; and Comparative Occupational Statistics for the United States, 1870–1940 (Washington, 1943), 87-89. Michael B. Katz elaborates on some of the weaknesses of occupational scales in "Occupational Classifications in History," Journal of Interdisciplinary History, III (Summer 1972), 63-88. More recently three scholars associated with the Philadelphia Social History Project, Bruce Laurie, Theodore Hershberg and George Alter, in "Immigrants and Industry: The Philadelphia Experience, 1850–1880," Journal of Social History, IX (Winter 1975), 219–67, question the validity of such scaling because of the fluidity of status within occupations over time. Their concern, however, is with an earlier period than is covered in this essay and they admit that the status of specific occupations underwent far less change as we approach the twentieth century. Donald Trieman disputes the idea that variance within occupations prevents the construction of a hierarchical scaling system in "The Validity of the 'Standard International Prestige Scale' for Historical Data," Paper delivered at the Conference on International Comparisons of Social Mobility in Past Societies, Princeton, New Jersey, June 1972. Clyde Griffin's "Comment" on this paper at the same conference should also be consulted.

[a]This occupational group includes such categories as Professionals, and Major Proprietors, Managers and Officials.

[b]Includes Clerks and Salespersons, Semiprofessionals, Petty Proprietors, Managers and Officials.

[c]Skilled who were not self-employed.

[d]Semiskilled and service workers.

[e]Unskilled and menial service workers.

Source: Sample data from Federal Census of Population, 1880, New York and Kings Counties; and New York State Census of Population, 1905, New York and King Counties.

factories and the men don't want them to do it. They must take the work home, especially if they are married."[5] Aside from the fact that such employment satisifed her husband's demands, it suited the Italian wife's schedule. She could work at home after picking up her bundle at the shop, planning her day around the household chores. Moreover, Italian women had familiarity with homework in the mezzogiorno where they had embroidered tableclothes, knotted fringes and constructed military uniforms around their kitchen tables.[6]

In New York, the garment trades and artificial flower work drew most of the Italian homeworkers. The clothing industry relied heavily on hand labor, especially for "finishing" garments which was generally accomplished at very low rates in lower East Side tenements. "Of the home finishers, in New York at least," Robert Foerster wrote, "the Italian women have been about seven in eight of all workers, earing 50 to 125 dollars a year." To an exploiting manufacturer they were "as cheap as children and a little better." By 1902 one investigator observed that Italian women monopolized the felling and finishing of garments: "Whenever [finishers] exist in large numbers we may be sure that they are Italians."[7]

Italian women also dominated the artificial flower industry which produced ornaments for the millinery trade. This field resisted mechanization because its processes required careful handcrafting. In this primitively developed trade, homework flourished. One Italian family, typical of many, consisted of a grandmother living with a couple and their four children, aged four, three, two years and one month. The mother and grandmother could not leave the house to work and it was, of course, illegal for the young children to do so. Nonetheless, all except the father and the two youngest babies made artificial flowers. The three-year-old worked on petals, her older sister, still too young for school, separated stems and dipped them into paste while the two women placed the petals on the stems. One hour's work for the four produced a gross of flowers and these 144 pieces earned them ten cents. A 12-hour day brought this team one dollar and twenty cents; a good week, seven dollars.[8]

Total earnings of Italian women engaged in homework on either textiles or flowers may appearl small, even insignificant, until set alongside total income for the entire household. By the early years of the twentieth century the average southern Italian family in New York reported an annual income of 688 dollars but only one-third of these households lived on the earnings of one worker. The majority of Italian families depended on their wives and children, working in factories or at home, to supplement the wages of the household head.[9]

As soon as they were old enough, Italian daughters left homework for the factories. Indeed, they took full-time jobs almost as often as their brothers, a parallel not repeated in the work records of Italian wives and husbands. In 1880 thirty wives and 450 husbands reported full-time jobs outside the home. Among their offspring, 110 of the sons and 78 of the daughters worked.

Although they took jobs outside the home more often than their mothers, Italian daughters did not enter all sectors of the city's economy. Not one young woman from the 1880 sample claimed professional status. About half of their number reported working as ragpickers, shoeshiners and unskilled laborers.

TABLE 2

OCCUPATIONAL DISTRIBUTION FOR ITALIAN OFFSPRING, BY SEX, NEW YORK CITY, 1880 AND 1905

	1880		1905	
Occupational Group	Males	Females	Males	Females
Upper white-collar	0%	0%	1.3%	0%
Lower white-collar	17.3%	12.8%	13.4%	8.8%
Skilled blue-collar	17.3%	20.5%	31.4%	45.1%
Semiskilled blue-collar	14.5%	21.8%	22.8%	35.8%
Unskilled blue-collar	50.9%	44.9%	31.2%	10.3%
Number	110	78	382	204
Total households sampled	456		1029	

Source: Sample data from Federal Census of Population, 1880, New York and Kings Counties; New York State Census of Population, 1905, New York and Kings Counties.

While jobs requiring skills and language facility went to groups with better connections and more urban experience, Italian girls, like their mothers, settled for the bottom rungs on the occupational ladder.

In flocking to the unskilled categories Italian women had the company of Italian males who show a similar occupational distribution. Male household heads, partly because they were older, reported more professionals and semiprofessionals than did either their male or female offspring. But all three groups, whether household heads, sons or daughters, reported about half of their number at unskilled labor. In the total picture, occupational distribution of male offspring falls midway between that of their fathers and their sisters. About one-quarter of the household heads claimed low white-collar status while 17 percent of the sons and 13 percent of the daughters did so. For combined skilled and semiskilled categories, the figures are 20 percent for the fathers, 31 percent for the sons and 42 percent for the daughters.

In the generation between 1880 and 1905, female offspring increased their hold on skilled and semiskilled jobs. The later sample indicates that four out of every five young women working reported such employment. This gain was registered by a corresponding escape from the unskilled categories where, by 1905, only one in ten still labored. Italian girls had still not penetrated the top professional sectors. Indeed their percentages in lower white-collar jobs actually diminished, but their rise out of the lowest paid categories marks a change unequalled by either their fathers or their brothers. In 1905, a full 42 percent of household heads and 31 percent of male offspring still filled unskilled jobs. As positions in the candy, cigar and clothing industries, which had been virtually closed to Italians in 1880, opened up by 1905, it was the young women who benefited most.

The girls reflected the effects of a system which encouraged them to cut schooling short. Thus, they did not show large numbers in the white-collar occupations. But they did learn skills from their mothers. Both sons and daughters felt pressures to keep formal education at a minimum but families with white-collar ambitions expected girls to sacrifice in favor of their brothers. Mary Van Kleeck, secretary of the Committee on Women's Work, explained: "It is by no means unusual to find girls... leaving school to go to work in order to give their brothers a chance to have a better education. One Italian girl, now earning ten dollars a week in busy season as a rose maker, left school... six years ago at the age of 13."[10] She worked sometimes until four and five in the morning to help send an older brother to medical school while another continued his high school education toward the same goal. By 1905, 15 percent of Italian male offspring wore white collars.

School was judged superfluous for girls. They could, it was felt, learn from their mothers at home. "The Italian girl," wrote Lillian Brandt, "more than the average girl expects to be occupied and at an earlier age than the average girl." "Why," asked one mother, "should she go to high school when she's going to get married anyway?" Other girls did not even get that far. Another signora explained to an investigator that she did not relish the prospect of her daughter's education: "Why should she learn to write, she'd only write to her fellas?" Yet another mother insisted on withdrawing her daughter from school just as she entered the graduating class. "That," said the unhappy girl, "is how Italians are."[11]

In spite of their limited academic preparation, Italian daughters learned tailoring and other skills which equipped them for participation in New York's manufacturing sector. The girls' contributions to family income continued to be a significant factor because of both amount and reliability. The 1029 families sampled in 1905 reported 382 working sons and 204 employed daughters but investigators of the period noted that the girls' work continued throughout the year while the young men labored during busy seasons but remained idle in slack periods. In one-quarter of the New York Italian families studied by Louise Odencrantz, daughters' earnings exceeded all others in the household. Besides, the girls willingly contributed their wages to their families. "It was not unusual," one observer wrote, "to find families in which the sons were not giving a cent to the support of the home." At the same time, 86 percent of the girls turned over their entire earnings.[12]

Italian women, both wives and daughters, appear to have made considerable progress out of unskilled jobs between 1880 and 1905. If this progress was unique to Italians or shared by other immigrants can best be answered by looking at the experience of their partners in the New Immigrant adventure, the Russian Jews. Together with the Italians they constituted the major foreign groups in New York City after 1905.

The 1880 sample of Russian households shows that shtetl-reared wives joined the city's work force even less frequently than their sisters from the mezzogiorno. Strong social attitudes prevailed among east European Jews regarding the proper role of married women, summed up in the prophet's aphorism that "a princess' honor resides indoors."

Having recently arrived from the constricted atmosphere of their Russian ghetto communities and buffeted by a variety of forces that threatened the old attitudes they carried with them, many Jewish men and women looked upon the American work environment as something to be saved from. The idea of married women pressed into close contact with men in factories violated their sensibilities. Married women were supposed to be discreet and modest, with hair covered and dresses that clothed both elbows and knees. This, a National Federation of Settlements Handbook warned, was not the sort of atmosphere to be found in crowded factories: "In many places girls work side by side with, or in the near vicinity of, men. They sometimes become careless in their conduct, slack in manners and conversation, immodest in dress and familiar to a degree that lays them open to danger. In many factories too, girls of low or even bad morals work."[13]

In the face of such warnings, few married Jewish women took jobs outside their homes. Only 2 percent of all eastern European households surveyed reported working wives (See Table 3). Not only mothers with young off-spring stayed home. Even those with no children rejected employment if it required leaving their apartments. With only 12 Jewish wives reporting employment in 1880, no conclusion of statistical significance can be drawn about the kinds of jobs they took. Yet similarities with the occupation picture of Jewish males cannot be ignored. Russian women's work classifications resembled those of their husbands far more than those of Italian women.

TABLE 3

OCCUPATIONAL DISTRIBUTION FOR RUSSIAN JEWISH WIVES AND HUSBANDS, NEW YORK CITY 1880 and 1905

	1880		1905	
Occupational Group	Husbands	Wives	Husbands	Wives
Upper white-collar	5.2%	0	15.1%	8.3%
Lower white-collar	38.9%	33.3%	30.8%	41.7%
Skilled blue-collar	50.0%	58.3%	34.8%	25.0%
Semiskilled blue-collar	5.3%	8.3%	17.7%	25.0%
Unskilled blue collar	.6%	0	1.7%	0
Number	524	12	963	12
Total households sampled	536		1008	

Source: Sample data from Federal Census of Population, 1880, New York and Kings Counties; New York State Census of Population, 1905, New York and Kings Counties.

As Table 3 shows, in 1880, when nearly half of all Italian working wives took unskilled jobs as ragpickers or common laborers, not one Russian Jewish wife reported such an occupation. One-third of the Russian working wives claimed white-collar status but only one-tenth of the Italians did so. Like their husbands, two-thirds of the Jewish women held skilled or semi-skilled jobs but less than one-half of the Italian women did. Plainly, those few Jewish women who worked trailed in the occupational paths of their husbands who may have secured jobs for their wives in their employment places.

In looking at Italians and Jews from both the 1880 and 1905 samples, gender proved less significant than ethnicity in shaping the occupational distribution of wives. Despite discrimination that reputedly set women apart as a class and barred them from a variety of jobs reserved for males, wives in these two ethnic groups resembled their husbands' job classifications more than those of women in the other immigrant group. By 1905 the segment of Jewish households reporting working wives decreased to 1 percent of the total but the jobs these women held continued to resemble those of their husbands more closely than their Italian sisters.

Italian and Jewish wives did share an interest in homework, especially in the years before 1900. The famous picture of the immigrant family toiling over a clothing-laden kitchen table originated in the Jewish Tenth Ward and it included the matriarch.[14] In the early "sweating" phase of the clothing industry Jewish women often engaged in homework, but mechanization, tenement legislation and competition from Italian women, who came into the clothing industry after 1890, sharply cut the participation of Jewish women.[15] Faced with the choice of leaving home for the shop or not working at all, many preferred the latter. Some joined their husbands in neighborhood stores or peddling but most retreated from income-producing endeavors.

Jewish husbands concurred in their spouses' refusing both factory work and home finishing. By 1907 one social worker observed: "No matter how great the poverty, the Hebrew men seldom allow the women of their family to do the [clothing] work at home even though they may have been shopworkers before marriage."[16] A neighborhood survey conducted the same year canvassed 488 home finishers in New York. Not one was a Jewish woman. Russian men who gained foreman status in factories often hired Italian women even though government investigators noted that this ran contrary to the general pattern in which "employees [are] recruited from the same race as the foreman."[17]

The reluctance of married Jewish women to engage in factory or office work was apparently not shared by their daughters. Younger women, often American-born or raised, proved more receptive to work outside the home. Status and wages were the significant factors, not modesty or fear of factory conditions. This attraction for work outside the home drew more Jewish than Italian girls into the city economy. In 1880 one of every three Jewish families reported a working daughter while for Italians the figure was one in five. Twenty-five years later the ratios remained about the same.

In 1880 the occupational distribution of young Jewish working girls reflected an ethnic differential. Like their mothers, fathers and brothers, they shunned jobs in the unskilled sector. Benefiting from a network of connections and experiences, they took skilled and semiskilled jobs in the clothing industry. A full 95 percent of their number claimed occupations in the middle categories. This compares with 61 percent of their brothers and 55 percent of their fathers.

TABLE 4

OCCUPATIONAL DISTRIBUTION FOR RUSSIAN JEWISH OFFSPRING, BY SEX, NEW YORK CITY 1880 and 1905

	1880		1905	
Occupational Group	Males	Females	Males	Females
Upper white-collar	1.1%	0	6.3%	2.7%
Lower white-collar	37.4%	3.5%	39.1%	23.8%
Skilled blue-collar	42.5%	57.6%	33.0%	26.5%
Semiskilled blue-collar	18.4%	37.5%	19.8%	45.9%
Unskilled blue-collar	.6%	1.4%	1.9%	1.0%
Number	174	144	430	294
Total households sampled	536		1008	

Source: Sample data from Federal Census of Population, 1880, New York and Kings Counties; New York State Census of Population, 1905, New York and Kings Counties.

The biggest differences within the Russian population involve the numbers with either professional or lower white-collar jobs. For household heads in 1880 the figure was 44 percent while sons reported 38 percent and daughters only 3 percent.

Twenty-five years later Russian daughters had clearly begun to penetrate the top sectors of the labor force. In the 1905 sample, one out of four young women worked as a school teacher, clerk, salesperson or shopkeeper.[18] They still did not approach their brothers and fathers who claimed about 45 percent of their number in white collar employment but they bore even less resemblance to Italian girls who reported fewer than one in ten in such higher level jobs.

In lagging behind their brothers at the white-collar levels, Russian girls, in part, reflected family values which favored careers for sons ahead of daughters. Mary Van Kleeck, who reported that Italian girls sacrificed educational opportunities in favor of their brothers, found similar instances in the Jewish community: "The oldest daughter in a Russian family left normal school teacher training] after the second year in order that her elder brother might attend college. Her father was a tailor. Two younger children were in school. She explained that she wanted to go back to normal college but for her brother a college education was a 'matter of life position' while for her it was not."[19]

Nevertheless, Jewish girls quickly gained a reputation for placing a high value on schooling and, while some of the deferred to their brothers, many went on to get a high school education. A study by two social workers explained that the young Jewish women entering the labor market were unique: "They seem to understand the increased power which preparation gives. As a result, Hebrew girls are everywhere crowding the high and commercial schools and taking their place beside the children of families with a start of one or more generations."[20]

While their better educations may have lifted some Jewish girls into the professional and lower white-collar occupations, many remained in the blue-collar class. Here Italian girls showed a greater hold on the skilled jobs where they gained praise for their training and tractability: "When the Italian girl exhibits an interest in her trade," one employer wrote, "it is an interest in craftsmanship or in her own wages rather than in general trade conditions. The Jewish girl, on the contrary, often displays an eager zest for discussion of her labor problems.... [She] will probably plunge at once into a discussion of her trade, its advantages and disadvantages, wages, hours of work, and instances of shabby treatment in the shops or of unsanitary conditions in the workrooms." Jewish girls retaliated with their own charges. "If they were more civilized," one Jewish girl complained about her Italian co-workers, "they wouldn't take such low pay. But they go without hats and gloves and umbrellas."[21]

In the last decades of the nineteenth century, women from these two immigrant groups confronted a changing economic environment. In 1880 fewer than 2 percent of the nation's non-agricultural working women found employment as clerks and stenographers. By 1900 this figure had climbed to over 9 percent and a decade later it stood at almost 15 percent. Positions in new, more highly mechanized fields opened up. At the same time the proportion of women employed as servants and waitresses declined from 47 percent to 26.[22]

New York City registered its own unique changes. Only about 6 percent of all employed women worked as clerks, salespersons and accountants in 1880 but the following two decades saw this segment spiral to about one in five. At the same time the percentages involved in manufacturing and domestic service declined slightly. The total number of women working in the two boroughs almost doubled between 1880 and 1900 but not all sectors of the economy witnessed equivalent increases. The lower white-collar jobs had belonged almost exclusively to men before 1880 but by the turn of the century one in six of these positions went to a woman.[23]

In the face of these rapid changes, Jewish and Italian married women reacted differently. Both groups shared a distaste for employment outside their homes but the Italians accepted such jobs more often than the Russians. In 1880 both engaged in homework for income-producing activity but by 1905 Jewish women had abandoned this field to the Italians who went on to monopolize it. Both groups progressed up the ladder of occupational status in the 25-year period. Italians, both husbands and wives, discarded unskilled jobs while a significant percentage of the Russians, whether male or female, moved even higher into white collars.

Female offspring of New York's Italians and Jews worked outside their homes more willingly than their mothers but ethnicity again shows significant effect. Russian girls, more likely to be employed than the Italians, traced occupational profiles more like those of their brothers than of Italian daughters. Ethnicity, with all its occupational implications, was more significant than sex in determining which jobs young women took. Neither Russian nor Italian women managed to enter white-collar classifications as often as their brothers but the former did so considerably more often than the latter who relied on their craft training to move into skilled sectors of the blue-collar category.

Between 1880 and 1905, New York's Russian and Italian female residents shared an economic environment bustling with rapid changes and new opportunities. But they confronted the city from different cultural and historical perspectives which produced different occupational priorities and objectives. These are reflected in the diverging paths which they forged for themselves, paths which may have divided married women from single girls within each group but which, more importantly, traced separate steps for the two ethnic groups.

*NOTES

*The authors acknowledge financial assistance from the National Endowment for the Humanities and from the American Council of Learned Societies.

[1]U.S. Department of the Interior, Tenth Census, 1880, Manufactures (2 vols., Washington, D. C., 1883), II, p. 155. The boundaries for New York City included only Manhattan. The inclusion of the other boroughs, heretofore independent municipalities, came with the charter of Greater New York and consolidation in 1898.

[2]U.S. Department of the Interior, Tenth Census, 1880, Statistics of the Population of the U.S. (Washington, D.C., 1883), 892 and 865. American immigration records did not provide information by religion, and only after 1899 was "Hebrew" included in the statistics as a racial category. Nonetheless, historians have commonly used Russian and Polish totals as proxies for the Jewish figures. This is a valid approach in cities, especially in New York. See United States Industrial Commission, Reports (19 vols., Washington, D.C. 1902), XV, pp. 475-6: "The Russians and Poles, practically all Hebrews..." Evidence for this substitution rests on more than impressionistic accounts. In his article, "Occupational Patterns of American Jews," The Jewish Review, III (April, 1945), 3-24, Nathan Goldberg provides the statistical undergirding for this assumption. His data indicate that for New York City, especially before 1900, Russian can safely be taken to mean Jewish. See also: Samuel Joseph, Jewish Immigration to the United States, 1881-1910 (New York, Reprint of 1910 Columbia University doctoral dissertation, 1969), 87-104, 164; Moses Rischin, The Promised City: New York's Jews, 1870-1914 (Cambridge, 1962), 270.

[3]U.S. Department of the Interior, Statistics of the Population, 1880, 892 and 865.

[4]The sampling procedure for 1880 concentrated on those wards that had high Italian or Russian Jewish concentration. At this point, the New Immigrants had not yet dispersed from their original neighborhoods on lower Manhattan and this brought most of them into the sample net. More precisely, those election districts in these wards that had over 10 new immigrant families were sampled by choosing every fifth Italian and Russian Jewish household. The Italian colony in Harlem was also sampled. Brooklyn neighborhoods were

scanned and a few households were included in the sample, but the number of Italians and Jews in Brooklyn was still small. For 1880 the following wards were sampled: 4, 6, 7, 8, 10, 12, 13, 14, 15 in Manhattan and wards 2, 6, 8, 10, 12, 14, 16, 18 and 25 in Brooklyn.

For 1905 the procedure was more complex, involving a three-stage stratified systematic sample. The first stage was to divide the target sample population for both Italians and Russian Jews into fractions that represented the proportional division of their populations between Manhattan and Brooklyn. The second stage was based on dividing Italian and Jewish populations of each borough into heavy, medium, and low concentration Assembly Districts. Then a proportional stratified sample was selected from each of the three strata. The 1905 Assembly Districts sampled were: 1, 2, 6, 8, 12, 14, 22, 28, 32 and 33 in Manhattan; 2, 3, 5, 6, 7, 11, 14, 18, and 21 in Brooklyn.

5 Mary Van Kleeck, Artificial Flower Makers (New York, 1913), 116. Louise C. Odencrantz makes a similar point in Italian Women in Industry (New York, 1919), 13 and 27.

6 For descriptions of women's work in Italy, see: Amy Bernardy, "L'emigrazione delle donne e dei fanciulli dal Piemonte," Bollettino dell'Emigrazione no. 10 (1912), 7 and 29; Amintore Fanfani, Storia del Lavoro in Italia (Milan, 1943), 121-24; Mary Argyle Taylor, "Italian Industries for Women," Atlantic, C (October 1907), 547-52; Ornello Vitali, Aspetti dello sviluppo economico italiano alla luce della ricostituzione della popolazione attiva (Rome, 1970), 378-83; Helen Stuart Campbell, Prisoners of Poverty Abroad (Boston, 1890), 230. Italian-American women's work is discussed in Robert Foerster, The Italian Emigration of Our Time (Cambridge, 1919), 347, 380-81; United States Department of Labor, Summary of the Report on Condition of Woman and Child Wage Earners in the United States (Washington, D.C., 1916), 97-103.

7 Foerster, Italian Emigration, 347; Mabel Hurd Willett, The Employment of Women in the Clothing Trade (New York, 1902), 99.

8 For a discussion of artificial flower making, see: Van Kleeck, Artificial Flower Makers, passim and Odencrantz, Italian Women, 45. Van Kleeck, Artificial Flower Makers, 94-95. As late as 1910, when a 15-year-old required a special employment certificate to work in a shop, 10 percent of those doing flower work alongside their mothers were under eight years of age and more than one-third, under 14.

9 U.S. Immigration Commission, Reports (41 vols., Washington, D.C., 1911), XXVI, p. 226, 232.

10 Van Kleeck, Artificial Flower Makers, 85-86.

11 Lillian Brandt, "A Transplanted Birthright," Charities, XII (1904), 494; Odencrantz, Italian Women, 205, 249-51, and 256.

12 Ibid., 21, 177.

13 Robert A. Woods and Albert J. Kennedy, eds., Young Working Girls, A Summary of Evidence from Two Thousand Social Workers (Boston and New York, 1913), 22-23.

[14]"Take the Second Avenue Elevated...and ride up half a mile through the sweater district. Every open window...gives you a glimpse [of Jewish] men and women bending over their machines...." Jacob Riis, How the Other Half Lives, 91.

[15]Joel Seidman, The Needle Trades (New York, 1942), 62-63; Jesse Eliphat Pope, The Clothing Industry in New York (Columbia, Missouri, 1905), 57, 155-60; Leo Grebler, Housing Market Behavior in a Declining Area (New York, 1952), 113-14.

[16]U.S. Bureau of Labor, Report on the Condition of Woman and Child Wage Earners in the United States (19 vols., Washington, D.C., 1911), II, pp. 53 and 221.

[17]U.S. Immigration Commission, Reports, I, p. 752. U. S. Bureau of Labor, Report on the Condition of Woman and Child Wage Earners, II, p. 53.

[18]This group also included one dentist.

[19]Van Kleeck, Artificial Flower Makers, 36 and 86. It is clear that these sacrifices were quite common and not restricted to immigrant daughters who were Italian or Jewish. See: Jade Snow Wong, "Puritans from the Orient," in Thomas C. Wheeler, ed., The Immigrant Experience (New York, 1971), 121.

[20]Woods and Kennedy, Young Working Girls, 11.

[21]Van Kleeck, Artificial Flower Makers, 34-37.

[22]U.S. Bureau of the Census, Abstracts of the Twelfth Census, 1900 (Washington, D.C., 1902), 24; Joseph A. Hill, Women in Gainful Occupations, 1870-1920 (Washington, D.C., 1929), 33.

[23]U.S. Department of the Interior, Statistics of the Population at the Tenth Census, 1880 (Washington, D.C., 1883), 892; U. S. Bureau of the Census, Abstract of the Twelfth Census, 126-27. The figure was actually 17 percent for Manhattan and 21 for Brooklyn. In 1880 a total of 180,259 women worked; by 1900 the number had grown to 351,329.

BEYOND THE STEREOTYPE: A NEW LOOK AT THE IMMIGRANT WOMAN, 1880-1924

Maxine S. Seller*

Much has been written about the achievements and experiences of the men who came to the United States from Southern and Eastern Europe between 1880 and 1924. Much less has been written, however, about the achievements and experiences of the immigrant women of this period. It is my opinion that the relative lack of material about immigrant women is not the result of a lack of activity on the part of these women. Rather, it is the result of the persistence of old, negative stereotypes, stereotypes making it appear that women did little worth writing about.

According to her native born contemporaries, the immigrant woman from Southern or Eastern Europe spent her life "confined within the four walls of her home and chained to her household routine."[1] According to a librarian, "(Immigrant) women are left behind in intelligence by the father and children. They do not learn English; they do not keep up with other members of the family."[2] The political influence of the foreign born woman was supposedly nil, both before and after the passage of the Women's Suffrage Amendment. As one observer put it, "The foreign born woman plays directly in American politics a part somewhat, but not much, more important than that played by snakes in the zoology of Ireland."[3] In summary, the native born who saw all immigrants as a threat to the American way of life, saw the immigrant woman in particular as backward, ignorant, and degraded. She was considered excellent raw material for the "uplift" programs of social workers and home missionary societies, but good for little else. To fervent advocates of Americanization of the immigrant mother was a "natural obstructionist" whose eventual death would enable the family to "move on much more victoriously to Americanization."[4]

These negative stereotypes from the early twentieth century have continued to influence our view of the immigrant woman. The second or third generation ethnic comedian romanticizes her as Super-Mom, a domestic wonder woman who solved the problems of the world with steaming bowls of chicken soup, spaghetti, or other appropriate ethnic food. Those less steeped in nostalgia are likely to think of her, if at all, as a shadowy, kerchiefed figure absorbed in the not very efficient care of a cluttered tenement apartment and an unending stream of offspring. If she had ambition, it was for her children, never for herself. Her own horizons were limited to the corner grocery and the parish church.

Historians, like others, have been influenced by these stereotypes. They have also been influenced by the knowledge that Southern and Eastern European immigrant groups usually had, and still have, a patriarchal family structure. Many share the general bias of our society that the activities of women are less important than those of men. Even in recent works on ethnic history far fewer

---

*Maxine S. Seller is a member of the Faculty of Educational Studies at SUNY, Buffalo.

women than men are mentioned by name, and women's organizations and activities are rarely treated as fully as the corresponding organizations and activities of men.

Is the stereotyped picture of the immigrant woman an accurate reflection of reality? There were women who did conform to the stereotype, but significant numbers did not. Women of energy and ability stepped outside the traditionally feminine spheres of home and child care to make a variety of contributions to their ethnic communities and to American life in general. Immigrant women built social, charitable, and educational institutions that spanned the neighborhood and the nation. They established day care centers, restaurants, hotels, employment agencies, and legal aid bureaus. They wrote novels, plays, and poetry. They campaigned for a variety of causes, from factory legislation to birth control, from cleaner streets to cleaner government.[5]

To illustrate the range of these activities, I will begin this paper with case studies of three non-traditional women, each from a different ethnic background, each making her contribution in a different area: Antonietta Pisanelli Alessandro, a founder of professional Italian theater in the United States; Josephine Humpel Zeman, Bohemian journalist, lecturer, and feminist; and Rose Pesotta, Russian Jewish labor organizer. After sketching the career of each of these undeservedly obscure women, I will explore how, coming from patriarchal ethnic cultures, they were able to achieve what they did. Then, by discussing briefly the activities of other immigrant women, I will show that these three were not unique. So many women's lives, traditional as well as non-traditional, departed from the stereotype in so many ways that much more research in this area is needed. As ethnic historian Rudolph Vecoli recently observed, the history of the immigrant woman remains to be written.[6]

Antonietta Pisanelli Alessandro came from Naples to New York as a child.[7] As a young woman, she made her living signing, dancing, and acting in the major eastern cities. She made her New York debut at an Italian benefit in Giambelli Hall. Then, as there were no professional Italian theaters in New York, she and some colleagues organized several. Personal tragedy marred her career, however; first her mother died, then her husband, then one of her two children.

With her remaining young son and few other resources but her ingenuity, she arrived in San Francisco in 1904. She assembled a group of amateur performers, rented a ramshackled hall, and opened an Italian theater. According to an early patron, the settings were so crude they were liable to fall apart at any moment--as were the actors. But the performance earned $150. By the time the fire department closed the building, Pisanelli was able to open the more substantial Cafe Pisanelli Family Circle, a combination theater, club, opera house, and cafe. Featuring the finest actors and singers imported from Italy, the Circle was soon known as the liveliest theater in San Francisco. Through road tours as well as home performances, Antonietta Pisanelli Alessandro and her company brought Italian drama and Italian music, from folk songs to opera, to Italian Americans and others throughout the country.

Josephine Humpel Zeman was born in Bohemia (Czechoslavakia) in 1870 and immigrated to Chicago as a young girl.[8] There she met Mary Ingersoll, a social worker at Hull House who became, in Humpel's words, "my second mother." Recognizing the young girl's ability, Mary Ingersoll helped her learn English and get an education. In 1895 Josephine Humpel Zeman was a member of the staff of Hull House, devoting her time to the study of the Bohemian community of Chicago. She was especially sensitive to the problems of women. In a published Hull House paper she complained that "nothing whatsoever has been done for the Bohemian working woman. No one has deemed her worthy of any effort. This is an interesting fact; for as long as these hundreds of thousands of girls shall be unorganized and uninformed, they will always be a great stumbling block in the path of the working women of Chicago."[9]

As social worker, author, journalist, and lecturer (both in her native language and in English) Josephine Zeman showed her concern for the welfare of immigrants, of women, and of all who were at the bottom of the nation's socio-economic pyramid. She wrote articles for the ethnic press, for American magazines such as Commons, and for the United States Industrial Commission on Immigration and Education. According to the Library of Congress catalog, a Josephine Zeman, presumably Josephine Humpel Zeman, wrote two novels, The Victim Triumphs: A Panorama of Modern Society published by Dillingham in 1903, and My Crime, published by Ogelvie in 1907. Thomas Capek, who described Zeman's career in his History of the Czechs in the United States, did not mention these novels, however, raising the question of whether she did in fact write them. He does mention her social critique of the United States, America in Its True Light, published in Prague in 1903. The book contained lectures she delivered on a tour to some thirty towns in Bohemia, and Silesia. Zeman's most important work was the founding of the Chicago-based Bohemian feminist journal, Zemske Listy, The Woman's Gazette, in 1894. Written, edited, and even printed by an exclusively female staff, the paper circulated throughout the United States. Avoiding the household hints and beauty advice common to most women's publications, the paper stressed the need to improve the lot of the working woman and campaigned for the adoption of the Women's Suffrage Amendment.[10]

Rose Pesotta was born in 1896 in the Ukraine, in the pale of settlement where Russian Jews were forced by law to live.[11] At the age of seventeen she came to New York City, where her older sister, who had emigrated earlier, got her a job in a garment factory. Familiar with the ideas of various peasant and worker revolutionary groups in Russia, Pesotta joined Waistmakers Local 25 of the International Ladies Garment Workers Union almost immediately. On May Day, 1914 she marched with her co-workers in a mass parade past the scene of the Triangle Waist Factory fire--an industrial disaster in which 126 garment workers, mostly immigrant girls like herself, burned to death.

Inspired by stories of the great labor battles of the recent past and by the distress of working people she saw all around her, Pesotta became actively involved in the organizational work of her union. She learned English at night school and continued her education, under the auspices of the Union, at Brookwood Labor College and at the Bryn Mawr Summer School for Working Girls.

According to Pesotta, the aim of the latter institution was "to stimulate an active and continuous interest in the problems of our economic life which vitally concern industrial women as wage earners."[12]

The Bryn Mawr Summer School realized its aim: Pesotta began by working to organize her fellow workers in New York, many of whom, like herself, were Jewish immigrants. Soon she was also organizing Italians and other workers of a wide variety of ethnic backgrounds. She traveled from coast to coast, unionizing garment workers in Los Angeles, San Francisco, Montreal, San Juan, and wherever else her services were needed. During the Great Depression of the 1930s she helped organize automobile and rubber workers also. She traveled in Europe and, upon her return, rallied aid for the cause of the Spanish Loyalists. In recognition of her valuable services, she was elected a vice president of the International Ladies Garment Workers Union for three consecutive terms. Rejecting the suggestion of a fourth term in 1944, she pointed out that a union with 300,000 members, 85% of whom were women, should have more than one token woman, herself, on its executive committee.[13]

The lives of Antonietta Pisanelli Alessandro, Josephine Humpel Zeman, and Rose Pesotta were not confined within the limits of customary women's activities. Why did these three women break with tradition? In the first place, like millions of other working women, immigrant and native born, they could not afford the luxury of full-time domesticity. Alessandro was a widow with a child to support when she opened her first theater in San Francisco. An "unfortunate" marriage made it necessary for Zeman to support herself. Pesotta, too, worked throughout her life to earn her own living.

For all three of these women, however, economic necessity was a less important motivating force than their inner drives to do meaningful and challenging work in the larger world. Antoinetta Alessandro began organizing theaters in New York while her first husband was still alive and continued to run her theater in San Francisco after a second marriage relieved her of the necessity to earn her living. Even before she left Russia, Rose Pesotta had decided that the traditional woman's life would not meet her needs. In her own words, "I can see no future for myself except to marry some young man returned from his four years of military service and be a housewife. That is not enough. . . . In America things are different. A decent middle class girl can work without disgrace."[14]

In each of these women motivation was matched by energy and ability. Alessandro impressed all who met her with her business acumen and resourcefulness, as well as with her unfailing charm. A fellow journalist dubbed Zeman "Mrs. General," a derisive acknowledgement of her forceful manner.[15] A colleague and former teacher described Pesotta as "possessing built-in energy... talk with her a few minutes as casually as you may and strength is poured into you, as when a depleted battery is connected to a generator."[16]

All three of these women came from ethnic backgrounds in which men were the dominant sex and women were relegated to domestic duties. Why, then, despite their obvious abilities, did they aspire to non-traditional careers in the first place? The journey to America opened new possibilities to these women, as it did to all immigrants. Still, early twentieth century America was scarcely more liberal than Europe in the roles it assigned to women. Also, by the time these three women arrived in the United States, their personalities and aspirations had already been shaped by old world environments. Undoubtedly there must be intensive investigation on the status of women in the mother countries if the immigrant woman is to be fully understood. Even a cursory investigation reveals, however, that there were cross currents in European ethnic cultures that supported the achievements of women like Alessandro, Zeman, and Pesotta.

Alessandro grew up in Southern Italy, where women were taught to be subservient to their fathers, husbands, uncles, brothers, even their male cousins. Still, Southern Italian women were respected, even revered, in their roles as mothers--perhaps because of the religious veneration of Mary as the mother of Jesus, or perhaps because of the critical economic importance of their work in a society where livelihood was marginal. Whatever the reasons, an Italian family could survive the death of the father, but not that of the mother.[17]

Alessandro was not above utilizing the respect due her as an Italian mother when it was to her advantage to do so. On one occasion, a road tour audience in St. Louis threatened to riot in the theater because of a misunderstanding about the program. (They had expected the opera Carmen instead of the folk song with a similar name that was actually presented.) Allesandro restored peace and probably saved the building from being torn apart by putting her young son on stage to sing "Wait Til the Sun Shines, Nellie"--while her husband slipped out of the back door to safety carrying with him the evening's cash receipts.

According to an old Slavic proverb, "the man who does not beat his wife is not a man." According to another, "one man is worth more than ten women." Women in the more remote areas of the Balkans were used, along with the animals, to carry the heavy burdens.[18] The Slavic societies of Eastern Europe were far from monolithic, however, in their views on religion, sex, or anything else. Josephine Humpel Zeman was from Bohemia, an area with a long tradition of opposition to established religious and political institutions.[19] The rationalism of Bohemian "free thinkers" was notorious both in the United States and in Europe, and provided a hospitable atmosphere for the radical social ideas and non-traditional behavior of someone like Josephine Zeman. Indeed, her lectures on feminism and social reform may have seemed less shocking in Bohemia than in Chicago.

Rose Pesotta, too, could find support for her chosen life work from within her own ethnic tradition. Sex roles were sharply defined in East European Jewish society, but not in precisely the same way as in Anglo Saxon society. In theory at least, the Jewish man was most admired for his religious scholarship rather than for his physical prowess or his economic achievement. It was not uncommon for a pious Jewish man to spend all his time in religious study, while his wife assumed full responsibility for earning the family livelihood. Thus, many East European Jewish women from religious backgrounds were at home in the world of the marketplace.[20]

In addition, by the turn of the century some young women had come under the influence of two new secular philosophies, socialism and zionism, both of which emphasized the equality of the sexes and offered a new range of roles for women. In 1880 Russia opened its universities to women. Although the government allowed few Jewish women to take advantage of this opportunity, increasing numbers found their way to some secular education. The "new" Jewish woman, intellectual, aggressive, and self-sufficient, brought her new lifestyle with her to the United States. According to journalist Hutchins Hapgood, who described the Jewish quarter of New York City in 1902,

> there are successful female dentists, physicians, writers, and even lawyers by the score in East Broadway who have attained financial independence through their industry and intelligence. They are ambitious to a degree and often direct the careers of their husbands. . . . There is more than one case on record where a girl has compelled her recalcitrant lover to learn law, medicine, or dentistry, or submit to being jilted by her. . . . The description of this type of woman seems rather cold and forbidding in the telling, but such an impression is misleading. . . . The women . . . are strikingly interesting because of their warm temperaments. . . .[21]

Certainly the old, limiting stereotypes of immigrant women do not apply to Allesandro, Zeman, and Pesotta. These three women were unusually able, but, as already suggested, they were not unique. The same combination of talents, motivations, necessities, and opportunities that turned these three to activities outside the traditional woman's sphere acted upon other immigrant women as well.

As many historians have noted, more men than women immigrated to the United States between 1880 and 1924, husbands often coming first and then sending for their wives and children. Still, surprisingly large numbers of single women did immigrate independently. Between 1912 and 1917, half a million single women under the age of thirty entered the United States. Many, like Rose Pesotta, were in their teens. Of 120,000 Polish women who came during this period, 84,000 were under the age of twenty-one.[22] Undoubtedly some came to join fiances, but others came entirely on their own. For them, the act of immigration itself was a breach of the stereotype.

In a family unit or on their own, immigrant women frequently became part of the labor force. In 1910 about a million and a quarter foreign born women were gainfully employed. Thus, contrary to the stereotype of the homebound immigrant woman, large numbers spent the greater part of their time somewhere other than in their own homes. Nor was this necessarily a new experience. The economic pressures that stimulated immigration had already forced tens of thousands of East European women into day labor fields or in the homes of the large landowners. Thus, even before immigration, many women were working outside the traditional family unit, beyond the immediate supervision of father or husband.

The women of Southern Italy were kept closer to home than their Slavic counterparts, but here too, economic pressures were causing breaks in the traditional patterns even before immigration. In the United States most Italian families preferred to have their women work at home, but the need to earn more money drove increasing numbers into the garment factories. So many entered the clothing industry that the Women's Trade Union League of New York found it worthwhile to establish a special Italian committee to organize Italian working women.[23]

Working outside the home did not always--or even often--lead to a new lifestyle. But the ability to earn money could be a first step toward change. New economic power among women caused an enormous change in the lifestyle of at least one immigrant group--those from the Middle East. Arabic immigrant men, who often earned their living peddling lace, underwear, and notions from door to door, discovered that their wives had easier access to American homes than they did. Arabic wives learned English quickly by peddling with or for their husbands. As the family fortunes advanced, some became active partners in large commercial enterprises. Such women moved in one generation from a subordinate, almost cloistered life in the old country to economic and social equality with their husbands in the United States and positions of importance in their communities.[24]

Whether an immigrant woman worked outside of her home or not, other aspects of life in the United States tended to break up traditional patterns. American courts could be appealed to prevent some of the abuses, such as repeated wife beating, against which there was no legal redress in many old world cultures. According to male Ukrainian immigrants, "the laws here are made for women."[25] In Middle Eastern societies the education and even the social life of the children had been controlled by their father. In the United States teachers, doctors, and social workers supported the mother in assuming control of these areas.[26]

Neighborhood problems pulled immigrant women into activities not traditionally associated with their homemaking and childbearing roles--politics, for example. An Italian woman, newly arrived in a Chicago neighborhood, was appalled at the presence of open ditches, a hazard to her young children. At the suggestion of a settlement worker, she canvassed the neighborhood to see how many other children were similarly endangered. Her survey led to a formal complaint to city hall, and the offending ditches were covered.[27]

Nor was this an isolated case. In Chicago Bohemian women organized to protest the use of open garbage wagons in their neighborhood. After the passing of the Nineteenth Amendment, Poles, Bohemians, and other immigrant women in Chicago helped organize a women's civic league, which registered five thousand women voters and campaigned against corrupt city administration. J. Joseph Huthmacher suggests that the success of Progressive Era reforms in urban states like Massachusetts and New York was at least partly the result of immigrant political pressure.[28] More investigation is needed on the role of immigrant women in these reforms.

In a study of today's working-class women, Nancy Seifer suggests that "When a wife comes home after testifying at a City Council hearing, from a meeting of the local school or hospital board, or from helping to out-maneuver a local politician or win a vote for day care in her union, she is changing the balance of power in her marriage in the most fundamental way, often without realizing it."[29] Did the pioneering ventures of immigrant women into the public life of their day have a similar effect on their marriages?

Immigrant women created a great variety of local organizations, sometimes with the aid of second generation women of their own ethnic group or sympathetic social workers from nearby settlements and sometimes entirely on their own. Singing societies and other cultural associations were common, but there were many others. In New York City a group of Finnish domestic servants pooled their money to rent a small apartment for use on their days off. Within a few years the Finnish Women's Cooperative Home, as it was called, grew into a four story building with sleeping accommodations for forty, lounges, clubrooms, a library, a restaurant, and an employment bureau--still owned and operated by the women themselves.[30] In Buffalo an immigrant Jewish women's club based at a settlement house bought and remodeled an old home where they established a day care center for their own children and the children of others.[31]

Slovenes, Lithuanians, Poles, Ukrainians, Lebanese, Syrians, Jews, and other immigrant women formed organizations that often expanded to include regions, or even the entire nation, to pursue charitable and educational work among the women of their own communities. Some of these groups functioned as auxiliaries to men's organizations. Others were independent. The Polish National Alliance, for example, was organized as one unit in which men and women were to be equal members. In practice, however, the Polish women discovered themselves an ineffective minority in a male dominated organization. A group of women decided, therefore, to establish a completely independent organization, The Polish Women's Alliance, so that Polish women could develop their own self-confidence and leadership ability.[32]

The varied and wide ranging activities of ethnic women's organizations are an appropriate subject for more intensive investigation. The Polish Women's Protective League gave free legal advice and other aid to Polish working women.[33] The Ukrainian Women's Alliance published a magazine offering its members information on homemaking, childcare, and women's suffrage.[34] The Lithuanian Women's Alliance provided insurance policies as well as social and educational programs.[35] Syrian, Lebanese, and Armenian women's groups had a virtual monopoly of social and charitable services within their communities. Another group of immigrant women whose contributions were great, and often overlooked, are the members of religious orders. Among these women were capable organizers and administrators of badly needed schools, hospitals, orphanages, and other social service institutions.

Contrary to the view expressed in the old stereotypes, then, many immigrant women had interests and commitments that extended beyond the care of their own homes and families. But what of those who did not? What of the very traditional wife and mother who had neither the time, the energy, the self-assurance, nor perhaps even the desire to participate in public life. The negative stereotypes are unfair to her too. They are unfair because they confuse illiteracy with ignorance and poverty with personal degradation. The woman who fed and clothed a large family on five dollars a week--to the astonishment of the social worker trained in home economics--may have been illiterate, but she was certainly not ignorant. The woman who worked a twelve hour night shift in a foundry and cared for her family and several boarders during the day had no time for the so-called "finer" things in life, but she was not therefore a degraded human being. To survive at all she must have possessed enormous inner resources.

Nor was the uneducated, homebound immigrant woman necessarily politically naive. While many women, like many men, sold their votes or did not vote at all, others were remarkably conscientious and astute. According to Jane Addams, Italian women who came in to vote knew more about the city's problems than their husbands, who were often away on construction or railroad jobs six months of the year. Addams writes of an illiterate Irish woman whom she was allowed to help at the voting booth in a Chicago municipal election. "The first proposition was about bonds for a new hospital. The Irish woman said, 'Is the same bunch to spend the money that run the hospital we have now? Then I am against it'. . . . There were ten propositions to be acted upon. I was scrupulous not to influence her: Yet on nine of them she voted from her own common sense just as the Municipal League and the City Club had recommended as the result of painstaking research.[36]

Undoubtedly life was too much for some immigrant women. Broken homes, physical and mental illness, despair, even suicide were all too often present in the ethnic ghetto. The amazing thing is that, given the cultural shock of immigration and the problems of poverty, and discrimination, and survival in urban slums, so many women were able to keep themselves and their families from being defeated. An early social worker, Katherine Anthony, described one such woman, a Hungarian immigrant, Mrs. Mary Grubinsky. Mr. Grubinsky worked in a furniture factory. The couple had seven children. Mrs. Grubinsky worked "a day here, half a day there" returning to her jobs within a month after the birth of each of her children.

> In addition she helps her husband with chair caning, makes the children's clothes, mends for her own family and also for hire, cooks, washes, irons, scrubs, tends her window boxes, minds the children of a neighbor who is doing a day's work, fetches ice from the brewery where it is thrown away, forages for kindling around warehouses, runs to the school when the teacher summons her--but a list of all that Mrs. Grubinsky does in the course of a week would be quite impossible. In her home nothing is lost. Even the feathers from a Thanksgiving turkey were made into cushions and dust brushes.[37]

It would be understandable if such a busy woman would lag behind the rest of her family in learning English and adjusting to the United States. But according to Katherine Anthony, this was not the case with Mary Grubinsky.

> She takes the lead in Americanizaing her husband and family. She insisted they move from a two to a three room apartment to have a sitting room. . . . Sees to it the girls have proper clothes, white shoes for confirmation. In these matters Mrs. Grubinsky feels that she must decide and that Martin must accommodate himself.

Like Allesandro, Humpel, and Pesotta, Mary Grubinsky was unusually capable. But also like them, she was not unique.

In conclusion, the current interest in ethnicity occurring simultaneously with the new interest in the history of women make this an opportune time for scholars to take a new look at the immigrant woman. "Forgotten" women, who like Allessandro, Humpel, and Pesotta, played an important role in the public life of their communities can be rediscovered by a careful study of the ethnic press and the papers of ethnic institutions (especially women's groups), labor unions, settlement houses, and political parties. The experiences of these women should become an integral part of our understanding of immigration history.

So, too, should the experiences of the more traditional women whose lives, like that of Mary Grubinsky, were centered around care of the home and the family. These women constituted too varied and complex a group to be ignored or dismissed with an inherited negative stereotype. More can be learned about them from their letters and diaries (where these exist), from the records of charities, hospitals, courts and other institutions, and from demographic sources such as census tracts and school surveys. Letters-to-the-editor columns in the ethnic press can be useful, as can the short stories, novels, and poetry of perceptive immigrant writers.[38] Research is needed on the impact of immigration and acculturation on the lives of all immigrant women, on the institution of marriage, and on child-rearing practices.

In conclusion, sources are available for the study of the Southern and Eastern European immigrant woman. With the use of some ingenuity on the part of historians, many more can probably be uncovered. It is time to begin writing the story of the immigrant woman--beyond the stereotype.

NOTES

[1]John Palmer Gavit, Americans By Choice, Harper and Row 1922. Reprinted in Americanization Studies: The Acculturation of Immigrant Groups into American Society. Patterson Smith, Montclair, New Jersey, 1971, p. 318.

[2]Gavit, p. 319.

[3]Gavit, p. 318.

[4]The Second Annual Report of the Commission of Immigration and Housing of California, California State Printing Office, San Francisco, 1916, pp. 151-2. See also Albert Kennedy and Robert Woods, Handbook of Settlements, Russell Sage Foundation, New York, 1911, pp. 16, 37, 191, 211, 245.

[5]Information about immigrant women's organizations can be found in Sophonisba Breckenridge, New Homes for Old and John Daniels, America Via the Neighborhood, both reprinted in Americanization Studies· The Acculturation of Immigrant Groups into American Society, Patterson Smith, Montclair, New Jersey, 1971. Examples of individual women active in public life are Teofila Samolinska, Polish poet, dramatist, and community organizer; Anzia Yezierska, Jewish author of short stories and novels; and Mrs. Mantura Frangierea, Lebanese businesswoman and advocate for the early Arabic community of Boston. Perhaps the best known national figure was Emma Goldman, spokeswoman for unpopular causes such as anarchism, labor reform, birth control, and the complete equality of women. Of course there were many more.

[6]Rudolph J. Vecoli, "European Americans: From Immigrants to Ethics," The Reinterpretation of American History and Culture, edited by William H. Cartwright and Richard L. Watson, Jr., National Council for the Social Studies, Washington, D.C., 1973, p. 104.

[7]For a full account of Antonietta Pisanelli Alessandro's career, see Lawrence Estavan, The Italian Theater in San Francisco, United States Works Progress Administration, North California Distric, San Francisco, 1939. Typescript copy is available at the Lincoln Center Theater Library in New York City.

[8]Information on Josephine Humpel Zeman can be found in Thomas Capek, The Czechs in America, Houghton-Mifflin Company, New York, 1920. I received additional information from the Balch Institute in Philadelphia, for which I am grateful to the Institute's bibliographer, Glen Skillen.

[9]Josephine Humpel Zeman, "The Bohemian People in Chicago," Hull House Maps and Papers, Boston, 1895. Reprinted by Arno Press, New York, 1970, p. 120.

[10]Emily Balch, Our Slavic Fellow Citizens, Charities Publications Committee, New York, 1910, p. 384.

[11]For an account of Pesotta's career, see her autobiography, Rose Pesotta, Bread Upon the Waters, Dodd, Mead & Company, New York, 1945.

[12]Pesotta, p. 15.

[13]Pesotta, p. 395.

[14]Pesotta, p. 9.

[15]Capek, p. 275.

[16]Pesotta, p. vii.

[17]Leonard Covello, The Social Background of the Italian-American School Child, Ph.D. Thesis, New York University, 1944. E. J. Brill, Leiden, 1967. p. 210.

[18]Gerald Gilbert Govorchin, Americans from Yugoslavia, University of Florida Press, Gainesville, 1961, pp. 188-189.

[19]Kenneth Miller, The Czech-Slovaks in America, George H. Doran Company, New York, 1922, pp. 128-130.

[20]Mark Zborowski and Elizabeth Herzog, Life is with People: The Culture of the Shtetl, New York Schocken, 1962, p. 131.

[21]Hutchins Hapgood, The Spirit of the Ghetto: Studies of the Jewish Quarter of New York, 1902. Schocken paperback edition, New York, 1965.

[22]Grace Abbott, The Immigrant and the Community, The Century Company, New York, 1921, pp. 55.

[23]Rudolph Glanz, Jew and Italian, Historic Group Relations and the New Immigration 1881-1924, New York, 1971, p. 47.

[24]Sabia F. Haddad, "The Woman's Role in Socialization of Syrian-Americans in Chicago," The Arab-American: Studies in Assimilation, edited by Elaine Hogopian and Ann Paden. Medina University Press International, Wilmett, 1969, pp. 89-97.

[25]Breckenridge, p. 215.

[26]Haddad, pp. 97-100.

[27]Daniels, p. 213.

[28]J. Joseph Huthmacher, "Urban Liberalism and the Age of Reform," Mississippi Valley Historical Review XLIX (September 1962), pp. 231-241.

[29]Nancy Seifer, Absent From the Majority, National Project on Ethnic America, American Jewish Committee, 1973, p. 45.

[30]Daniels, pp. 78-81.

[31]Daniels, pp. 185-186.

[32]Breckenridge, pp. 205-209.

[33]Breckenridge, p. 294.

[34]Breckenridge, p. 215.

[35]Breckenridge, p. 214.

[36]Gavit, p. 324.

[37]Katherine Anthony, Mothers Who Must Earn, New York, 1914, pp. 186-190.

[38]See, for example, the works of Anzia Yezierska, Hungry Hearts, The Bread Winners, Salome of the Tenements, and All I Could Never Be.

URBANIZATION WITHOUT BREAKDOWN

Italian, Jewish, and Slavic Immigrant Women in Pittsburgh, 1900 to 1945

CORINNE AZEN KRAUSE
American Jewish Committee, and
University of Pittsburgh

In 1951 Oscar Handlin published a Pulitzer prize-winning book in which he advanced the provocative thesis that immigration, which brough some 35 million persons to our country in the century after 1820, represented a traumatic, potentially devastating experience to the 35 million who made the daring crossing to American life.[1] Handlin pointed out that the vast majority of the immigrants came from traditional peasant societies, usually from villages where the way of life had hardly changed for centuries. The disintegration of peasant economy made it impossible to make a living in traditional ways in Europe and thrust rural villagers into America's industrial, technologically developed urban society. Handlin wrote of the personal costs of this migration to

Author's note: *I thank Professor Richard Schoenwald of Carnegie-Mellon University for his helpful suggestions for this article.*

the individual in terms of alienation and loss of status and self-esteem. In recent years historians have reexamined Handlin's theory and found it unduly pessimistic. Later theory considers that in view of the extent of change, immigrants made amazingly successful adjustments.[2] Psyches and physiques did not shatter completely. Indeed, immigrants not only survived, they adjusted to the requirements of the American economy, government, and mores while maintaining something of traditional culture that strengthened them and enabled them to keep a sense of identity distinguishing them from carbon copies of some stereotyped "American" model. Handlin himself has revised his original thesis and in his more recent work has focused on factors within American society that made possible the absorption of the immigrants by America and the absorption of America by the immigrants.[3]

Sociologists have long been interested in the adjustment of rural migrants to the city, frequently citing negative results.[4] On the other hand, anthropologist Oscar Lewis developed a compelling theory, "urbanization without breakdown," based upon years of work with peasant families who moved from a rural Mexican village to Mexico City. After long-term observation and in-depth interview with families who had made the move from village to urban life, he concluded that the transition of the Mexican villagers was accomplished without significant symptoms of personal maladjustment or breakdown of family life.[5]

An oral history study of ethnic women recently completed in Pittsburgh provides data on women that tend to support the Lewis theory.[6] Considering the culture shock and alienation faced by all immigrant women and the special nature of Pittsburgh, a city devoted to heavy manufacturing, immigrant women were surprisingly successful in the transition from European peasant of small town life to industrial urban Pittsburgh, although a few tragic exceptions lend support to Handlin's original thesis.

Pittsburgh was "a man's town." The city made iron, steel, and electrical products—rails, engines, turbines, generators. With the exploding demand for iron and steel that followed the Civil War, Pittsburgh became "the hearth of the nation," and increased in population from 343,904 in 1890 to 533, 907 in 1910. The population of Homestead and Braddock, steel producing towns bordering the city, tripled during the same period.[7]

Early settlers in the Pittsburgh area were chiefly English and Scotch-Irish Protestants. By the mid-nineteenth century large scale immigration from Ireland and Germany began the diversification of the city's population. By 1890 job opportunities for men offered by the steel industry, coupled with political and economic unrest in eastern and southern Europe, resulted in the influx of thousands of eastern European Jews and tens of thousands of Italians, Slovaks, and Poles as well as large numbers of Croatians and other southern Slavic peoples. By 1920 Pittsburgh had become the prototype of a multiethnic city, a living example of cultural pluralism. Over 120,000 of the city's inhabitants were foreign-born, and 54,899 of these were women.

Pittsburgh was not an attractive city for women at the turn of the century. While expanding industry sparked demand for all kinds of goods and services that men produced, there was little demand for women in the labor force. In addition, public services and utilities were abysmally inadequate, making living conditions primitive and difficult in poorer neighborhoods.[8] Most immigrants settled in ethnic enclaves in the poorest neighborhoods.[9]

In spite of these difficulties, the evidence points to a successful adjustment for most immigrant women. This article explores the transition of women from southern and eastern Europe who settled in Pittsburgh and surrounding mill towns between 1900 and 1937. Evidence from selected tape-recorded interviews of 45 foreign-born Italian, Jewish, and Slavic women between the ages of sixty-eight and eighty illustrates factors that proved helpful to women in the transition period.

No single factor can be deemed responsible for the adjustment of these immigrant women. Indeed, a wide variety of elements contributed to their adaptation to America, demonstrating that women did find a niche for themselves and achieved a degree of self-esteem without transforming themselves into any single "American" model. The varied avenues of adjustment testify to the reality of cultural pluralism.

The data indicate that for the majority of eastern and southern European women in Pittsburgh, informal networks of friends, relatives, neighbors, and their own children were the most significant agents of successful adjustment. In addition, the establishment of ethnic churches and the celebration of religious festivals frequently proved means of forming crucial ties between old and new societies.

The actual process of acquiring citizenship provided a sense of accomplishment and belonging to women from all three immigrant groups. Formal agencies such as the settlement houses and Carnegie Libraries reached relatively few immigrant women. While their children would be active members, immigrant women comprised the group least likely to participate in such activities.[10]

Paid employment also came within the experience of only a small minority of immigrant women in Pittsburgh. Pittsburgh had no textile mills or ladies' garment factories, industries which employed thousands of women in New England and Manhattan. Nor were there opportunities for homework, making artificial flowers, men's ties, buttons, and bows. Here, "the black smoke of the mills determined the scope of industry." In fact, only 16.5% of Pittsburgh's foreign-born women were reported as "engaged in gainful occupations" in 1920, a figure much lower than the average of 22.4% in other major cities.[11]

Even though only a small proportion of immigrant women worked in paying jobs (and most of those were young and single), for those who did, the work experience contributed significantly to the transition to America. Frequently work provided a comfortable social setting with others who spoke the same language; in other cases a job broadened the horizons of immigrants, bringing them into contact with other immigrant groups as well as with native Americans. Perhaps most important, work contributed to a sense of competence that women carried over into other life situations.

Ethnic patterns were discernible among working women in Pittsburgh. Young Slavic girls worked in canning factories and molasses plants, washed dishes in restaurants, cleaned other people's houses, and fed the mangles in commercial steam laundries. Single Jewish immigrant women worked in the lowest paid jobs in the city's 203 stogy factories or home sweatshops, or at sewing machines in factories where men's work clothes were made. In contrast, Italian immigrant women were likely to remain out of the labor market, unless need drove them to seek work compatible with traditional cultural values.[12]

As one example, Anna Porto* (starred names are pseudonyms requested by respondents; real names are unstarred) immigrated alone to Pittsburgh where her married sister lived. Her brother-in-law and a cousin found work for her at the Italian bakery where they were employed. This work was considered acceptable for an Italian woman since it was in a traditional occupation, presented no threat to a male in the family, and was performed at a place where other family members were present.[13]

Slavic women, on the other hand, felt no such restrictions. In Europe they had worked side by side with fathers and husbands in the fields. American observers, noting that Slavic women were willing to take the most arduous and physically demanding jobs, seemed unaware that grueling work and abysmal poverty was the usual condition of the "old country," where even little girls were put to work in the fields. Anna Vasil* related how, at five and six years old, she and her sister followed harvesters picking the gleanings in the fields. "Believe me, that was hard work for little girls. . . . I've worked hard all my life, but that was the hardest of all. . . . And I still remember how hard and that was seventy years ago."[14] Also, Slavic people valued hard work and "doing a good job." The highest praise for a man or woman was that he or she "was a good worker."[15] Slavic women who had not worked for 50 or more years described in detail, when interviewed, the techniques of bunching cigars by hand and of rolling mica at an electrical equipment plant. Housework, an area almost totally unexplored by historians, broadened the experience and worldliness of peasant women, bringing them into contact with middle class life which they would strive to achieve for their children. As one example, Anna Fovich* said, "I raised my children like rich children. I knew what to do, and I made them go to school."[16]

While most employed immigrant Jewish women worked in Jewish cigar and work clothes industries, for one Jewish woman interviewed, work in a department store proved the major vehicle for adjustment by enhancing her competence and self-esteem. For such work, knowledge of English was a necessity. Esther Bernstein Green came to Pittsburgh from Austria-Hungary after

World War I at the age of 21. When asked by the interviewer "What was the best part about coming to America?" Mrs. Green answered:

> I'll tell you, the best part was when I got a job for myself and was able to stand on my own feet. When I came here, what could I do? I went to school at night and I learned English. Then I went to a department store—it's Gimbel's now—and I got a job as an interpreter. See, when foreigners came in to buy and they could talk only Russian, or Slovak, or Polish, I interpret for them. Someone else interprets Italian, someone else French; all kinds of interpreters. . . . And I sold a lot of merchandise, and I worked after I was married until I was pregnant seven months.[17]

Work outside the home after marriage was unusual in Pittsburgh. Employment rates were far below the average 7.3% of foreign-born married females employed in other major cities. Only 6% of all married women in Pittsburgh held paying jobs, and in the case of foreign-born married women the rate was 3.8%. Most importantly, the overwhelming majority of immigrant women were married.[18] Although women remained at home, many performed important economic functions. In a city where immigrant men far outnumbered women, the married woman was likely to augment the family income by keeping boarders in her tiny quarters. Shopping, cooking, packing lunch buckets, and washing mountains of laundry in outside tubs for as many as 10 or 12 men consumed all her time and energy.[19]

Josephine Lucca,* who immigrated with her parents from Italy when she was only four, described her mother's arduous responsibilities in a household without indoor water or oven. Her account also indicated the Italian practice of introducing responsibility to the daughter of the family at a very early age:[20]

> Mother had a new baby every year and a houseful of boarders. The house was small, only five rooms, but they used to sleep down the cellar where my father made a flat place like a floor. . . . Then Mother had to go for wood that she used to carry on her head. Wherever they were building homes they would cut the pieces of wood. She would go near the park and pick this wood up and carry it on her head back down about a mile to our house. We had no warm water, we had no gas. . . . And, plus the fact she used to go

> for dandelions and she used to wash them outside in a tub in the backyard. . . . Then, I would take those dandelions in a basket and sell them for ten cents a bunch to people on the street. My mother used to buy flour bags and bleach them to get the printing out and make pillowcases and nightgowns out of them. I hardly went to school. I went until I was thirteen, but I couldn't go on Mondays or Fridays because Mother washed and I had to take care of the kids. I always worried about my brothers and sisters, even when I used to go to school. It was a part of me. I carried them around all the time. I just felt responsible for them.

When she married and had her own five children, the same pattern continued—housework, child care, bleaching flour sacks to make clothes. In Josephine Lucca's words, "We were poor, really poor." In later years Mrs. Lucca contributed directly to the family's rise to middle class life by helping her illiterate husband get his start in the landscaping business.[21]

In Italian families the woman's role was of central import, for it was her responsibility to see that signs of family well-being emanated from the household. Within her domain were keeping the home, managing the finances, and doing what best served the interests of the family. Thus, one Italian woman could say with satisfaction, "He took care of the business and I took care of the house. That's what we decided and it worked fine for us." By the same token, a wife who laundered barber shop towels, cooked for the restaurant, or acted as bookkeeper for her husband's business was simply fulfilling her woman's role as the center of the family.[22]

Jewish women traditionally shared with men the burden of supporting the family. In the eastern European *shtetl* (small Jewish community) the large majority of women participated in some gainful occupation, and the combination of managing a business and a home was so common that no one recognized it as special. For the woman whose husband was a scholar (the highest status for a Jewish man), it was essential for the wife to be "realist and mediator between his ivory tower and . . . everyday life."[23]

Thus, it was in keeping with Jewish tradition when Esther Green set out to augment the family income. As Mrs. Green related:

> My husband got a job with the Metropolitan Life Insurance Company. He was a wonderful man, a scholar, but not a businessman. One night he came home and said, "I been fired." It was winter, and it was cold, dark, ten o'clock at night. I say, "Why was you fired?" He said, "Because I don't have any business this week." I said, "Okay." I got up and dressed and across from me lives a new immigrant family, just moved in. I went in to her. I sold her industrial insurance for the children, five policies. I came home and I said, "Hear this. You ain't going to be fired." Then in the morning I got some more business. He went to work, but he was such an honest man. When his boss says, "How come you have more business than the whole office?" he says, "Not me, due to my wife." Oy, when he came and told me, I nearly fainted. I said, "You're the one who has the license. You're the one that has the job. Don't tell him."

During the Depression she took in boarders. When her husband became ill, she took over as insurance saleswoman to sustain the family.[24]

While Italian and Jewish women often helped their husbands in their work, this economic role was closed to most Slavic women, whose husbands were employed in Pittsburgh industries. While World War II was a turning point for women throughout the United States, in Pittsburgh the change was dramatic. The shortage of men coupled with peak demand for the products of the city's industry opened laboring jobs to women. Many Slavic immigrant women responded to this opportunity, and for their families these war-time jobs provided savings that raised the economic level from bare survival to a measure of security. For two of the women interviewed, savings from jobs of only 18 months' and two years' duration made reality of the long-cherished dream of owning their own homes. For a Serbian born woman on the South Side, a daughter's ambition for a college education was the motivation behind her taking a heavy laboring job at the railroad yard.

Milka Vuyjic* expressed their common feeling of satisfaction when she answered the interviewer's question, "Was there anything in your life that made you feel very good because you did it?":

> Well, when I was working on the railroad I loved my job. I was working hard, like a man . . . two hundred pounds of ice I carried

> and chopped in the diner. My pants were still full of ice when I came home, but I was never tired. I was more than satisfied to put that money away for my daughter's college. That's what made me more satisfied like anything, and more happy.[25]

The women who did war work, except for one, were not new immigrants. They had long before made the transition to American life, and most of the immigrant women interviewed expressed deep patriotism and love of the United States.[26] For many, the acquisition of citizenship contributed greatly to self-esteem as well as a sense of belonging. This example from Anna Laver's oral history speaks for itself:

> I got a letter from United States of America; it's time to go for citizen papers to downtown Pittsburgh. I said to my daughter, "Mary, you have to teach me something." And, she asked me different things. I don't know nothing. Okay, but I had to go get my citizen paper because I got letter. I get two witnesses; two friends from old country went with me. They were already citizens. We wait with lots of people. And then it was my turn. My judge asked me something. I don't know what he said, but I said, "Freedom of speach, freedom of religion, freedom of the press and trial by jury." And, you know what? I'm perfect! We were in a big room, full of people, and the judge looked at me, and he said, "You see this woman? This woman just came from old country but two years, and some of you come twenty years, and you don't know nothing. She pass. Okay, everything correct." I got citizenship papers. Well, everyone look at me—that's true. I was bigger than a prizefighter.[27]

Most women who became citizens had friends to help them. Indeed, friends and relatives were perhaps the most significant agents of adjustment for immigrants. Usually, immigrant women settled in ethnic neighborhoods where neighbors became friends, and frequently earlier immigrants from the same European town helped the newer arrivals find housing and jobs. They acted as matchmakers, and they introduced the immigrants to church, to friends, and to proper American clothes.[28]

In many cases the friends were also relatives. A few women, like Eva Dizenfeld, perceived the Hill District as totally made up of relatives. Mrs. Dizenfeld said:

We lived in the little Russian town of Pliscov. My mother's parents and my father's parents, and all their brothers and sisters all lived close together. We never met anybody but our own family, and do you know what? It was almost the same thing here in America. We all lived together down in the Hill District and really never mingled with the others. All Father's brothers and sisters came to Pittsburgh and we all lived in the Hill close to each other. My father made one dollar and a quarter a day, and with this, he was able to buy a house—1609 Webster Avenue. And this is the address that everybody from our little town that came to America came to. Everybody was a relative. Before they came to America they all knew this one address—1609 Webster Avenue. I lived in Pittsburgh from 1902 until 1920 [returning later], and I never met any stranger outside the family while I lived in Pittsburgh.[29]

For other women, the neighborhood took the place of family. For Mary Vasil, City Farm Lane in Homestead "was a nice place to live":

In the evening the ladies would all bring their stools out and sit around and talk about Europe. It was very interesting, even for me, because I remember Europe, and everybody, even the people born in this country, wanted to know. Even now when we ladies meet at church to sew and make quilts, we talk about Europe and what we remember, and how bad it was and it makes us all feel good to be here. My mother never did learn English. The people from Europe—they didn't have anybody to talk to them in English. They talked in Slavish. They had each other, and they felt good to be here because in Europe there was nothing. My mother was happy here. The ladies were all the same; they were like one family.[30]

For single women the neighborhood provided a comfortable social setting where young immigrant men and women could meet. Ruth Hirsh came alone from Russia to live with an aunt in the Hill District. She reported:

All the immigrant boys and girls would meet on Center Avenue and we were friends. I worked sewing pants for a pants factory, and all the girls who worked there were immigrants like me. So, I had friends and we met on the street and we went sometimes to the Irene Kaufmann Center. That's how I met my husband, just on the street where all the immigrant people walked.

The Hill District also played a role in easing the transition of Anna Fodorovich, a young Russian Orthodox woman. She lived with her brother on the South Side. She related:

> The Russian Church was in the Hill District then. So every Sunday morning my brother would take me and we would walk over the bridge to church. That's where we met people; that's how we socialized, walking back and forth. And, in the Hill District were lots of Jewish people from Russia. And there were all kinds of Russian stores. So, we bought herring and black bread and got together. That's how we met people.[31]

Mrs. Fodorovich mentioned the Russian church. This is only one example pointing to the ethnic church as an agent of adjustment for immigrant women. Several women made such comments as "Church came first," or "Everybody went to church." One said, "I love church; I go every day; a day that I don't go to church is double long. And we ladies bake every week for the church." Among all the Slavic groups, men, women, and children went to church. Among the Jewish immigrants the synagogue was a man's institution, and the role of the woman was limited to visiting in the balcony where some women read the prayers in Yiddish.

During the decade 1900 to 1910, ethnic churches of every denomination were built in the Pittsburgh area, and 11 Jewish synagogues, organized by nationality, were established in the Hill District alone.[32] The establishment of the ethnic church provided what might well have been the single most important source of continuity in a world changed in so many ways. Religion was a basic value in Europe, and the ethnic church represented the continuation of the most important institution in the lives of many poor immigrants.[33] Aside from its religious function, the church played a vital social role. Here was a meeting place and social center where immigrants carried out the traditional observance of holy days and fiestas with festive foods, familiar dances, and meaningful ritual.

Church played a central role in the lives of most Italian women, but many men were ambivalent or even hostile toward organized Catholicism. For Italians, the recreation of the feast day of the patron saint took on even greater importance than it had in

Italy. Nicolette DiLucente described an elaborate annual celebration in Braddock. Musicians were hired, a grandstand constructed, and a chapel built. Men carried a statue of the saint through the streets followed by a procession of musicians and excited children. Mrs. DiLucente explained:

> All the people were from the same town, San Angelo del Pasco. We decorated the whole street, made special foods, and we celebrated. We did this every year from when I came in 1920 to the 1960s.[34]

Rudolph Vecoli suggests that "The cult of the patron saint was perhaps the strongest emotional bond, outside the family, which tied the Italian immigrants to each other and to the distant past."[35]

Church and religious celebrations were important to both immigrant men and women. For immigrant women, however, the one most emotionally satisfying experience, the one thing in life that could heal the wound of separation from parents and loved ones left behind, was the creation of their very own families.

For some, giving birth to a child brought the first real sense of joy in America. For example, Dianna Jordanoff, an immigrant bride from Bulgaria, expressed her elation at having a child,saying, "My Pat was my rebirth. I felt that I was born again . . . having my own baby, that was heaven."[36]

Immigrant women wanted children above all else. Difficulty in conceiving, miscarriages, stillbirths, and infant deaths caused women who had never known a physician to consult medical specialists. Mrs. DiLucente chose to undergo surgery even though her doctor warned her that there was little chance of a successful pregnancy. "I didn't care," she said "I didn't have children, and I wanted."[37] On the other hand, Eva Dizenfeld, whose stillborn child was delivered by a physician, resorted to folk magic when she feared for the life of her second child. A Jewish (or perhaps Russian) folk belief reputed to bring long life and luck to an endangered child was to sell that child to parents of a healthy family. "So," said Eva Dizenfeld, "I sold my son to Mrs. Pittler for a nickel. . . . It was only a superstition, but my son did grow up wonderful." Mrs. Dizenfeld continued, "My children meant everything in the world to me. To this day . . . my great grandchildren mean to me as much as my children; my Belle's children are my children, and I don't feel any different towards my grandchildren and my great grandchildren . . . my children mean the world and all . . . that's all."[38]

Motherhood was (and is) a goal of most women, but for immigrant women, beginning a family carried special significance. In Italian, Jewish, and Slavic cultures, motherhood was highly valued, and a woman was valued for the number and beauty and behavior of her children.[39] In addition, for immigrant women separated from their own parental families, children represented the beginning of continuity in America. While there are several alternate explanations, the deep desire for one's own family may go far to explain why immigrant women had much larger families than American-born women.[40] Certainly, among the elements fostering adjustment, motherhood appears to be the one universal factor.

Not every woman was able to make the kind of successful adjustment described in this article. Study of those who could not cope is beyond the scope of this paper, but the incidence must have been significant. In this study, which included 45 immigrant women over age 68, each woman had at least one living child and one adult grandchild, and each was willing to record her life history. These characteristics are in themselves a measure of adjustment; our sample is admittedly skewed toward success. Yet, even in this "successful" sample, women mentioned mothers and friends who did not adjust. One 75 year old Jewish woman described moving back and forth from Philadelphia to Pittsburgh during her childhood because, "My grandmother was, you know, nervous. She never got used to America. Today you would say she was emotionally disturbed." And a Serbian-American woman reported, "I was born here, but my mother was always sick. She wanted to go back to Yugoslavia. She said she would only get well if she could go home. When I was four years old, Mother took me back to Europe. Daddy came there three times to visit, but Mother never came back to America." Thus, although she was born here, this woman arrived in Pittsburgh at age 25 as an immigrant. One Italian immigrant woman who leads a full and satisfying life here, in spite of poverty, told of her sister-in-law who was killed when she walked in front of a streetcar. "She never got used to things here. She didn't know what she was doing."[41]

Certainly evidence exists to support Handlin's original thesis. On balance, however, immigrant women did adjust to Pittsburgh's industrial urban environment. Certain factors, true of Pittsburgh, apply equally to most American cities. Improvement in the material conditions of life, the creation of their own families, and close ties maintained with children and other family members aided the positive adjustment of immigrant women throughout the United States. The Pittsburgh environment, however, encouraged the maintenance of a certain amount of traditional culture. Ethnic neighborhoods, ethnic churches, and community celebrations of traditional religious rituals provided the opportunity for association with others of similar background, helping to smooth the transition from European village to this industrial city. These factors overcame the major limiting characteristic of Pittsburgh, an economy based on male-oriented heavy industry. Most Italian, Jewish, and Slavic women did become "at home" in the Pittsburgh area and achieved "urbanization without breakdown."

NOTES

1. Oscar Handlin, *The Uprooted* (New York, 1951).

2. See Rudolph Vecoli, "Contadini in Chicago: A Critique of *The Uprooted*," Journal of American History, 51 (1964), 405-417.

3. Oscar Handlin, *The Americans* (Boston, 1963), and *The Uprooted*, (rev. ed.; Boston, 1973).

4. See William I. Thomas and Florian Znaniecki, *The Polish Peasant in Europe and America* (New York, 1919-1920).

5. Oscar Lewis, "Urbanization Without Breakdown," Scientific Monthly, 75 (1951), 31-41.

6. Women, Ethnicity, and Mental Health, an oral history study of three generations of Italian, Jewish, and Slavic women in the Pittsburgh area, included 50 oral history interviews with immigrant women. The study, directed by this author, was sponsored by the American Jewish Committee and funded by the Maurice Falk Medical Fund. Cassettes and transcripts are available for research at the Historical Society of Western Pennsylvania; transcripts at Hillman Library, University of Pittsburgh.

7. All census data are from Thirteenth, Fourteenth, and Fifteenth *Decennial Census Reports*, Population Volumes (Washington, D.C., 1910, 1920, 1930).

8. Susan J. Kleinberg, "Technology and Women's Work: The Lives of Working Class Women in Pittsburgh, 1870-1900," Labor History (Winter, 1976), 58.

9. Map (Figure 1) illustrates selected neighborhoods with large Italian, Jewish, or Slavic populations. The Hill District was primarily Jewish; Larimer, Italian; South Side and Homestead, Slavic.

10. Elizabeth Beardsley Butler, *Women and the Trades* (New York, 1909), 324-333.

11. Joseph A. Hill, *Women in Gainful Occupations, 1870 to 1920*, Census Monograph 9 (Washington, D.C. 1929), 13.

12. Butler, *Women and Trades*, 21-27, 101.

13. Interview I-14-A, Women, Ethnicity; Virginia Yans McLaughlin, "Patterns of Work and Family Organization: Buffalo's Italians," Journal of Interdisciplinary History, 2 (Autumn, 1971), 308-312.

14. Interview S-1-A, Women, Ethnicity; Bessie Olga Petovsky, *The Slavic Immigrant Woman* (Cincinnati, 1925), preface; Butler, *Women and Trades*, 24-27.

15. Interviews S-1-A, S-7-A, S-11-A, S-16-A, S-20-A. Paul Wrobel, "Polish-American Men: As Workers, As Husbands, As Fathers," paper presented to American Association for the Advancement of Science, February, 1976.

16. Interviews S-11-A, S-23-A, S-8-A. See also Thomas Bell, *Out of This Furnace* (Pittsburgh, 1974), 126-138.

17. Interview J-7-A.

18. Hill, *Women in Occupations*, 79 and 276; Thirteenth Decennial Census Report (1910).

19. Margaret Byington, *Homestead: Households of a Mill Town* (Pittsburgh, 1974), 136-144; Kleinberg, "Technology," 62.

20. Richard Gambino, *Blood of My Blood, The Dilemma of Italian-Americans* (New York, 1974), 146-166.

21. Interview I-19-A.

22. Francis Femminella and Jill S. Quadagno, "The Italian-American Family," in Charles H. Mindel and Robert W. Habenstein, eds., *Ethnic Families in America* (New York, 1976), 65; Interviews I-13-A, I-2-A, I-3-A, I-19-A.

23. Mark Zborowski and Elizabeth Herzog, *Life is With People* (New York, 1962), 31.

24. Interview J-7-A.

25. Interviews S-3-A, S-12-A, S-2-A.

26. See particularly Interviews I-4-A, I-8-A, J-5-A, J-7-A, J-13-A, J-16-A, S-1-A, S-3-A, S-7-A, S-16-A; also Byington, *Homestead*, 271-276.

27. Interview S-3-A.

28. Interviews I-14-A, I-24-A, I-25-A, J-5-A, J-24-A, S-5-A, S-8-A. See also Herbert Gans, *The Urban Villagers* (New York, 1962), 62; Byington, *Homestead*, 136; Nathan Glazer and Daniel Patrick Moynihan, *Beyond the Melting Pot* (Cambridge, 1964), 186-191.

29. Interview J-14-A.

30. Interview S-1-A.

31. Interviews J-5-A, S-8-A.

32. Byington, *Homestead*, 133; Charles Cooper, "History of the Jews of Pittsburgh," The Jewish Criterion (Pittsburgh, May, 1918).

1. Downtown
2. Hill District
3. Polish Hill
4. Larimer
5. South Side
6. Homestead

FIGURE 1: City of Pittsburgh and Homestead/Munhall Selected Ethnic Neighborhoods

33. Randall M. Miller and Thomas R. Marzik, eds., *Immigrants and Religion in Urban America* (Philadelphia, 1977), xi-xxii, 87-99.

34. Interview I-25-A.

35. Rudolph Vecoli, "Cult and Occult in Italian-American Culture: The Persistence of a Religious Heritage" in Miller and Marzik, *Immigrants and Religion*, 25-47.

36. Interview S-12-A.

37. Interview I-25-A.

38. Interview J-14-A.

39. Cecyle S. Neidle, *America's Immigrant Women* (New York, 1976), 85-113.

40. William H. Grabill, *The Fertility of American Women* (New York, 1958), 103-108.

41. Interviews J-8-A, S-2-A, I-21-A.

Bei Fragen zur Produktsicherheit wenden Sie sich bitte an:
If you have any questions regarding product safety,
please contact:

Walter de Gruyter GmbH
Genthiner Straße 13
10785 Berlin
productsafety@degruyterbrill.com